TASCHEN

100
ALL-TIME FAVORITE
MOVIES

1915–2000

TASCHEN

100
ALL-TIME FAVORITE
MOVIES

Volume 2: 1960–2000   Ed. Jürgen Müller

In collaboration with
**defd and Cinema, Hamburg
Deutsche Kinemathek, Berlin
British Film Institute, London
Bibliothèque du Film, Paris,** *and*
**Herbert Klemens Filmbild
Fundus Robert Fischer, Munich**

TASCHEN

y Jürgen Müller and Steffen Haubner

on the Wild Side 406

Introduction by Jürgen Müller and Jörn Hetebrügge

The Sceptical Eye 522

The 80s

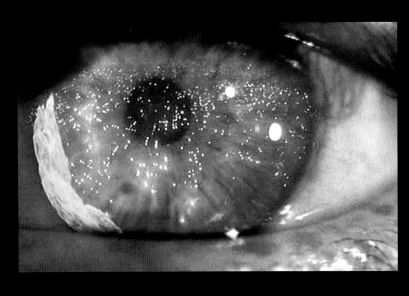

The 90s

THE 60^s
WALK ON THE WILD SIDE

WALK ON THE WILD SIDE
Notes on the Movies of the 60s

The buildings of Fifth Avenue are still submerged in darkness, but the sun is already rising at the end of the street. It's a timeless moment, as if the world had paused for thought before the day gets going. A yellow cab drives slowly up the street and stops on the corner of 57th; a young woman gets out. She's wearing a black evening dress and a pearl necklace. She stops in front of a department store and glances up at the sign above the door: "Tiffany & Co." Then she moves over to look in the window.

We see her in profile while she studies the display, lost in thought. She reaches into a paper bag and pulls out a coffee and a croissant. The camera follows this elegant apparition from one window to the next, and then there's a change of perspective: we're watching from the store, and before us stands Audrey Hepburn, lost to the world as she gazes at the costly jewels on display. Behind the glass, she herself seems the quintessence of beauty and worth – as far beyond our reach as Tiffany's glittering gems. And the beauty of this entire sequence consists in the fact that we never actually see a single valuable item of jewelry.

Instead, we've spent the whole time observing a wide-eyed girl, and though her loveliness is apparently only celebrated in passing, it actually represents a touchstone of value. Audrey Hepburn's looks are breathtaking,

and her elegance is surpassed only by her perfect, unaffected naturalness. And though Miss Hepburn's hats do become ever more extravagant in the course of the movie, they only serve to accentuate the classical simplicity of her dresses and coats. It's as if Irving Penn, who celebrated a modern kind of beauty, had accompanied the director as an aesthetic advisor.

Few opening sequences can match the elegance of this one. In *Breakfast at Tiffany's* (1961, p. 442), Audrey Hepburn is the icon and harbinger of a stylish and style-conscious decade. Yet there's something undeniably idiosyncratic about the ideal of female beauty presented by this film and its star; for the focus is not just on Hepburn's looks, but on the extravagance of her character, Holly Golightly. Evening dress, pumps, pearl necklace and sunglasses in the first light of dawn: what we have before us is a glamorous and matchlessly beautiful creature of the night. But every mortal human casts a shadow… and Holly Golightly is no exception.

For a discreet visit to the powder room with a gentleman, she picks up 50 dollars; and she's quite prepared to accept the financial support of a fat millionaire, before eventually letting herself be snapped up by a rich Brazilian. Yet for all the "rats and super-rats" she uses and is used by, Truman

An icon on the verge
of a nervous breakdown

Svelte, sylph-like, indeed positively elfin, Audrey Hepburn embodied an ideal of beauty for the new decade. But although she bestowed the face of an angel on Holly Golightly, it was this very film that saved her from being typecast as the nice girl waiting for Mr. Right. However fragile in appearance, Holly is a confident woman who needs no 50s curves to draw the attention of every man – and every woman – in her vicinity. She refuses to accept any limits, even to her feelings. Her worries about her brother Fred culminate in a fit of aggression that sees her demolishing part of her furniture. This pairing of sadness and anger reveals both the intensity and the poverty of her emotional life. Nonetheless, there are occasions when *Breakfast at Tiffany's* remains stuck in the clichés of its time. Sometimes, for all her incomparable grace, Audrey Hepburn does lay it on a bit thick. Her character's fervent inner life is acted out so excessively, and so very visibly, that Paul – and the audience – can be forgiven for wanting to offer her something a little *quieter*. And ultimately, that means the safe haven of a bourgeois marriage.

For such apparently amoral figures, this is the prescribed moral stance, and we can see it in the symbolic language of the film: Holly's cat and the stolen mask cast this animal as her familiar and her alter ego. Certainly, she's a girl who desires her independence. Tellingly, she's never given her adopted housecat a name, because she never felt she had a right to do so. But when she tries to set Cat free, the animal refuses to leave her: he's grown used to domesticity and he no longer misses his freedom. The message is clear: life can't be lived as a permanent Walk on the Wild Side.

The cry for sexual liberation prompted huge controversy in the 60s. The changed behavior of young people, especially young women, divided the generations. And so it's very noticeable that *Breakfast at Tiffany's* is elaborately indirect. Holly's source of income is only ever hinted at, and her night of love with Paul is indicated discreetly in a single image: the dog's mask he'd been wearing now graces the statue of Amor beside his bed. (His wealthy patroness had given him this kitschy figurine as a token of her esteem.)

Blake Edwards' film toys with the topic of sexuality rather than dealing with it frankly. In any case, Audrey Hepburn's innocent face seems capable of taking the steam out of any situation. Take the scene with the stripper in the nightclub: as Holly and Paul watch her slowly undressing, they talk without looking at one another; they're watching themselves, each other and the dancer in the mirror at the back of the bar. Holly muses aloud on how much the stripper earns, and comments critically on the quality of the girl's performance. In a roundabout way, she makes it quite clear how she feels about sex, which in her eyes has a lot to do with money and nothing at all to do with love. Holly looks quite as friendly as ever, but she's clearly just not very interested. It all seems harmless, trivial, nothing to get very much worked up about. The couple might as well be discussing the purchase of a new vacuum cleaner.

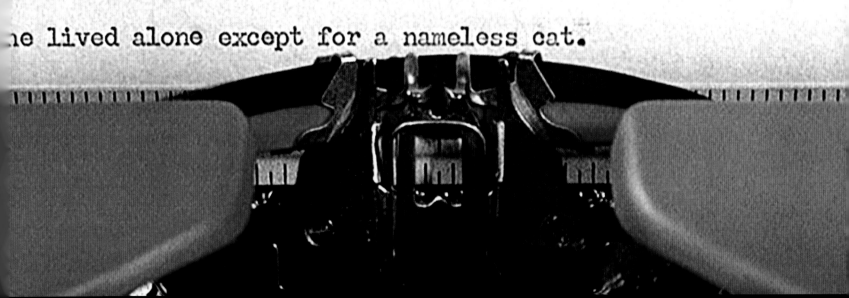

There was once a very lovely, very frightened girl.

he lived alone except for a nameless cat.

Breakfast at Tiffany's, however, is also a film about New York in particular and big city life in general. In this urban jungle, only those who can commandeer a taxi with brio will survive. Manhattan is a major character in this movie: Paul and Holly move among the skyscrapers, up and down the Avenues, across Central Park and into Tiffany's; and even Sing-Sing penitentiary gets a look-in, as an image of the criminality inseparable from a world like this. NY's fire escapes, finally, permit people to move around in secret, and they certainly facilitate amorous encounters. This city is a place of seduction, in which a kid from the sticks can become a playgirl and a poet may earn his keep by warming the bed of his patroness. But it's also a place of enormous promise; here, it might be possible to marry a millionaire, to meet the love of your life or to publish the Great American Novel.

Seen today, *Breakfast at Tiffany's* seems curiously prudish. With much less kerfuffle than Blake Edwards' film, Truman Capote's work of fiction had told the story of a girl on the make; and with far greater honesty, the book had denied its protagonists a happy ending. Yet however justified this criticism may be, it's also somewhat naive; for not everything can be said with the same directness in every generation. In this respect, no decade is more ambivalent than the 60s. In Edwards' film, we see the start of a process of liberation that still hasn't reached its conclusion; here, taboos are gently knocked without ever really being broken; and here, we see the first tentative sketch of an autonomous woman, taking charge of her sexuality without ever having heard the word "feminism." Though it may look a little strait-laced today, this movie was certainly free-and-easy by the standards of the early 60s.

But perhaps even at that time, it was the apparent contradictions that made *Breakfast at Tiffany's*, like its leading actress, so charming and so strangely sexy. The movie is nicely emblematic of a decade of incongruities and a period of transition. For just as it celebrated the sophisticated new-jet-set lifestyle of the early 60s, that lifestyle was showing the first clear signs of decay. Soon, a new mode of existence would take its place, after trampling on everything it stood for.

Wild angels

The chi-chi glamour of Holly Golightly's world shouldn't deceive us. In Hollywood, the 60s began, not with wild parties but with the near-bankruptcy of the studio system. The TV lured millions away from the movie palaces and led to thousands of lost jobs at the major studios. It seemed people were no longer prepared to leave their homes in order to escape reality when the box in the corner could do the job more cheaply and just as well.

The crisis of the studios and the dawning realization that society was changing eventually led to the end of the Production Code, which had stipulated for decades what was and wasn't permissible on the silver screen. Though their chains were now broken, it still took the Majors a while to start moving. Like lame giants, the rulers of Hollywood gaped at the transformations going on around them and played it safe, preferring to rent out their un-

derused studio space to the producers of low-budget movies than engage in any experiments themselves.

But surely the success of these cheap pictures was precisely the proof needed that a new, young audience could indeed be enticed to the movie theaters any weekend of the year? Surely it was clear that Hollywood had to find an answer to the *cinema des auteurs* emerging in other countries? And if anyone feared that "difficult," frightening and highly sexualized films were box-office poison, hadn't Hitchcock's *Psycho* (1960, p. 436) demonstrated that precisely the opposite was true?

In the late 50s, it had become clear that the High School public was bored by expensive, big-budget epics, flocking instead to cheap AIP productions such as *The She-Creature* (1956) and *I Was a Teenage Werewolf* (1957). This formed a starting point for the next generation of filmmakers. Under the patronage of the ubiquitous Roger Corman, there appeared a series of seminal films such as Monte Hellman's Western *The Shooting* (1967), while directors like Francis Ford Coppola (*Dementia 13*, 1963) took their first tentative steps in movie making. And it's no accident that Peter Bogdanovich's *Targets* (1968) raised a monument to the B-Movie icon Boris Karloff, for in doing so, the young director was simply acknowledging his own roots. A little later, significantly, it was also Corman who had his hand most firmly on the pulse of the age: in films such as *The Wild Angels* (1966) and *The Trip* (1967), he was one of the first directors to seek ways of expressing the burgeoning youth culture of the decade.

Beyond the mainstream, more and more filmmakers were finding their voice and living out their opposition to Hollywood values — boldly, aggres-

sively and joyfully. Words like "trash" and "exploitation" simply don't do justice to this wildly creative fusion of good old sex and violence with an anarchist spirit and the stylistic resources of the avant-garde. A prime example is the cheerfully destructive Russ Meyer, who refused to play by the rules and ran amok against etiquette and art. In *Faster, Pussycat! Kill! Kill!* (1966), we are confronted, not for the first time in the U.S. cinema, with the endless vistas of the West. But the mythical landscape is now a cross between Nirvana and Pandemonium, where lustful go-go girls meet All-American boys and throttle them with their bare hands. Traditional Westerns had depicted the pioneering farmer as a bold and resourceful man amongst men. Meyer confronts us with a drunken wreck who exploits his strapping but mentally challenged sons as stooges fit only to do the dirty work. It's a bitterly funny satire on the way America eats its own children.

Though they come in the guise of cheap horror movies, Herk Harvey's *Carnival of Souls* (1962) and George A. Romero's *Night of the Living Dead* (1968) are genuine works of art that quickly acquired cult status, and their influence on later generations of filmmakers can hardly be overstated. Romero's film is a morality play about a secluded community threatened more from within than without. Despite its visual power and psychological acerbity, years passed before most critics came to appreciate its qualities.

Yet it wasn't just the cineastic underground that showed new signs of life. There was plenty of potential in the younger generation of Hollywood directors too. John Frankenheimer's *The Manchurian Candidate* (1962) was a disturbing satire on the anti-Communist witch-hunts of the McCarthy era, but

(1962) and John Ford's *The Man Who Shot Liberty Valance* (1962). These directors realized that the time had come for a less starry-eyed view of the Western hero. Movies emerged that were a little more "realistic," showing gunmen who cared only for themselves, and endeavoring to correct the cruel misrepresentation of Native Americans in most early Westerns. Among the outstanding attempts to save a genre that was fast losing its credibility were John Sturges' *The Magnificent Seven* (1960) and Ford's *Cheyenne Autumn* (1964).

Then came the year 1964… and a young Italian turned the "classic" Western on its head with a movie made in Spain starring a young unknown called Clint Eastwood. *A Fistful of Dollars* (*Per un pugno di dollari*, 1964) replaced the hero of old with a shady, tight-lipped pistolero addicted to cheap cigars. Though the Spaghetti Western phenomenon lasted only a few years, a few mischievous Europeans succeeded in revitalizing a genre that had needed to change or die. And in passing, they also provided Hollywood with one of its greatest-ever stars and directors.

All in all, the Late Western reflects an important insight of the 1960s: that even in the land of unlimited opportunities, the chances for any individual have never been unlimited, to say nothing of equal. These films asked a simple question: If contemporary society is built on self-interest, steeped in envy, hatred and violence, filled with corrupt politicians and crooks of all sizes – why should we believe things were any different in the Age of Pioneers? The Italian directors turned the Western hero into a cynical, egotistical survivor. In America itself, the cowboy said a melancholy and satirical farewell

to his own moribund myths (as in Arthur Penn's *Little Big Man*, 1970) before riding off for ever into the sunset: see *The Wild Bunch* (1968), Monte Hellman's *Ride in the Whirlwind* (1965) and *Butch Cassidy and the Sundance Kid* (1969).

The movies hit the streets

The French *cinema des auteurs*, which would later become known as *la Nouvelle Vague* ("The New Wave"), had an immense influence on American filmmakers; but it had itself begun by taking a bow towards Hollywood. A beautiful young woman in a *New York Herald Tribune* T-shirt meets a contemporary urban outlaw, a man with the air of a young Humphrey Bogart and a cigarette hanging permanently from his lower lip; with *Breathless* (*À bout de souffle*, 1959) Jean-Luc Godard ushered in a new epoch.

The Gaullist government's decision to introduce a special tax to subsidize the French film industry – and to combat "American cultural imperialism" – enabled a number of film critics to leave the safe haven of their studios and embark on the adventure of making movies. They filmed on location (often in the open air), their scripts left plenty of room for improvisation, and their previously static cameras seemed suddenly weightless. Rejecting the studio-bound French cinema of the past (which they contemptuously dubbed "Le Cinéma de Papa"), they chose the raw authenticity of the streets. This was an attitude inherited from the neorealists of post-war Italy.

Films like Claude Chabrol's *Le Beau Serge* (1958) and *Les Cousins* (1959) and François Truffaut's *The 400 Blows* (*Les quatre cents coups*, 1958/59, p. 378) attracted a new audience of moviegoers: people who were prepared to open up to new forms of visual expression and to recognize films as the work of autonomous artists. The concept of the *auteur* saw the director as an independent creator in full control of his work. One can imagine the explosive force this idea must have had in the Hollywood Dream Factory, where movies have always been regarded as a commercial product constructed by a team. Nonetheless, America's young filmmakers were grateful for the impulses given by their colleagues in France. These included a group of former critics from the legendary film journal *Cahiers du cinema* – Eric Rohmer, Jacques Rivette, Jean-Luc Godard, François Truffaut – as well as directors such as Alain Resnais, Louis Malle and Jean-Pierre Melville, who had themselves been deeply influenced by American movies. One might say that the French cinema was ultimately responsible for saving the American film from petrifying in its own stereotypes and worn-out genre motifs.

Perhaps this is going too far. Nonetheless, the U.S. cinema was obsessed with dreams – and there was one task the Americans would probably never have managed alone. For all their insistence on immediacy and closeness to real life, France's young generation of filmmaking film critics were equally radical in their insistence that a film is *a work of art*. These movies demanded no direct identification with the protagonist, and their directors scorned cinematic illusion and time-honored narrative conven-

tions as the merest self-deception. In so doing, they initiated a process without which today's cinema would be unthinkable; and, to name only two American examples, this includes the work of Martin Scorsese and Woody Allen. The self-reference and self-irony of these French films were the first manifestations of a cinematic art that could truthfully be called intellectual.

The women's decade

While young French directors turned away in disdain from the sterile and impersonal cinema of their fathers, American movie heroes were being tipped off their pedestals. Epic adventures were going out of fashion, and their stars along with them. Moviegoers now wanted characters like Holly Golightly and actors who could carry a film with nothing more than their natural presence and charisma. It was, in short, the women's decade.

Here too, the *Nouvelle Vague* set new standards with actresses such as Jean Seberg, Anna Karina, Jeanne Moreau and Catherine Deneuve. Though even the U.S. cinema had been forced to start recognizing the signs of the times, these rising French stars made the prevailing American image of womanhood look almost reactionary. In France, the dominance of the narrative element was combated more effectively than in any other country, and this seemed to lend women an unprecedented freedom. Take Luis Buñuel's *Belle de Jour* (1967), a film without any discernible plot and no clear distinction be-

by his father's generation. Thus the poster bore a picture of the tiro Dustin Hoffmann, plus the following caption: "This is Benjamin. He's a little worried about his future…"

As the decade came to an end, women were no longer merely decorative accessories – a sexual promise to the victorious warrior – but (almost) equal partners. A disillusioned anti-hero like Steve McQueen's Frank Bullitt (*Bullitt*, 1968) was given a strong female partner like Jacqueline Bisset, who drives him around in her snazzy convertible and functions as his conscience. While Bullitt's ethics have been worn ragged by his job, she embodies the radiantly beautiful hope for a better life – a counterblast to the dead, affectionless existence of the men who still rule her life. In *Bonnie and Clyde*, the female sidekick is even permitted to die in a hail of bullets at the side of her man. Before expiring, however, Faye Dunaway's Bonnie Parker is a wonderfully erotic *femme fatale* (in the truest sense of the term), posing in front of her car, dressed to kill in a chic hat, a silk scarf and a pistol. This is a woman who has finally freed herself from the dictates of morality – even if sexual liberation has had to make way for indiscriminate violence.

Swinging cinema

A side-on view of Paul Newman's face – and behind it, the same profile as a luminous red silhouette against an orange background (*Cool Hand Luke*, 1967); Liv Ullmann in black and white and extreme close-up (*Persona*, 1966),

her face divided by a series of monochrome bars; Sue Lyon, glancing over the heart-shaped lenses of her plastic sunglasses (*Lolita*, 1962) – three instantly datable movie posters. Sixties design is unmistakable, and hardly any other decade has had a greater sense of style.

The psychedelic orgies of color in *Barbarella* (1968) or *Yellow Submarine* (1968) are extreme examples of an aesthetic stance that owed a lot to the burgeoning fashion for comics. Not only were Superman, Flash Gordon and Modesty Blaise brought to new life on the screen; they were also stylistic trendsetters. Propelled by the LSD-inspired color whirls of the hippie generation and fuelled by the new possibilities offered by plastic, this "will to design" gradually penetrated all areas of life, eventually achieving a kind of respectability as Pop Art.

All this is in keeping with a tendency one might describe as "the urbanization of the cinema." Everywhere, moviemakers were focusing on city life, filming in clubs, discos and hip concert halls, establishing their credentials as artists alive to the power of the present. In *2001: A Space Odyssey* (1968, p. 496), a vision of the future, Stanley Kubrick gave his interiors and costumes a Pop Art design with skintight overalls and lurid plastic furniture. It was as if he were saying: "We are the future – and it's only just begun…"

Yet the example of *2001* demonstrates another characteristic of the decade: a certain critical and ironical distance from itself. In *Blow Up* (1966), it's no accident that it's a fashion photographer who attempts to discover some kind of truth behind a world of superficial appearances. The director, Michelangelo Antonioni, takes this as an opportunity to lead

Man on the moon

While 007 fought the supercrooks and American and French cineastes had their differences, the most dramatic struggle was taking place elsewhere, between two rival media. Television was establishing itself as *the* mass medium, forcing the film industry to come up with ever more thrilling spectacles in order to resist this potent new challenger. At the same time, TV had a profound effect on moviegoers' ways of seeing, and it also raised their expectations. The murder of Kennedy, the Olympic Games, or a war of your choice anywhere in the world: you could watch it all from the comfort of your own armchair, frequently while it happened. Until the moon landing, science fiction had been a B-movie genre; thereafter, the big studios lavished money on it.

With sumptuous "production values" and increasingly explicit sex and violence, the movie business fought desperately against the growing dominance of the box. Yet this was only one side of the coin. For the very fact that TV was becoming the natural home of the entertainment industry enabled the cinema to develop as an artistic medium. Faced with the mass-produced visual pabulum churned out by TV, many artists now saw film as an attractive alternative. Directors such as Stanley Kubrick and Jean-Luc Godard created works of genius, preparing the way for film's entry into the annals of art history. More than this, the work of these directors set new standards for all who followed – aesthetically, intellectually and in the quality of its engagement with social and political realities. With *Lolita* (1962), Kubrick used an

adaptation of a morally precarious novel by a Russian exile to plumb the sexual depths of affluent America. In France, Godard shattered the stylistic and narrative conventions of the classical cinema and pieced together a new film language from the fragments.

There is another reason for TV's central role in the intellectualization of the cinema: the more moving images became an ordinary part of everyday life, the more practiced people became in dealing with them. This created a basis for self-reflexive discourse and the ability to tackle heterogeneous forms of representation. Thus John Frankenheimer – who never denied his origins in television – could make a feature film (*Grand Prix*, 1966) that looked like a documentary, adding authentic film material to the fictitious story. In this way, the film also become a homage to television and its ability to show us the unscripted stories generated by life itself – unmediated by art, and broadcast live from anywhere in the world.

At the same time, the cinema was becoming a place where serious questions could be asked. Did public discourse in the mass media have to be so *breathless*? How trustworthy were the official accounts of political and social realities? The TV emissary John Frankenheimer also made *The Manchurian Candidate*, a surreal satire on America's fear of communism. In this movie, the apparently most vehement anti-Commies are actually controlled from Moscow; but the terrible truth about the ease with which people can be manipulated is lost without a trace amongst the milling reporters and TV cameras.

The old morality is immoral

"Today, we have a cinema that no longer has any lasting temporal structures at its disposal (...). The films being made today are wholly determined by the imperative of the present." Jacques Rivette made this statement as early as 1963, yet it is an unusually fitting description of the situation at the end of the decade. The images rush by, instants of light that briefly illuminate the dreams and nightmares of a liberalized society. In *Woodstock* (1970), a generation presented itself as a new model of society, and also as a big, happy American family, spreading the word about births and marriages with the help of a monstrous sound system. *Alice's Restaurant* (1969) celebrated the commune as a surrogate nuclear family; and Disney's *The Jungle Book* (1967) dreamt the old dream of a peaceful natural world free of division and strife.

Yet this new vision of politics and society was flawed from the very beginning. In *Midnight Cowboy* (1969, p. 512), Dustin Hoffman went to look for America and ended up coughing his guts out on a Greyhound bus. On the Highway to Hell between Texas, Manhattan and Miami, heroes had become superfluous. In the same film, Jon Voight – a wannabe gigolo in a slowly disintegrating Stetson – makes it painfully clear that the myth of endless freedom lies buried in the alleyways of New York.

The Establishment carried on exploiting the young, the reactionaries stood firm against renewal, and the cinema reflected a deep and widespread conviction that the old morality was hopelessly corrupt. The movies showed

us a counter-culture that oscillated wildly between self-realization and self-destruction. The genuine charm of *A Hard Day's Night* (1964) is highly precarious, always threatening to collapse into a whimsical sequence of vapidly slaphappy moments. The orgies of violence in *The Wild Angels* or *Easy Rider* (1969, p. 508) are accompanied by gestures of rebellion, but a demand for freedom as absolute as this can have no clear destination. And in the druggy and strikingly inert arthouse cinema of *Zabriskie Point* (1969), the frustration of the young generation leads to the explosion of a hyper-modern villa that symbolizes the hated status quo. This pocket apocalypse is in fact only imagined, yet it does express an awareness of the fact that time moves only in one direction. There's simply no way back to a state of original innocence.

And so the rebellious note struck by Godard's *Breathless* eventually modulates into a cacophonous emotional feedback loop. "Live fast, die young and leave a beautiful corpse" – the deadly intransigence of Bonnie and Clyde was reiterated by many of the generation's heroes, from Jimi Hendrix to Brian Jones and Janis Joplin. An abyss divides the comparatively harmless Holly Golightly from the bullet-riddled pariah Bonnie Parker, and the contradictions at the heart of this decade mark it out as a period of transition.

It is precisely these contradictions that make the 60s such an astonishingly vital epoch: the temporary decline of Hollywood and the fresh impulses from Europe; the sense of infinite possibilities – expressed not least in a re-definition of the role of women – and the sardonic fatalism of the cinematic underground; the bombastic million-dollar epics and the brave low-budget

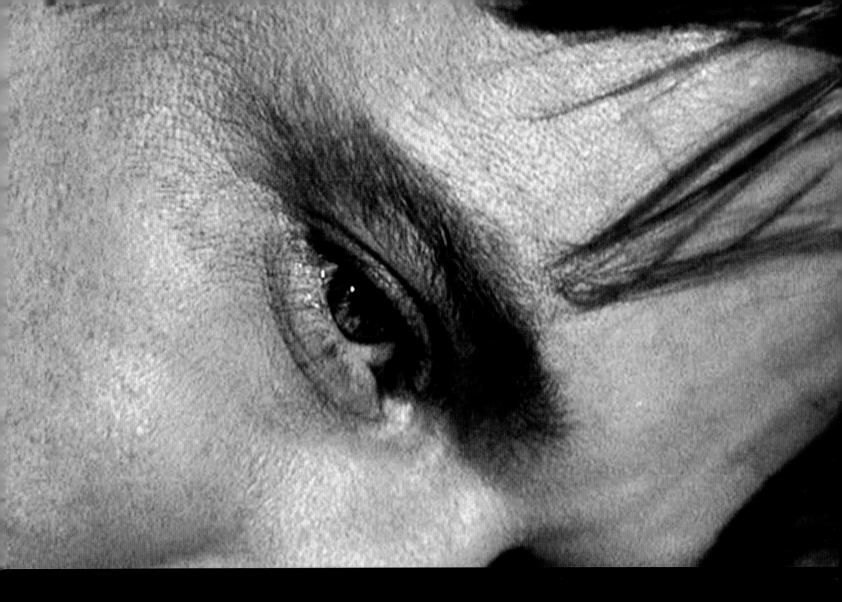

experiments of innumerable independent artists. Ultimately, the movies of the decade reflect its inherent contradictions, and humanity is still suffering from the failure to overcome them. In uncompromising form, *Bonnie and Clyde* embodies the grimmest of insights: in an unfree society, a personal struggle for peace and freedom may well terminate in death and destruction. It's an insight that has lost nothing of its validity. Yet this world is the only one

we have! Or as they say in the film adaptation of Joseph Heller's most famous novel (*Catch 22,* 1970):

– "That's some catch, that Catch 22."
– "It's the best there is."

Jürgen Müller / Steffen Haubner

LA DOLCE VITA – THE SWEET LIFE ⚲

La dolce vita

959/60 - ITALY / FRANCE - 177 MIN. - B & W - DRAMA

DIRECTOR FEDERICO FELLINI (1920–1993) SCREENPLAY FEDERICO FELLINI, TULLIO PINELLI, ENNIO FLAIANO, BRUNELLO RONDI DIRECTOR OF PHOTOGRAPHY OTELLO MARTELLI EDITING LEO CATOZZO MUSIC NINO ROTA PRODUCTION GIUSEPPE AMATO, ANGELO RIZZOLI for RIAMA FILM, PATHÉ CONSORTIUM CINÉMA, GRAY-FILM.

STARRING MARCELLO MASTROIANNI (Marcello Rubini), ANITA EKBERG (Sylvia), ANOUK AIMÉE (Maddalena), YVONNE FURNEAUX (Emma), ALAIN CUNY (Steiner), WALTER SANTESSO (Paparazzo), ADRIANO CELENTANO (Singer), LEX BARKER (Robert), ALAIN DIJON (Frankie Stout), ANNIBALE NINCHI (Marcello's Father), NADIA GRAY (Nadia), NICO (Partygoer).

ACADEMY AWARDS 1961 OSCAR for BEST COSTUMES (Piero Gherardi).

OF CANNES 1960 GOLDEN PALM (Federico Fellini).

"Rome is simply marvelous. A kind of jungle – humid and beautiful, loud at times, peaceful at others – it's a place where you can hide behind the foliage."

"Scandalous!" The cries of the Italian press were heard far and wide: *La dolce vita* was a wanton, permissive, blasphemous piece of celluloid and nothing short of appalling. The Vatican condemned it to the last circle of hell, and the in-crowd turned up their noses. Federico Fellini was spat at and even challenged to a duel. With *La dolce vita*, the filmmaker immersed himself in a world of stars and hopefuls, artists and intellectuals, and supplied his audience with superficiality and decadence instead of the traditional content and good morals. As Fellini saw it, desire had won out over reason, speechlessness over communication, and filth over purity …

A stone-carved Jesus glides over the rooftops of Rome, sanctifying arms outstretched. Suspended by cables, the gigantic statue is being flown to the Vatican via helicopter, followed by a second chopper in which reporter Marcello (Marcello Mastroianni) and photographer Paparazzo (Walter Santesso) keep a close eye on the action. The two men are tabloid journalists, riff-raff propagators of the flashbulb storm that hits the city whenever a movie star struts down a runway. Their notebooks are always within arm's reach in case they spot an aristocrat canoodling with his mistress at a nightclub. Paparazzo chomps at the bit for a potential photo opportunity of Rome's A-listers – preferably with their pants down. The suave Marcello, however, is discrete in his approach, offhandedly ensnaring his quarry while as he shadows them from one haunt to the next. The chic cafés of the Via Veneto are his second home, the heart of the action and a breeding ground for young ladies itching to get discovered.

Marcello is not an impartial observer, more an active member of the lofty company he keeps tabs on. Accompanied by Maddalena (Anouk Aimée), a local billionaire's daughter, he gallivants through the night until sunrise, then rushes off to the side of a Hollywood glamour girl (Anita Ekberg), giving her a personal tour of all Rome has to offer … He'll attend a palace soirée, and promenade with blue bloods across the expanse of the princely estate. At an outdoor party where starlets and movie producers fill the dance floor, Marcello's the one who puts a sizzle in their step, only to watch from the sidelines as the night nearly ends in an orgy. Sunset comes and goes, and he completes the circle at a gathering hosted by his intellectual buddy Steiner (Alain Cuny), bringing a tone of calm to the evening while rediscovering his calling in life as a writer – only to let it slip through his fingers once more.

By openly depicting sexuality to an extent that had been virtually unheard of until then – from a barefooted Anita Ekberg getting down and dirty

2

"This sensational representation of certain aspects of life in contemporary Rome, as revealed in the clamorous experience of a free-wheeling newspaper man, is a brilliantly graphic estimation of a whole swath of society in decay and a withering commentary upon the tragedy of the over-civilized."

1 Couldn't aspire to anything higher: The statuesque Anita Ekberg soaks up the sweet life during a midnight bath in Rome's Trevi Fountain.

2 Passing up the paparazzi: And wouldn't you know it, the man that coined the term 'paparazzi' was none other than former tabloid journalist gone film director, Federico Fellini.

3 Sweets for the sweet: Within minutes, this sober pair will be utterly drunk on life and ready to brave the shallows.

to the sound of young Adriano Celentano's wild rock'n'roll stylings to Nadia Gray baring it all at a party to the pack of hungry eyes – Fellini's film was immediately the target of a heated debate. The outcome: even in the more remote provinces, audiences lined up in their thousands to see a three-hour picture that would normally have only run in art house cinemas. *La dolce vita* instantly became Federico Fellini's greatest hit, regardless of its episodic narrative structure and the absence of an exciting storyline. Marcello is the film's sole connecting thread, leading us through a labyrinth of nightly escapades across Rome.

The film's opulent visuals meant that it was often compared to a painting, deemed either a "portrait of society" or "Baroque fresco." Much of that in fact is the result of Swedish actress Anita Ekberg's performance. Her nighttime dip in Rome's Trevi Fountain is one of the most illustrious images ever to grace the screen; her viewing of St. Peter's Dome in a slinky priest-like garment created a furore among the Catholic churchmen sensitive to the use of symbols. Ekberg, in fact, was a sensation throughout Rome even before shooting commenced, and Fellini made shrewd use of her celebrity status. He drew from actual tabloid anecdotes – the slap Ekberg takes from

4   Wiggle and jiggle your way across the dance floor: Fellini's depiction of high society's decadence-till-dawn mentality awakens images of the Fall of Rome.

5   Caught up in the glamour: An ordinary woman loves the unexpected media attention she is showered with. Little does she suspect her husband's suicide and the murder of their children is the reason for it. Without a doubt, Fellini's criticism of the media has even more clout today than it did then.

6   Undulating Undine: A former 'Miss Sweden,' the real life Anita Ekberg also lost her heart to Italy's capital city. Shortly after the shoot of *La dolce vita* wrapped up, she relocated there permanently.

7   Va-va-va-voom! A woman, dressed in her own rendition of the holy cloth, awaits Marcello at the top of the cathedral. It was one of the many scenes that shocked the Vatican, especially considering that St. Peter's Square can be spotted in the background.

8   Maestro Mastroianni: *La dolce vita* marked the beginning of a collaboration between Mastroianni and Fellini that spanned several decades and six films. As the director's on-screen alter ego, the suave actor plays Marcello Rubini, a man desperately trying to escape the frustrations of life as a tabloid journalist.

"... an allegory, a cautionary tale of a man without a center." *Chicago Sun-Times*

her on-screen husband (Lex Barker) was directly lifted from a public incident with her real life spouse – and shamelessly blurred the distinctions between real life people and film characters. Likewise, he had numerous aristocrats and models portray themselves, thus hoping to get the episodes to play as naturally and authentically as possible. His choices paid off. The German newspaper *Die Welt* wanted to know why there was so much controversy surrounding the film, claiming that Fellini had simply spliced together a chronicle of scandals to unmask Rome's nitty-gritty demimondes.

What *La dolce vita* does succeed in unmasking is the inter-dependency of the media and media sensations, and journalists and stars. The former needs material to write about, and the latter needs the publicity in order to exist in at all. Long before this habitual feed-off became a point of public interest with regard to World Trade Center attacks in 2001, Fellini began to ask himself whether an event without media attention can be regarded as an event *per se*. It is precisely this question which still makes the film read like something hot off the press.   NM

**NINO ROTA
(1911–1979)**

It all started with a bus stop. This was the site where Fellini was to happen upon a fellow caught up in his own thoughts and waiting for a line that normally took a totally different route. Fellini wanted to inform him of his error, but the gentleman's desired bus stopped right in front of them before he got the chance. The event left a lasting impression on Fellini, who was convinced that he had met someone capable of performing magic. Although the particulars of the account vary – sometimes the director placed the bus stop at Rome's Via Po, sometimes in front of Cinecittà Studios – this is allegedly how Fellini got to be friends with composer Nino Rota just after the end of World War II. Their genial relationship gave rise to many a magical moment in cinematic history. Be it Gelsomina's lament in *The Road* (*La strada*, 1954) or the circus march in *8 1/2* (*8 1/2 / Otto e mezzo*, 1962) Nino Rota's music was, as one critic wrote, very much an invisible player within a film's narrative. Nino Rota Rinaldi was born into a Milano family of musicians in 1911. It wasn't long before he was deemed a prodigy and schooled in classical music throughout Italy and abroad in American conservatories. He started out composing orchestra and choir pieces, before trying his hand at film scoring in the early 1940s. By the time he scored Alberto Lattuada's *Without Pity* (*Senza pietà*, 1948) it became clear just what the distinguishing factors of Rota's music were: he had a knack for pursuing known melodies, transforming them, and integrating existing snippets here and there. Later, for example, he was awarded an Oscar for scoring, Francis Ford Coppola's *The Godfather – Part II* (1974), a project largely inspired by the musical compositions he created for Eduardo de Filippo's *Fortunella* (1957).

Rota produced dozens of readily recognizable melodies. His music seesawed between pathos and irony, and it was not unheard of for melancholy bars to suddenly switch into something snappier, or for a loud note to subside into an extended undertone. He collaborated with big name directors like Luchino Visconti, King Vidor, and René Clément. Nonetheless, his lifelong partnership with Fellini is the stuff of legend. Starting with *The White Sheik* (*Lo sceicco bianco*, 1952), Rota wrote the music to all Fellini's pictures for the remainder of his life. The two men would sit together at the piano with Rota composing and testing out combinations, while Fellini provided feedback. This was to be the birthplace of some of the cinema's most magical music. *The Orchestra Rehearsal* (*Prova d'orchestra*, 1978) was the last project they would work on together. Nino Rota died in Rome the following year. He was one of the 20th century's most influential film composers.

L'AVVENTURA / THE ADVENTURE

L'avventura

1960 - ITALY / FRANCE - 145 MIN. - B & W - DRAMA

DIRECTOR MICHELANGELO ANTONIONI (1912–2007) SCREENPLAY MICHELANGELO ANTONIONI, ELIO BARTOLINI, TONINO GUERRA DIRECTOR OF PHOTOGRAPHY ALDO SCAVARDA EDITING ERALDO DA ROMA MUSIC GIOVANNI FUSCO PRODUCTION LUCIANO PERUGIA, CINO DEL DUCA, AMATO PENNASILICO for CINO DEL DUCA, PRODUZIONE CINEMATOGRAFICHE EUROPEE, ROBERT & RAYMOND HAKIM COMPANY, SOCIÉTÉ CINÉMATOGRAPHIQUE LYRE.

STARRING GABRIELE FERZETTI (Sandro), MONICA VITTI (Claudia), LÉA MASSARI (Anna), DOMINIQUE BLANCHAR (Giulia), JAMES ADDAMS (Corrado), RENZO RICCI (Anna's Father), ESMERALDA RUSPOLI (Patrizia), LELIO LUTTAZZI (Raimondo), GIOVANNI PETRUCCI (Goffredo), DOROTHY DE POLIOLO (Gloria).

UN FILM DI MICHELANGELO ANTONIONI

L'AVVENTURA

JAMES ADDAMS · DOROTHY DE POLIOLO · GIOVANNI PETRUCCI · ESMERALDA RUSPOLI

IL FILM CHE HA TRIONFATO AL FESTIVAL DI CANNES 1960 · PREMIO SPECIALE DELLA GIURIA PREMIO FEDERAZIONE INTERNAZIONALE AUTORI CINEMATOGRAFICI · PREMIO FI PRES CI · PREMIO NOUVELLE CRITIQUE

"The thought of losing you kills me. But I no longer feel your presence."

This film needs some effective defenders, such as the famous Spanish director Pedro Almodóvar, who said: "When I first saw *L'avventura*, I was shaken. I felt just like Monica Vitti in the film. Like her, I could say: 'I don't know what to do… Good, let's go to a nightclub … I think I have an idea … I've forgotten it already…'" Or the great American film critic Pauline Kael, who wrote (in *Film Quarterly*): "*L'avventura* is, easily, the film of the year, because Antonioni demonstrated that the possibilities for serious, cultivated, personal expression in this medium have not been exhausted."

The reason why *L'avventura* needs some persuasive advocates is simple: at first glance, it looks forbidding, unfocused and long-winded. At the premiere in Cannes, the audience made its feelings very clear, with some people shouting "Cut!" during scenes that seemed too protracted. Others disliked the characters' strange behavior. The ending was even greeted with mocking laughter, which is hard to understand, given the symbolic power of the final image: a panorama platform in the light of dawn; on the left, in the distance, the snowcapped peak of Mount Etna; in the middle, with his back to the camera, a man in a suit, sitting hunch-shouldered on a park bench. Standing beside him, also with her back to us, a blonde woman in a dark skirt and sweater; she strokes his head, but says nothing. The right half of the frame is filled with the windowless wall of a house. The man and the woman are in some kind of limbo, or purgatory, or no-man's land; they are caught between the dense presence of the architecture and the vast distances of the natural world, between prison and escape. It's a powerful metaphor for the state of their relationship, as they are about to decide whether or not they will part. The film ends before we learn their decision.

The blonde woman is Claudia (Monica Vitti), a girlfriend of Anna (Léa Massari). Anna comes from a wealthy family, and she has a relationship with Sandro (Gabriele Ferzetti), though his work as a structural engineer means they rarely see each other. Together with some friends, they take a trip to the Liparian islands on a small private yacht. They are a typical bunch of Roman

"Director Michelangelo Antonioni has given this a good beginning as he incisively blocks out the characters and the lack of roots in a life where emotion and love have been lost in an almost meaningless chain of attempts at love."

Variety

1   It's nothing personal: Claudia (Monica Vitti) doesn't take to serious discussions first thing in the morning. Or could it just be that she wants to avoid talking about love with the man she's bedding? (Gabriele Ferzetti as Sandro). Director Michelangelo Antonioni once said of his films,

"You can't know what's really going on in a film unless you surrender yourself to its logic."

2   Lacking content? There are times when Claudia finds patterned wallpaper more interesting than her beau.

3   Nancy Drew ventures abroad: Giulia (Dominique Blanchar) and Claudia go off in search of Anna. It won't be long before Claudia finds herself assimilating aspects of the missing woman's character; in this scene, she's already wearing her clothes.

bohemians: vain, jaded and cynical. When they stop off at a rocky island near Panarea, Sandro suddenly mentions marriage, but Anna no longer wants this as she no longer has any feelings for him. A short time later, she disappears – and we never see her again.

Sandro and Claudia go off in search of her. Separately, then together, they follow vague clues across the island of Sicily, from Milazzo to Messina to Noto, and finally to Taormina. Though they never succeed in finding Anna, they do develop an interest in each other, and eventually they're a couple. Then Sandro meets an American starlet at a party … and Claudia runs away,

deeply hurt. On that terrace above the sea, he catches up with her. Both of them are crying; he, perhaps, out of regret, or because he realizes he is actually incapable of love.

Perhaps. In the world of Michelangelo Antonioni, things are seldom clear and simple. This is partly because the viewer is thrown in at the deep end, and told very little about the characters' past history. They seem impulsive and unpredictable, always acting on the spur of the moment. *L'avventura* was the first film in Antonioni's so-called Italian Trilogy, which continued with *La notte* (1960) and *Eclipse* (*L'eclisse*, 1962). These movies reflect the frag-

SICILY IN FILM

Lanterns dangle from the bows of little boats as they row across the sea in the darkness: night after night, the fishermen of Acitrezza, a small village near Catania, perform the same hard work for starvation wages. Luchino Visconti's *The Earth Trembles* (*La terra trema*, 1948) was not the first film about Sicily, its sometimes rough people, and its idiosyncratic language; but it was the first great one. As someone says: "only the rich speak Italian here." *The Earth Trembles*: exploitation, tradition, rebellion and pride on a stunningly beautiful island. The film is based on a novel by Giovanni Verga, a native of Catania. As the most important writer of the Italian realist tradition, he had a huge influence on Italian cinema. His novel of Sicilian jealousy, *I Malavoglia*, was published in 1881, and formed the basis of *The Earth Trembles*. Even more successful still was the short story Cavalleria rusticana, adapted for the first time in 1916 by Ugo Falena, and remade many times. The Mafia made its movie debut no later than 1949, in Pietro Germi's *In the Name of the Law* (*In nome della legge*), a neorealist movie depicting a young judge's struggle against entrenched corruption. His next movie, *Il cammino della speranza* (1951) also focused on the miserable social conditions so prevalent in the south of the country, showing unemployed miners from Sicily forced to seek work in France. *Divorce Italian-Style* (*Divorzio all'italiana*, 1961) was a humorous satire on absurd marriage laws, and it cast an ironical eye on Sicilian ideas about honor and manliness.

One Sicilian in particular was an object of fascination for filmmakers: the bandit Salvatore Giuliano, whose heyday was in the 40s. Variously presented as a nationalist, a freedom fighter, or a would-be politician, he was always seen as a victim, either of society as a whole, or of powerful individuals pulling the strings from behind the scenes. Towards the end of the 20th century, the bloody wars against the Mafia took pride of place in cinematic portraits of the Italian island, resulting in films such as Francesco Rosis' *The Palermo Connection or To Forget Palermo* (*Dimenticare Palermo / Oublier Palerme*, 1989) or Ricky Tognazzi's *The Escort* (*La scorta*, 1993). A warmer take on Sicily was crafted by Giuseppe Tornatore in his films about the cinema such as *Cinema Paradiso* (*Nuovo cinema Paradiso*, 1989) and *The Star Maker* (*L'uomo delle stelle*, 1995), idyllic views of a past and so much more appealing island in the sun.

5

4   Gone with the wind? After Anna vanishes, Giulia and Claudia look for clues near her last known whereabouts – the rocky island, Lisca Bianca. As can be seen in numerous Antonioni films, the director was partial to the seaside.

5   I'll be at the office if you need me: Whereas the Italian filmmaker consistently made pushovers of his male characters …

6   … he made sure his female leads always had a lot going on upstairs. And indeed, most of them gave new meaning to the term 'lady liberty.'

"His photography is exquisite – sharp and immensely picturesque. Much of it is shot on location, in the cities and countryside of Sicily, and there is a great deal of beauty and excitement in the pure composition of movement against architectural forms." *The New York Times*

mentation of experience in the modern world. People have lost all orientation, traditional values have grown questionable, and there is no longer any real connection between the individual and society or between man and the natural world. Everything is growing more and more complicated, and more and more abstract.

L'avventura sketches this progress towards abstraction. After 25 minutes of the film, its main character simply vanishes, after a conversation in which she rejects the time-honored identity of a bourgeois wife. She is replaced by Claudia, an equally self-confident woman who is equally unsure of the role she will adopt in life. Then there's Sandro, whose new job as a

structural engineer pays him a lot more money than his creative work as an architect. And finally we have the Sicilian ghost town, possibly the result of property speculation, whose empty houses may be seen as a symbol of the vacuum at the heart of the protagonists. *L'avventura*, then, is a study of the social abyss between the old world and the new, between the Roman sophisticates and the rooted Sicilians, who greedily eye any unaccompanied woman.

It may well be Antonioni's best work. Certainly, few other films have examined their time with such elegance and acuity, from such a distance and yet with such emotional power.

PSYCHO

1960 - USA - 109 MIN. - B & W - PSYCHO THRILLER

DIRECTOR ALFRED HITCHCOCK (1899–1980) SCREENPLAY JOSEPH STEFANO, based on the novel of
the same name by ROBERT BLOCH DIRECTOR OF PHOTOGRAPHY JOHN L. RUSSELL EDITING GEORGE TOMASINI
MUSIC BERNARD HERRMANN PRODUCTION ALFRED HITCHCOCK for SHAMLEY PRODUCTIONS INC.

STARRING ANTHONY PERKINS (Norman Bates), JANET LEIGH (Marion Crane), VERA MILES
(Lila Crane), JOHN GAVIN (Sam Loomis), JOHN MCINTIRE (Al Chambers), MARTIN BALSAM
(Milton Arbogast), LURENE TUTTLE (Mrs. Chambers), SIMON OAKLAND (Doctor Richmond),
PATRICIA HITCHCOCK (Caroline), MORT MILLS (Policeman).

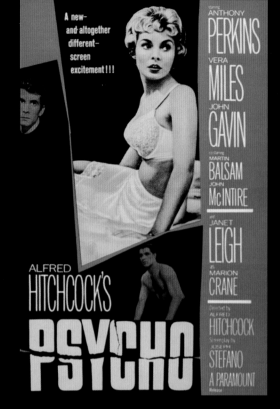

"Mother, she's just a stranger!"

It's what you might call a *twisted* fate. Marion Crane's (Janet Leigh) illicit affair with the married Sam Loomis (John Gavin) awakens deviant impulses within her. Entrusted with 40,000 dollars in company funds, she promptly invests in the future, making off with a sum that will allow her to start a new life with Joe. But the cops are on to her, and Marion thinks twice about executing her plan. The choice, however, isn't hers: a storm forces Marion to seek sanctuary at a remote motel, where a relaxing shower ends as a bloodbath. The murderess, it seems, suspected the overnight guest of making advances toward her son, the motel's introverted manager Norman Bates (Anthony Perkins), and decided to nip danger in the bud. Attempting to cover up his mother's regrettable actions, Bates wipes the scene clean, stuffs Marion's corpse into her car, and sinks the vehicle in a swamp – forty grand and all.

Then the real investigation begins. Despite all their hard work, the gruesome twosome don't get to close shop just yet. Sam, Marion's sister Lila (Vera Miles) and a private detective named Arbogast (Martin Balsam) come in search of the missing woman and the stolen funds. Sticking his nose in the wrong place, Arbogast is also disposed of by the deranged old lady, who apparently resides in the seclusion of the familial estate overlooking the motel. After Sam and Lila wise up to the horrors of the Bates' mansion, they are dumbfounded to learn from the authorities that Mrs. Bates has been dead for a good ten years ...

Psycho is undoubtedly Hitchcock's boldest film – although the critical uproar of the time, fixated on a close up of a toilet bowl, seemed to miss the point. Tauntingly, the master of suspense plays with the viewer's expectations time and again: mercilessly killing off his leading lady in the first third of the picture, and introducing plot elements like the suitcase of money that amount to nothing more than red herrings. Arguably, the entire plot is a network of setups and visual suggestions meant to keep the audience unnerved until the

"**What makes Psycho immortal, when so many films are already half-forgotten as we leave the theater, is that it connects directly with our fears: Our fears that we might impulsively commit a crime, our fears of the police, our fears of becoming the victim of a madman, and of course our fears of disappointing our mothers.**"

Chicago Sun-Times

curtain falls. And the seamless manner in which these subversive images undermine the story and suck it into the background makes *Psycho* more reminiscent of an experimental art-house piece than a Hollywood blockbuster. The most striking example of this is the shower scene, where a total of 70 camera shots fill forty-five seconds of scream time – the hard cuts between shots and Bernard Herrmann's screeching score viscerally tuning us to each stab of the killer's knife. The scene was so shocking that Hitchcock abstained from the further inclusion of similarly violent displays in the rest of the film for he clearly already had the audience just where he wanted them.

Equally remarkable is how ingeniously the filmmaker and cinematographer John L. Russell come up with excuses not to reveal the face of Norman's mother until just before the end. We never suspect that Arbogast's stairwell death is shot from a bird's eye for anything other than artistic reasons.

1 Who? *Moi?* Mama's boy Norman Bates (Anthony Perkins) fears the gaze of foreign eyes – especially when they belong to his attractive hotel guests.

2 Heartbreak hotel: The Bates' Mansion, a set-piece replica of an existing building, is among the most readily recognizable homes ever to grace the screen. The original is located in the 6th circle of hell.

3 Behind bars and closed doors: All the conniving Marion Crane (Janet Leigh) ever wanted in life was to run off and elope with lover Sam Loomis (John Gavis). And she would have, had it not been for one little, but fatal, mistake. But then you only get to make one now darling, don't you?

3

JANET LEIGH
(b. 1927)

Jeanette Helen Morrison, born in Merced, California, was just 15 years old when she finished high school and began her studies in music and psychology. Her rise to fame is something of a Hollywood fairy tale: actress Norma Shearer apparently saw her while vacationing at a ski resort where Janet's father was working. Soon the young woman was cast in films opposite some of the industry's biggest names, including Robert Mitchum in *Holiday Affair* (1949), James Stewart in *The Naked Spur* (1953), John Wayne in *Jet Pilot* (1957), and both Charlton Heston and Orson Welles in *Touch of Evil* (1958). With *Psycho* (1960), Alfred Hitchcock supplied her with her most memorable role: Marion Crane, a heroine who is murdered before the first half of the picture is over. The part earned Leigh an Oscar nomination. John Frankenheimer's classic political drama *The Manchurian Candidate* (1962) proved to be one of the last high-caliber Hollywood films she would appear in; playing the girlfriend of the brainwashed Bennett Marco (Frank Sinatra), Leigh relies on her particular brand of aloof understatement to help him get his life back on track. From 1951 to 1962, the actress was married to favorite co-star Tony Curtis. They had two daughters, Kelly and Jamie Lee Curtis, both of whom followed in their parents' professional footsteps. Janet made a recent appearance in front of the camera at the side of daughter Jamie Lee in *Halloween H20 – 20 Years Later* (1998), the eighth installment in the horror film series made popular by Janet Leigh's world-famous child.

4

"After Hitchcock's suspense pictures and romantic adventure stories could he come up with a shocker, acceptable to mainstream American audiences, which still carried the spine-tingling voltage of foreign presentations such as *Diaboliques*? The answer is an enthusiastic yes. He blended the real and the unreal in fascinating proportions and punctuated his film with several quick, grisly and unnerving surprises."

San Francisco Chronicle

Psycho's narrative takes just as many experimental liberties. Much like in a television drama, lengthy dialog clarifies plot and subtext. Of prime importance is Norman and Marion's conversation at the motel, in which a bond is established between the killer and his victim. It is here that the viewer learns of Norman's interest in taxidermy, with the stuffed birds themselves acting as an eerie congress of witnesses: no amount of money can make them divulge the grizzly acts they've seen. These petrified beasts, and the peephole that Norman uses to spy on Marion as she undresses, are reminders of the camera's voyeuristic nature.

Everywhere we turn, *Psycho* confronts us with visual analogies of watching and being watched: from the eye-like shower drain into which Marion's blood disappears, to the smirking toilet seat that stares us down in one of the final shots. And there is no misunderstanding the accompanying dialog: "They're probably watching me. Well, let them. Let them see what kind of person I am. I hope they are watching. They'll see. They'll see and they'll know."

It's more than just a coincidental choice of words Hitchcock placed in Bates' mouth. In truth, the soliloquy is as much a personal confession on the part of the director as of its speaker. At the peak of his career, Hitch couldn't have picked a more poignant moment to make it. For beyond the façade of terror, what is *Psycho* if not a great master's artistic manifesto?

SH

4 Drowned out screams: How many cuts does it take to kill Marion Crane? Hitchcock used approximately seventy. Urban legend would have you believe that renowned cinema graphic artist, Saul Bass, staged *Psycho's* shower scene. But it's a bloody lie!

5 Checking in and checking out: Norman is among the few hotel managers who hate having guests.

6 Don't tell mama: Mother will be livid if she finds out who's been sleeping in one of Norman's beds.

5

BREAKFAST AT TIFFANY'S ♟♟

1961 - USA - 115 MIN. - LOVE STORY, LITERARY ADAPTATION

DIRECTOR BLAKE EDWARDS (*1922) SCREENPLAY GEORGE AXELROD, based on the novel of the same name by TRUMAN CAPOTE DIRECTOR OF PHOTOGRAPHY FRANZ F. PLANER EDITING HOWARD SMITH MUSIC HENRI MANCINI PRODUCTION MARTIN JUROW, RICHARD SHEPERD for PARAMOUNT PICTURES.

STARRING AUDREY HEPBURN (Holly Golightly), GEORGE PEPPARD (Paul "Fred" Varjak), PATRICIA NEAL (2-E), BUDDY EBSEN (Doc Golightly), MICKEY ROONEY (Mr. Yunioshi), MARTIN BALSAM (O. J. Berman), JOSÉ LUIS DA VILLALONGA (Villalonga), JOHN MCGIVER (Tiffany's Sales Clerk), ALAN REED (Sally Tomato), DOROTHY WHITNEY (Mag Wildwood).

ACADEMY AWARDS 1961 OSCARS for BEST MUSIC (Henri Mancini), BEST SONG: "Moon River" (Music: Henry Mancini; Text: Johnny Mercer).

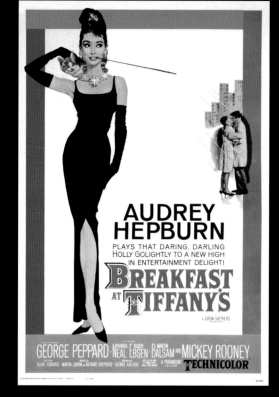

"You know those days when you've got the mean reds?"

Night dissolves into day over an all but empty 5th Avenue. As the rest of New York brushes the sleep from its eyes, a willowy figure, still fragrant with dreams of yesterday, is reflected in the front window of the world's most famous jewelry store. Hidden behind tortoise-shell sunglasses, a slinky black cocktail dress, and a mane of upswept hair, she is a vision of aloof elegance softened only by the brown sandwich bag and paper coffee cup she holds. This is Holly Golightly (Audrey Hepburn) as we best remember her: a lone and radiant gem amongst so many lesser diamonds as she indulges in an unforgettable breakfast at Tiffany's.

Unlike her clients, Holly herself is not a member of the upper echelons of New York society who patronize her beloved jewelry store. Although it's toned down in the movie, Truman Capote made it clear in his original novella that the 18-year-old powder room princess, described as "a creature of chic thinness with a face beyond childhood… yet this side of belonging to a woman," is indeed a professional call girl.

Holly has bolted from her May-December marriage to a Dust Bowl vet-

erinarian without so much as a kiss goodbye for a stab at happiness in the Big Apple. This, naturally, involves pressing her luck on the Bohemian circuit, trying to make ends meet (or maybe even a fortune) amongst playboys and snobs in a world of masks, affectations and countless mirrors. Whenever this party girl tires of the whole scene, she stays up the night with a case of the "mean reds," only to seek sanctuary and a glimmer of self-reflection the next morning in the Tiffany's storefront.

Sharing a Manhattan brownstone apartment with her nameless cat, she is utterly alone in the presence of countless aging millionaires, who look after her financial welfare in exchange for a bit of companionship. There are, however, several men who expect nothing in return, at least not on the surface. She visits imprisoned drug-runner Sally Tomato once a week in Sing-Sing, thinking he just wants someone to talk to and never suspecting that he's really using her as an illegal messenger pigeon.

It's just as well – he's not her idea of relationship material anyway. And so she continues to seek out a man, preferably a millionaire under 50, who

1 Looking for a girl's best friend: Holly Golightly (Audrey Hepburn) sizes men up to make sure they can support the lifestyle she's grown accustomed to – and hopefully move her up a notch.

2 Nine lives: Despite being penniless, Paul (George Peppard) tries to land on his feet with Holly.

3 Nickel and diming: In Holly's hands even a little nightshade can be a deadly weapon.

can fill the ever-increasing void in her life. The person she eventually turns to, neighboring tenant and penniless writer Paul Varjak (George Peppard), hardly fits the bill. Nonetheless, these two lost souls have a few points in common. Much like Holly, Paul's precarious existence is financed by a married benefactress who expects a little sugar for supporting the arts.

It's only a matter of a time before floozy and gigolo warm up to one another other and set off on a relationship full of highs and lows. They establish a rare and precious sense of trust, gradually revealing themselves to one another while discovering moments of clarity in a superficial and mixed-up world.

Deviating from Capote's literary work, in which Holly continues the search for her Mr. Right Millionaire in Brazil, the film's conclusion leaves us with one of the most poignant happy endings Hollywood has ever put forth. We are left witnessing an emotional storm in the streets of New York as Holly chooses Paul over money. They kiss and then the cat nestles in between their

AUDREY HEPBURN Edda Hepburn van Hemmstra was born into a wealthy, influential family in Brussels, Belgium on May 4th, 1929. Her mother was a Dutch baroness and her father a British banker. After several years at a London boarding school, twelve-year-old Edda headed to Amsterdam with her mother, who had severed ties with her husband because of his affiliation with English fascists. From their new home base, mother and daughter were active in resistance efforts against the Nazi occupation.

A fairy tale career followed the war. Hepburn had her first small speaking part as a cigarette girl in Mario Zampi's *Laughter in Paradise* (1951), in which she could be heard saying "I'm not a lady, I'm a girl" to numerous elderly gentlemen. It wasn't long before French writer Colette cast her as the lead in the Broadway adaptation of her novel *Gigi*. The European ingénue played the courtesan 217 times until director William Wyler took her on a Hollywood style *Roman Holiday* (1953). Wyler's film starred Audrey Hepburn as an inexperienced young princess eager to sow her wild oats at Gregory Peck's side. The doe-eyed actress became an instant postwar icon, a new type of woman which replaced the blonde bombshell. Hollywood approved wholeheartedly and Tinsel Town's infatuation with Audrey earned her a Best Actress movie for her debut performance as Princess Ann in *Roman Holiday*.

Hepburn's designer, Givenchy, quickly transformed her into a trend-setting sensation and, together they succeeded in wiping the slate clean of the buxom female ideal. Tastes shifted from the full blonde mane to the pageboy or ponytail, from pumps to flats, from form-fitting sweaters to draping gowns.

Audrey Hepburn went on to shoot 26 more features and became an ambassador for Amnesty International in her later years. Indisputably, her final role in Steven Spielberg's *Always* (1989), four years prior to her passing, couldn't have been more fitting: Audrey Hepburn left Hollywood an angel.

embrace and somehow completes a spectacularly unorthodox image of family. Rain pours down in sheets, as if the heavenly banks of "Moon River," had overflowed and spilled onto earth. The tune that accompanied the lovers throughout the entire picture (and won Oscars for composer Henry Mancini and lyricist Johnny Mercer) crescendos as Holly and Paul arrive at their train's final destination – simple happiness. These two drifters' days of running on empty, fleeing reality, and blindly chasing rainbows are over. Theirs is a distinctly urban quest for meaning, which Woody Allen would pick up again in his New York stories some twenty years later.

Two things in particular make *Breakfast at Tiffany's* a Hollywood standout to this day. The first is the film's feel for fashion. It wasn't Marilyn Monroe who was cast in the role of 18-year-old Holly Golightly, but rather 32-year-old Audrey Hepburn, a former model for French designer Hubert de Givenchy, who used to her to create a new style of dress and a new type of woman. For Hepburn made the busty blonde bombshell of the 1950s obsolete. Cultivated, reserved, tender and somewhat girlish, Audrey Hepburn became the 1960s Hollywood trademark for the worldly and refined female, an image so perfectly assimilated by Jacqueline Kennedy.

The picture's other characteristic is its utterly self-contained moments, celluloid snapshots that have become as famous as paintings. Be it Holly stowing her shoes in a fruit bowl or using her 20-inch long cigarette holder to maneuver through a packed crowd of partiers – they are images that remain emblazoned in our mind. Nonetheless, the most memorable of these moments is the one the picture is named after, in which a traveling girl reflects on where she really belongs. RV

4   A little sugar in his bowl: Holly finds out that she and Paul are in the same line of work. Patricia Neal as 2-E.

5   Two drifters off to see the world discover a little magic in their own backyard.

6   Bohemian rhapsody: Partygoers in need of a nice cold shower.

7   Timber! Hostess plays lumberjack and clears the way for drunken partygoers.

> **"She (Audrey Hepburn) didn't go to acting schools, she didn't hear the word Strasberg, she did not repeat in front of the mirror. She just was born with this kind of quality and she made it look so unforced, so simple, so easy."**
>
> *Billy Wilder*

LAWRENCE OF ARABIA ♟♟♟♟♟♟♟

1962 - GREAT BRITAIN - 222 MIN. - HISTORICAL DRAMA, BIOPIC

DIRECTOR DAVID LEAN (1908–1991) **SCREENPLAY** ROBERT BOLT, MICHAEL WILSON
DIRECTOR OF PHOTOGRAPHY FREDDIE YOUNG **EDITING** ANNE V. COATES **MUSIC** MAURICE JARRE
PRODUCTION SAM SPIEGEL for HORIZON.

STARRING PETER O'TOOLE (Thomas Edward Lawrence), ALEC GUINNESS (Prince Feisal),
ANTHONY QUINN (Auda Abu Tayi), JACK HAWKINS (General Allenby), OMAR SHARIF
(Sherif Ali Ibn El Kharish), ANTHONY QUAYLE (Colonel Harry Brighton), CLAUDE RAINS
(Mr. Dryden), ARTHUR KENNEDY (Jackson Bentley), JOSÉ FERRER (Turkish Governor),
DONALD WOLFIT (General Murray).

ACADEMY AWARDS 1962 OSCARS for BEST PICTURE (Sam Spiegel), BEST DIRECTOR (David Lean),
BEST CINEMATOGRAPHY (Freddie Young), BEST EDITING (Anne V. Coates), BEST MUSIC
(Maurice Jarre), BEST ART DIRECTION (John Box, John Stoll, Dario Simoni), BEST SOUND
(John Cox).

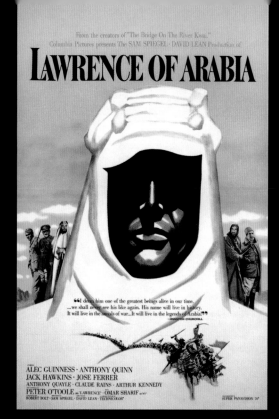

"The best of them won't come for money. They'll come for me!"

"I'm different," announces Thomas Edward Lawrence (Peter O'Toole) right at the start of the film. He's trying to explain to a Bedouin what distinguishes him from the rest of his compatriots in "a fat country with fat people." Different… yes. But in what way? Who was this British officer from Oxford, who led the Arab tribes to rebel against their Turkish rulers during the First World War? An idealistic dreamer? A narcissistic megalomaniac? A homosexual sadomasochist? He died young after a motorcycle accident, and his acquaintances and superior officers answered as one: we don't know who he was – we hardly knew him at all.

Indeed, T. E. Lawrence hardly knew himself, and the more he made his own acquaintance, the more he recoiled from what he saw. This is one major theme of David Lean's monumental film biography, which shows various facets of this strange character without ever really solving the mystery that surrounds the man.

Lawrence of Arabia is not so much a film about war, politics and British colonial history as a visually splendid record of one man's trip to the limits of sanity in the hope of finding himself. Only the most impossible challenges are enough for Thomas Edward Lawrence. He crosses deserts no one has ever ventured into; he plans surprise attacks on seemingly impregnable Turkish positions; he forges fragile alliances amongst bitterly opposed tribes; and eventually, he takes Damascus with his Arab army. Lawrence was once asked what he liked so much about the desert, and he replied, "its cleanliness." But far from achieving the purified soul he longed for, he paid for his self-torturing expeditions with a loss of innocence. Originally inspired by the

"In his performance, O'Toole catches the noble seriousness of Lawrence and his cheap theatricality, his godlike arrogance and his gibbering self-doubt; his headlong courage, girlish psychasthenia, Celtic wit, humorless egotism, compulsive chastity, and sensuous pleasure in pain."
Time

2

3

1 Hitchcock mirage: Director David Lean and cinematographer Freddie Young reeled in the Oscars for their desert magic.

2 Desert Storm: Omar Sharif emerged from the Arabian sands as Sherif Ali Ibn El Kharish and rose to international stardom.

3 Eagle eyes: Major Lawrence (Peter O'Toole) is a singular force and sees what he wants to see.

ideal of helping the Arabs to achieve their independence, Lawrence was eventually forced to recognize that his masters, the British, would never allow it. This is why, at the end of the film, Mr. Dryden (Claude Rains) calls him "a man who tells half-lies." Dryden is a British government representative in Arabia, and in his view, such "half-lying" is worse than mouthing complete falsehoods in the interests of political expediency. By this time, however, Lawrence is barely concerned with political considerations anymore. His courage and willpower have so impressed the Arabs that they have honored him with a new name, and Lawrence, with his tendency to narcissism, luxu-

riates in his popularity and the splendor of his triumphs. As his megalomania grows, he behaves increasingly as if he were the Messiah to the Arab people.

What's more, in the course of his military campaigns, he has learned to kill, and the power he feels while doing so is a source of genuine pleasure. On one occasion, he is captured, tortured and raped by the Turks; and the film hints discreetly that even this is a somewhat ambivalent experience for Lawrence. Speaking to Jackson Bentley, the American reporter (Arthur Kennedy), the Englishman's comrade in arms Prince Feisal (Alec Guinness) sums him up as follows: "With Major Lawrence, mercy is a passion; with me,

PETER O'TOOLE   In 1962, the title role in David Lean's *Lawrence of Arabia* shot the unknown 29-year-old Irishman Peter O'Toole into the major league of international movie stars. Previously, he had only played a few minor roles, such as a bagpiper in Robert Stevenson's *Kidnapped* (1959). In Britain, however, he had already made a name for himself on the stage, thanks to his appearances with the Royal Shakespeare Company in Stratford-upon-Avon. The 60s were to be O'Toole's great decade, in which he would be nominated for the Academy Award on several occasions without ever winning it. With his Irish charm, his piercing blue eyes, his impish sense of humor, and his faintly ironical air, he was perfectly cast in eccentric comedies such as *What's new, Pussycat?* (1965), and *How to Steal a Million* (1966). He had less luck with later roles, apart from his appearance as Robinson Crusoe in Jack Gold's *Man Friday* (1975), a new take on Defoe's tale that depicted the "native" Friday as the cleverer of the two men. By this time, O'Toole's problems with alcohol were gradually becoming noticeable.

O'Toole is still active in film and television today. His most recent movie was *The Final Curtain* (2001), released in 2002, in which he played an age-ing entertainer. In 2003, Peter O'Toole was given an honorary Academy Award: a "Lifetime Achievement Award." Against his will, incidentally; for he announced in no uncertain terms that he still reckoned he had a chance of winning the Oscar in fair competition with his peers.

"Lean and cameraman Young have brought out the loneliness and pitiless torment of the desert with an artistic use of color, and almost every take is superbly framed and edited." *Variety*

4   Taking out the big guns: Aristocrat Sherif Ali shows his impatient friend Lawrence that he is a man be reckoned with.

5   Head in the sand? Lawrence mobilizes the Arabs against a Turkish attack.

6   At a loss for words: Lawmaking and bureaucracy are certainly not among Lawrence's strengths. His patience wears thin as disputes between the Arab tribes sour the spirit of newfound liberty.

7   Listening to his inner clock: Auda Abu Tayi (Anthony Quinn) fears that Lawrence is acting out of self-interest.

it is merely good manners. Judge for yourself which motive is the more reliable."

Lawrence certainly has reasons to be worried about his enthusiasms. When his desperate application for an "ordinary job" is turned down, his next mission ends in the insane butchery of an exhausted Turkish regiment, and in the course of the massacre Lawrence works himself into an ecstasy of bloodlust.

Before *Lawrence of Arabia* Peter O'Toole was an almost completely unknown actor, yet his portrayal of is one of his greatest-ever performances. The background to that portrait is almost equally spectacular: using Technicolor and Super-Panavision-70, director David Lean and cameraman Freddie Young created astonishing panoramas of the beautiful and pitiless desert,

with its fiery sun, its sandstorms, and a horizon like a line drawn through the world. Filming took two years, and ten months alone were spent filming exteriors in Jordan. At one surreal moment, we see a ship sailing through the sands: Lawrence has arrived at the Suez Canal. Equally impressive is the first meeting between Lawrence and Sherif Ali Ibn El Kharish (Omar Sharif): a shimmering mirage that suddenly materializes into a real figure.

For all its beauty, the film is never merely interested in "strong images" for their own sake. Despite the overwhelming landscapes and the dynamic battle scenes, this is an actors' film performed by an outstanding ensemble, and its fascinating central character is always the main focus of interest. *Lawrence of Arabia* is one of the biggest *and* best movies ever made.

LP

TO KILL A MOCKINGBIRD 🏆🏆🏆

962 - USA - 129 MIN. - DRAMA

DIRECTOR ROBERT MULLIGAN (*1925) **SCREENPLAY** HORTON FOOTE, based on the novel of the same name by HARPER LEE **DIRECTOR OF PHOTOGRAPHY** RUSSELL HARLAN **EDITING** AARON STELL **MUSIC** ELMER BERNSTEIN, MACK DAVID **PRODUCTION** ALAN J. PAKULA for PAKULA-MULLIGAN, BRENTWOOD PRODUCTIONS, UNIVERSAL INTERNATIONAL PICTURES.

STARRING GREGORY PECK (Atticus Finch), MARY BADHAM (Jean Louise "Scout" Finch), PHILLIP ALFORD (Jeremy "Jem" Finch), ROBERT DUVALL (Arthur "Boo" Radley), JOHN MEGNA (Dill Harris), BROCK PETERS (Tom Robinson), FRANK OVERTON (Sheriff Tate), ROSEMARY MURPHY (Maudie Atkinson), RUTH WHITE (Mrs. Dubose), ESTELLE EVANS (Calpurnia), COLLIN WILCOX (Mayella Ewell), JAMES ANDERSON (Bob Ewell), ALICE GHOSTLEY (Stephanie Crawford).

ACADEMY AWARDS 1962 OSCARS for BEST ACTOR (Gregory Peck), BEST ADAPTED SCREENPLAY (Horton Foote), and BEST ART DIRECTION (Alexander Golitzen, Henry Bunstead, Oliver Emert).

"I was to think of those days many times. Of Jem and Dill and Boo Radley, and Tom Robinson, and Atticus."

America is a land of unlimited optimism and perilous incongruity, and the history of the USA is also the history of its hopes, its fears and its myths. Amongst the great tales of all the races and generations that have inhabited this country is *To Kill a Mockingbird* – written by Harper Lee and filmed by Robert Mulligan. Indeed, perhaps only Tom Sawyer and Huckleberry Finn have etched themselves into the collective unconscious as indelibly as this novel and this movie.

The story is set in the Depression years. The southern States are particularly hard-hit by the crisis, and countless idyllic small towns are threatened by poverty, racial hatred, ignorance and bigotry. Yet for the children of the widowed lawyer Atticus Finch (Gregory Peck), life is one big adventure. To ten-year-old Jem (Phillip Alford) and his kid sister Scout (Mary Badham), everything is a source of wonder: an old car tyre becomes an exciting toy; a box containing nothing but a few chalks, a broken clock and a pocket-knife is their jealously-guarded treasure chest; and they have a burning interest in the house of the mysterious Boo Radley (Robert Duvall). It's been years since

anyone saw him; and in the children's imagination, every step they take towards his scary, dilapidated house is a terrifying test of their courage. Yet their father's latest case also captures their attention: a black man, Tom Robinson (Brock Peters), has been accused of raping a white woman – and Atticus, bravely, is defending him. The case for the prosecution, and the trial itself, are outrageously unfair; but Jem and Scout gradually learn some lessons for life from their father, who looks evil in the eye and stands up firmly against it. And it's Atticus' tolerance and sympathy that finally enables the children to overcome their greatest fear: the fear of Boo Radley.

As the tomboy Scout, Mary Badham captured the hearts of generations of moviegoers, big and small. Her inimitable mixture of cheek and innocent curiosity disarms everyone she meets; and at the end of the film, she need only speak two words to build a bridge across an abyss: "Hey, Boo." A deathly pale Robert Duvall also gives a touching performance as Boo Radley. To prepare himself for this tiny but unforgettable role (his film debut), he stayed indoors for six weeks, avoiding the sun. And then, of course, there is Gregory

1 The walls have ears: Scout (Mary Badham), Jem (Phillip Alford) and neighborhood friend Dill Harris (John Megna) get caught eavesdropping at the door.

2 Growing pains: The children follow the proceedings from the landing above the courtroom and learn that the grown-up world isn't always fair. Scout

begins to wonder whether her father has any chance of getting his innocent client off the hook.

Peck as Atticus Finch, father and lawyer. An ideal combination of gentleness, intelligence and strength, he became something of a model for all the fathers (and lawyers) who came after him. Peck's Atticus Finch is the very image of integrity.

What really made this quiet film such a huge success was its faithful adherence to a basic tenet of the novel: the story is told exclusively from the children's perspective. Each of their daily adventures is a journey into the shadow-world that lies between Good and Evil. When they encounter the terrors of the adult world, they're armed with the power of their imagination and an absolute trust in the strength of their father; and so they're capable of moving mountains. Nowhere is this clearer than in the scene at the jailhouse,

where a lynch mob demands that Atticus hand over the prisoner Tom Robinson. Though Scout is barely even aware of the crowd's aggression, she manages to defuse the situation merely by asking a few simple questions. The lengthy trial scene is also attended by Scout and Jem, and it ends in a moving demonstration of support for Atticus by the entire black population of the town. *To Kill a Mockingbird* is studded with such miniature highpoints, and quite free from the melodramatic tendentiousness of many films with a political or anti-racist "message."

This is in every respect an extraordinary film — and it was nominated for no less than eight Academy Awards, including Best Film Music. Elmer Bernstein's remarkable score is an assemblage of simple melodies, of the

GREGORY PECK (1916–2003) He embodied the American ideal of modest integrity like no other actor – not even Gary Cooper, whose role in *High Noon* (1952) he had politely declined. Just a couple of years previously, he had played a dignified cowboy in *The Gunfighter* (1950), and he didn't want to be typecast. Yet the big man with the piercing eyes always remained true to himself, however varied the actual roles he played, from a dedicated journalist in *Gentleman's Agreement* (1947) to a New York office worker in *The Man in the Grey Flannel Suit* (1956) and a hard-bitten General in *The Guns of Navarone* (1961). Even ambivalent characters such as the innocently guilty lawyer in *Cape Fear* (1962) had a touch of quiet nobility about them. In *Moby Dick* (1956), his Captain Ahab bore a strong resemblance to Abraham Lincoln, with whom Peck himself had often been compared. Despite chalking up successes in *Roman Holiday* (1953) and *Arabesque* (1966), he never really felt comfortable playing comedies. But those who regarded him as the biggest bore in Hollywood not only failed to notice his immense charisma; they also overlooked the fact that he lived out his ideals, and not merely on screen. He was a committed worker for many charities, he took part in protest marches alongside Martin Luther King, and in 1970, he seriously considered standing as a candidate against the Governor of California, Ronald Reagan. Gregory Peck died in 2003 at the age of 87. His funeral eulogy was given by Brock Peters, the actor who played Tom Robinson in *To Kill a Mockingbird* (1962).

3   Hostile witness: Bob Ewell (James Anderson) is more fired up than a loose cannon. But his fervor leaves defense attorney Atticus Finch (Gregory Peck) cold.

4   In the hot seat: A simple parlor room trick proves that the allegations are false. The defendant, Tom Robinson (Brock Peters), is left-handed.

5   Taking a stand: In the name of the truth, Atticus and Tom combat latent racism in their small Southern town.

"If you just learn a single trick, Scout, you'll get along a lot better with all kinds of folks. You never really understand a person until you consider things from his point of view… Until you climb inside of his skin and walk around in it."

Film quote: Atticus (Gregory Peck)

6 Rabid gunfire: With a steady hand and the eye of marksman, Atticus silences a mad dog terrorizing the neighborhood.

7 Is there no justice? Despite presenting a compelling case, Atticus couldn't sway the jury from finding him guilty.

8 Ominous shadows: Dill and the other children may still be young innocents. However, a day will come when they'll have to have to ward off the darkness themselves.

"*To Kill a Mockingbird* is, first and foremost, a re-creation of a children's world, and a rather grizzly, ghoulish world at that: where the main center of local interest is a lunatic reputed to be dangerous; where dogs run mad in the streets every now and again; and where the half-noticed adult dramas impinge on the children only occasionally. The violence is all the more frightening for being totally unpredictable." *Sight and Sound*

kind a child might produce while tinkering around on the piano. But this sensitive literary adaptation was up against the desert epic *Lawrence of Arabia* (1962)… and ultimately, the only Oscars it received were for Horton Foote's reworking of the novel (which the novelist, unusually in the movie business, thoroughly admired); for the Art Direction, a loving reconstruction of Harper Lee's home town Monroeville on the premises of Universal Studios; and for Gregory Peck, as Best Actor. Till the day he died, he described *To Kill a Mockingbird* as his favorite among all the films he had made, and he maintained a friendship with Harper Lee for many years. In 2003, the American Film Institute voted Atticus Finch the greatest film hero of all time. Among the runners up were Indiana Jones, James Bond – and Lawrence of Arabia.

DR. STRANGELOVE OR: HOW I LEARNED TO STOP WORRYING AND LOVE THE BOMB

963 - GREAT BRITAIN - 93 MIN. - COMEDY, SOCIAL SATIRE

DIRECTOR STANLEY KUBRICK (1928–1999) SCREENPLAY STANLEY KUBRICK, PETER GEORGE, TERRY SOUTHERN, based on a novel by PETER GEORGE DIRECTOR OF PHOTOGRAPHY GILBERT TAYLOR EDITING ANTHONY HARVEY MUSIC LAURIE JOHNSON PRODUCTION STANLEY KUBRICK for HAWK.

STARRING PETER SELLERS (Capt. Lionel Mandrake / President Merkin Muffley / Dr. Strangelove), GEORGE C. SCOTT (General "Buck" Turgidson), STERLING HAYDEN (General Jack D. Ripper), KEENAN WYNN (Colonel "Bat" Guano), SLIM PICKENS (Major T. J. "King" Kong), TRACY REED (Miss Scott), PETER BULL (Ambassador de Sadesky), JAMES EARL JONES (Lieutenant Lothar Zogg).

"Gentlemen, you can't fight in here! This is the War Room!"

The story was meant to be taken very seriously indeed – and it was written by a man who knew what he was talking about. In the 1950s, Peter George, a former officer of the Royal Air Force, published a thriller under the pseudonym Peter Bryant. Its title: *Two Hours to Doom* (in the U.S.: *Red Alert*). Stanley Kubrick had been considering making a film about the nuclear threat for quite some time, and when George's book was recommended to him, he knew he'd found what he was looking for.

Together with Peter George, he started working on the script. At first, they stuck with the dramatic tenor of the original novel, but as time went on, Kubrick was struck by the comic potential of the military subject matter, and

he changed his initial plans. *Dr. Strangelove* became an absurd, coal-black comedy about the end of the world. It united the exceptional visual gifts of this brilliant director with the witty writing of the satirist Terry Southern – who was hired to work on the dialogue – and the unique presence of the comedian and character actor Peter Sellers, who improvised many of his own lines. Sellers' importance to this movie can hardly be over-estimated: not only did Kubrick entrust him with three roles; he even shifted filming to England (where he himself would eventually settle), because Sellers was in the throes of a divorce case and couldn't leave the country. In *Dr. Strangelove*, Kubrick sets out to thwart all our usual expectations. Right at the start, most movie-

goers will miss the customary musical accompaniment, as a disclaimer announces: "It is the stated position of the United States Air Force that their safeguards would prevent the occurrence of such events as are depicted in this film. Furthermore, it should be noted that none of the characters portrayed in this film are meant to represent any real persons living or dead."

The opening titles show a sea of clouds and a bomber being refueled in mid-air. And then we hear the music: "Try a little tenderness." In combination with the selection and editing of the images, this tender foxtrot melody transforms a complex military docking manoeuvre into a bizarre and comical act of love.

The actual story begins at Burpleson Air Base. The paranoid Commander-in-Chief, General Jack D. Ripper (Sterling Hayden), sends a squadron of

"Stanley Kubrick's nightmare comedy – the extraordinary story of a psychotic American general who triggers off a mass nuclear attack on Moscow!" *Film Review*

1   Watch the hand: Scientist Dr. Strangelove's (Peter Sellers) prosthetic appendage has a mind of its own. Don't go pressing any buttons now.

2   Oral fixation: General Jack D. Ripper (Sterling Hayden) mutters bizarre incantations about the mixture of bodily fluids and exhibits a fondness for phallic symbols.

3 Knights of the round table: President Merkin
   Muffley (Peter Sellers) causes an uproar amongst
   his generals by inviting red sheep de Sadesky

(Peter Bull) to graze among his herd in the top
secret war room.

4 Practice what you preach.

GEORGE C. SCOTT General "Buck" Turgidson is the hard-bitten antithesis to Peter Sellers' soft-spoken President Muffley. He is played by an actor whose "unique qual-

"Once again, Peter Sellers demonstrates his versatility and fine comedy sense with three widely varied portrayals: A mild-mannered British liaison officer, the calm, serious President of the U. S. and the heavily accented crippled German scientist, who gives the film its title (certainly the longest ever)." *Box Office Magazine*

8

5   Bollocks! British group Captain Mandrake (Peter Sellers) goes into a frenzy upon hearing of mad U. S. General Jack D. Ripper's (Sterling Hayden) plan to launch World War III.

6   All very hush, hush: The Pentagon's phone call reaches General Buck Turgidson (George C. Scott) after wrapping up a flagrante delecto session with secretary Miss Scott (Tracy Reed).

7   Nothing like a little personality to brighten a place up.

8   Gripping the joystick: "King" Kong opts for a cowboy hat rather than flying helmet for his final mission in pioneering the great frontier.

bombers to the Soviet Union, seals off his airbase from the outside world and activates a special code that makes it impossible to communicate with the pilots. British contact officer Mandrake (Peter Sellers) has no success with his attempts to exercise a moderating influence. Meanwhile, a crisis team chaired by President Muffley (Peter Sellers) is meeting at the Pentagon. Despite the protests of the Air Force Chief of Staff Buck Turgidson (George C. Scott), the Soviet ambassador Alexi de Sadesky (Peter Bull) is also permitted to enter this military Holy of Holies. When de Sadesky and Muffley inform the President of the Soviet Union that his country is in danger, they learn to their horror that the Communist state is in possession of a "Doomsday Machine," which reacts automatically to a nuclear attack and cannot be switched off.

Muffley has no choice but to reveal the target coordinates to the Soviets, in the hope that the bombers can be intercepted in time. Mandrake manages to decipher the codeword and communicate the solution to Washington, and all the bombers are recalled – with the exception of one. The Russians have fired a missile at the B52 of Major T. J. "King" Kong (Slim Pickens) and destroyed his communications equipment. He is now unreachable, and still on his way. Though the damage to the plane is considerable, Kong is determined to accomplish his deadly mission. When the release mechanism refuses to function, he climbs down personally into the bomb bay. Sitting astride an atom bomb, he sets to work on the electronics. Sparks fly, the bay doors open and the bomb falls free – and Kong, happily whooping and waving his Stetson, rides off into the sunset of the world.   HK

"*Dr. Strangelove*'s humor is generated by a basic comic principle: People trying to be funny are never as funny as people trying to be serious and failing." *Chicago Sun-Times*

GOLDFINGER ⚊

1964 - GREAT BRITAIN - 106 MIN. - SPY FILM, BOND FILM

DIRECTOR GUY HAMILTON (*1922) **SCREENPLAY** IAN FLEMING, RICHARD MAIBAUM, PAUL DEHN
DIRECTOR OF PHOTOGRAPHY TED MOORE **EDITING** PETER R. HUNT **MUSIC** JOHN BARRY
PRODUCTION ALBERT R. BROCCOLI, HARRY SALTZMAN for EON PRODUCTIONS and UNITED ARTISTS.

STARRING SEAN CONNERY (James Bond), HONOR BLACKMAN (Pussy Galore), GERT FRÖBE
(Auric Goldfinger), SHIRLEY EATON (Jill Masterson), TANIA MALLET (Tilly Masterson),
HAROLD SAKATA (Oddjob), BERNARD LEE (M), MARTIN BENSON (Martin Solo), CEC LINDER
(Felix Leiter), LOIS MAXWELL (Miss Moneypenny).

ACADEMY AWARDS 1964 OSCAR for BEST SOUND EFFECTS (Norman Wanstall).

"This heart is cold – he loves only gold."

Sixties siren Shirley Bassey sings forebodingly of a man's stone-cold heart and his affinity with a certain precious metal; fragmented images of a female figure dipped in gold flash against a pitch-black screen: we are bid welcome in the world of Goldfinger, a scoundrel with a singular fixation.

Fireballs, high-speed chases and love scenes hint at the action about to explode in this early James Bond thriller. The third picture in the British secret agent series – Bond spoof *Casino Royal* excluded – *Goldfinger* is a shrine to Cold War hysteria. This time round, 007 (Sean Connery) is out to stop unscrupulous German super-criminal Auric Goldfinger (Gert Fröbe) from monopolizing the metal that shares his name and which was associated with so much economic and political power in the 1960s. To succeed, this modern-day Midas has come up with a diabolical scheme…

For Mr. Goldfinger intends no less than to wipe out the Western World's economy by detonating an atomic bomb inside Fort Knox, home to the Unit-ed States' gold reserve and democracy. With the entire supply of American

gold radioactive and worthless, the value of his own resources would sky-rocket. A piece of cake, except James Bond tails Auric Goldfinger to the States and wises up to the despicable plan. However, 007's attempts to fill his colleagues in on the matter are foiled by Goldfinger's right-hand man, a femme fatale known as Pussy Galore (Honor Blackman). Not to worry; after a night of spiritual cleansing with our favorite secret agent, she awakens a new woman, switching sides and informing the American authorities of her ex-employer's machinations.

In *Goldfinger*, female characters are all too readily seduced by gold's luster. There are even a few who meet an untimely demise as a result of its sparkle. Jill Masterson (Shirley Eaton), for example, suffocates when coated with an ever so fine layer of gold paint. Evidently, regardless of what form it takes, this high-carat poison can reduce women to little more than paper dolls and film décor. Pussy Galore is the only exception. She too is initially transfixed by the lure of its immeasurable wealth and power, but her en-

1

2

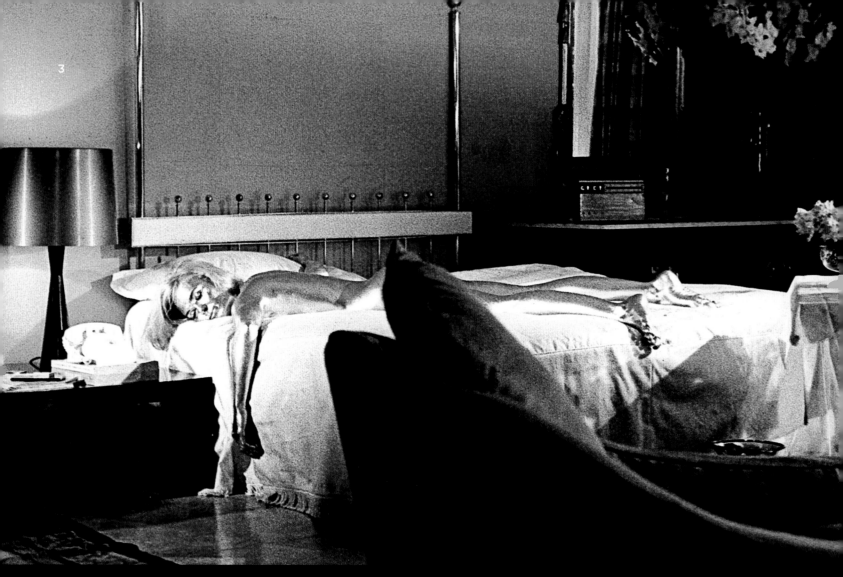

1 The evil eye: Someone's watching 007's (Sean Connery) every move.

2 Rear window, revisited: Even during a stakeout, there's always time for a little hanky panky.

3 The Midas touch: Jill Masterson's (Shirley Eaton) body has increased in value.

"There is an assumption – which you find, at quite the other end of the spectrum, in the Godard films – that we all know the clichés and can have a little fun with them." *Sight and Sound*

counter with 007 changes all that. As the agent's prim secretary Miss Moneypenny (Lois Maxwell) might put it, after a girl lays eyes on James, the only golden trinket of any interest is a wedding band.

To the picture's male leads, gold is a means to an end, and to Auric Goldfinger that end is world domination. He enlists the aid of North Korean communists and is willing to put the lives of thousands of innocent bystanders on the line. His idea of a hostile takeover is gassing the opposition – literally. More central to the film's plot, however, is Goldfinger's intention to hoard as much gold as he possibly can and paralyze the global cash flow in the process. But James Bond, like Moses tempted by the golden calf, does not let all that glitters get the best of him. Instead, the secret agent is intrigued by the practical value of bullion which during the showdown in

Fort Knox, proves a vital tool in the struggle to defuse Goldfinger's atomic bomb.

Considering the era in which it was made, the film races across the screen at top speed, fuelled by countless audio-visual effects and the simmering sex appeal of its cast. The same can't be said of its one-time extravagant set, which today looks more like a relic that could use a good dusting.

The picture's undisputed saving grace is its funny bone – especially with regard to its hero. James Bond may appear to be acting in the name of God, but, in truth, he is a servant of her Majesty's economy. By current standards, his character's impeccable playboy veneer and compliance to passé gender stereotypes read like a highly entertaining persiflage of what was intended to be taken seriously – very seriously.

PLB

5

4   Nights in white satin: Bond is guaranteed more than just a few steamy rendezvous if he keeps sports threads like these.

5   Out of the frying pan, into the fire: Bond doesn't know which of these guys is the worse of two evils – German Goldfinger (Gerd Fröbe) or mute manservant Oddjob (Harold Sakata).

6   Cracker jack: Whenever he's in a jam, James counts on Q's nifty gadgets for a novel rescue.

BOND GIRLS   With the exception of Miss Moneypenny (played throughout the 60s and 70s almost exclusively by Lois Maxwell), most female characters who appear at Bond's side readily bare all for the British secret agent (played by Sean Connery). Teasing monikers that play up the hanky panky like "Pussy Galore" (Honor Blackman) and "Honey Ryder" (Ursula Andress) take the edge off the fact that all of Bond's beauties succumb to his charms without knowing the slightest thing about him. That's not to say that there's no price to pay for being a bad girl. Rosie (Gloria Hendry), Tiffany (Jill St. John), Kissy (Mie Hama), Bambi (Lola Larson), Tilly (Tania Mallet), Bonita (Nadja Regin) and many others all got the kiss of death after shagging 007. It almost makes one wonder whether it's more than just coincidence: for as everybody knows – all of James' actions are performed in the service of her Majesty. How else can we explain why 007 goes for someone as subversive as Pussy – a known lesbian in the Ian Fleming novel, *Goldfinger* (1964)? Too bad that Honor Blackman, who made a name for herself as Cathy Gale in *The Avengers* (1961–69), didn't get a chance to explore this aspect of her character in the movie. Still, much like her literary counterpart, it is a sexual awakening *à la* Bond that enables Ms. Galore to see the light and take her proper place in society. It was only in the 1990s that sexual tables began to turn in the super spy series. Ever since *Golden Eye* (1995) Judi Dench has stood at the MI5 helm as Bond's no-nonsense superior. Slowly but surely, James seems to be developing a taste for the dominatrix thing.

6

DOCTOR ZHIVAGO ♟♟♟♟♟

1965 - USA - 200 MIN. - MELODRAMA, LITERARY ADAPTATION

DIRECTOR DAVID LEAN (1908–1991) SCREENPLAY ROBERT BOLT, based on the novel of the same name by BORIS PASTERNAK DIRECTOR OF PHOTOGRAPHY FREDDIE YOUNG EDITING NORMAN SAVAGE MUSIC MAURICE JARRE PRODUCTION CARLO PONTI for MGM.

STARRING GERALDINE CHAPLIN (Tonja), JULIE CHRISTIE (Lara), TOM COURTENAY (Pasha Antipova / Strelnikov), ALEC GUINNESS (Gen. Jevgraf Zhivago), SIOBHAN MCKENNA (Anna), RALPH RICHARDSON (Alexander Gromeko), OMAR SHARIF (Yuri Zhivago), ROD STEIGER (Victor Komarovsky), RITA TUSHINGHAM (The Girl), ADRIENNE CORRI (Amelia).

ACADEMY AWARDS 1965 OSCARS for BEST ADAPTED SCREENPLAY (Robert Bolt), BEST CINEMATOGRAPHY (Freddie Young), BEST MUSIC (Maurice Jarre), BEST ART DIRECTION (John Box, Terry Marsh, Dario Simoni), BEST COSTUME DESIGN (Phyllis Dalton).

"The personal life is dead in Russia. History has killed it."

Love, affection and sentimentality did not color the rainbows of Social Realism – at least not officially. As Soviet commander Strelnikov (Tom Courtenay) tries to impress upon poet and physician Yuri Zhivago (Omar Sharif), Russia's new social order has been painted a uniform tone: a grand, uncompromising red, which has turned his once admired verse into meaningless displays of formalism. Though fired by the same fanatic idealism that made a general of him, the bloodthirsty Bolshevik's commentary on art and politics leaves the good doctor unfazed. Enslaved by distant echoes of individualism, Zhivago retreats to what has become a taboo private life, losing himself in his literary craft and the freedoms of the countryside. Yet the revolutionary goings-on that surround him refuse to be ignored, and soon he is plunged into the throes of war and away from Lara (Julie Christie) – his mistress and the inadvertent cause of his undoing.

Based on a novel with a background as intriguing as the content of its pages, David Lean's film adaptation of Boris Pasternak's *Doctor Zhivago* was the inevitable conclusion of what had ballooned into a widely publicized East-West political scandal. First brought into the public eye by an Italian publisher in 1957, *Doctor Zhivago* became a run-away literary hit throughout Western Europe and the United States within a year of its appearance. But success proved hollow for Pasternak, whose work remained banned in the Soviet Union for the next thirty years. Although recognized with the Nobel Prize for Literature in 1958, his government coerced him to decline the honor. Two years later, the author was dead.

The events were still very much alive in the collective consciousness of the West when David Lean decided to take on the film adaptation as the project to succeed his critically acclaimed *Lawrence of Arabia* (1962). Paster-

nak's tale about the fate of a conforming non-conformist, whose only desire is to avoid being engulfed by the overwhelming backdrop of a new social order, seemed perfectly suited to Lean's cinematic style. Based on his track record, the self-proclaimed "sensualist of spectacle" promised to deliver yet another intricate character portrait that luxuriated in the contours of absolutely lavish scenery. And indeed, the stunning visuals of Lean's picture leave audiences breathless. Under the guiding hand of masterful production designer John Box, a crew of approximately 800 worked at reconstructing the streets of Moscow for two years straight on a lot located just outside Madrid. These are the resplendent, broad stretches of promenade we cast our eyes upon from the loggia adjoining the apartments of Zhivago's surrogate parents (Ralph Richardson and Siobhan McKenna), whilst the Czar's cavalry march upon a sea of Bolshevik demonstrators.

Together with his returning cinematographer Freddie Young, Lean again succeed in delivering spectacular landscape shots, making superb use of the Panavision wide-screen format to capture the snow-covered masses fighting desperately against the brutal Russian winter (these sequences were actually filmed in eastern Finland near the Soviet border).

In opposition to these monumental scenes and to Lean's larger-than-life protagonist in *Lawrence of Arabia*, Yuri Zhivago emerges as an unassuming character, who peers dreamily out his window while the rest of the world comes crashing down around him. Omar Sharif endows the role with an air of naiveté that plays up the reluctant hero's indecisiveness and lack of moral fiber as he traverses the many historical events he is powerless to influence.

Zhivago's passivity provides other members of the ensemble, like his half-brother Jevgraf (Alec Guinness), with an opportunity to take the helm.

1 Somewhere, my love: Yuri (Omar Sharif) holds onto antiquated ideals and chases a rainbow named Lara (Julie Christie).

2 Waltz with the wicked: The opportunistic Victor Komarovsky (Rod Steiger) offers Lara his experience and protection.

3 Cold front: The merciless Russian winter is indifferent to politics.

4 White nights and the White Guard: The Russian people run off to join the revolution. Interestingly, these Moscow scenes were filmed on a Madrid movie lot in Franco's dictatorial Spain.

5 Love without passion: Yuri demonstrates tenderness and compassion for wife Tonya (Geraldine Chaplin), but denies her the fires of his soul.

"The bitter cold of winter (the only section of film made outside Spain, these Finland settings are at once beautiful and foreboding), the grime of Moscow, the lush countryside, the drabness of life in a dictatorship, the brutality of war, and the fool's paradise of the declining Czarist era are forcefully conveyed in full use of camera, color, sound and silence." *Variety*

A Bolshevik officer with the secret police, Jevgraf uses his influence to bail Yuri out of numerous impossible entanglements, just as he does with the entire film whenever a narrator is required to bridge scenes separated by years.

There's no doubt about who is the picture's most spellbinding character. Komarovsky (Rod Steiger), a cynical womanizer and color-blind political opportunist, is a shifty businessman who caters to the highest bidder, successfully negotiating one deal after the next with whoever he considers the man of the hour. He's flawed, but not entirely despicable, and his steady concern for Yuri and Lara win him the sympathies of the audience, even though the central couple despise him. Manifesting neither Strelnikov's fanaticism nor Yuri's introspection, he is high-spirited and resilient, and therefore Lara's true male counterpart. This would explain why before allowing Lara to be-

come Strelnikov's wife or Zhivago's mistress, Pasternak had Komarovsky deflower her himself. Indeed, Lara's character is of significance to those around her. To Komarovsky, she is a mere plaything to be enjoyed – a view he expects her to accept as a simple matter of fact, but which she doesn't take lightly. Yuri, of course, only sees the muse in her, and even his understanding wife Tonja (Geraldine Chaplin) deems the once-virtuous nurse a truly fine woman. In truth, Lara is a composite of all their assessments, but is first and foremost a survival artist.

Beyond the characterizations, Lean's unmistakable symbolism does a brilliant job communicating the struggle for individual and artistic survival in times of sheer adversity, and each merciless winter is followed by a spring bloom of daffodils. Likewise, a steadfast belief in legacy and greater mean-

6 Red, white and dead: The October Revolution according to Hollywood.

7 Do you play the balalaika? Gen. Yevgraf Zhivago (Alec Guinness) looks for some clue that might indicate that the girl before him (Rita Tushingham) is indeed Lara and Yuri's lost child.

ing appears throughout the film in the form of Yuri's balalaika, the sole heirloom and recollection he has of his mother, who was a great musician. Although he cannot play the instrument himself, he carries it with him for most of his life, until finally passing it on to Lara, who in turn leaves it to their daughter – a child Yuri never meets, but who, nonetheless, inherits his mother's great gift for music.

Russia never looked this glamorous, but then again, with its predominantly British cast and Egyptian leading man speaking what Lean must have taken to be the Czarina's English, *Dr. Zhivago* never looks quite like Russia. Screenwriter Robert Bolt cut major portions of Pasternak's book, relying on voice-overs to tie together his somewhat sporadic, three-and-a-half-hour tragic love story. It is therefore hardly surprising that this triumph of schmaltz and romance was eaten alive by the critics and went on to become one of the biggest box-office smashes of the entire decade! Eager moviegoers stood in lines that wrapped around blocks to get a glimpse of Soviet snuggling, and some theaters ran the film for years on end.

Cynics continually attribute *Zhivago's* popularity to Maurice Jarre's score and the folkloric balalaika melody that flows through the film. So what? It's evidence that music lovely enough to fill the harsh Siberian winter with jingling bells can warm even the coldest of hearts. LP

8 Country cottage: Yuri and family take refuge in what used to be the servants' quarters of their summer residence. However, without Lara, it will be a fallow season for Zhivago's poetry.

9 Healing with dreams: Caught up in reverie, Dr. Yuri Zhivago tends to patients wherever the winds of war blow him.

OMAR SHARIF Omar Sharif (*1932) made a name for himself throughout the Western world with his role as Sherif Ali ibn el Kharish in *Lawrence of Arabia* (1962). Nonetheless, the actor born Michael Shalhoub on April 10th, 1932 in Alexandria was already a big-screen heartthrob in his native Egypt, and had founded a thriving production company by the time international acclaim rolled around. His next move was to win the hearts of women worldwide with his role as the daydreaming poet Yuri in David Lean's adaptation of Boris Pasternak's *Doctor Zhivago* (1965). The role of Yuri as a boy was played by Sharif's son Tarek. The cavalier Sharif's career flourished throughout the 1960s, and he had the great fortune of being cast in a breadth of roles alongside *Lawrence* and *Zhivago*. He played a the war-faring Sohamus in *The Fall of the Roman Empire* (1963), a priest in *Behold a Pale Horse* (1964), and a jealous husband whose suspicious nature ends up destroying his marriage in Sidney Lumet's *The Appointment* (1969). As Sharif's popularity began to dwindle in the 1970s, he took up philandering as an international playboy, ensuring that his face would at least be on the tabloids. A man of leisure, Sharif also earned a reputation as a world-class bridge player. Today, Omar Sharif enjoys a steady career in made-for-TV movies and mini-series, although his César-winning turn as a sentimental shopkeeper in François Dupeyron's *Monsieur Ibrahim* (2003) showed a marked return to form.

PIERROT LE FOU

Pierrot le fou

1965 - FRANCE / ITALY - 110 MIN. - DRAMA, CRIME FILM

DIRECTOR JEAN-LUC GODARD (*1930) SCREENPLAY JEAN-LUC GODARD
DIRECTOR OF PHOTOGRAPHY RAOUL COUTARD EDITING FRANÇOISE COLLIN MUSIC ANTOINE DUHAMEL,
BORIS BASSIAK, JEAN-BAPTISTE LULLY, ANTONIO VIVALDI PRODUCTION GEORGES DE BEAUREGARD
for ROME PARIS FILMS, SOCIÉTÉ NOUVELLE DES CINÉMATOGRAPHIE, DINO DE LAURENTIIS
CINEMATOGRAFICA.

STARRING JEAN-PAUL BELMONDO (Ferdinand "Pierrot" Griffon), ANNA KARINA (Marianne Renoir),
GRAZIELLA GALVANI (Ferdinand's Wife), DIRK SANDERS (Fred), PASCAL AUBIER
Second Brother), PIERRE HANIN (Third Brother), JIMMY KAROUBI (Dwarf), ROGER DUTOIT
Gangster), HANS MEYER (Gangster), KRISTA NELL (Madame Staquet),
SAMUEL FULLER (Himself).

"If you're gonna be crazy, then be really crazy!"

Disgusted by his bourgeois existence, Ferdinand (Jean-Paul Belmondo) runs off with Marianne (Anna Karina). She's been involved in the shady business carried out by her brother Fred (Dirk Sanders), a weapons dealer, and now there's a body and several guns lying around her flat. There's also a suitcase full of dollars there… so the couple head south with the money, pursued by gangsters with political connections. When their car goes up in flames along with the cash, the couple are forced into a series of petty thefts in order to make it to the Mediterranean. For a while, they live in perfect freedom in a lonely house on the beach; but eventually differences arise, and their crimi-nal past catches up with them.

With a plot like this, *Pierrot le fou* might well have been a thoroughl[y] average American-style thriller. Naturally, the name of Jean-Luc Godar[d] ensures that it isn't. Even his legendary debut *Breathless* (*À bout de souffle* 1959) was much more than a mere variation on a familiar genre; indeed, i[t] was one of the most brilliant works of the *nouvelle vague*, subverting the conventions of narrative cinema with playful ease. With *Pierrot le fou*, the French director continued the tradition he had initiated.

Godard did without a script and relied on free improvisation, producing a strikingly spontaneous movie that follows its own associative logic. Struc-turally, it is a kind of collage rather than a classical film narrative, and it man

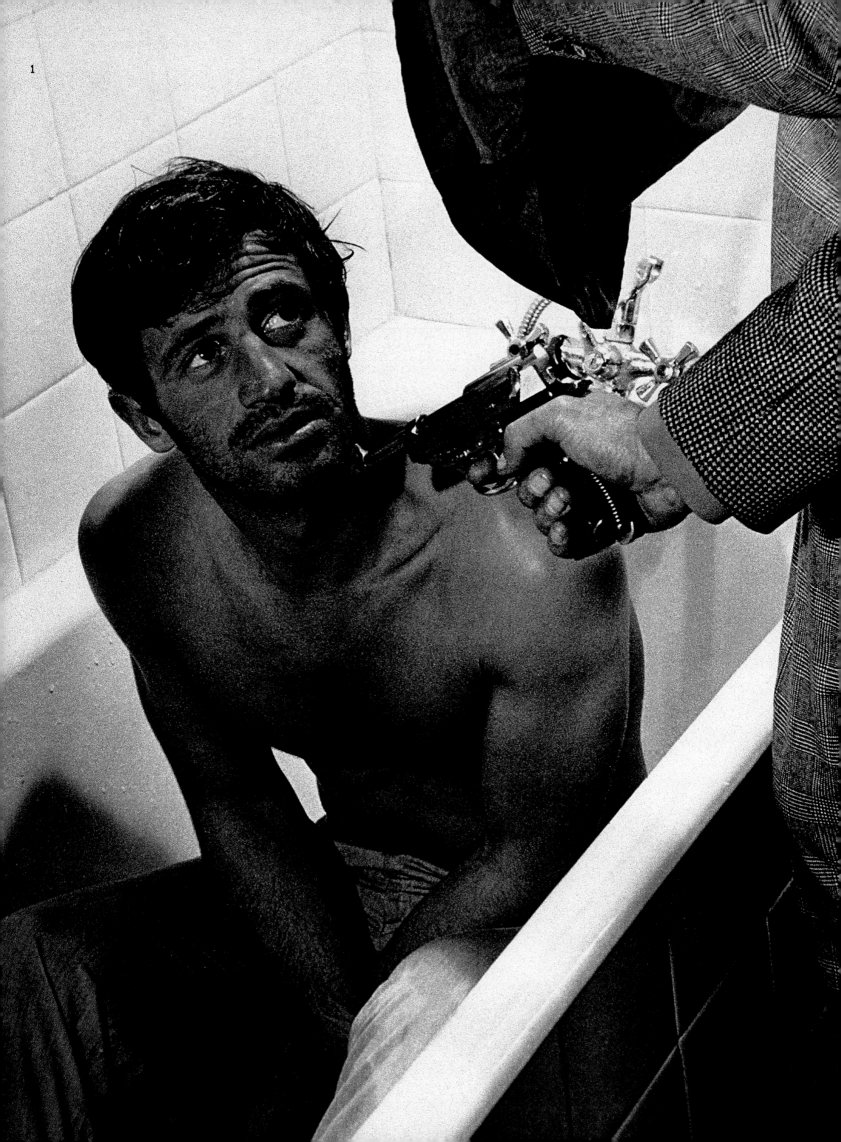

2

3

JEAN-PAUL BELMONDO   He acquired his trademark as a young boxer: a very conspicuously broken nose. Jean-Paul Belmondo was born in Paris in 1933 and both his parents were artists. By the time he made his cinema debut in the mid-50s, he had acquired a solid acting training and some experience on stage. In 1959, he became famous practically overnight with his performance as the cheeky but romantic crook in Godard's *Breathless* (*À bout de souffle*). From then on, Belmondo bore the nickname "Bebel," and French sociologists pondered the phenomenon of "le belmondisme" – a wave of imitation among the country's youth.

François Truffaut described Belmondo as the best French actor of his generation, and there's no denying his presence in a whole series of outstanding 60s films. These included Godard's comedy *A Woman is a Woman* (*Une femme est une femme*, 1961) and Truffaut's adventure movie *Mississippi Mermaid* (*La Sirène du Mississippi*, 1969), in which he gave a convincing performance in a romantic role – just as he had done in *Pierrot le fou* (1965). Jean-Paul Belmondo made three films with Jean-Pierre Melville, including the brilliant gangster movie *L'Aîné des Ferchaux / Lo scia-callo* (1963). He also appeared in some of the biggest box-office hits of the 60s and 70s. Of these, Philippe De Broca's *That Man from Rio* (*L'Homme de Rio / L'uomo del Rio*, 1963) best displayed his charm, temperament and athletic physique. In the 70s, Belmondo concentrated increasingly on action-oriented thrillers and comedies that provided a more or less ironical take on his incomparably virile image. One exception was Alain Resnais' *Stavisky* (1974), which Belmondo himself produced. From then on, he mainly cropped up in run-of-the-mill entertainments. In the late 80s, however, with his pulling power at the movies in decline, he attracted a lot of attention with a successful comeback in the theater.

ages to hold a number of very disparate elements in equilibrium. Paintings, advertising billboards and comic strips are edited into the flow of images alongside quotes from various films and books, and the movie changes its tone and style abruptly, seeming at various moments to be a thriller, a musical, a melodrama or a grotesque comedy. It has room for a satirical mime-show on the Vietnam war and a guest appearance by Sam Fuller, who provides Ferdinand with his personal definition of the cinema: "Film is like a battleground," he explains: "Love, hate, action, violence, death. In one word: emotion."

Fuller's statement doesn't just anticipate the tragic development of the plot; it also indicates the extent to which *Pierrot le fou* reflects on its own making. For Godard's movie is also a confrontation with the cinema, a piece of film criticism in the form of a film. The regular shattering of the "realistic" illusion – the actors often speak directly to the camera, for instance – is typical of Godard, and such moments are of course also a challenge to follow the film with open eyes and a clear head. Those who do so experience *Pierrot le fou* as a fascinating attempt to approach reality in all its complexity. Godard shows the private, economic, cultural and political influences that have made his film what it is. In the process, he proves himself to be a more skilful chronicler of his times than any of the other French New Wave's *auteurs*.

Not least, *Pierrot le fou* is a memorably beautiful love film that gave two stars the opportunity to exploit their enormous acting potential to the full. Anna Karina, at that time still married to Godard, imbues Marianne with emotional depth and anarchic charm. And Belmondo, for all his nonchalance,

1 Death of Marat: Guess again. 1960s French heartthrob and superstar Jean-Paul Belmondo plays Ferdinand a. k. a. "Pierrot le fou" (*Crazy Pete*) – slave to circumstance and dumb luck.

2 Fleeing south for the winter: Marianne (Anna Karina) seduces Ferdinand into abandoning his bourgeois existence.

3 Sand pebbles: Anna Karina and Jean-Paul Belmondo indulge in a bit of the *nouvelle vague's amour fou*.

4 Hard eight: Danish born Anna Karina filmed a total of eight films under the direction of ex-husband Jean-Luc Godard.

5 Climb aboard, we're expecting you: Ferdinand, the vulnerable *homme faible*, falls for an adventuress and succumbs to her every whim. Just a few years later, Belmondo would play a similar role in Truffaut's *Mississippi Mermaid* (*La Sirène du Mississippi*, 1969).

"Two or three years ago, I had the impression that everything had already been done, that there was nothing left to do that hadn't been done before. In short, I was a pessimist. Since *Pierrot*, I no longer have this feeling at all. Yes; one has to film everything, to talk about everything. Everything remains to be done." *Jean-Luc Godard*

reveals a vulnerability that was already discernible behind the tough brittleness of the wise guy he played in *Breathless*. His Ferdinand – Marianne calls him "Pierrot," the clown – is a melancholy brooder in search of the truth. It's a mission that can only collide with Marianne's sensual and concrete approach to the world.

Raoul Coutard's gently-moving camera luxuriates in the radiant Mediterranean light and captures the intoxicating freedom of the lovers in the widescreen Cinemascope format. But the promise of happiness contained in these images will eventually turn out to be deceptive. When Ferdinand realizes that Marianne has been lying to him – that Fred is not her brother but her lover – he shoots the two of them, paints his face blue, wraps two dynamite belts around his head and blows himself to pieces.   JH

ANDREI RUBLEV
Strasti po Andreju

1966 - USSR - 205 MIN. - HISTORICAL EPIC, BIOPIC

DIRECTOR ANDREI TARKOVSKY (1932–1986) SCREENPLAY ANDREI TARKOVSKY,
ANDREI MIKHALKOV-KONCHALOVSKY DIRECTOR OF PHOTOGRAPHY VADIM YUSOV
EDITING LYUDMILA FEIGINOVA, T. YEGORYCHYOVA, O. SHEVKUNENKO
MUSIC VYACHESLAV OVCHINNIKOV PRODUCTION MOSFILM.

STARRING ANATOLI SOLONITSYN (Andrei Rublev), IVAN LAPIKOV (Kirill), NIKOLAI GRINKO (Daniil),
NIKOLAI SERGEYEV (Feofan Grek), IRMA RAUSCH (Idiot Girl), NIKOLAI BURLYAYEV (Boriska),
YURI NAZAROV (Grand Prince), ROLAN BYKOV (The Jester), IGOR DONSKOY (Christ),
MIKHAIL KONONOV (Foma), YURI NIKULIN (Patrik).

"You found bells, I paint icons – what a feast day for mankind!"

A peasant stares, flabbergasted as he watches a man slowly rise up into the air. "Now you're going to heaven!" he shouts, as the patchwork hot-air balloon drifts ever higher across a bizarre winter landscape. The makeshift aircraft reaches a dizzying height, when the whistling wind and the groaning rope make us fear the worst; and seconds later, the journey's over and the balloon crashes to the ground.

In this allegorical opening sequence, Andrei Tarkovsky anticipates the central theme of *Andrei Rublev*. By showing us the rise and fall of a man who reached for the sky, the Russian director illustrates a yearning for freedom and the desire to overcome humanity's limitations. On a surface level, *Andrei Rublev* is a biopic about a 15th-century Russian icon painter. In essence, however, it's a reflection on the nature of art itself, and the eight episodes of his three-hour black and white masterpiece amount to a panoramic vision of the Russian nation under the heel of the Tatars.

On an epic scale, yet without a trace of nationalistic pathos, director Andrei Tarkovsky portrays a world in which the line between good and evil is impossibly blurred. Despite all the horrors of this earthly existence, monk and painter Andrei Rublev (Anatoli Solonitsyn) is convinced of the essential goodness of mankind, and he regards art as a source of comfort and power

for change. But his sublimely idealistic worldview collapses as the Tatars storm into his homeland: Russians fight Russians, slaughtering each other like cattle, and he himself is forced to kill a would-be rapist. Shaken to the core, he loses all faith in art, lays down his paintbrush and retreats into silence.

His faith in life and art is finally restored by a young man called Boriska (Nikolai Burlyayev). In an unforgettable sequence, Rublev observes how the young man gives his all to cast a colossal bell for the local prince. Deeply impressed by the joy this heroic endeavor gives to the people, Rublev takes up his work once again. For he now realizes that the artist, like any other man or woman engaged in the struggle for existence, must fight to achieve his destiny.

Many critics have pointed out that Rublev, the monk, was a kind of cinematic avatar of Tarkovsky himself – the Russian title is *The Passion of Andrei* – and that the film's true subject was contemporary reality. So it's no surprise that, in 1966, the Soviet authorities weren't prepared to release the completed movie as it stood. The censors objected to some particularly harrowing torture scenes, and to an allegedly unpatriotic rendering of Russian history. Tarkovsky stood his ground and refused to tolerate the mutilation of

1   Brothers in arms: The Grand Duke's brother (Yuri Nazarov in a dual role) enjoys the benefits of influence, but would prefer to occupy the prestigious position himself. Flexing his military muscles, he leads troops to pillage Vladimir's cathedral.

2   The passion: The jester (Rolan Bykov) and the painter Andrei Rublev (Anatoli Solonitsyn) fight for more humanity.

3   Sacred spaces: Andrei's meeting with the mighty Grand Duke is set in an eerie, vacuous church, an echoing the emptiness in his heart.

his work, which was originally 220 minutes long. Finally, though, he did agree to shorten a few scenes, without, however, affecting the film's essential content and meaning. It was February 1969 before *Andrei Rublev* received its first "semi-official" showing, but this was enough to capture people's attention. In the same year – though the film had still not been officially approved for showing abroad – *Andrei Rublev* was screened at Cannes, where it received the International Critics' Prize. Only in 1973 was it finally released for public distribution.

By this time, *Andrei Rublev* had already been recognized as one of the most important and multifaceted films ever made about art. Few movies reflect on the subject so seriously. The episodic narrative structure allows Tarkovsky to incorporate a wide range of positions and perspectives. This enables him, not least, to deliver a variety of answers to the difficult question: "What is a work of art?" In the very first episode, for example, the jester's jokes about Popes and potentates broach the issue of the relationship between art, politics and social criticism. Several episodes contrast the

"A violently poetic film, Dostoyevskyan in its furious intensity, yet breathtakingly precise and at times almost shockingly calculating."

quiet and thoughtful Andrei with his talentless but striving apprentice Kirill (Ivan Lapikov), who eventually suffers the consequences of his own excessive ambition. Kirill is prepared to betray both himself and Andrei if it will gain him the public recognition he so desperately craves. This is a clear allusion to Judas and Christ, and it implicitly assigns a redemptory function to the creation of true art.

In Tarkovsky's cinematic cosmos, non-linear narrative plays a central role, and in this film his use of the technique reached its maturity. The camera meditates at length on the natural world behind and beyond humanity: snow-covered hills and swampy forests, wild horses and endless rain. It's as if the director were looking for a primary visual language, concealed within nature yet pointing to a dimension outside it.   AZ

FILM BIOGRAPHIES OF ARTISTS

A well-established sub-genre of the biopic examines the lives of artists, both real and fictional, including painters, musicians and writers. Although they occasionally verge on the didactic, these "artist films" have often been highly successful. Artists frequently lead spectacularly interesting lives, and the processes and techniques of creation are fascinating themes in themselves.

Most of these movies deal with the life, work and reputation of artists already reasonably familiar to the general public. Great pains are therefore taken to recreate the settings, characters and costumes with a maximum of historical accuracy. Only a few films break with this tradition, preferring a timeless or contemporary look instead (as in Derek Jarman's *Caravaggio*, 1986).

In popular mythology, the artist is a lonely genius, suffering for his art and generally neglected by a philistine public. The movies are an ideal platform for variations on this theme, from Michelangelo as "divino artista" (*The Agony and the Ecstasy*, 1965) to Goya as a useful member of society (*Goya*, 1971), from the crazed creator as social outcast (*Vincent & Theo*, 1990) to the modern "mad and tragic hero" (*Pollock*, 2000).

4   I don't mean to shock anyone: Rublev explains his view of art and turns his back on the power-hungry.

5   Borscht bully: Kirill (Ivan Lapikov) is the sly counterpart to the woeful Andrei.

6   Lightweight: Boriska's (Nikolai Burlyayev) youthful courage makes Andrei painfully aware of his own shortcomings.

BONNIE AND CLYDE 🏆🏆

1967 - USA - 111 MIN. - GANGSTER FILM

DIRECTOR ARTHUR PENN (*1922) SCREENPLAY DAVID NEWMAN, ROBERT BENTON
DIRECTOR OF PHOTOGRAPHY BURNETT GUFFEY EDITING DEDE ALLEN MUSIC CHARLES STROUSE,
LESTER FLATT & EARL SCRUGGS (Song "Foggy Mountain Breakdown")
PRODUCTION WARREN BEATTY for TATIRA-HILLER PRODUCTIONS, SEVEN ARTS, WARNER BROS.

STARRING WARREN BEATTY (Clyde Barrow), FAYE DUNAWAY (Bonnie Parker),
MICHAEL J. POLLARD (C. W. Moss), GENE HACKMAN (Buck Barrow), ESTELLE PARSONS
(Blanche), DENVER PYLE (Frank Hamer), DUB TAYLOR (Ivan Moss), EVANS EVANS
(Velma Davis), GENE WILDER (Eugene Grizzard)

ACADEMY AWARDS 1967 OSCARS for BEST SUPPORTING ACTRESS (Estelle Parsons),
and BEST CINEMATOGRAPHY (Burnett Guffey).

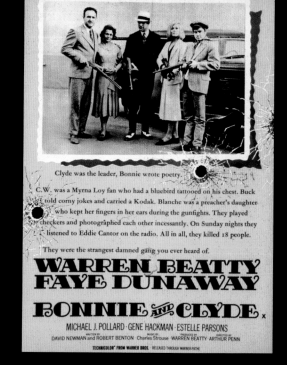

"Now Mrs. Parker, don't you believe what you read in all those newspapers. That's the law talkin' there."

Faces of country folk unfold in a sequence of black and white photographs, yellowed by time. We hear the camera click, as it captures one image after the other of hunger and despair, and we could easily believe we're watching a documentary by Dorothea Lange, the most honest chronicler of the age. Then the final image appears, a photo of a young man and a thin blonde woman. The confusion disappears and the connection is explained: these were America's poor during the Great Depression, and among them were Bonnie and Clyde.

Back in 1967, it was probably fair to say that the public memory of Bonnie Parker and Clyde Barrow had accumulated as much dust as the photos we are shown. But when the cobwebs vanish, the tired faces of the amorous outlaws are replaced by a close-up of luscious ruby lips. The camera pulls back, revealing their owner, Bonnie Parker (Faye Dunaway), a woman thoroughly bored with her mundane existence as a waitress in some podunk Texas diner. Half-dressed, she undulates atop her bed, disturbed by the reflection of her body in the mirror and fit to burst with sexual frustration. The attractive young man in the front yard presents a welcome diversion. Bonnie is clearly taken by the swanky affectations of Clyde Barrows (Warren Beatty), a self-proclaimed crook in a suit and fedora. Before long Clyde robs a mom-and-pop store, giving some clout to his big talking ways. Tailed by the state cops and powered by adolescent giddiness, the couple blaze across the Texas border on "hot" wheels. These bandits quickly adopt a charming, anar-

chic attitude toward the law and, stripped of their innocence, earn a much-publicized reputation as serial killers.

Parting studio head Jack Warner harbored serious reservations about *Bonnie and Clyde*. To his mind, the film was an all-too-explicit example of how the Hollywood system had changed in the 1960s. This was a project that an actor had produced with an independent production company, with a renegade artist in the director's chair. It was a sign of the studio's dwindling influence and of its relegation to the realm of marketing and financial sponsorship. With its point-blank depiction of sex and violence, *Bonnie and Clyde* proved that the so-called production code could be nullified at a major studio. For decades, the code had ensured that Hollywood movies contained only "morally harmless" content and the film's no-holds-barred visuals ruffled the

"The excellent script, with its strong characterizations, telling dialogue and gripping suspense, has benefited from the fresh and original directorial touch of Arthur Penn." *Herald Tribune*

1   Killer style: Faye Dunaway's public deified her far beyond anything the real Bonnie Parker had ever known. Dunaway's 1930s inspired costumes took 1960s fashion by storm and her performance transformed her into an equal rights icon.

2   A shooting star: Clyde Barrow (Warren Beatty) opens fire against the authorities and walks out of the bank a few dollars richer.

3   Two gun-slinging lovers: Clyde's impotence could force Bonnie to put a pistol to her own head, if the police don't beat her to it.

4   Fireworks: Robbing banks used to be more fun than being a kid at Christmas.

4

feathers of several highly-regarded film critics. Premiering at the 1967 Montreal film festival, it was branded a tasteless display of ostentatious violence. After a poor initial run, the picture returned to theaters thanks to a massive counter-offensive launched by another set of film critics, including the then little-known Pauline Kael.

Although the movie's protagonists were rooted in the past, it was primarily young viewers who identified with the outlaws. Their forays into crime were regarded as anti-establishment acts of rebellion. The international and national political crises of the 1960s had shaken the people's trust in political authority, and created a need for critical reflection. *Bonnie and Clyde* allowed U. S. audiences to recognize themselves in the commoners of the Depression era, who had also lost a great deal of faith in the government. This is no minor aspect of the film, and may explain its unpopularity with hostile critics.

Bonnie and Clyde is sometimes reproached for being a romanticized

gangster ballad, but its depictions of death are undeniably blunt. The bullet the bank teller takes in the face is as gruesome as the killing of Clyde's brother Buck (Gene Hackman), who dies like a flailing animal hours after being shot in the head. Still, the most poignant moment of violence undoubtedly comes at the film's conclusion as Bonnie and Clyde are riddled with bullets by the authorities. It is a scene that becomes surreally macabre as a result of slow motion photography, constantly changing camera angles, and the prolongation of the act itself. Their bodies convulse in a terrifying dance of death as they are shot through with enough lead to wipe out a small town. The execution transforms them into the stuff of legend, but it doesn't cleanse them of their sin or turn them into martyrs.

The final shot shows the man who carried out these official orders of police brutality. He looks on in total disgust until the screen goes blank, leaving nothing in its trail but anguish. DG

DEDE ALLEN *Bonnie and Clyde* (1967) presents an almost endless spectrum of dynamically innovative cinematic elements. This is firstly due to the screenplay

THE GRADUATE 🏆

1967 - USA - 105 MIN. - LOVE STORY, SOCIAL SATIRE, LITERARY ADAPTATION

DIRECTOR MIKE NICHOLS (*1931) **SCREENPLAY** CALDER WILLINGHAM, BUCK HENRY, based on the novel of the same name by CHARLES WEBB **DIRECTOR OF PHOTOGRAPHY** ROBERT SURTEES **EDITING** SAM O'STEEN **Music** DAVE GRUSIN, PAUL SIMON **PRODUCTION** LAWRENCE TURMAN for EMBASSY PICTURES CORPORATION, LAWRENCE TURMAN INC.

STARRING ANNE BANCROFT (Mrs. Robinson), DUSTIN HOFFMAN (Benjamin Braddock), KATHARINE ROSS (Elaine Robinson), WILLIAM DANIELS (Mr. Braddock), MURRAY HAMILTON (Mr. Robinson), ELIZABETH WILSON (Mrs. Braddock), BUCK HENRY (Hotel Desk Clerk), WALTER BROOKE (Mr. McGuire), ALICE GHOSTLEY (Mrs. Singleman), NORMAN FELL (Mr. McCleery).

ACADEMY AWARDS 1968 OSCAR for BEST DIRECTOR (Mike Nichols).

"Mrs. Robinson – you are trying to seduce me... aren't you?"

"I just want to say one word to you, Benjamin. Just one word…" At a welcome home party on his parents' Beverly Hills estate, recent college graduate Benjamin Braddock (Dustin Hoffman) can't mask his bewilderment as business associate, Mr. McGuire (Walter Brooke) rants and raves about the wonders of…"plastics!"

Plastics may be the wave of the future, but the new miracle substance has yet to corner a market with young Braddock – emerging voice in the next generation of American consumers. The young man has too many other things on his mind to be concerned with the "revolutionary" business propositions of his father's crowd. Actually, no one's really sure just what Benjamin wants from life – least of all him. Until now his future has fallen into his lap thanks to his parents, his social circle, and his class. He himself has no idea about the person he'd like to become, except that he doesn't want to end up like his well-dressed, superficial parents. That's one thing he knows for sure.

Taking cover in his room, he sits down beside his old aquarium, where a figurine diver floats about aimlessly. Then Mrs. Robinson (Anne Bancroft) sails onto his horizon, and suddenly things start to look up…

What follows is one of the most suggestive seduction scenes in all Hollywood history. Mrs. Robinson has Ben drive her home in his new, candy-apple red Alfa Romeo. A sultry siren in her mid-forties, she is the wife of his father's most trusted business associate, and one of his mother's dearest friends. After coming up with an array of pretexts, she manages to lure Ben up to her bedroom. And before he knows it, there she is standing stark naked in front of him, making a proposal that no one could misunderstand. At that instant, Mr. Robinson's (Murray Hamilton) car pulls into the driveway, and Ben bolts from the scene in a panic.

But it's not over yet. For those who are granted this sort of audience with Mrs. Robinson can't easily shake her off. Two days pass, and suddenly

1   Would you like me to seduce you? Mrs. Robinson (Anne Bancroft) is on the prowl and about to de-flower the newly graduated Benjamin Braddock.

2   Too funky: As Benjamin (Dustin Hoffman) builds up his ego he begins to turn his back on the persistent Mrs. R.

3   Hello darkness my old friend: Benjamin is fed up with being an obedient son and rejects the comforts of his existence. But it is only after meeting Mrs. Robinson's daughter, Elaine, that his life really begins to take on meaning.

4   Trying to stay afloat: Even at what should be a relaxing poolside gathering, Benjamin's prospective employers try to drown him with responsibility.

5   A little R & R: Mrs. Robinson wants to lock lips, but poor Benjamin is tongue-tied.

> "Simon & Garfunkel's score fills *The Graduate* with a gloominess and somber quality. 'Sounds of Silence,' 'Scarborough Fair,' and 'Mrs. Robinson' are great songs and while, inside the movie they sound a bit like elevator music, they do add a sort of quiet in an otherwise pungent movie."
>
> *Andrew Chan, Filmwritten Magazine*

Ben is ready to take her up on the offer. He rings his seducer from a secluded hotel room. Two hours later, the deed has been done. It may have been Ben's first time, but from then on not a day goes by without them meeting. In seamless cross-fades, the film deftly fans out the progression of these days as one continuous cycle between hotels and Ben's childhood bedroom; from a firm white bed to a flimsy air mattress. Mrs. Robinson doesn't make many demands of him, but she does make one. Ben is to never meet with her daughter Elaine (Katharine Ross). However, Ben cannot resist temptation, and suffers dire consequences as a result. He embarks on a crusade of love and

rebellion, leading to a pathetic stalking and, finally, a spectacularly romantic rescue at the wedding altar. After a comic beginning, Mike Nichols' second feature climaxes as a melodrama, turning a fresh-faced Dustin Hoffman into an overnight sensation.

The film maps Benjamin Braddock's rite of passage from aimless graduate to self-sufficient young man. With zoom shots and practically invisible cross-fades, which elegantly mirror the spirit of the changes in Ben's life, the film masterfully matches content and form. It is in this way that *The Graduate* bridges temporal gaps with the greatest of ease, and relays the sense of time experienced by the characters. Simon and Garfunkel's "Sounds of Silence" album emerges as the cinematic ballad that enables Benjamin's maturation to unfold as a gradual realization of his own feelings and desires. It's not by chance that watery images appear throughout the film – shots of aquariums, the familiar swimming pool as well as the sequence meant to be seen from behind a set of diving goggles. These visions are constant reminders of Benjamin's odyssey, sense of drifting, and need to give direction to his life. It is an arduous awakening to adulthood in a fractured, uncertain environment. Yet we always see light at the end of *The Graduate's* tunnel in the form of vibrant imagery and the bright, carefree superficiality of an utterly decadent milieu.

SR

ANNE BANCROFT

When Anne Bancroft made her grand entrance at the hotel room bar, clad in a tiger-striped coat and black tights, she was supposed to be a woman in her mid-forties. Provocatively removing both blouse and bra back at *The Graduate's* hotel room, after teasing herself out of her mile-long hose, she has no difficulty unpeeling the 21-year-old like a ripe banana. Indeed her domineering brass exudes the experienced air of a much older woman. But in truth Anne Bancroft had just turned 36 at the time she was cast as Mrs. Robinson – wife on the prowl. Her severe, angular face, set-off by the silver highlights in her raven hair, a reminder of her trademark chain-smoking, imbued her character with a vampish vitality. Combined with her talent, it made for a virtuoso performance that went on to define eroticism for an entire generation.

Still, the acting range of the woman born Anna Maria Italiano on September 17th, 1931 in New York City can hardly be measured by this role alone. A veteran of the theater, she triumphed in many roles on Broadway including Brecht's Mother Courage. Raised in the Bronx, Bancroft was always a pro at integrating her upbringing into her artistry. In Arthur Penn's *The Miracle Worker* (1961) she lit up the screen as Annie Sullivan, Helen Keller's visually impaired teacher and mentor, and won herself the Best Actress Oscar for breathing life into an uncompromising character. She exhibited her prowess again in David Lynch's *The Elephant Man* (1980), playing a stage diva who voices her admiration for the deformed John Merrick before her theatrical public. It was a cinematic spectacle as unforgettable as her ruthless seduction of Benjamin Braddock.

2001: A SPACE ODYSSEY 🏆

1968 - GREAT BRITAIN - 141 MIN. (ORIGINAL VERSION 160 MIN.) - SCIENCE FICTION

DIRECTOR STANLEY KUBRICK (1928–1999) **SCREENPLAY** STANLEY KUBRICK, ARTHUR C. CLARKE, based on a short story by ARTHUR C. CLARKE **DIRECTOR OF PHOTOGRAPHY** GEOFFREY UNSWORTH, JOHN ALCOTT (additional shots) **EDITING** RAY LOVEJOY **MUSIC** ARAM KHACHATURYAN, RICHARD STRAUSS, JOHANN STRAUSS, GYÖRGY LIGETI **PRODUCTION** STANLEY KUBRICK for POLARIS, HAWK, MGM.

STARRING KEIR DULLEA (David Bowman), GARY LOCKWOOD (Frank Poole), WILLIAM SYLVESTER (Dr. Heywood Floyd), LEONARD ROSSITER (Smyslov), DANIEL RICHTER (Moonwatcher), ROBERT BEATTY (Halvorsen), FRANK MILLER (Mission Controller), MARGARET TYZACK (Elena), SEAN SULLIVAN (Michaels), BILL WESTON (Astronaut).

ACADEMY AWARDS 1968 OSCAR for BEST SPECIAL EFFECTS (Stanley Kubrick).

An epic drama of adventure and exploration

taking you half a billion miles from Earth...
further from home than any man in history.
Destination: Jupiter.

MGM PRESENTS A STANLEY KUBRICK PRODUCTION

2001 a space odyssey

CINERAMA Super Panavision® and Metrocolor

"What are you doing, Dave?"

A gate of light opens and swallows up the space capsule with its pilot Dave Bowman (Keir Dullea). He flies through a corridor of light: rays, flecks, waves and nets of luminosity, constantly dissolving and reforming into new patterns and shapes. He flies over crevices riddled with burning rivers, through shimmering mists, over glittering oceans. His mouth opens in a silent scream. His staring eye reflects a fireworks display of exploding colors. He sees what no one has ever seen. And suddenly, the journey ends, in a white room sparingly furnished with antiques. The astronaut looks out from his capsule: he sees a man in a space-suit – himself, several years older; he discovers an old man eating at a table – himself again; he throws a glass to the floor, where it breaks, and he glimpses a decrepit bedridden figure – himself. At the end of the bed stands the black monolith that has led him here, beyond Jupiter. And now there's an embryo in the bed. Reborn as a star-child, he floats through space towards the earth in an amniotic sac.

The final sequence of *2001: A Space Odyssey* is a cinematic wonder, a baffling and visually overwhelming passage to another dimension where space and time are meaningless. The famous psychedelic trip through the corridor of light, made even more marvelous by the music of György Ligeti, is the crowning glory of Stanley Kubrick's masterpiece. Moreover, this virtuoso piece of special effects, a team effort, was created entirely without computers, using only models and light. There is still nothing to match this film in its

quest for authenticity and sheer visionary power. It's a monolith of the science-fiction genre, and all questions about its meaning rebound off its smooth black surface.

In three separate episodes, Kubrick describes the emergence of new forms of existence: the development from ape to man; the leap from artificial intelligence to real, emotional life; and the transition from our own dimension to something entirely strange. The witness to these changes – and perhaps their cause – is a black monolith from God-knows-where. One day it's simply there, standing in the savannah amidst a horde of apes. In the shade of this monolith, one of the apes abruptly understands that a bone can be used as a weapon. The apes kill other animals and start eating meat, and their technological superiority enables them to defeat a rival horde. It's the first stage in the conquest of nature, and the birth of humankind. Several evolutionary stages later, an American scientist is traveling to the moon on a secret mission. Beneath the surface of the earth's satellite, a black monolith has been discovered, and the mysterious object is transmitting a powerful signal in the direction of Jupiter. Scientists are in no doubt: the monolith is four million years old, and it was buried deliberately.

The spaceship "Discovery" on the way to the moon. Only the computer HAL knows the true reason for the journey – the search for extraterrestrial life. Three of the crewmembers are in hibernation while two others take care

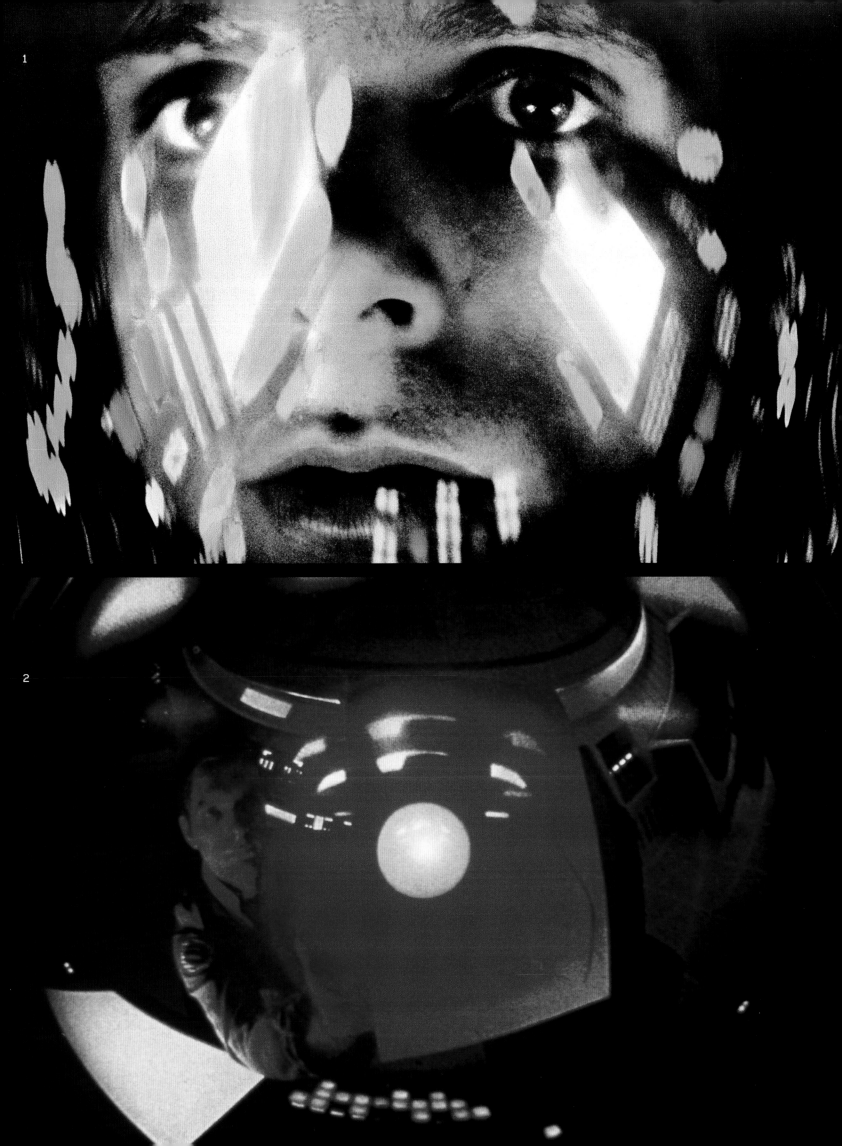

3

1   Space – the final frontier: Special effects designer Douglas Trumbull helped blast *2001* into cinematic history. Within just a few light years later, he gathered speed and took the helm of *Silent Running* (1972).

2   "Good afternoon, gentlemen. I am a Hal 9000 computer. I became operational at the H-A-L lab in Urbana, Illinois on the twelfth of January, 1992. I am completely operational and all my circuits are functioning perfectly." Although film co-writer

Arthur C. Clarke insisted that HAL stood for Heuristic Algorithmic Computer, there's no denying that if all three letters were shifted a notch, you'd get I B M.

"I tried to create a visual experience, one that bypasses verbalized pigeonholing and directly penetrates the subconscious with an emotional and philosophical content." *Stanley Kubrick*

4

3   Small sacrifices: Mama Hal is ready to severe the umbilical cord if need be. Meaning that astronaut Frank Poole (Gary Lockwood) had better gain independence fast if he intends to survive.

4   It can only be attributable to human error: Keir Dullea as astronaut David Bowman, the last human member of the Jupiter mission crew.

5   I can see you're really upset about this. I honestly think you ought to sit down calmly, take a stress pill and think things over: An ape (Dan Richter with a flawless makeup job) takes one bold step for his kind and discovers the benefits of organized violence.

of the flight. HAL, the most complex electronic brain ever constructed, makes an error, and the men consider switching it off; but the machine starts fighting for its life, and kills the crew. Only Bowman manages to escape, and he succeeds in shutting down the computer. Outside the spacecraft, a black monolith is floating. Bowman boards a space capsule and follows it to Jupiter…

The film doesn't make things easy for the spectator. It follows no conventional narrative pattern, it makes enormous leaps in time and space, and the figures in it are mere functions rather than characters. Technically and formally perfect, *2001: A Space Odyssey* offers us nothing and nobody we can identify with. It is a cool and somewhat forbidding film. Only around one quarter of its 160 minutes are taken up with dialogue: Kubrick lets his pictures do the talking.

2001 wasn't just an incredible enrichment of the science fiction genre, but also changed the way we look at the universe. The dazzling sun, its rays

5

6

6 The dark side of the moon: An artifact whose "origin and purpose is still a total mystery," is discovered on the earth's sleeping satellite.

7 Pulling the plug: Just what do you think you're doing? Poole and Bowman revolt against technology.

8 No need to reinvent the wheel: Although Stanley Kubrik originally commissioned Alex North to compose *2001's* entire score, the director eventually opted to have his space stations turn to the tune of Strauss' "Blue Danube" and other classics.

MATCH CUT Triumphantly, the ape stands up. In its right hand it holds the animal bone it has just used to kill another ape. It seems to understand just how much power it has gained by discovering how to use the bone as a weapon. The hairy arm swings back, and the creature hurls the bone into the air. The camera follows this bone in close-up as it rises, turning, towards the sky; and as it drops back towards the earth – there's a sudden cut: the blue of the sky has become the blackness of interplanetary space, and instead of a bone, we see a spaceship. A single cut surmounted millions of years and millions of miles, linking the prehistoric past to the distant future. It's a cut that contains all of human history. This sequence, from *2001: A Space Odyssey* (1968) is perhaps the most famous "match cut" in movie history. The term describes a cut between two shots that may be far apart spatially or temporally, yet contain striking visual similarities. Identical plot elements, a similar movement or the same person can create a connection between these two shots, thus preserving a feeling of continuity. A match cut may cause a moment of surprise or uncertainty, yet it is an important element in the economy of film narrative, for it can leap over barriers of space and time.

reflected from the snow-white body of the spaceship, while the dark side is sunk in inky blackness; the fountain pen floating through the cabin, dropped by a sleeping passenger on the way to the moon; the ghostly silence enveloping a dead astronaut in his yellow spacesuit, as he spins eternally through space; the circular space station turning like a gyroscope on its own axis; the blue, shimmering planet Earth. Outer space is Stanley Kubrick's invention. Never before and never since has a film so brilliantly succeeded in conveying an impression of infinity.

A few years later, the pictures of the Apollo missions showed that Kubrick's vision was also highly realistic – much to the director's relief, incidentally.

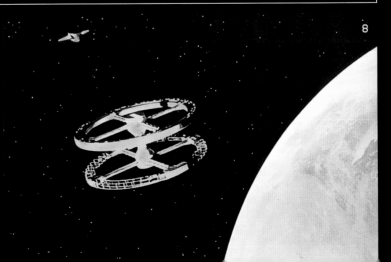

8

ONCE UPON A TIME IN THE WEST

C'era una volta il West

968 - ITALY / USA - 165 MIN. - SPAGHETTI WESTERN

IRECTOR SERGIO LEONE (1929–1989) SCREENPLAY SERGIO DONATI, SERGIO LEONE, based on
a story by DARIO ARGENTO, BERNARDO BERTOLUCCI, SERGIO LEONE
IRECTOR OF PHOTOGRAPHY TONINO DELLI COLLI EDITING NINO BARAGLI MUSIC ENNIO MORRICONE
RODUCTION FULVIO MORSELLA for RAFRAN, EURO INTERNATIONAL, PARAMOUNT.

TARRING CLAUDIA CARDINALE (Jill MacBain), HENRY FONDA (Frank), CHARLES BRONSON
("Harmonica" / The Man With No Name), JASON ROBARDS (Cheyenne), GABRIELE FERZETTI
Morton), FRANK WOLFF (Brett MacBain), KEENAN WYNN (Sheriff), PAOLO STOPPA (Sam),
LIONEL STANDER (Barkeeper), WOODY STRODE (Gang member), JACK ELAM (Gang member).

"What's he waiting for out there? What's he doing?"
"He's whittlin' on a piece of wood.
I've got a feeling when he stops whittlin'… somethin's gonna happen."

Three men in long coats are waiting at a lonely railroad station. A pinwheel creaks in the wind. A droplet from a water tank plops on to one man's (Woody Strode) hat; it's followed by another, and another. A fly buzzes around the unshaven face of the gang's leader (Jack Elam); the insect lands on his lip, he drives it away, it buzzes back again. Eventually, he catches the fly in the barrel of his Colt, and listens to the trapped creature with a smile on his face. We hear the distant sound of a train whistle. The men get ready. The train arrives – no sign of any passengers disembarking – and departs again. Suddenly, a doleful tune: on the other side of the tracks stands a man playing a mouth organ. He puts his bags down, and a dialogue ensues: Harmonica: "And Frank?" – The gang leader: "Frank sent us." – "Did you bring a horse or me?" – "Well… looks like we're… looks like we're shy one horse." –

"You brought two too many." They draw their guns, open fire and collapse to the ground.

This incredibly slow beginning lasts a quarter of an hour, ending abruptly in a shoot-out that leaves only one man alive (but slightly injured): the man with the harmonica (Charles Bronson). It's a sequence that displays all the stylistic elements of the Spaghetti Western: extreme close-ups that reveal every pore in a man's face; warped perspectives, with characters shot from below; the sudden transition to panoramic views of a vast, empty landscape; terse dialogue; time stretched unbearably, then shattered in an eruption of gunfire. "Harmonica" – we never discover his real name – has come to avenge the death of his brother. Two-and-a-half hours of the film will pass before he finally encounters the man who didn't have time to meet him at the

"Sergio Leone... seems to have improved as he has gone along, and *Once Upon a Time in the West* I consider his masterpiece, even surpassing *The Good, the Bad and the Ugly*, which is actually more efficient if less ambitious. Indeed, I am convinced that Sergio Leone is the only living director who can do justice to the baroque elaboration of revenge and violence in *The Godfather.*" *The Village Voice*

1 Play dead for me: Like in opera, Ennio Morricone had individual theme music composed for each of his main characters. Charles Bronson as Harmonica.

2 O. Henry: Sergio Leone looks his characters straight in the face and makes villains like Frank (Henry Fonda) break out in a cold sweat.

3 Still life: Bernardo Bertolucci hangs 'em high and turns glorified violence into visual masterpieces. The film's script was a joint effort between Bertolucci, director of *Ultimo tango a Parigi* (*The Last Tango in Paris*, 1972) and horror flick aficionado Dario Argento.

station. Frank was busy – massacring an entire family of defenseless settlers, including a little boy who'd looked right in his cold blue eyes.

As the face of the killer Frank was revealed for the first time, American moviegoers allegedly gasped in dismay; for it was none other than Henry Fonda. The living embodiment of Good as the face of pure Evil... This shocking casting-against-type was a straight declaration to the audience: *What you're watching here has absolutely nothing to do with the classical Holly-*

wood Western. That's why Woody Strode and Jack Elam, familiar faces from countless Westerns of the past, got blown away right at the start. What you're watching here is the Myth of the Wild West turned on its head; no more shining heroes, not an honorable motive in sight. Sergio Leone later stated that he had wanted to sweep away all the lies that had been told about the colonization of America. *Once Upon a Time in the West* tells of the blood and the dirty money that lubricated the wheels of "civilization."

ENNIO MORRICONE The success of *Once Upon a Time in the West* (*C'era una volta il West*, 1968) was due not least to the music of Ennio Morricone. For each of the

"They wanna hang me! The big, black crows. Idiots. What the hell? I'll kill anything. Never a kid. Be like killin' a priest."

Film quote: Cheyenne (Jason Robards)

4   Death Valley: Jill (Claudia Cardinale) arrives at her new home on the frontier only to find that her entire family has been assassinated. Save for Jill's thought-provoking journey to the farm – filmed in the California desert – the picture was shot exclusively in Spain.

5   Sweetwater: Jill is set on the idea of founding an oasis town. It's a commentary in itself that Leone picked a whore to serve as mother of the civilization that grew out of the Wild West.

4

Besides the revenger's tale, Leone also tells us of the building of the railroad and the passing of the old-style gunslinger. Frank is the right-hand-man of a sickly entrepreneur who dreams of reaching the Pacific with his railroad line. It's Frank's job to remove any obstacles in the path of this project. The settler and his kids had to die because their land contained the only water source for miles around. The guy knew this, and dreamed of being the stationmaster and founder of a new town. What Frank doesn't know is that the widowed settler had previously married a high-class whore (Claudia Cardinale) in New Orleans. It takes her a while to grasp what a valuable piece of real estate she's inherited in the desert, but with the help of Harmonica and the desperado Cheyenne (Jason Robards), she sets out to realize her dead husband's plans.

With the three films that made up his "Dollar Trilogy" – *A Fistful of Dollars*, *For a Few Dollars More*, and *The Good, The Bad and The Ugly* – Sergio Leone became the most innovative director of European Westerns (along with Sergio Corbucci). Today, these three films look like preliminary studies for his ultimate masterpiece: *Once Upon a Time in the West*. It is perfect, in more ways than one: in its casting, its relentless build-up of suspense, and in its sheer visual power. Each shot is meticulously composed, and its use of zooms, complicated camera moves and slow motion in the flashback sequences give it the quality of a bold formal experiment. Some accused Leone of mannerism; other critics and colleagues such as Wim Wenders were appalled because the movie represented "the ultimate Western," and was therefore "the end of the road." It may well be the most breathtaking Western ever made.   NM

EASY RIDER

1969 - USA - 95 min. - ROAD MOVIE

DIRECTOR DENNIS HOPPER (*1936) **SCREENPLAY** PETER FONDA, DENNIS HOPPER, TERRY SOUTHERN **DIRECTOR OF PHOTOGRAPHY** LÁSZLÓ KOVÁCS **EDITOR** DONN CAMBERN **MUSIC** STEPPENWOLF, ROGER MCGUINN, THE BYRDS, THE BAND, THE JIMI HENDRIX EXPERIENCE **PRODUCTION** PETER FONDA for PANDO, RAYBERT PRODUCTIONS, BBS, COLUMBIA PICTURES CORPORATION.

STARRING PETER FONDA (Wyatt), DENNIS HOPPER (Billy), JACK NICHOLSON (George Hanson), LUKE ASKEW (Hitchhiker), LUANA ANDERS (Lisa), SABRINA SCHARF (Sarah), TONI BASIL (Mary), KAREN BLACK (Karen), WARREN FINNERTY (Rancher), ROBERT WALKER JR. (Jack).

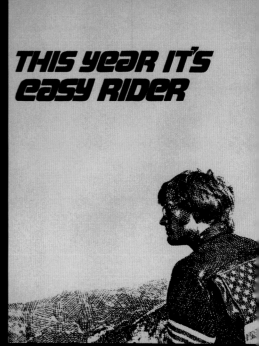

"This used to be a helluva good country. I can't understand what's gone wrong with it."

Freedom… and the impossibility of freedom in a country where people are scared to be free. Billy (Dennis Hopper) is sitting at the campfire with the lawyer George Hanson (Jack Nicholson). The legal eagle is no longer perfectly sober, and Billy is a little slow-witted because he's permanently stoned. But George is doing his best to clarify a few matters for Billy: why the motel owner slammed the door on him and his buddy Wyatt (Peter Fonda); why the girl behind the bar in the one-horse town refused to serve them; why the mob and their sheriff chased them out of town instead. The lawyer explains that these people are not scared of Billy personally; they're scared of what he represents: an easy, unforced existence outside of society – a life in which the only things that matters are self-realization and life itself.

Billy and Wyatt ran into the lawyer in a jail cell, where he'd been sleeping off his latest bout with the bottle. Now he's joined them on their motorcycle odyssey, all the way from Los Angeles to Mardi Gras in New Orleans. They cruise down endless empty highways, through stunningly beautiful landscapes, rarely stopping before the sun goes down. Wyatt has spurs on his boots and a star-spangled banner on the back of his leather jacket; Billy wears suede pants, and he sports a Stetson on his long, matted hair. They're two 20th-century cowboys on a quest for space and freedom, chasing an ideal America that disappeared many moons ago.

Easy Rider cost only $400,000 to make, but it quickly became one of the cult movies of the 60s. It's a piece of celluloid that evokes an entire generation's outlook on life, a road movie about youth, drugs and the dream of revolution, with a soundtrack as hugely successful as the movie that spawned it. Far from merely accompanying the pictures, songs by The Byrds, The Band and Fraternity of Man provide a running commentary on the film. "Born to Be Wild," Steppenwolf's hymn to freedom, is a programmatic opening number; and Roger McGuinn's cover version of Bob Dylan's "It's Alright Ma (I'm Only Bleeding)" paves the way for the sober and melancholy conclusion. Producer and protagonist Peter Fonda reported that Dylan had refused to allow the original version to be used because he felt the movie offered too little hope. For Wyatt and Billy are ultimately blown out of existence by a reactionary hick with a rifle; they're on their bike and he's in his truck, and he kills them just for the hell of it.

This pessimistic ending casts doubt on the whole freewheelin' on-the-road adventure. In an interview with the German magazine *Filmkritik*, Peter Fonda commented: "We knew there couldn't be any more heroes, yet we still tried to *live* like heroes. This yearning is there in the film – along with the disillusionment." The project began with the simple desire of two real-life friends, Hopper and Fonda, to travel through the country by motorbike, and the end result was this movie. All the various episodes took place on the road, from the visit to a hippie camp in New Mexico to the meeting with a farmer whose entire extended family lived off the land. Like the characters they play, Hopper and Fonda were verbally abused by rednecks – and even threatened with guns – while filming. They also smoked a lot of grass.

In a cemetery in New Orleans, the two protagonists team up with a couple of hookers and embark on an acid trip that turns completely nightmarish. Hopper shoots the drug experience not as a cleansing of the doors of per-

3

1   Made in the shades: Peter Fonda as the reflective and easy-going Wyatt.

2   Fireside chats: The erratic and eccentric Billy (Dennis Hopper) just loves chewin' the fat – no matter who's listening. It's no coincidence that the film's two main buddies share their first names with legendary cowboys Wyatt Earp and Billy the Kid.

3   The thrill of the open road: Attorney George Hanson (Jack Nicholson) heads down south to New Orleans. Good thing his mom kept his football helmet of his high school glory days intact for him.

"*Easy Rider* is a Southern term for the whore's old man, not a pimp, but the dude who lives with a chick. Because he's got the easy ride. Well, that's what happened to America, man. Liberty's become a whore, and we're all taking an easy ride." *Peter Fonda*

DENNIS HOPPER

"I'll fuck anything that moves!" As Frank Booth in David Lynch's *Blue Velvet* (1985), he celebrated his unforgettable comeback – as an obscenely violent psychopath horribly dependent on an unnamed gas. Ever since then, Dennis Hopper has embodied the unpredictable, the explosive and the insane. He played variations on these themes in *Red Rock West* (1992) by John Dahl, *Speed* (1994) by Jan de Bont, and *Waterworld* (1995) by Kevin Reynolds and Kevin Costner. All told, Hopper has now appeared in over 100 films, more than 40 of them made in the 90s alone. "I no longer wait to be offered great roles," said Hopper in an interview with the German newspaper *Süddeutsche Zeitung*: "I just work. I make sure I'm always busy, because I love doing what I do."

Dennis Hopper came to Hollywood at the age of 18. Just a year later, after a few TV jobs, he appeared alongside his role model James Dean in Nicholas Ray's *Rebel Without a Cause* (1955) and George Stevens' *Giant* (1956). But Hopper acquired a reputation for being "difficult," and after studying at the Actors' Studio in New York he worked mainly in the theater. In 1969, with *Easy Rider*, he returned to Hollywood as director and protagonist of his own movie. The film's enormous success took its toll on him, however, as he embarked on a wild life marked by excessive drug use. After the failure of *The Last Movie* (1969/71), Hopper disappeared from view for a while, before returning in European films such as Wim Wenders' *The American Friend* (*Der Amerikanische Freund*, 1977) and Roland Klick's *White Star* (1982). He also worked as a photographer and collected artworks, including some important pieces of Pop Art.

Later, he began making his own films again, such as the mesmerizing *Colors* (1988), a police movie set in L. A. But the decisive turning point in his career was undoubtedly *Blue Velvet*. With this film, he began his *third* career, after his successes in the 50s and 60s; and the words of Frank Booth seemed to encapsulate Dennis Hopper's situation yet again: "Let's hit the fuckin' road!"

4   The fall guy: Billy gets pinned with the crime. Is he a victim of circumstance or menace to society?

5   Alien abduction: Hanson gets a first taste of Mary Jane and starts spacing out. Talk of extra-terrestrials who already have the world under their control circulates around the campfire.

6   Road hogs: And hog wild at that. Peter Fonda was already an experienced biker at the time of the shoot – a clue as to why his cycle got more souped up than Dennis Hopper's.

ception, but as a splintering of reality, a kaleidoscope of terror and despair. A short time later, the thoughtful Wyatt comments to Billy: "We're duds." They've reached New Orleans but missed their true goal. A drug deal has brought them several thousand dollars, which Wyatt hides in the tank. It's this money that's supposed to guarantee their freedom. But anyone who wants a free life beyond bourgeois society must break their dependence on its symbols and material values – like that farmer, reaping the fruits of his honest labor, far from the snares of civilization.

Hopper and Fonda seem to feel an almost religious sense of connection to their native country, and this is evoked in gorgeous, panoramic views of the American landscape. In truth, they're in mourning, for they know that the America they revere has long since passed way. If God didn't exist, you'd have to invent him, says Wyatt, as the original duo arrive in New Orleans. George didn't make it with them; in the middle of the night, he was beaten to death by a mob. And in a sudden moment of vision, Wyatt sees his own approaching end.   NM

MIDNIGHT COWBOY ♟♟♟

1969 - USA - 113 MIN. - DRAMA, LITERARY ADAPTATION

DIRECTOR JOHN SCHLESINGER (1926–2003) SCREENPLAY WALDO SALT, based on the novel of the same name by JAMES LEO HERLIHY DIRECTOR OF PHOTOGRAPHY ADAM HOLENDER EDITING HUGH A. ROBERTSON MUSIC JOHN BARRY, FLOYD HUDDLESTON, FRED NEIL PRODUCTION JEROME HELLMAN for FLORIN PRODUCTIONS, JEROME HELLMAN PRODUCTIONS.

STARRING DUSTIN HOFFMAN (Enrico Salvatore "Ratso" Rizzo), JON VOIGHT (Joe Buck), SYLVIA MILES (Cass), JOHN MCGIVER (Mr. O'Daniel), BRENDA VACCARO (Shirley), BARNARD HUGHES (Towny), RUTH WHITE (Sally Buck), JENNIFER SALT (Annie), GILMAN RANKIN (Woodsy Niles), PAUL MORRISSEY (Party Guest), VIVA (Gretel McAlbertson).

ACADEMY AWARDS 1969 OSCARS for BEST PICTURE (Jerome Hellman), BEST DIRECTOR (John Schlesinger), and BEST ADAPTED SCREENPLAY (Waldo Salt).

"Frankly, you're beginning to smell and for a stud in New York, that's a handicap."

Midnight Cowboy is a portrait of urban life that can also be read as a revisionist Western. For beyond this bittersweet tale of the concrete jungle lies a melancholy ballad that bids adieu to the ideals of the American West. An ode to innocence lost, the movie follows the story of young Joe Buck (Jon Voight), the last urban cowboy, as he tries to hold onto a rapidly disappearing dream in the 1960s. A strapping Texan, Buck has come to the Big Apple to fulfill the sexual fantasies of the city's affluent lonely hearts. What he finds is a world with little need for such services. And soon, after a series of empty encounters with homosexuals, junkies and religious fanatics, he's down and out as a second-rate male prostitute on 42nd Street. Stripped of everything but a fading dream, all that accompanies Buck on his travels is a transistor radio emitting a hollow stream of promises, and a TB-stricken runt in a tattered dress suit known as Rico "Ratso" Rizzo (Dustin Hoffman).

As his dubious name suggests, Ratso is quick to scam the bright-eyed cowboy in the hopes of running off with his money. Mr. Buck however seems too caught up in his polished appearance to take any notice, preferring instead to steal prideful glances in the mirror before hitting the town. In fact, all the Texan can think about is how his cowboy get-up is sure to be all the rage of the New York penthouse scene. Hearing opportunity knock, the hobbling Ratso appoints himself the kid's manager and sets him up on "dates" with women and men alike – sordid little encounters that slowly but surely rub the shine off the cowboy's illusions.

Ratso and Joe soon become partners in crime, living hand to mouth as small-time crooks and spending most of their waking hours in a squat without even electricity and running water. Their cohabitation is dominated by fantasies of a better life, where they would move to Florida and mingle with the rich and famous. And tragically, the men only realize how much they mean to each other when it is too late. Transcending the picture's wretched ending, their curious love story is a tender message that still strikes a chord with contemporary audiences. Wistfully underscored by "Everybody's Talkin'" (performed by Harry Nilsson), the strength of this paean to friendship lies in John Schlesinger's ingenious visuals and the astonishing talent of the movie's two principle actors. The interaction between a then virtually unknown Jon Voight and his co-star Dustin Hoffman inspires immediate

> "This is obviously the sort of film in which people argue endlessly about which of the principals steals it, and the argument is irresistible, if pointless. Both are very good, in different ways. Against Mr. Voight's unnoticeable acting Mr. Hoffman has a field day with all the fireworks — ugly, crippled eccentric, and dying by degrees, he is always at the very edge of his being, which, as we all know, is a very comfortable place for an actor. He does it very well, but finally I think Mr. Voight has the more difficult part, and carries it off impeccably."

The Times

1   Bridge over troubled waters: Don Quixote and Sancho Panza are reincarnated in 1960s New York as Joe Buck (Jon Voight) and Rico Salvatore Rizzo (Dustin Hoffman).

2   Cry me a river: Dustin Hoffman made fans see just how sexy a black sheep can be.

3   Pop goes the weasel: Rico 'Ratso' Rizzo has killed time long enough and is ready to turn his know-how into a moneymaking scheme as Joe Buck's manager.

4   Life's little fetishes: Joe gets to know a couple of gay guys really well and finds out what life in the big bad city is really all about.

5   Back off. I'm contagious: Ratso is the kind of guy who'd think up anything to get out of danger's path, and so Joe doesn't realize just how ill he really is.

empathy. Whereas Joe's unfaltering optimism in a world where raw need overshadows all emotion is the only ray of hope, Ratso's tenacious pride is no less impressive. No scene encapsulates the nature of their struggle to survive so dramatically as Ratso's unforgettable outburst when a taxi nearly runs him over in the midday traffic. Screaming "I'm walking here! I'm walking here!" he claims his and Joe's stake to life with these words of retaliation.

This unscripted moment came about when a real New York City cab driver recklessly motored onto the scene and nearly shut down the shoot. Rather than breaking character, Hoffman spontaneously adlibbed an already difficult take.

It is scenes like this that attest to the extraordinary precision of British director John Schlesinger's gutsy experimental techniques and give the film

6

6 Flim flam man: Ratso doesn't want anyone's compassion; he'd much rather have a meal ticket and a cash cow.

7 Hopalong Cassidy: All that's missing to complete this image of American naivety is a broomstick

pony. Jon Voight as Joe Buck, the sexy innocent, a role which made the actor an overnight sensation.

such undeniable urban authenticity. Yet somehow *Midnight Cowboy's* nightmarish images accurately capture the darkness and violence of 1969 New York without losing sight of the era's underlying hopefulness. For even though the only remnants of the utopia once promised by flower power and the sexual revolution are the pornography and prostitution beckoning at every corner, Joe Buck goes through life shielded by a diehard innocence.

The cowboy's naive sexuality, played up by his childish misconceptions, is undoubtedly the picture's major riddle. While sex is peddled on the city streets like any other commodity, Joe Buck inexplicably regards physical in-

timacy and its sale as the most natural thing on earth. No less unsettling are the chilling flashbacks that tell of the Texan's traumatic childhood marked by abuse and rape. But even so, this leaves us far from a psychological diagnosis

In awarding *Midnight Cowboy* the Oscar for Best Picture, mainstream cinema paid homage to an innovative form of filmmaking that would go on to shape New Hollywood and Indie Cinema. From a contemporary standpoint, i is hard to understand that several of the movie's scenes were considered drastic enough to warrant the X rating usually reserved for pornography.

PE

DUSTIN HOFFMAN

Dustin Hoffman (*1937) is among the world's best-known actors and one of the few to gain international acclaim through character roles. His striking features, nasal voice and seeming lack of self-confidence cut him out for difficult parts. A Los Angeles native, he studied music at Santa Monica City College and acting at the Pasadena Playhouse before gaining admission to Lee Strasberg's Actor's Studio in 1958. His big break in Hollywood came at the age of thirty with Mike Nichols' timeless classic *The Graduate* (1967) in which he played Benjamin Braddock, a character ten years his junior. The part brought him his first Oscar nomination.

It took two years and much persistence before the allegedly "difficult" actor delivered his next incomparable performance as the sickly Ratso in *Midnight Cowboy* (1969). It was the beginning of a sterling career, and soon he was cast as a 121-year-old Western pioneer in *Little Big Man* (1970), a title that incidentally became the 5'5" tall actor's nickname. He went on to play a prisoner opposite Steve McQueen in *Papillon* (1973) and claim the stage all for himself as scathing satirist Lenny Bruce in *Lenny* (1974).

A master of disguise, he dazzled audiences in *Tootsie* (1982), one of his few blockbuster romantic comedies, playing an actor who has to dress up like a woman to get work. Hoffman also shone in the political thriller *Marathon Man* (1976) and in the sensitive divorce drama *Kramer vs. Kramer* (1979), which won him his first Oscar. After poignantly portraying an autistic *Rain Man* (1988), his reputation as an insufferable perfectionist started to get the better of him and great roles became more of a rarity. Be that as it may, Hoffman is still a box-office favorite and has continued to impress audiences in recent productions like *Billy Bathgate* (1991), *Outbreak* (1995) and *Wag the Dog* (1997).

THE WILD BUNCH

1969 - USA - 145 MIN. - WESTERN

DIRECTOR SAM PECKINPAH (1925–1984) SCREENPLAY WALON GREEN, ROY N. SICKNER, SAM PECKINPAH DIRECTOR OF PHOTOGRAPHY LUCIEN BALLARD EDITING LOU LOMBARDO MUSIC JERRY FIELDING PRODUCTION PHIL FELDMAN for WARNER BROS., SEVEN ARTS.

STARRING WILLIAM HOLDEN (Pike Bishop), ROBERT RYAN (Deke Thornton), ERNEST BORGNINE (Dutch Engstrom), EDMOND O'BRIEN (Sykes), WARREN OATES (Lyle Gorch), BEN JOHNSON (Tector Gorch), JAIME SANCHEZ (Angel), EMILIO FERNÁNDEZ (Mapache), STROTHER MARTIN (Coffer), L. Q. JONES (T. C.), ALBERT DEKKER (Pat Harrigan).

"We all dream of being a child again, even the worst of us. Perhaps the worst most of all."

To judge by their faces, the men riding slowly into town have done some serious living. Their path takes them along a railroad line, where some kids are laughing and playing. The men stare at them sullenly as they pass. Only the close-up shows the cruelty of the children's game. While two scorpions struggle in vain to avoid being eaten by a horde of red ants, the kids are using sticks to block the tormented animals' escape route.

Under a tarpaulin, a travelling preacher is fulminating against the evils of drink. A little later, the Temperance Union sets off on a parade, accompanied by a brass band. By this time, Pike Bishop (William Holden) and his men have reached their destination: they're in the wages office of the railroad company, and they're quietly robbing it while holding the customers at gunpoint. Then one of Bishop's men spots the rifles on the roof... There are some pretty rough-looking men positioned all around them, and they're hungry for the bounty on the Wild Bunch's heads. In cold blood, Bishop organizes the breakout. Though the streets are filled with innocent passers-by, the bounty

hunters open fire and start shooting wildly into the crowd. Bullets whine, horses whinny, people panic while others die. The bandits know no mercy, but use the crowd and the Temperance parade for cover. Only four members of Bishop's gang survive the massacre, and one of them is so badly wounded that he can't ride a horse. When he asks to be shot, Bishop doesn't hesitate. There is no time for a burial.

These first scenes already contain the essence of Sam Peckinpah's film. Noble heroes like John Wayne or Randolph Scott are nowhere to be found in this Western, and the Law has no claim to moral superiority. The sleazy gunmen hired by railroad boss Harrigan (Albert Dekker) are a bunch of trigger-happy fools and money-grabbers. Only their leader Deke Thornton (Robert Ryan) demonstrates a certain amount of backbone, but even he is driven by self-interest: he's been promised amnesty for his crimes if he manages to hunt down his former friend Pike Bishop.

Peckinpah disposes ruthlessly of the old Western cliché that conflicts

1   King of the wild frontier: Pike Bishop (William Holden) isn't going to let renegade leader Mapache pull the wool over anyone else's eyes.

2   Following the leader: Dutch (Ernest Borgnine) has his reservations about Bishop's motives but joins up with him just the same.

3   Let me entertain you: Pike Bishop and Deke Thornton get a rude awakening from their assailants while frequenting a house of ill repute. When Pike leaves him in the lurch, his buddy changes sides quicker than most people change clothes.

4   Always let your conscience be your guide: Demanding the release of their friend Angel, the remaining bunchies head back to Mapache's hideout.

5   White bishop takes black queen – check: Bishop and his men storm Mapache's headquarters, where the dastardly gaucho is being serviced with a smile.

6   Tending to a paper cut: Despite a gaping wound, Bishop refuses to give up the fight against his mighty opponents. But his impassioned battle can only end in defeat.

like these can be solved cleanly, in a heroic dual of individuals. His protagonists and their henchmen are fighting a filthy miniature war. Across the border, in Mexico, where the militias of General Mapache (Emilio Fernández) have established a reign of terror, life is even more brutal: soldiers move through Indian villages, raping, torturing and killing – and are hunted in turn by the troops of Pancho Villa. The violence makes no exception of women and children. With unsparing exactness, Peckinpah shows us what bullets are really capable of: he shows us how blood spurts, and how human bodies are torn and tossed around by flying metal. In Peckinpah's vision, the moment of death is extended, as the victims perform a horrible slow-motion dance.

The Wild Bunch can only be understood in the context of the late 60s. For the first time, the mass media were bringing uncensored images of warfare

ERNEST BORGNINE   He was born Ermes Effron Borgnino in 1917 and in the course of his lengthy career, he got to know every aspect of the acting trade. Ernest Borgnine, as he later became, appeared in provincial theaters, B-movies and prestigious big-budget productions. And just once, in 1956, he stood in front of his peers at the Oscars ceremony, when he received the Academy Award for his performance in Delbert Mann's Marty (1955). The quiet butcher Marty was one of the few leading roles Borgnine played, and the film was exceptionally good. But his unmistakeable physiognomy, with gappy teeth, bushy brows and boxer's nose, was never going to make him a matinee idol. Nonetheless, in the 50s and 60s he soon became a familiar face to keen moviegoers.

Borgnine, who spent ten years in the army, gave a rambunctious performance as the sadistic Sergeant Judson in Fred Zinnemann's From Here to Eternity (1953). After appearing as the titular hero in the TV series McHale's Navy (1962–66), he also co-starred in two well-known movies directed by Robert Aldrich: The Flight of the Phoenix (1966) and The Dirty Dozen (1967). He also acted in several Westerns and historical epics, as well as turning up in the odd obscure European production. Though he often played the burly bad guy, he was just as memorable playing the rough diamond or the buddy with a heart of gold. Moviegoers liked the warmth and energy he brought to such roles, and when he played Dominic Santini in the TV adventure series Airwolf (USA, 1984–86), these qualities won him a whole new generation of fans.

"Violent, thoughtful and authoritative, it keeps Peckinpah out on his own among the Western directors of his generation." *Sight and Sound*

to the attention of the public and it was becoming impossible to ignore the dreadful suffering of civilian populations. Even if some of Peckinpah's interviews reveal a sneaking sympathy with the doomed desperadoes of his Wild Bunch, he never left us in any doubt that these were ruined men, souls in hell.

Although the film's outstanding artistic quality was almost universally recognized, its outrageously realistic depiction of violence led to some heat-ed discussions. Peckinpah himself was furious at his producers, who re-leased an allegedly more marketable shortened version of the film without his consent. In some countries, including Germany, further passages were cut, with the result that several different versions were in circulation world-wide. In 1982, a so-called "director's cut" lasting the originally planned 145 minutes was finally released.   HK

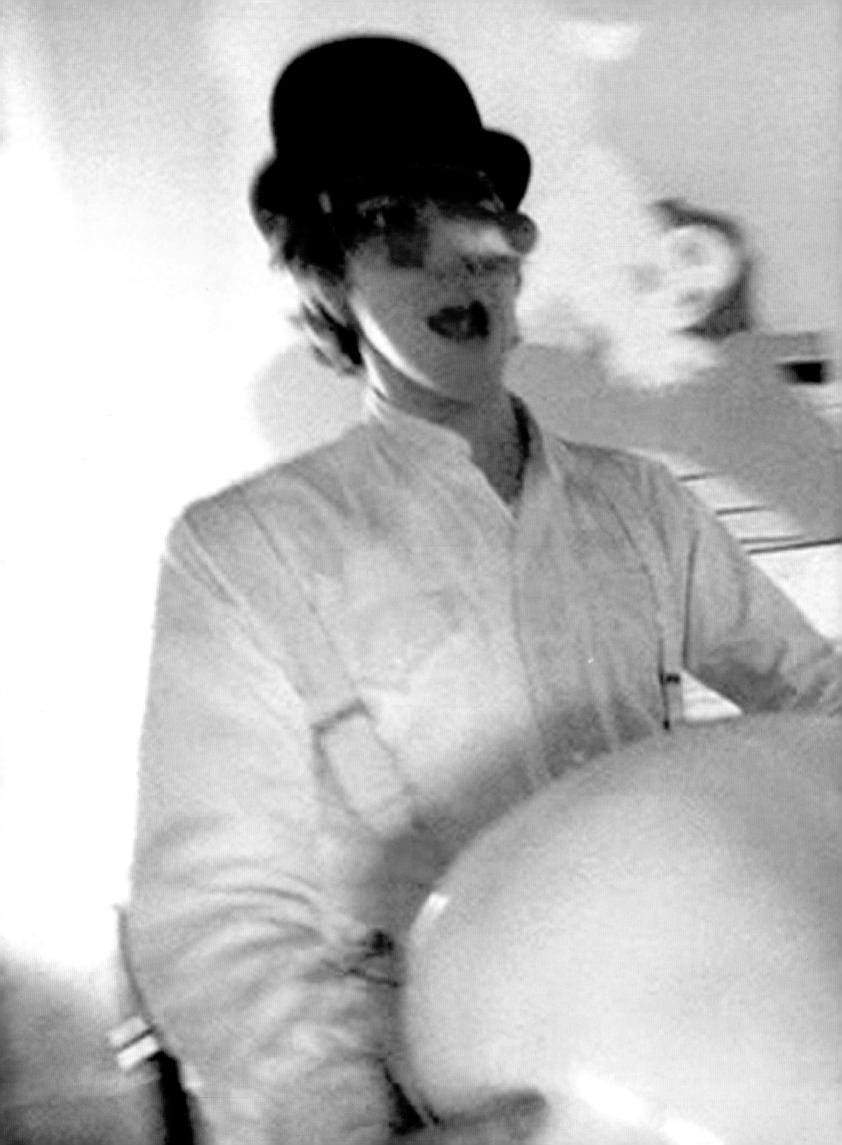

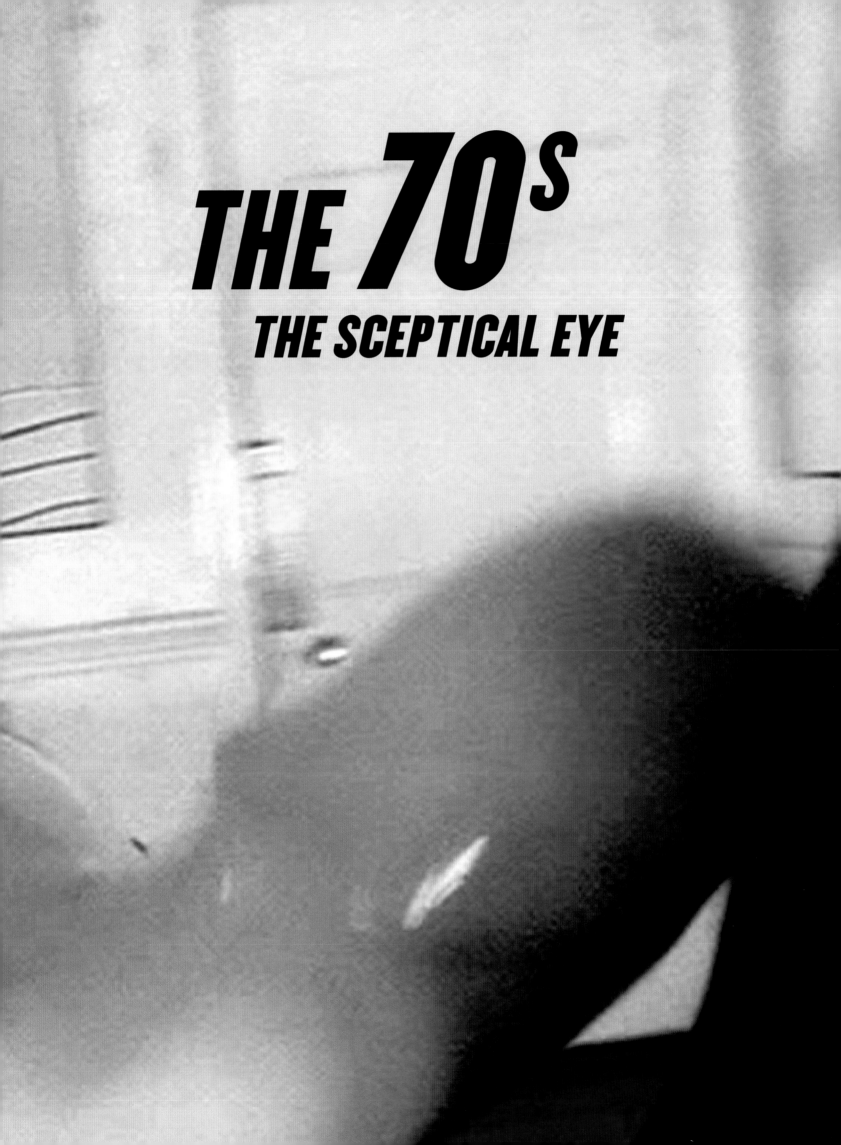

THE 70s
THE SCEPTICAL EYE

THE SCEPTICAL EYE
Notes on the Movies of the 70s

"Municipal Flatblock 18a, Linear North. This was where I lived with my dadda and mum," says Alex (Malcolm McDowell), as he strolls home whistling between the houses of a suburban housing development somewhere in the middle of nowhere. The place is like a labyrinth. Lights burn in a few windows, weakly illuminating the protagonist's path. There's something strangely static about the camera that accompanies him through these streets in a single parallel tracking shot. The dramatic impression is not created by Hollywood's standard techniques – shot/reverse shot – but by a camera that glides like a ghost through dilapidated flowerbeds full of discarded junk.

In this dismal environment, the film's young hero is the only sign of life, and he's just enjoyed a good night out. Alex and his droogs have tolchocked an old tramp and a writer, raped a devotchka, stolen a car, and forced a respectable number of fellow-drivers into the roadside ditch. Horrorshow.

Alex is in a splendid mood. Accompanying him homewards, we become highly aware of the camera's presence. We're waiting for a cut, but the camera does not blink, staring persistently at Alex as it slides along at his side. What we see here is more than a happily whistling hoodlum; we're seeing the fact that we see him.

Stanley Kubrick's *A Clockwork Orange* (1971, p. 544) is one of the key cult movies of the 70s, and certainly the most controversial. It might be described as the hinge that links the 60s with the 70s, for Kubrick's film may well be seen as a skeptical critique of the ideals formulated by the 60s student movement. Yet although the movie makes constant allusions to the progressive optimism of that decade, its purview includes the entire century and the inhuman ideologies that marked it out.

It's hard to think of another film that assigns us the role of voyeur so effectively. In a shocking way, *A Clockwork Orange* makes all of share responsibility for the things it shows. Thus the eloquent off-screen narrator who tells us his story never doubts for a second that he has our sympathy – and our consent. Again and again, he addresses us as "brothers." Still, the risk remains that we might have to see things from another perspective; and once, indeed, we find ourselves in the role of the victim – with Alex insisting we take a *veddy* good look… In this respect, Kubrick plays with the viewer's expectations. The film insists on breaking the bounds of fiction and assigning a series of different roles to us, the spectators. It's as if the director wanted to demonstrate his awareness of the pleasure we take in voyeurism, while also demanding that we see the world through Alex's eyes.

But Kubrick takes possession of us to an even greater extent than this, using all cinematic means available to give an authentic representation of Alex's world. We don't just see through Alex's eyes; we hear through his ears; and the music that accompanies his atrocities "allows" us to share his visceral pleasure in cruelty. As we watch a vicious brawl in a disused cinema, we hear Rossini's *La gazza ladra*; but this doesn't mean that Kubrick is trivializing violence.

On the contrary; the fighters' fun is simply being made plain to us. Kubrick is attempting to show – to make us *feel* – what violence looks like from the inside. Here, violence is presented as a creative principle. It signifies lust, intoxication, as described by Nietzsche in the "The Birth of Tragedy." The film sketches a theory of ecstasy as the true fulfillment experienced by any human being who escapes the limits of his individuality. One scene shows this with particular vividness: like a satyr of the ancient world, Alex embraces a stone phallus – life petrified into art – and reawakens it in a grotesque balletic dance.

As we accompanied Alex back to the flat, we got so close to him that we almost entered his Holy of Holies – home itself, with dadda and mum. In the entrance hall of his apartment block, the camera blinks; and now we're gliding along in front of a mural. Once again, the director has flouted our expectations. Naturally, we interpret this tracking shot as if we see what we're seeing through Alex's eyes, or as if we had just escorted him into the foyer; yet now, to our surprise, we see him enter the frame from the opposite direction. And while we wait for him to arrive, there's time to ex-amine the heaps of garbage, the parched and trampled lawns. With the passage of time, this once impressive stairwell, with its murals and its potted plants, has adapted itself to the forbidding and inhospitable concrete jungle that surrounds it. The tenants' rage is directed at the "beautifications" – and especially at the mural, which is now disfigured by paint smears and obscene graffiti. The building's inhabitants, waiting in vain for the broken-down elevator, can only have taken pleasure in this fresco for a very short period. For they've "improved" it by adding enormous male sex organs, along with some helpful advice: "Suck it and see," says a boy bearing a narrow barrel, as he gazes down on his beholders from the painting on the wall.

Yet even without the obscenities, these heroic images of the working class don't really fit into their grim concrete environs. We see men and women of all ages united in their praise of skilled labor, agriculture and industry, an assurance of the happy future awaiting mankind. Here, careful planning and conscientious work are two sides of the same coin. Thinkers and doers, young and old, farmers, laborers and craftsmen, all striving together in the service of a better life, a new world forged by a vigorous humanity. At the center of the painting stands a man whose physique and headgear mark him out as a leader; brave and strong, he gazes heroically towards the future.

The fresco in the foyer of Alex's parents' apartment block seems very familiar – as if we had encountered it all over Europe in course of the 20th century. We know this kind of agitprop art; we've seen it in Berlin and

Rome, in Bucharest and Moscow. It's as if Kubrick wished to comment, in passing, on a century marked by totalitarian systems. But this director doesn't make it easy for the audience; for he's set us a trap by asking us to sympathize with this apparently peaceful world, now defiled by vandalism. But who in fact are the vandals? The kids who've desecrated the artwork with filthy graffiti? Or the state technocrats who think they know the fate of humanity, and who paint a rosy future to conceal the inhumanity of the present?

Alex and his droogs counter moralists of all colors with the growled refrain, "If it moves, kiss it," while attaching outsized phalli to the heroes of classical antiquity. The droogs are shamelessly, indeed proudly, evil, and they're clearly convinced that work is for jerks.

Commentators who have written about this film have so far failed to notice that the mural in question is based on designs by Fritz Erler, a German painter and Hitler portraitist who readily adopted the themes of National Socialist art. Kubrick confronts us with two separate examples of state-ordained schemes to improve the world – modern urban architecture and the painted image of a utopian society – before letting loose their anarchistic adversaries. For the patently starry-eyed idealism debunks itself, leading inexorably as it does to a world in which the only choices left are between violence or boredom, hurting or being hurt; a world inhabited solely by brainless conformists and evil geniuses.

"Viddy well"

Alex, the hoodlum, is pure literature. His language is a bizarre patois invented by Anthony Burgess, a potpourri of adolescent slang, onomatopoeia and Russian. In Kubrick's apocalyptic vision, Alex mutates into a creature of cinema whose "Gulliver" is haunted by the dreams and nightmares of 60s movies, from Warhol's *Vinyl* (1965) via Hammer's *Dracula* (1958, 1960, 1965; further productions of the same subject were realized by the Hammer Studios in 1968, 1970, 1972 and 1974) to Antonioni's *Zabriskie Point* (1969). We all have the freedom to worship our own personal graven images; and in Alex's case, these happen to be Beethoven, manslaughter, rape, and the products of the Deutsche Grammophon record label.

The paradoxical truth of Kubrick's film consists in the assessment that there can be no morality as long as human beings are not free to flout it – even if the upshot is the collapse of civilization while Free Will stands by and applauds. *A Clockwork Orange* aestheticizes violence in order to express the autonomy of creativity; indeed, this is one of the film's central theses. Implicitly, the American director Kubrick is narrating the Fall of Man in the 20th century. He is showing us how the dictators – Hitler first and foremost – became conscious of the power of film and realized that the medium could do much more than merely tell stories and deliver snapshots of reality. In the 20th century, the camera became a perpetrator of violence. What's more, the camera is the viewers' ally, and it presupposes they will acquiescence – and relish the experience – when it shows them images of brutality. "Viddy well, little

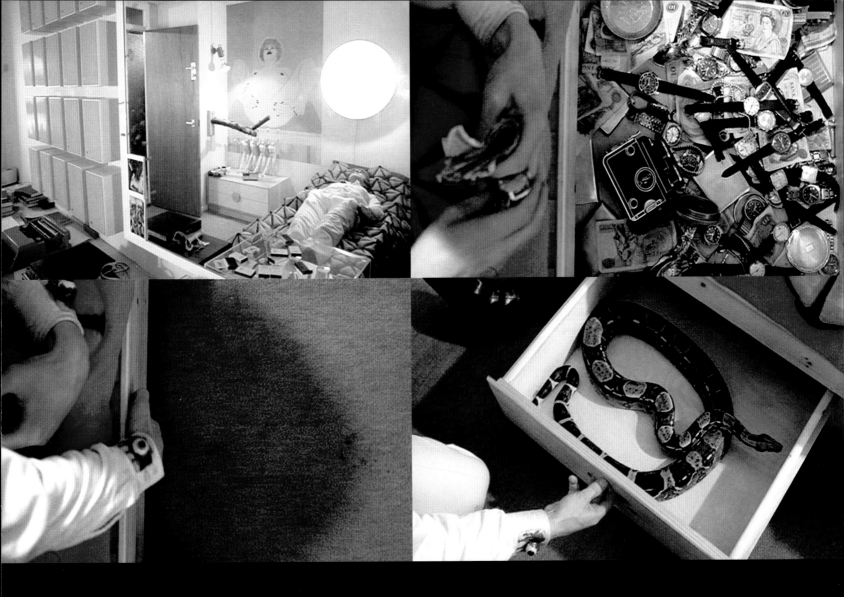

brother. Viddy well," says Alex, getting ready to rape, as he stares into the camera and makes direct contact with the viewer.

In *A Clockwork Orange*, the camera does not move enquiringly through cinematic space: instead, the camera's large-scale movements constitute and confirm this space's right to exist. It forms the stage on which the camera operates with icy precision, putting the beloved protagonist through his paces; first with pathos, later with pity, the camera follows its hero, bending the cinematic space to its will, so that Alex may bestride it like a king. When he struts through the record store, it's his spatial environment that seems to adjust to his trajectory, rather than vice-versa.

The few scenes we have described are enough to make it clear that *seeing* constitutes one of the major themes of *A Clockwork Orange*. The film sketches seeing as a sensual pleasure, if not an instinctual drive, and shows us as no more than its agents: cheerful voyeurs and accomplices, gourmets of the violence displayed with such narcissistic vanity. Thus it's no surprise that we even continue watching as Alex pisses blissfully in the toilet bowl.

Only a few films in the history of cinema have provoked such varying reactions. The legendary Pauline Kael, for example, was one film critic who despised this movie, and it inspired her to pen a veritable tirade: *A Clockwork Orange*, said Kael, "might be the work of a strict and exacting German professor who set out to make a porno-violent sci-fi comedy." Well, Alex would probably be delighted by this judgment; but why, one wonders, a "German" professor…?

In any case, the peasants and proletarians in the foyer mosaic do seem to be German; and this grandiloquent glorification of social upheaval is lost in the midst of an urban landscape that has now buried Utopia in a concrete crypt. Though Anthony Burgess tells us that the story takes place "somewhere in Europe," the location could as easily be anywhere else in the world.

Yet there's even more German in Kubrick's film: the uniforms sported by Billy Boy's gang, for instance; and of course the music of Ludwig van Beethoven, which fills Alex's head with magnificent dreams of death and destruction. (In this respect at least, he may well resemble some German professors before him…) In the conglomerate of qualities regarded as "typically Teutonic," Kubrick finds a paradigmatic relationship between genius and madness, high art and barbarism, the creative powers of genius and the horror of mass murder.

A Clockwork Orange is also, and not least, a film about the power of music. Though the book describes a lover of classical music in general, Kubrick makes him a fanatical fan of Beethoven in particular. Alex describes his auditory experiences with his usual inimitable eloquence: "Oh bliss! Bliss and heaven! Oh, it was gorgeousness and gorgeousity made flesh. It was like a bird of rarest-spun heaven metal or like silvery wine flowing in a spaceship, gravity all nonsense now. As I slooshied, I knew such lovely pictures!"

The second movement of Beethoven's Ninth Symphony (*Molto vivace*) is accompanied by a wild carnival of images; this associative montage does not balk at mocking Jesus as a naked, quadrupled, porcelain Messiah, flinging his arms around to the strains of the glorious Ninth. In this world, there is

Alex after his therapy demonstrate Dr. Brodsky's success: for Alex, the very thought of violence has become equivalent to the violent act itself. The image has replaced the deed.

A Clockwork Orange conveys a significant and pervasive mood in the cinema of the 70s. With this film, an American director expresses his skepticism about the emancipatory potential of technology, science and morality. Kubrick doubts whether any of these can ever lead humanity, driven as it by fears and instincts, onto the right path – whatever that may be. At the same time, the director is providing a commentary on the 20th century, which began with unparalleled aspirations to improve the world, and soon led to the most dreadful catastrophes. In the 20th century, the cinema became an important artistic medium; and at the same time, it turned out to be the most effective method of manipulation (as with the propaganda of the totalitarian systems). But Kubrick is not content to leave it at that. For it's significant that two of Alex's droogs have become policemen in the second half of the movie. Although his former friends have now changed sides, they haven't had to give up their passion for brutality. Humankind, whatever it does, is always stuck with violence.

The Wunderkinder

Even today, the films of the 70s have an astonishing potency. This applies not least to the American cinema of the decade, which experienced an un-

precedented renewal that few would have considered possible. It was a time of unparalleled freedoms, and many felt they were living through a kind of revolution.

By exploiting the possibilities of commercial cinema with a new vigor, and by examining the myths as critically as the social realities, cinematography achieved a new truthfulness, which emancipated it once more from the pre-eminence of TV. Though the monumental Cinemascope epics of the 60s may have paraded the silver screen's superiority to the box, the cinema only realized its true strength when it began to fill that screen with new subject matter. In America, there were particularly good reasons to do so, for the USA was a deeply traumatized and divided nation. The war in Vietnam continued to drag on unbearably, consuming more and more victims; and the political justification for the military intervention was in any case more than questionable. What little trust was left in the political administration was destroyed by the Watergate scandal. America had lost its credibility as a moral instance, and U.S. cinema traced the causes and effects of this trauma in a series of memorable films. The basic skepticism of 70s cinema is balanced by the filmmakers' huge enthusiasm for their medium. Their curiosity, creative will and refusal to compromise now seem more fascinating than ever, for we live in an age in which Hollywood seems ever more rationalized and conformist.

At the end of the 60s, a period described by Hans C. Blumenberg as "the most dismal and boring decade" in American cinema history, Hollywood was on the ropes, both economically and artistically. In the face of the prevalent societal crisis, the cinema had lost its power to form identity; and for anyone

after mere distraction, the TV was clearly the simpler and cheaper alternative. As the movies declined in importance, the old studio system was doomed to collapse, for it had been showing signs of sickness since the early 1950s. The last of the old-style Hollywood moguls stepped down, and a younger generation took over the management of the studios, which were now almost all owned by major corporations. By this time, the studios were barely developing a single project themselves.

Such was the situation as the 60s drew to a close; until a few small movies, most of them produced independently, turned out to be surprise hits – simply by encapsulating the rebellious spirit of the age. In *Bonnie and Clyde* (1967, p. 486), for example, Warren Beatty and Faye Dunaway blaze an anarchic trail through the mid-West, each bank heist and shoot-out a token of their mutual love and a gesture of defiant revolt. In *Easy Rider* (1969, p. 508), Peter Fonda and Dennis Hopper transverse the vastness of America, ostensibly to sell drugs, but in fact quite simply for the hell of it – to be on the road, to be free. These new heroes were not just excitingly beautiful and cool; they also embodied a truth irreconcilable with the truth of their elders. And this is what the young wanted to see at the movies: actors who gave a face to their yearnings.

These films gave a decisive impulse to the New Hollywood. From now on, the studios would give young filmmakers a chance. And they knew how to use it; with Francis Ford Coppola, Brian De Palma, George Lucas, Steven Spielberg, Peter Bogdanovich, William Friedkin, Paul Schrader and Martin Scorsese, the 70s produced a generation of "child prodigies," who defined

a new kind of Hollywood cinema. These young movie-maniacs helped the American film industry to make an unexpected and lasting commercial comeback. For their films included some of the biggest box-office hits of the decade – *The Godfather*, (1972, p. 562; Part II, 1974), *The Exorcist* (1973), *Jaws* (1975, p. 588), *Close Encounters of the Third Kind* (1977) and *Star Wars* (1977, p. 606).

Naturally, one has to be careful when comparing the *Wunderkinder* with European *auteurs* in the tradition of the *Nouvelle Vague*, but the influence of the latter on the New Hollywood is readily apparent. In the 70s, American directors enjoyed a stronger position than any of their predecessors since the days of Griffith – and this in a film industry characterized by specialization. The decade marked a highpoint of directorial independence. Having begun with the death of the old Dream Factory, it ended with the invention of the blockbuster: an "event-movie" swaddled in a tailor-made marketing strategy, with which today's Hollywood continues to rule the commercial cinema practically worldwide.

The Back Doors of Power

The most important American director of the decade is Francis Ford Coppola. He is also the one who most radically upheld his position as a "film author." As the first director of the New Hollywood, he scored a major triumph. *The Godfather* was an artistic and commercial success, and he even managed to

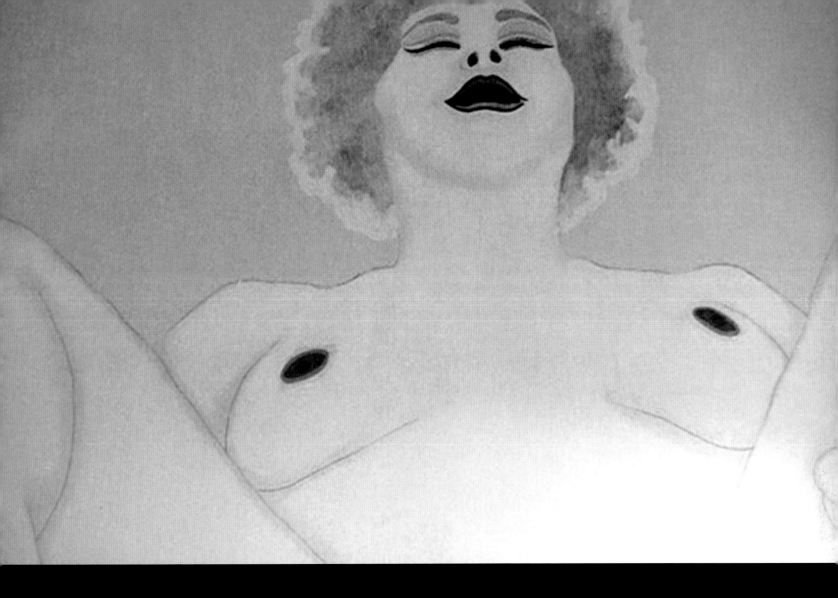

top this with the second part. Marlon Brando, the one-time embodiment of rebellious youth, was an indubitable sensation as Don Vito Corleone, the massive patriarch with the rasping voice. There were, however, other reasons for the film's enormous popularity.

The epic tale of the Corleone Mafia clan marked the first cinematic treatment of a non-WASP American family history. Until this film appeared, the white Anglo-Saxon protestant majority had enjoyed uncontested cultural dominance. *The Godfather* shows how the Corleones succeed in transplant-ing their Sicilian ideas of family ... onto American soil ... are they

he read in the newspaper. Coppola showed us insulated centers of power, impervious to external influence. In the terrifying final scene of Part I, Kay (Diane Keaton) realizes that her husband Michael is the new Godfather. The door is ajar, and she sees him greeting his accomplices; as a sign of defer-ence, they kiss his hands. Then the door closes before Kay's eyes, and the picture fades to black. This film's pessimism captured the mood of an entire nation.

Scorsese, De Niro immersed himself in the filmmaking process with an almost fanatical intensity; and he, too, wanted to explore the depths of his own psyche.

The most spectacular film Scorsese made in the 70s was *Taxi Driver* (1975, p.600). As the flipped-out Vietnam Vet Travis Bickle, De Niro gave definitive, threatening form to the existential nausea, frustration and blocked-up aggression of the lonely city-dweller. It was all the more disturbing because the film allowed us the opportunity to identify with Bickle. The scene in which De Niro, armed to the teeth, poses in front of the mirror must be one of the most frequently quoted in film history.

Taxi Driver shows New York through the eyes of its psychotic protagonist. Night after night, he drives his yellow cab through a sick city that infects its inhabitants, a monstrous metropolis that mirrors the decadence of society. The film's atmosphere is dark and the use of color is disturbing, a typical example of how even non-political films gave expression to distrust of the American political system and showed the growing brutality of a society undergoing cataclysmic change. Certainly, the corruption of the political classes was directly addressed in various political dramas, such as Alan J. Pakula's Watergate thriller *All the President's Men* (1976) or Sydney Pollack's *Three Days of the Condor* (1975). But in the American cinema of the 70s, a general loss of confidence is perceptible almost everywhere – in disaster movies such as *The Towering Inferno* (1974) and in countless paranoia thrillers. In such a situation, the return of the horror film is no surprise – and George A. Romero, Tobe Hooper, Wes Craven and John Carpenter created some real classics, though William Friedkin's *The Exorcist* is probably the most notable example of the genre.

Towards the end of the 70s, the U.S. cinema began dealing explicitly with the Vietnam War. Here, too, Coppola was the pioneer. In *Apocalypse Now* (1979, p.634), he attempted to grasp the nature of war. The film depicts a regression to an anti-humanist world in which good and evil have become indistinguishable. Here, Coppola made a radical break with the alleged realism of the war-film genre, by combining the greatest possible degree of authenticity – the film was made on location in the jungle – with a lurid, expressive artificiality.

Apocalypse Now is one of the most daring projects in cinematic history. It stands as proof of a passionate filmmaker's unbroken faith in himself, for Coppola was prepared to risk both his livelihood and his health in order to realize his vision. In retrospect, however, the project's very radicalism seems to presage the end of large-scale "authorial cinema" in the New Hollywood era. Soon after, Michael Cimino's box-office disaster *Heaven's Gate* (1980) supplied the death certificate.

It took so long to complete *Apocalypse Now* – while the media speculated avidly about the project's impending collapse – that other Vietnam films reached the theaters sooner. Hal Ashby scored a considerable success with his melodrama *Coming Home* (1978), the story of a soldier's wife (Jane Fonda) who falls in love with an invalid war veteran (Jon Voight). This was a relatively conventional tale, told in the best liberal Hollywood manner.

By contrast, Cimino's *The Deer Hunter* (1978, p.618) was the source of considerable controversy, with the negative representation of the Vietcong arousing particular criticism. If truth be told, the film is completely uninterested in a balanced representation of events, and less interested in the conflict itself than in what the American film scholar Robin Wood called "the invasion of America by Vietnam" – the war's penetration of the American psyche. In Wood's reading of the film, Cimino is examining the myth of an ideal America at the moment of its dissolution. Vietnam initiated a process of increasing awareness, a terrible dawning. At the end of the film, the survivors join together in singing "God Bless America," and the song is heavy with grief. These people are in mourning, not just for their dead friend, but for a lost ideal.

The Comeback of the Classics

Following the lead of the French auteurs, young American cineasts discovered the great classics of U.S. cinema. For not a few of these new directors, the older movies were their declared models, and they paid tribute to them in their own films. Peter Bogdanovich began his career as a film journalist, interviewing Hollywood legends such as Orson Welles and John Ford. When he himself took up directing, most of his films were homages to the Hollywood movies of the past. With *What's Up, Doc?* (1972), he attempted to create a screwball comedy *à la* Howard Hawks. "Reclaiming" such classic genres was typical of the "Wunderkinder." In this case, the re-

sult was a splendidly exuberant film-buff's jamboree, packed full of movie quotations and amusing nods to past classics. Nonetheless, the film worked even for those who were less in the know, partly thanks to the comic talent of Barbra Streisand, one of the top female stars of the 70s.

New York, New York (1977) was Martin Scorsese's extravagant attempt to revive interest in the musical. To evoke the Golden Age of the genre, he placed all his bets on the glamour and star quality of a Broadway icon: Liza Minnelli. Although the daughter of Vincente Minnelli and Judy Garland had received a lot of attention for her lead role in Bob Fosse's *Cabaret* (1972, p. 556), *New York, New York* failed to attract a big audience. Instead, moviegoers flocked to pop musicals like *Hair* (1978) and the tongue-in-cheek *The Rocky Horror Picture Show* (1975). These were two films that achieved remarkable cult status – yet ultimately, they too were isolated, one-off hits.

Of course, Neo-Noirs such as *Taxi Driver* were also modeled on classic films of the past; yet they reveal much more than the cinematic preferences of their creators. In the pessimistic perspective of Film Noir, it's obvious that these filmmakers saw clear parallels to their own take on American reality. And so they didn't merely adopt the dark visual style of 40s and 50s thrillers; they also facilitated the comeback of a genre with a supremely skeptical outlook on social mechanisms: the detective film.

Roman Polanski's *Chinatown* (1974, p. 582) is a masterpiece of the genre, and one of the best films of the decade. The Polish-born director created a magnificent portrait of universal corruption and violence, while

also managing to conjure up the glory that was Hollywood. Nonetheless, his film was much more than a mere homage, thanks not least to some fabulous actors. Faye Dunaway perfectly embodied the mysterious erotic allure of a 30s film vamp, without ever seeming like a mere ghost from movies past. Jack Nicholson's private detective was also far more than yet another Bogart clone: J. J. Gittes is an authentic figure, a tough little gumshoe made of flesh and blood, who maintains his credibility even with a plaster on his nose. For a moralist like Gittes, a sliced nostril is just another hazard that goes with the job.

The U.S. cinema of the 70s took a skeptical and pessimistic attitude to the myths of the nation, and this had its effect on the most American film genre of them all – the Western. John Ford, Howard Hawks and John Wayne all died within a few years, and these were the personalities who had stamped the genre for decades. Ever since the late 50s, a process of demystification had been at work; and now the *content* of the Western was also taken to its logical conclusion.

The classical Western had always taken an optimistic attitude to history and progress. Sam Peckinpah's *Pat Garrett and Billy the Kid* (1973) is a sorrowful elegy for the old Western, and a complete reversal of its basic worldview. As the film sees it, the growing influence of capital on social relationships meant the end of the utopia of freedom. Individuals can only succumb and conform to a corrupt society, or else they are doomed to perish, like Billy the Kid. Kris Kristofferson gave Billy the aura of a hippie idol – and with the outlaw's demise, the film also buried the hopes and ideals of the Woodstock generation.

It was clear that Western heroes would no longer serve as the icons of reactionary America. Their successors were "urban cowboys" like the protagonist of Don Siegel's controversial *Dirty Harry* (1971): Clint Eastwood plays a cynical cop who takes the law into his own hands – because the legal system only serves crooks – and who makes no bones about despising the democratic legitimation of power. When Dirty Harry Callahan has completed his mission by killing the psychopath, he gazes down on the floating corpse – and throws his police badge in the water.

The primordial American yearning for freedom and the open road were now better expressed in road movies such as *Easy Rider*, Monte Hellman's *Two-Lane Blacktop* (1971) or even star vehicles like *Smokey and the Bandit* (1977), featuring Burt Reynolds. But as demonstrated by Steven Spielberg's feature-film debut *Duel* (1971), even the endless highway offered no refuge from the paranoid nightmares of the 70s.

The Triumph of the "Jedi Knights"

During the 1970s, Vietnam and Watergate cast their dark shadows across the cinema screens. The divisions in the national psyche came to expression in horror and paranoia movies as well as pessimistic thrillers, war films and do-it-yourself-justice potboilers. In the midst of the crisis, many people wanted one thing and one thing only from the cinema: a short vacation from real life. Hollywood was more than happy to cater for their

needs. At the end of the decade, the science fiction genre boldly went where no films had gone before. The sensational success of George Lucas' *Star Wars* and Steven Spielberg's *Close Encounters of the Third Kind* laid the foundations for the blockbuster movies of the decades to come.

One reason for this triumph of these films was their sheer technical perfection, which made a substantial contribution to the credibility of their plots. In addition, Lucas and Spielberg succeeded in bringing together so many different elements of popular film so convincingly that these movies, however fantastic their premises, offered a huge potential for identification. *Close Encounters* and *Star Wars* are also remarkable for their overwhelming visual power. These were cinematic adventures that even adults could enjoy with childlike pleasure, and millions were happy to do so. The escapism of these films anticipated the cinema of the 80s.

The Return of German Film

The enlivening influence of the French *Nouvelle Vague* was felt not only in America. "New Waves" arose everywhere, including West Germany. Artistically, the 70s were the most interesting decade in German cinema since the Golden Age of the 20s and early 30s. Film authors such as Werner Herzog, Rainer Werner Fassbinder, Wim Wenders and Volker Schlöndorff drew the world's attention to the New German Cinema.

Many of these young filmmakers forged conscious links to the traditions of classic German cinema, seeing themselves as the legitimate heirs to a body of work supplanted by Nazism and forgotten ever since. In this respect, Werner Herzog's *Nosferatu* (*Nosferatu – Phantom der Nacht*, 1978) seems almost programmatic, for it is a spectacular remake of a famous silent film by Friedrich Wilhelm Murnau.

Like most of Herzog's films, *Nosferatu* bears witness to the director's sympathy for outcasts, for lonely and eccentric personalities. Klaus Kinski provided the ideal embodiment of such figures, in this and in five other Herzog films. Artistically at least, the two men complemented each other perfectly: an obsessive director with a touch of genius, and a wildly eccentric actor who endowed each of his roles with all the strangeness and seemingly unrestrained intensity of his personality. In their jungle projects *Aguirre, Wrath of God* (*Aguirre, der Zorn Gottes*, 1972) and *Fitzcarraldo* (1978–81, p. 662), this was a constellation that almost led to catastrophe; but the final results were two utterly original film creations. As was *Nosferatu*, in which Kinski added a tragic dimension to the vampire's existential loneliness – an astonishing achievement when we consider the grotesque horror of the vampire's appearance. In a world of bourgeois businessmen, Kinski's Nosferatu is a creature crucified by despairing love.

The tragedy of an individual life is also the focus of each of the films made by the most productive German director of the time. In a tempo that can only be described as feverish, Rainer Werner Fassbinder made more than 40 films in the 12 years before his early death (in 1982). These included genre

films, literary adaptations, melodramas, radically "committed" films, intimate character studies, and even movies with popular appeal, such as *The Marriage of Maria Braun* (*Die Ehe der Maria Braun*, 1978). Both in form and content, Fassbinder's films are uncompromising studies of society's brutality and emotional coldness. At the same time, they are also reflections on his work as a filmmaker and his personal demons. Fassbinder's fame is also founded on his genius as an actor-director; and the female members of his "film family" – first and foremost, Hanna Schygulla – stamped the image of the New German Cinema.

Volker Schlöndorff, by contrast, made his name by adapting works of literature. *The Tin Drum* (*Die Blechtrommel*, 1979, p. 624), brought him the Oscar for Best Foreign Film, and he is the first German director to have won this award. (The second German is Caroline Link who won an Oscar for *Nirgendwo in Afrika*, 2001) In the role of the little drummer boy Oskar Matzerath, David Bennent played a large part in assisting the New German Cinema to its greatest triumph. Only a few years later, however, Fassbinder's death marked the almost complete collapse of the German *Autorenfilm*. The sole director to preserve his status was Wim Wenders, whose films displayed a fascination for the American cinema. At that time, however, his enthrallment was also tempered by critical reflection.

An "authors' cinema," in spite of everything

By the time the 60s ended, most people in France regarded the *Nouvelle Vague* as essentially over. Not least under the impact of the student revolts of May 1968, the movement's former protagonists – Jean-Luc Godard, François Truffaut, Claude Chabrol, Eric Rohmer und Jacques Rivette – moved apart, or began to pursue their own ideas more assertively.

Since the mid-60s, Godard, the most important force for change in European cinema, had increasingly seen the film medium as an instrument of political dissent. Post-'68, he turned his back completely on the commercial cinema, devoting his time to experimental, political film-projects. The one exception was *Everything's Fine* (*Tout va bien / Crepa padrone, tutto va bene*, 1972). Only in 1980 did Godard return to the mainstream cinema with his "second first film:" *Every Man for Himself* aka *Slow Motion* (*Sauve qui peut [la vie]*) was a resigned, allegorical commentary on the state of cinema and society.

While Godard chose radical opposition to commerce, the 70s saw François Truffaut, Claude Chabrol and other French *auteurs* become increasingly established as popular filmmakers. With *Day for Night* (*La Nuit américaine*, 1973), Truffaut achieved a considerable feat: this intelligent and entertaining movie tells the story of how a film is made, and managed to appeal both to

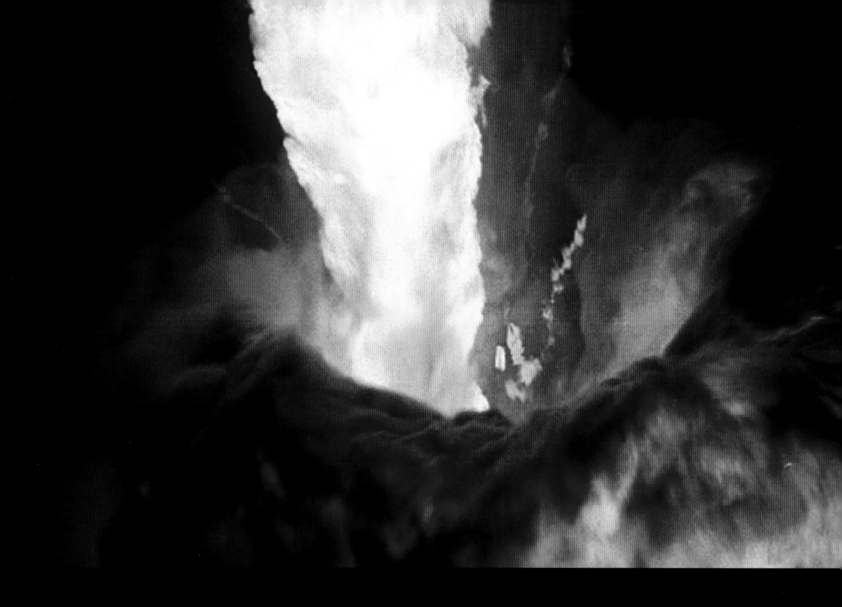

cineasts and a broad movie-going public. In 1974, Truffaut's wonderful homage to filmmaking earned him the Oscar for the Best Foreign Film.

The Last Metro (*Le dernier métro*, 1980) even succeeded in reconciling the art-cinema of the French *auteurs* with the perennial appeal of the stars. It tells the tale of a love triangle during the German occupation of Paris, and brought Truffaut an exceptional box-office success. As the woman beside Gérard Depardieu and Heinz Bennent, Catherine Deneuve gave a performance that established her reputation as the *grande dame* of French cinema. Some critics, though, were less than complimentary; to them, the film's classical brilliance exemplified the kind of sterile, workmanlike cinema that Truffaut had so doggedly opposed in his days as a film journalist. Despite his detractors' polemics, however, Truffaut remained one of the leading theorists and practitioners of the French cinema until his death in 1984. His influence on the European cinema can be felt even today.

For Britain's film industry, the 70s were a difficult decade and the continuing success of the James Bond films could do nothing to alter this fact. The problematic situation had much to do the industry's traditional economic dependency on foreign (especially American) film productions made in British studios. Though there had been many such productions in the past, their numbers were now in decline. In addition, the Free Cinema directors had by now lost their clout. Though they had initiated a renewal of the style and subject matter of British film from the late 50s onwards, the time of the Angry Young Men had clearly been and gone. The number of films produced in Britain sank rapidly, and even more English filmmakers than pre-

viously now felt forced to seek work in America. Many of them, indeed, remained on the other side of the Atlantic.

Nonetheless, pronounced individualists such as Nicolas Roeg continued to work frequently in Britain. Roeg's extravagant thriller *Don't Look Now* (1973) was a British production that included a wonderfully sensuous love scene between Julie Christie and Donald Sutherland, a sequence unrivaled in any other U.S. production of the time.

The American Stanley Kubrick was another director who valued the freer production conditions outside Hollywood. He had emigrated to England in the 60s. With *Barry Lyndon* (1975) he made an outstandingly beautiful costume drama that seemed gloriously indifferent to any kind of commercial consideration. Kubrick did return temporarily to the States to make his Steven King adaptation *The Shining* (1980), but he shot the interiors of the Overlook Hotel in the time-honored Elstree Studios near London.

Sceptics in the Empire of the Senses

In Italy, the situation looked very different. At the beginning of the decade, many commercially successful films were being made. Spaghetti Westerns were still selling well abroad, but the genre had long since passed its artistic zenith, with Sergio Leone's *Once Upon a Time in the West* (*C'era una volta il West*, 1969, p. 502). Directors such as Luchino Visconti, Michelangelo Antonioni and Federico Fellini, many of whom had their roots in the neo-

realism of the 40s and early 50s, sustained the Italian cinema's international reputation.

But it was another director, one of the leading members of the intellectual avant-garde, who was responsible for the most ambitious Italian project of the decade: Bernardo Bertolucci's *1900* (Part I and II) (*Novecento*, 1975/76) was a monumental two-part epic featuring a cast of international stars. It traced the history of Italy in the 20th century by following the lives of a few people from a single country estate – and might well have been entitled "Once Upon A Time In Italy."

Three years previously, Bernardo Bertolucci had caused a different kind of hullabaloo. His *Last Tango in Paris* (*Ultimo Tango a Parigi / Le dernier Tango à Paris*, 1972) examined the self-destructive sexual relationship between a cynical, ageing American in Paris (Marlon Brando) and a younFrenchWoman (Maria Schneider). The film's representation of sexuality was extreme for its time, and provoked a storm of protest. Attempts to ban screenings of the movie led to an avalanche of court cases in Italy.

The sexual revolution continued in the cinema. Particularly in European films, there was more and more sex on the screen. Nevertheless – or rather, for that very reason – the 70s were also a decade of "scandal films." Bertolucci's *Last Tango* was by no means an isolated exception. Many moviegoers were also outraged by Pier Paolo Pasolini's *Salo, or The 120 Days of Sodom* (*Salò o le 120 giornate di Sodoma*, 1975). A deeply pessimistic film that transferred the plot of a De Sade novel to the Italy of the Fascist era, it depicted the sadistic fantasies of a decadent *grande bour-*

geoisie in images of icy perversion that are hard to watch even today. In many countries, the film was censored. Another movie to hit the headlines was Nagisa Oshima's Japanese-French co-production *Ai no corrida / L'Empire des sens* (1976). A ballad of sexual dependency, the film tells the story of an *amour fou* that ends in physical mutilation. During Berlin's International Film festival in 1977, the German authorities temporarily confiscated the film, as it was suspected of being pornographic. Isolated actions such as these, however, did little to hinder the general tendency towards liberalization. Naturally, this was not entirely unconnected to the fact that sex sells.

Looking back at the movies of the 70s, it seems that the freedoms brought by the influence of the film authors are reflected in a highly heterogeneous range of visual styles. Quite clearly, the director's personality determined the look of a film much more strongly than in previous decades. There was certainly a trend towards stylization apparent in many Neo-Noirs, SF and horror films. Yet the realistic elements and faith in a good storyline were just as new, and more significant. Movies shot on location increasingly supplanted those made on studio sets. In the 70s, films were made in real streets, real backyards, and real apartments.

The recording technology too developed an unprecedented, dynamic mobility. Nervous hand cameras were soon practically standard, and opened up new frontiers, even for the commercial movie business. The Steadycam made it possible to film smooth pans and tracking shots without laying down cumbersome tracks; and for the simulation of amateur film sequences in *Mean Streets* and *Raging Bull*, Martin Scorsese even used an 8 mm camera

Clearly, many 1970s directors were looking for something closer to real life – which doesn't mean they were trying to slavishly reproduce the world around them. Though Coppola set up his cameras in the primeval jungle, what he produced was a war film that looked liked an acid trip: "This is not a movie about Vietnam. It is Vietnam."

In the 70s, it became clear at last that the old myths would no longer suffice. Vietnam and Watergate were only the most blatant symptoms justifying the terrible diagnosis of the decade's filmmakers: the Enlightenment had failed, and reports of humanity's progress had been premature. The American cinema of the period cast a strong light on the murky depths of American society. This was a country that felt recklessly secure in its possession of democracy and free speech. And the filmmakers were as skeptical about personal relationships as they were about politics. Predictions of sexual liberation, apparently as much of a myth as the Enlightenment itself, remained stubbornly unfulfilled.

If we turn our thoughts once again to Kubrick's *A Clockwork Orange*, the prophetic quality of the film becomes clear. For the American director is questioning nothing less than the idea of a world without violence. By postulating a future in which there is nothing but oppression, revolt and opportunism, he is rejecting the utopia of a conflict-free society. In Kubrick's film, sadism and ignorance are more than merely "lapses" by an individual, a group, or an institution.

The film takes its leave of the idea that humanity is perfectible. If the cinema nonetheless remains an instrument of enlightenment, then the main

reason is this: it forces us to undergo a paradoxical experience. For film can only retain its integrity by refusing to shield us from the irrational nature of the world. But it's not only the filmmakers' findings that undermine rationality. Our simple desire to *look* sometimes makes the movies seem more real us to us than our own lives. As Alex remarks during the therapy inflicted on him by Dr. Brodsky: "It's funny how the colors of the real world only seem really real when you viddy them on a screen."

Jürgen Müller / Jörn Hetebrügge

DEATH IN VENICE
Morte a Venezia

1970 - ITALY - 135 MIN. - LITERARY ADAPTATION, DRAMA

DIRECTOR LUCHINO VISCONTI (1906–1976) SCREENPLAY LUCHINO VISCONTI, NICOLA BADALUCCO,
based on the novella *DER TOD IN VENEDIG* by THOMAS MANN
DIRECTOR OF PHOTOGRAPHY PASQUALE DE SANTIS EDITING RUGGERO MASTROIANNI
MUSIC GUSTAV MAHLER PRODUCTION LUCHINO VISCONTI for ALFA CINEMATOGRAFICA.

STARRING DIRK BOGARDE (Gustav von Aschenbach), SILVANA MANGANO (Tadzio's Mother),
BJÖRN ANDRESEN (Tadzio), ROMOLO VALLI (Hotel Director), MARK BURNS (Alfred),
MARISA BERENSON (Frau von Aschenbach), FRANCO FABRIZI (Hairdresser),
ANTONIO APPICELLA (Vagabond), SERGIO GARFAGNOLI (Polish Boy),
NORA RICCI (Gouvernante).

"Your music is stillborn."

Venice, in the early 20th century. Gustav von Aschenbach (Dirk Bogarde), an aging German composer, is visiting the city of canals, hoping to recover from a nervous breakdown. He moves into an exclusive hotel facing the beach, where his fellow guests include an aristocratic Polish lady (Silvana Mangano) with her children and servants. Aschenbach immediately notices her son Tadzio (Björn Andresen), a pale, slender boy with long blond hair. Soon, Aschenbach is so fascinated by this beautiful youth that his daily schedule is increasingly dominated by the need to observe him. This obsession leads to a resolve to make contact with the boy – despite the threat posed by the cholera epidemic that is spreading through the city. Aschenbach ultimately succumbs to the disease and dies.

Few film adaptations of literary classics manage to surpass the original. Luchino Visconti's *Death in Venice* is one of the few exceptions, not least because the director refused to be intimidated by Thomas Mann's famous novella. His film version is strikingly different from the book, and he made these changes in order to realize his own cinematic vision.

In the course of his career, Visconti directed opera as well as films, and it shows. The importance of music to *Death in Venice* can be judged by the

1

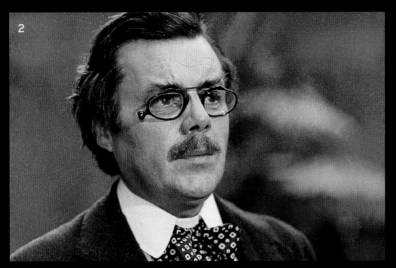

fact that Visconti made Aschenbach a composer; in Mann's novella, Aschenbach was a writer, though the character was in fact based on Gustav Mahler.

Mahler's music is of essential importance to the film. His Fifth Symphony is heard over the opening titles, and it accompanies Aschenbach's arrival in Venice on a steamship emerging into the light of dawn. This musical motif recurs throughout the film, and the elegiac gravity of the piece is mirrored in the almost lethargic rhythm of the images. The drama is contained, and develops, in a series of slow zooms and meticulous tracking shots that capture the morbid and sensual atmosphere of Venice, in the strong but subdued colors of the sultry summer and in the broad Cinemascope format. There is a remarkably serene quality to Visconti's film, strengthening the impact of the music, which is used very sparingly. The film has no narrator, Aschenbach is

"A film to be savored and one to be enjoyed and studied more than once." *Variety*

1   Angel of death: Frail aesthete Gustav von Aschenbach is overtaken by youth's fleeting beauty when he lays eyes on Tadzio (Björn Andresen).

2   Music to our ears: The role of composer Gustav von Aschenbach was the crescendo of Dirk Bogarde's acting career.

3   Eternal flame: Much like Visconti, Silvana Mangano's (left) film career rode the wave of postwar Italian neo-realism. She was one of the movement's shining stars.

4   Phoenix from the ashes: Visconti and cameraman Pasquale de Santis masterfully translate Thomas Mann's prose to the screen with sensuous visuals, gliding cinematography and seamless zoom-ins.

allowed no internal monologues, and indeed, no one says very much at all. Instead, the camera feels its way around the story discreetly, and Dirk Bogarde's expressive acting does the rest. Thomas Mann's polished descriptions and the fine irony of the text are perfectly translated into a purely visual language. Visconti traces the beginnings of Aschenbach's downfall in a series of flashbacks: the destruction of a happy family, sexual frustration and, above all, failure as an artist. In his ambition to express a pure, absolute beauty through his music, Aschenbach is not merely an anachronism; he is also in fatal rebellion against the claims of the body. When his friend Alfred (Mark Burns) insists on the dual nature of music, Aschenbach resists desperately. These are the moments in which Visconti interrupts the tranquil flow of his narrative and allows the past to erupt into the sluggish present like a fever-ish memory. The lie that has ruled Aschenbach's life catches up with him in Venice: for in recognizing that Tadzio embodies both perfection *and* sensuality, the noble aesthete is thrown back upon his own physical desire, which is more clearly homosexual in Visconti than in Mann.

By the time Aschenbach realizes what's driving him, it's too late: he's an elderly man with a decaying body. With the bitterest of irony, Visconti shows us how the composer attempts to regain his youth in the hairdresser's salon. At the end of the film, a cadaverous Aschenbach lies slumped in his deckchair on the beach, with black hair-dye trickling down his sweat-soaked face. Tadzio, standing on the shore, turns towards him and points off into the distance: it's a last greeting from an angel of death.

JH

LUCHINO VISCONTI (1906–1976) He was the scion of a noble Italian family, and he described himself as a Marxist – though his politics didn't stop him enjoying the best that life had to offer. The apparently disparate sides of Luchino Visconti's personality left their traces in his filmography. After learning his trade with Jean Renoir, he made his directing debut while Mussolini's Fascist regime was still in power: the naturalistic style of *Obsession* (*Ossessione*, 1943) was the starting point for Italian *neorealismo*. Visconti's *The Earth Trembles* (*La terra trema*, 1948), the story of a fisherman exploited by wholesale merchants, is regarded as one of the masterpieces of the neorealist movement. His sympathy for ordinary people is also evident in later films: see *Rocco and His Brothers* (*Rocco e i suoi fratelli*, 1960), which shows the disintegration of a family that moves from southern Italy to Milan in search of work. With *Senso* (*Senso*, 1954) however, he created the first of the splendidly operatic color films that would dominate his later career. Of these major productions, many critics feel the best was *The Leopard* (*Il gattopardo*, 1963), based on a novel by Giuseppe Tomasi di Lampedusa. This spectacular epic about a family of Sicilian aristocrats in the 19th century won him the Golden Palm at Cannes and made him an international star director. He sustained his reputation with films such as *Death in Venice* (*Morte a Venezia*, 1970) and *Ludwig* (*Le Crépuscule des dieux*, 1972), the latter a biography of the eccentric King of Bavaria. In parallel to his work in the cinema, Visconti was also a successful theater and opera director. The career of Maria Callas was closely linked to his own.

4

A CLOCKWORK ORANGE

1971 - GREAT BRITAIN - 137 MIN. - LITERARY ADAPTATION, THRILLER

DIRECTOR STANLEY KUBRICK (1928–1999) SCREENPLAY STANLEY KUBRICK, based on the novel of the same name by ANTHONY BURGESS DIRECTOR OF PHOTOGRAPHY JOHN ALCOTT EDITING BILL BUTLER MUSIC WALTER CARLOS PRODUCTION STANLEY KUBRICK for POLARIS PRODUCTIONS, HAWK FILMS LTD., WARNER BROS.

STARRING MALCOLM MCDOWELL (Alex), PATRICK MAGEE (Frank Alexander), MICHAEL BATES (Chief Guard Barnes), WARREN CLARKE (Dim), JOHN CLIVE (Stage Actor), PAUL FARRELL (Tramp), ADRIENNE CORRI (Mrs. Alexander), CARL DUERING (Doktor Brodsky), CLIVE FRANCIS (Joe), MICHAEL GOVER (Prison Governor), MIRIAM KARLIN (Miss Weatherly).

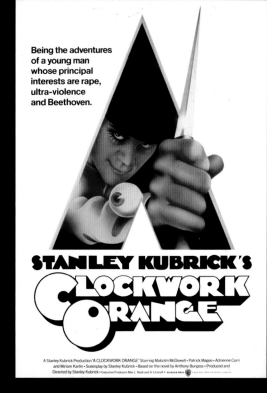

"Viddy well, little brother, viddy well."

A Clockwork Orange was banned in England until Stanley Kubrick's death in 1999. The director himself had withdrawn it in 1974, and the motivation for his self-censorship remains obscure. Perhaps he had simply grown tired of being blamed for glorifying violence, but it's possible he had actually been threatened. This is not as outlandish a suggestion as it may seem, for the film had occasioned a great deal of heated debate. No film before *A Clockwork Orange* had depicted violence in such an aestheticized manner, and with such a laconic refusal to justify itself. The critics accused Kubrick not merely of fomenting an appetite for extreme brutality, but of failing to challenge or even question that appetite. The violence on screen, they felt, was crying out to be imitated in real life. But Kubrick is no moralist, and no psychologist either; he doesn't explain what he shows. The audience is forced to decide for itself what it wants to see in his film, and the price we pay for this freedom includes accepting the risk that Nazi skinheads will love it.

Black bowler and bovver boots, white shirt and pants, tastefully topped off with an eyecatching, fortified codpiece; this is the uniform of Alex (Mal-

colm McDowell) and his Droogs, a teenage gang in constant search of some real "horrorshow" action. On a particularly enjoyable night out, they start off with a few drinks in the Korova Milkbar before going on to kick a drunken bum to pulp, indulge in a rumble with a rival gang, and play "road hogs" in a stolen car. Having warmed up, they proceed to break into the country house of a successful author and take turns at raping his wife, making very sure that the elderly writer – bound and gagged – gets a first-class view of her lengthy ordeal. Back at the bar, "feeling a bit shagged and fagged and fashed," they chill out with a "moloko plus" (milk with a little something added) before heading "bedways."

It's not so much the brutality that makes *A Clockwork Orange* such a haunting experience: it's the choreography. Alex above all, adoring fan of Ludwig Van, celebrates and savors his own "appearances" like works of performance art. In the writer's villa, he parodies Gene Kelly in "Singin' In The Rain," keeping time to the music with a series of kicks to his victim's guts. In contrast to his three mates, who expect to pick up some booty on their raids, he has

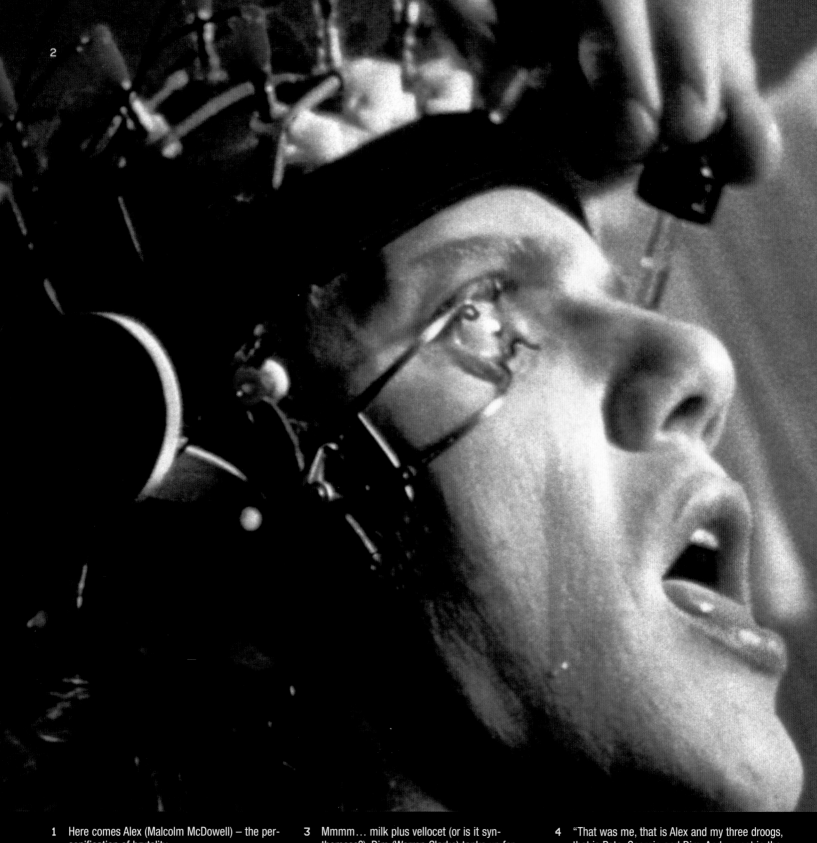

2

1   Here comes Alex (Malcolm McDowell) – the personification of brutality.

2   Doomed to look: Alex undergoes the Ludovico therapy.

3   Mmmm… milk plus vellocet (or is it synthemesc?): Dim (Warren Clarke) tanks up for a night of the old ultra-violence.

4   "That was me, that is Alex and my three droogs, that is Pete, Georgie and Dim. And we sat in the Korova Milkbar, trying to make up our razudoks what to do with the evening."

"In my opinion, Kubrick has made a movie that exploits only the mystery and variety of human conduct. And because it refuses to use the emotions conventionally, demanding instead that we keep a constant, intellectual grip on things, it's a most unusual – and disorienting –

little interest in money. To show them who's "Master and Leader," he beats them up. This will turn out to be a fateful difference of opinion. For later, when Alex inadvertently kills a woman with an *objet d'art* (a giant phallus), his disgruntled and mutinous droogs smash a bottle in his face and leave him to be found by the police. He is sentenced to 14 years in jail, but thanks to a new resocialization program and a revolutionary therapeutic technique, he is granted an early release. From now on, Alex will be violently sick whenever he's tempted to indulge in "a bit of the old ultra-violence." But though he can't hurt a fly, his past is inescapable: the world is full of people who suffered under his rule, and who will now exact revenge on their helpless ex-tormentor.

A Clockwork Orange is a complex discourse on the connections between violence, aesthetics and the media. The film gives no answers, it

MALCOLM MCDOWELL *A Clockwork Orange* (1971) would not have been made without him. For Stanley Kubrick, Alex simply had to be Malcolm McDowell. At that time, the 27-year-old had almost nothing to show for himself. He had just made his very first major film, the impressive *If...* (1968), set in an English boarding school and directed by Lindsay Anderson. But Kubrick was convinced of the qualities of the young, unknown actor, for he saw in him the human being in a natural state. And so Malcolm McDowell became a star. His instant success was also a kind a curse, for his face came to stand for everything evil, incalculable and dangerous, and he has rarely been permitted to play anything but the villain.
Born in Leeds in 1943, McDowell worked as a coffee salesman before going to drama school in London. Later, he acted with the Royal Shakespeare Company. After *A Clockwork Orange*, he went on to make two more films with Lindsay Anderson, both of them intelligent satires: *O Lucky Man!* (1973) and *Britannia Hospital* (1982). In 1979, he caused another stir, this time as the notorious dictator in Tinto Brass' controversial *Caligula*. He then disappeared from view, showing up almost only in B-movies, although he did have some interesting supporting roles in movies such as Paul Schrader's *Cat People* (1982). In the 90s, however, MacDowell was a very busy man, making around 50 appearances in movies or TV series, for example in *Star Trek: Generations* (1994), where he faced off Captains Kirk and Picard, and in Paul McGuigan's *Gangster No.1* (2000).

4

5   "A truly Satanic cinematic satire, made with almost unimaginable perfection," said *Der Spiegel*. In this scene, Kubrick himself operated the hand-held camera.

6   The writer Alexander (Patrick Magee), a victim of Alex and his droogs. But he'll wreak his revenge.

7   Pop art: Alex batters a woman to death with a giant phallus.

merely asks questions, and it calls some assumptions into doubt: for example, that violence in the cinema will inevitably lead to violence in the world. Alex's therapy consists of forced viewings of brutal films. The longer he's bound to his seat with his eyes propped open, the worse he feels – an effect reinforced by the drug he's been given. Alex the Doer is transformed into Alex the Watcher. For the former hoodlum, it's a terrible torture; for the average moviegoer, it's a regular delight: to become a mere seeing eye, with no obligation to act; to watch, entranced, happily "glued to the seat." Kubrick almost literally pulls the audience into the film. Alex often looks straight into the camera, apparently addressing the spectators. Before he rapes the writer's wife, he kneels down before her on the floor: "Viddy well," he says to the captive woman, and to the captivated audience in the argot of the droogs: "take a good look." The real scandal of *A Clockwork Orange* is that we catch ourselves looking forward with excitement to whatever is going to come next. It's not what Kubrick shows us that shocks, but how we react as spectators, fascinated by a masterly and unforgettable film.   NM

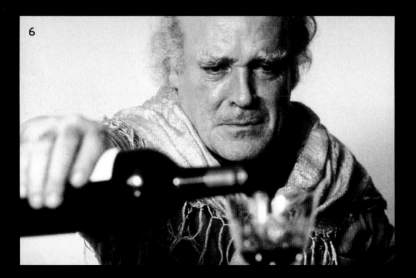

"Objectively, it has to be said that there has seldom been a film of such assured technical brilliance"

Der Tagesspiegel

DELIVERANCE

1972 - USA - 105 MIN. - ACTION FILM, THRILLER

DIRECTOR JOHN BOORMAN (*1933) SCREENPLAY JAMES DICKEY, based on his novel of the same name DIRECTOR OF PHOTOGRAPHY VILMOS ZSIGMOND EDITING TOM PRIESTLEY MUSIC ERIC WEISSBERG, STEVE MANDEL PRODUCTION JOHN BOORMAN for ELMER PRODUCTIONS, WARNER BROS.

STARRING JON VOIGHT (Ed Gentry), BURT REYNOLDS (Lewis Medlock), NED BEATTY (Bobby Trippe), RONNY COX (Drew Ballinger), ED RAMEY (Old Man), BILLY REDDEN (Lonny), SEAMON GLASS (First Griner), RANDALL DEAL (Second Griner), BILL MCKINNEY (Mountain Man), HERBERT "COWBOY" COWARD (Toothless Man), LEWIS CRONE (First Deputy), JAMES DICKEY (Sheriff Bullard).

"That's the game, survival."

A river winds softly through a pristine landscape of craggy cliffs and dense virgin forest. Four men from the city are here to relax while exploring the area by canoe. Lewis (Burt Reynolds), Ed (Jon Voight), Bobby (Ned Beatty) and Drew (Ronny Cox), are paddling downriver in two fragile boats. They've paid some farmers to drive their cars to the final destination, which they expect to reach two days later; but this is an adventure holiday that will turn into pure terror.

The first day is idyllic, a boy-scouts' paradise for four grown men: paddling boats, pitching tents, fishing with bows and arrows, and playing guitar round the campfire. On the second day, the horror begins. Ed and Bobby have gone on ahead in their canoe, and a welcoming-party is waiting for them: two of the farmers, ugly rednecks with very bad teeth. After tying Ed to a tree, they beat, rape and humiliate Bobby. As they turn their attentions to Ed, one of them keels over, pierced by an arrow; Lewis and Drew have caught up with their friends. The other attacker flees, and the four friends bury the corpse. They're sick of adventures and hungry for home, and the canoes are their only means of transport. But down on the river, between the sheer cliffs, they're as open to predators as a hamburger on a plate…

With its breathtaking journeys through whitewater rapids and overwhelming images of natural splendor, *Deliverance* is a wonderful action and adventure film. Director John Boorman, his editor Tom Priestley (both of whom received Oscar nominations) and the cameraman Vilmos Zsigmond (who got an Oscar for *Close Encounters of the Third Kind*, 1977) created a visual language of great beauty, combining careful composition with a directness and immediacy that pulls the audience right into the story. The

1   Hell bent over: Ed (Jon Voight) gets a close-up view of prison in the wild.

2   "The voyage down the river echoes the journey of Conrad's demonic Mr. Kurtz to the Congo's heart of darkness." (*The New York Times*)

3   A grassroots movement: Ed hunts his attackers with a bow and arrow.

"A repugnant but fascinating portrait of human beings out of their environment, forced to defend themselves where the laws of civilization no longer apply."

4

immensity and indifference of the natural world and the threat of sudden attack are almost physically present. Boorman also demonstrates a fine feeling for effective but inconspicuous symbolism: In a famous scene, early on in the film, Drew and a retarded farmer's boy begin a tentative musical dialog on guitar and banjo. The game of question-and-answer develops into a regular duet – or duel – in which the city-dweller is eventually defeated by the sheer speed and skill of the hillbilly kid. In a beautifully understated manner, this joyful encounter anticipates the deadly power struggle to come.

The film's surface is brilliant, and the depths below it are multi-layered and hard to fathom. With a screenplay by the poet James Dickey, who adapted it from his own novel of the same name (1970), the film resists any easy interpretation. "Man Against Nature" won't do, for the dumb-but-crafty hill-

"It's the best film I've ever done. It's a picture that just picks
you up and sends you crashing against the rocks.
You feel everything and just crawl out of the theater."

Burt Reynolds, in: Motion Picture Guide

4   Bobby (Ned Beatty), Lewis (Burt Reynolds), Drew
    (Ronny Cox) and Ed are looking forward to some
    male bonding – two days in virgin nature.

5   Sneak attack: Ed resorts to archery.

6   The men park their cars in a tiny hamlet –
    and sacrifice a link to civilization.

5

billies can hardly be seen as symbols for a state of unspoilt nature. "Arrogant City-Slickers versus Disadvantaged Rural Population" is an equally unusable model, for neither the canoeists nor their antagonists can be reduced to this kind of cliché. What remains is the story of four men in an alien environment, defending their lives with alien methods; solid citizens far from civilization, struggling to survive with the aid of bows and arrows. Events take their course inexorably, and we are granted no comforting explanations. Lewis, the fittest of the four, is quickly incapacitated by an injury, while the cerebral pipe-smoking Ed is forced to kill in self-defense. When the survivors finally reach safety, they're still far from peace; the Sheriff (author James Dickey in a guest appearance) is a highly skeptical interrogator, and their dreams will long be haunted by memories of their hellish ordeal.   HJK

JOHN BOORMAN   Civilized human beings forced to come to terms with barbarism: this is as good a summary of *Deliverance* (1972) as any, and it's also the ground-plan for many of John Boorman's films. In the SF movie *Zardoz* (1973/74) Sean Connery struggles against a terroristic slave system; in *The Emerald Forest* (1985), the son of an engineer (Boorman's own son, Charley) falls into the hands of an archaic forest-dwelling tribe.
England's John Boorman (*1933) has made highly idiosyncratic films in a wide range of standard genres. In *Hope and Glory* (1987), he called on his own childhood memories to tell the story of the war from a boy's perspective. The gangster in *The General* (1998) behaves like the gangsters he's seen in the movies. And in *The Tailor of Panama* (2001), Boorman portrays his "hero" (sex symbol and 007 Pierce Brosnan) as a deeply repellent character. Boorman made his cinema debut in 1965 with the Dave Clark Five pop vehicle *Catch Us If You Can* (*Having a Wild Weekend*). The big break came in 1967 with his second film, the gangster drama *Point Blank*.

7   Concealing evidence: Lewis hides the corpse of a redneck he's just neutralized. The men think their nightmare is over, but it's only just begun.

CABARET ♟♟♟♟♟♟♟♟

1972 - USA - 124 MIN. - LITERARY ADAPTATION, DRAMA, MUSICAL

DIRECTOR BOB FOSSE (1927–1987) SCREENPLAY JAY PRESSON ALLEN, based on
the Broadway musical of the same name by JOE MASTEROFF, JOHN KANDER
and FRED EBB, the drama *I AM A CAMERA* by JOHN VAN DRUTEN,
and the collection of short stories *THE BERLIN STORIES* by
CHRISTOPHER ISHERWOOD DIRECTOR OF PHOTOGRAPHY GEOFFREY UNSWORTH
EDITING DAVID BRETHERTON MUSIC JOHN KANDER, RALPH BURNS
PRODUCTION CY FEUER, HAROLD NEBENZAL; MARTIN BAUM for ABC PICTURES
CORPORATION and EMMANUEL WOLF for ALLIED ARTISTS.

STARRING LIZA MINNELLI (Sally Bowles), MICHAEL YORK (Brian Roberts),
HELMUT GRIEM (Maximilian von Heune), JOEL GREY (Master of Ceremonies),
FRITZ WEPPER (Fritz Wendel), MARISA BERENSON (Natalia Landauer),
ELISABETH NEUMANN-VIERTEL (Fräulein Schneider), HELEN VITA
(Fräulein Kost), SIGRID VON RICHTHOFEN (Fräulein Mayr), GERD VESPERMANN
(Bobby).

ACADEMY AWARDS 1972 OSCARS for BEST DIRECTOR (Bob Fosse), BEST ACTRESS
(Liza Minnelli), BEST SUPPORTING ACTOR (Joel Grey), BEST CINEMATOGRAPHY
(Geoffrey Unsworth), BEST MUSIC (Ralph Burns), BEST FILM EDITING
(David Bretherton), BEST ART DIRECTION (Rolf Zehetbauer, Hans Jürgen
Kiebach, Herbert Strabel), and BEST SOUND (Robert Knudson).

"Divine decadence, darling!"

Berlin 1931. Despite a severe economic crisis, the German metropolis is determinedly cosmopolitan and exudes sensuality. Leave your worries at the door and come on into the Kit Kat Club, a dazzling night club where evening after evening an enthusiastic emcee greets you in three languages: "Willkommen, Bienvenue, Welcome!" His diabolically painted white face is reflected on the shimmering stage. And like a funhouse mirror, the film presents the cabaret to movie audiences as a caricature of the outside world. "Life is a cabaret!" exclaims Liza Minelli in an unforgettable song that is meant to be taken at face value.

Like so many other foreigners, British student Brian (Michael York) feels drawn to this thriving urban center. Arriving at a boarding house, he quickly makes the acquaintance of American Sally Bowles (Liza Minnelli), who works as a singer at the Kit Kat Club and dreams of making it big one day as a movie star. She's not only willing to capitalize on her charisma to get there, but will

readily exploit her body too if need be. Sexually uninhibited with a taste for luxury, Sally is a hedonistic modern whose deep-seated, hidden desire is to find true happiness. Beneath her decadent exterior we are shown more and more of the childish, vulnerable woman she really is. Brian, who at first seems immune to her erotic advances, eventually falls madly in love with her. It is a happy romance until the wealthy, young and rather attractive Baron Max von Heune (Helmut Griem) enters their world. Sally, mesmerized by his charms and riches, becomes more impractically minded with each passing day. Brian is jealous and turned on at the same time. Their love triangle is only spoken of in jest initially, but it soon becomes reality. Both of them have slept with the affluent Baron, and Sally, it turns out, is pregnant. While Sally and Brian are busy tackling their personal catastrophes, the Nazis take to the streets of Berlin in preparation for their rise to power. It seems the couple's lifestyle is doomed, for the epidemic of fascism spreading throughout the

"*Cabaret* is dance routines and hit songs. It's a murky tale inspired by the novels of Christopher Isherwood. It's the myth of 30s Berlin. And above all, it's Bob Fosse. He has a marvelous grasp of the world of cabaret, its pathos and its poetry: fleeting, illusory, and poignantly authentic."

Le Monde

nation seeks to extinguish all that is urban and modern. In its place, the Nazi movement prescribes conservative and provincial values for the German people. Brian decides to return to England. Sally, however, stays on in Berlin to try her luck at acting.

Cabaret was one of last great Hollywood musicals. (Eat your heart out Chicago! [2002]) It was awarded an astounding eight Oscars at the Academy Awards. The movie version was based on John Kander and Fred Ebb's Broadway musical, which premiered in 1966. This, likewise, drew heavily from the short stories "The Last of Mr. Morris" and "Goodbye to Berlin" by Christopher Isherwood, which were published in a volume entitled *The Berlin Stories*. Unlike the majority of Hollywood musicals, such as *An Ameri-*

can in Paris (1951) or *Singin' in the Rain* (1952) there is nothing anachronistic about *Cabaret* even today. This is due to its songs, as popular as those of Kurt Weill's *Three Penny Opera* (*Dreigroschenoper*), and to the then 25-year-old Liza Minnelli, whose image is more intrinsically linked to *Cabaret* than almost any other actress' has ever been to a single production. Yet above all else, it is the film's narrative structure that plays the decisive role in its timelessness. Deviating from the traditional Hollywood musical format, *Cabaret* markedly separates its musical numbers from its plot. In other words, none of the characters in the film burst into song for no given reason. Instead, director and choreographer Bob Fosse brilliantly lets the stage acts at the nightclub serve as commentary on both the surrounding political situation

1   Cigarette, lipstick and a voice that won't quit: The role of Sally Bowles made Liza Minelli an international superstar.

2   "Life is a cabaret:" The stage as a world of entertainment and politics.

3   A pink-tinted love triangle: Only later does Sally discover that Brian (Michael York) and Maximilian (Helmut Griem) have been playing house.

4   Babe in the woods: When Brian comes to Berlin, he's a shy young writer. Sally's attempts to seduce him are initially unsuccessful.

"*Cabaret* may make a star out of Miss Minnelli, but it will be remembered as a chilling mosaic of another era's frightening life-style." *Films in Review*

LIZA MINNELLI The extent to which her image was shaped by one single film is itself a Hollywood phenomenon. Her belting voice and touching yet extravagant flair breathed so much life into *Cabaret's* (1972) nightclub singer Sally Bowles that from then on world audiences viewed Liza Minnelli as virtually inseparable from the role she had played. The daughter of Hollywood legend Judy Garland and director Vincente Minnelli was literally born into show business in 1946. She made her first appearance in front of a Hollywood camera when she was just two years old. Be it on Broadway, in film, in TV movies or in the music industry, her work has always met with instant success. She received a Tony in 1965 for her performance in the Broadway musical *Flora, the Red Menace*. Her first Oscar nomination came for her portrayal of the eccentric Pookie in *The Sterile Cuckoo* (1969). Another nomination followed in 1970 for Otto Preminger's *Tell Me That You Love Me, Junie Moon*, and in 1973 she won the Best Actress Academy Award for *Cabaret*. She became more popular with audiences than ever before, and in 1972, NBC aired the award winning television special *Liza with A Z*. Liza Minnelli, who describes herself as both "hopeful and cynical," is a star to this day, even though not all her films are smash hits. She collaborated with her father Vincente Minnelli on *A Matter of Time / Nina* (1976). Images of her superstar mother, who died in 1969, pop up in many of her movies, including Stanley Donen's *Lucky Lady* (1975) and most prominently in Martin Scorsese's musical drama *New York, New York* (1977). She experienced one of her greatest commercial successes in 1981 with *Arthur*. Shortly thereafter, her film career started to dry up. She disappeared completely from the public eye for several years. Alcohol and prescription drug addictions contributed to her personal downfall. In 1984 she sought professional help. She staged a comeback in 1985 in the form of an NBC made for TV movie *A Time to Live*, winning the Golden Globe for her performance. She then went on a star-studded tour at the end of the 80s with Frank Sinatra and Sammy Davis Jr. and even recorded a single with the Pet Shop Boys entitled "Losing My Mind" that reached number six on the U.K. charts. In 1997, Liza Minnelli was celebrated on Broadway in Blake Edwards' "Victor/Victoria," yet another great comeback after a twelve-year absence.

5 Tomorrow belongs to... whom? It remains unclear how fascism will change Sally's wild and extravagant lifestyle.

6 Mirror, mirror on the wall, *Cabaret* was Liza's best picture of all.

and the lives of characters themselves. In particular, the stage appearances of the emcee (Joel Grey), whose character doesn't exist within the framework of the plot outside the nightclub, do a poignant job of this. Plot elements and musical numbers are occasionally brought together through the ironic use of parallel montage. Such is the case when a scene of a staged Bavarian folk-dance is cut between rapidly appearing images of Nazis brutally beating up the Kit Kat's manager elsewhere. This sequence feeds violence into the musical number and choreography into the street fight. *Cabaret*, with its strikingly dark palette, is highly reminiscent of the 1920s, as is the music inspired by Kurt Weill and Fosse's stylized dance numbers, which clearly draw from that era's expressionist tradition. Commendably, it does this without trying to ignore the cinematic conventions of the 1970s. The overall im-

pact of the film is born out of its song and dance sequences which, with one exception, all take place on stage. The only time we witness music outside the cabaret setting is when a young blond boy begins to sing what is meant to sound like a traditional German folk song at a beer garden. We just see his face at first, but soon the camera pulls back to show us his swastika arm-band. One beer garden patron after the next joins in his chant. The rhythm of the piece transforms into a military march and by the end, all have their hands extended in a Hitler salute. It may sound ludicrous, but at the time of the picture's European premiere, this scene was to be cut out for German audiences. Only after a number of critics were up in arms about the decision, was the sequence restored.

KK

THE GODFATHER ♔♔♔

1972 - USA - 175 MIN. - GANGSTER FILM, DRAMA

DIRECTOR FRANCIS FORD COPPOLA (*1939) SCREENPLAY FRANCIS FORD COPPOLA, MARIO PUZO, based on his novel of the same name DIRECTOR OF PHOTOGRAPHY GORDON WILLIS EDITING MARC LAUB, BARBARA MARKS, WILLIAM REYNOLDS, MURRAY SOLOMON, PETER ZINNER MUSIC NINO ROTA PRODUCTION ALBERT S. RUDDY for PARAMOUNT PICTURES.

STARRING MARLON BRANDO (Don Vito Corleone), AL PACINO (Michael Corleone), DIANE KEATON (Kay Adams), ROBERT DUVALL (Tom Hagen), JAMES CAAN (Santino "Sonny" Corleone), JOHN CAZALE (Frederico "Fredo" Corleone), RICHARD S. CASTELLANO (Peter Clemenza), STERLING HAYDEN (Captain McCluskey), TALIA SHIRE (Constanzia "Connie" Corleone-Rizzi), JOHN MARLEY (Jack Woltz), RICHARD CONTE (Don Emilio Barzini), AL LETTIERI (Virgil Sollozzo), AL MARTINO (Johnny Fantane), GIANNI RUSSO (Carlo Rizzi), SIMONETTA STEFANELLI (Appollonia Vitelli-Corleone).

ACADEMY AWARDS 1972 OSCARS for BEST FILM (Albert S. Ruddy), BEST ACTOR (Marlon Brando), and BEST SCREENPLAY (Mario Puzo, Francis Ford Coppola).

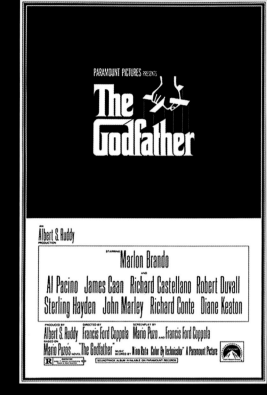

"I'll make him an offer he can't refuse."

The unmentionable words are never heard. No one dares speak of the "Mafia" or the "Cosa Nostra" in this film, despite the fact that it tells a tale whose roots are at the heart of organized crime. The contents are categorized by another word: family. "It's a novel about a family, and not about crime," said its author, Mario Puzo. Francis Ford Coppola initially rejected the offer to direct the film after reading the book over-hastily and dismissing it as just another Mafia-vehicle. He eventually changed his mind for a number of reasons, principally because he discovered the family aspect of the story and was fascinated by it.

It is no coincidence that the film begins and ends with traditional family celebrations – a wedding and a baptism. The marriage of Connie Corleone (Talia Shire) and Carlo Rizzi (Gianni Russo) is the occasion for an enchanting celebration. An orchestra plays in the Corleone's garden, filled with a mass of dancing guests. Feasting and joking, children run wild and glasses are repeatedly raised to toast the bride. During the festivities, FBI agents mill outside the gates of the villa and scrawl down license plate numbers of the guests. The father of the bride, Vito Corleone (Marlon Brando) is one of the five Dons of the Italian community in the New York area and the guest

"Like practically no other Hollywood film of recent years, the tale of the New York Mafia clan Corleone reflects the divisions, the compulsions and the fears afflicting American society. Damaged by Vietnam and shaken by a profound crisis of faith in the nation, America's hallowed norms of good and evil are looking more beleaguered than ever." *Kölner Stadt-Anzeiger*

list is accordingly illustrious. According to old Sicilian tradition, the father of the bride cannot refuse any favor on his daughter's wedding day. Surrounded by his sons and confidants he aristocratically sits in his darkened reception room, glowing in a golden brown light, the perfect expression of dignity and power. He patronizingly receives the supplicants, listens to their dilemmas, accepts congratulations, and basks in the respect offered from all sides.

Like every scene with Marlon Brando in the role of the Godfather Vito Corleone, these scenes are filled with warmth. The colors fade when his son Michael (Al Pacino) flees to the family's ancestral home in sunny Sicily after committing two murders. Later Michael, who once strived for an honorable life and distanced himself from his family, will become the ringleader

of a blood bath: the images change with him, slowly acquiring a cold, bluish tinge.

The cause of the violent clash is Vito Corleone's decision to deny his backing to Virgil Sollozzo's (Al Lettieri) plans to branch out in the drug dealing business. Vito's temperamental son Sonny (James Caan) seems to disagree with his father, which inspires Sollozzo to try and topple the patriarch. Five shots bring Corleone down, but the old tiger survives. Michael, who to this point has held himself out of the family business, is shaken. His outsider role makes him seem unsuspicious, and he is therefore sent to the negotiation table. Michael promptly uses the opportunity to murder both Sollozzo and the corrupt police captain McCluskey (Sterling Hayden), and flees to Sicily. His unsuspecting girlfriend Kay (Diane Keaton) remains behind.

1   A man that won't take "no" for an answer: Marlon Brando takes life in stride as Don Corleone.

2   In sickness and in health: Making a deal with Don Corleone is more than a business transaction – it's a life-long bond.

3   One wedding for fifty funerals: *The Godfather* opens with the Corleone family renewing its vows, whilst Carlo (Gianni Russo) and Connie (Talia Shire) take theirs.

MARLON BRANDO   Among the many curiosities surrounding the legendary *The Godfather* (1972) is that its success sprung from a series of coincidences and imponderables. Mario Puzo was unhappy writing the screenplay, Francis Ford Coppola initially didn't want to direct the film, and the studio had problems with the choice of the male lead. At this time, Marlon Brando was at a low point in his career, which began in the 1940s in the theaters of New York City. In 1947, his portrayal of Stanley Kowalski in *A Streetcar Named Desire* was a triumph and in 1951 he played the character in Elia Kazan's film adaptation. Schooled in "method acting," Brando graduated to Hollywood big-time – four Oscar nominations in a row speak for themselves. Initially he was repeatedly cast as the youthful rebel, but he soon proved his versatility in costume films and musicals. In the 1960s, his notorious moodiness and a string of flops caused him to fall from grace with Hollywood producers. In 1972 he made his comeback with *The Godfather* and *The Last Tango in Paris* (*Ultimo tango a Parigi* / *Le Dernier Tango à Paris*), receiving Oscar nominations for both films. Though he was awarded the Oscar for his role as Vito Corleone in *The Godfather*, he refused to accept it for political reasons.

4 European vacation: A hunted man, Michael Corleone (Al Pacino) decides it's time to go back to his roots.

5 Like father like son: After some initial stumbling, Michael learns how to fill his father's shoes.

6 Deadlock: Michael Corleone and bride-to-be, Kate (Diane Keaton).

7 The emissary wore black: Michael holds out a Sicilian olive branch to Virgil Sollozzo (Al Lettieri).

8 When in Rome: During his time in Sicily, Michael fares the local cuisine and develops a taste for Appollonia (Simonetta Stefanelli).

"And all the while, we think we're watching a Mafia crime story; but we're actually watching one of the great American family melodramas."

The Austin Chronicle

7

In Sicily, Michael's hardening process continues. He falls in love and – with old-fashioned etiquette – asks the bride's father permission for his daughter's hand. But the long arm of vengeance stretches to Italy – his young wife, Appollonia is killed in a car bomb that was meant for Michael. In New York, the war between the families rages on. Michael's brother Sonny is the next victim. The slowly recovering Vito Corleone is devastated, but forgoes his right to vengeance in an attempt to put an end to the killing. Michael returns to the United States. He marries Kay, who has become a teacher. Michael, whose eyes now have a cold, hard expression, knows that the old feud is not over. He plans a large liberating coup. While he is in church at his nephew's baptism, and is solemnly named as the child's godfather, the enemies of the Corleones are killed off one

In scene after scene – the long wedding sequence, John Marley's bloody discovery in his bed, Pacino nervously smoothing down his hair before a restaurant massacre, the godfather's collapse in a garden – Coppola crafted an enduring, undisputed masterpiece."

San Francisco Chronicle

8

9   Big brother: When Carlo makes putty of wife
    Connie, Sonny puts a little love in his heart.

10 Gone with the wind: Sonny Corleone (James
    Caan) walks into a trap and goes up in smoke.

11 Paying the piper: An attempt to rescue sister
    Connie from a violent marriage proves more
    dangerous than Sonny had imagined...

"Cast and designed to perfection, this epic pastiche of 40s and 50s crime movies is as rich in images of idyllic family life as it is in brutal effects." *Der Spiegel*

by one. Among them is Connie's husband Carlo, who lured Sonny into a deadly trap.

Connie has become a nervous wreck and Kay begins to ask critical questions. Michael coldly denies responsibility and Kay is forced to experience her utter exclusion from the male circle. Before the doors close in front of her, she sees her husband, the new Don, Michael graciously receive the best wishes of his confidants and associates.

The film stands out for its clever dramatization of the balance of power enjoyed by Vito Corleone and his successor, Michael, as well as its scenes of heavy violence, such as the severed horse's head in film producer Jack Woltz's bed, Sonny's bullet-riddled body, or the gunshot through the lens of casino owner Moe Green's glasses. The brilliant finale has an Old Testament-like intensity about it. But these drastic images are mere moments compared

to the extensive family scenes. The business activities of the Corleones, which include murder and extortion, invariably take place outside the inner circle – they often follow car rides and trips, literally at a distance from the family core. This distance represents a lack of protection – the attempted hit on Vito Corleone occurs when he spontaneously stops to buy fruit from a street vendor, and hothead Sonny is killed when he leaves the family fortress with too great haste.

In a poignant reversal, Michael Corleone, the initially modern man, is unable to escape the chains of his family. Though he always considered himself an independent individual, he becomes a victim of the family tradition, a marionette whose strings are moved by the hands of fate, a metaphor the image on the book cover and film poster captures with perfection.

HK

THE DISCREET CHARM OF THE BOURGEOISIE

Le Charme discret de la bourgeoisie

972 - FRANCE - 102 MIN. - SOCIAL GROTESQUE

DIRECTOR LUIS BUÑUEL (1900–1983) **SCREENPLAY** LUIS BUÑUEL, JEAN-CLAUDE CARRIÈRE
DIRECTOR OF PHOTOGRAPHY EDMOND RICHARD **EDITING** HÉLÈNE PLEMIANNIKOV **MUSIC** GUY VILLETTE
PRODUCTION SERGE SILBERMAN for GREENWICH FILM PRODUCTIONS.

STARRING FERNANDO REY (Rafaele Costa, Ambassador of Miranda), PAUL FRANKEUR
(Monsieur Thévenot), DELPHINE SEYRIG (Madame Thévenot), BULLE OGIER (Florence),
STÉPHANE AUDRAN (Madame Sénéchal), JEAN-PIERRE CASSEL (Monsieur Sénéchal),
MILENA VUKOTIC (Ines, the Maid), JULIEN BERTHEAU (Bishop Dufour), CLAUDE PIÉPLU (Colonel),
MICHEL PICCOLI (Minister).

ACADEMY AWARDS 1972 OSCAR for BEST FOREIGN FILM.

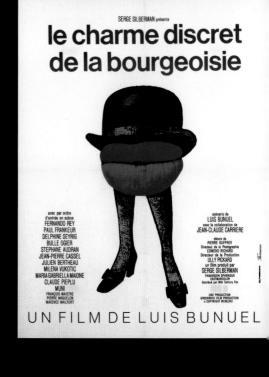

"There's nothing like a martini, especially when it's dry!"

An anecdote from Oscars Night, 1972, encapsulates the spirit of this film. When Luis Buñuel's movie was officially nominated, the 72-year-old Surrealist and scourge of the bourgeoisie made a statement to Mexican journalists: he was quite sure, he announced, that he would indeed be awarded the Oscar; after all, he insisted, he'd forked out the 25,000 dollars demanded for the prize – and though Americans might have their faults, they could always be relied on to keep their word… The story hit the press, and all hell broke loose in Hollywood. Buñuel's producer, Serge Silbermann, had his work cut out pouring oil on the troubled waters. When *The Discreet Charm of the Bourgeoisie* actually went on to win the Academy Award for the Best Foreign Film, Buñuel smugly told anyone who'd listen: "The Americans

may have their faults – but you can always count on them to keep their word."

In his last film but three, the Old Master unleashed the beast of surrealism once more. This time, however, the result was less visually disturbing than the early masterpiece *An Andalusian Dog* (*Un chien andalou*, 1929) made in collaboration with Salvador Dali. After years of struggle and exile, in his hard-boiled but still vital old age, Buñuel no longer had any need to prove his credentials as an anarchic, subversive, and unconventional artist. And though one might complain that the film has no plot, that its characters are as lifeless as marionettes, or that they're forced to caper through an all-too theatrical set, this kind of criticism simply fails to recognize the film's truly

1 The Mirandan ambassador (Fernando Rey) is a connoisseur of good food. Madame Thévenot (Delphine Seyrig) admires his excellent taste.

2 The more unattainable the goal, the more authoritative the moral law, the more unsuspecting the husband… the more desire grows.

3 Everybody's nightmare: Suddenly on stage without a line in your head.

revolutionary quality, as a grotesque cinematic carnival of bourgeois ideals, values and clichés.

The story is easily summarized: six *grands bourgeois* are doing their damnedest to meet for an exquisitely cultivated evening meal – but something or other keeps stopping them from doing so. Either they mysteriously get the dates mixed up, or they're inconvenienced by a sudden death in the restaurant. So they try again; and this time, a squad of paratroopers burst into the house in order to carry out a maneuver. The would-be diners persist undeterred; and just as they've all taken their places and lifted their

cutlery, they realize they're on a theater stage; the chicken is made of rubber, the audience are booing, and the actors appear to have forgotten their lines…

This last scene is not the only one that turns out to have been dreamt by one of the protagonists. Various other nightmares disturb the diners, whose faultlessly polite but utterly trivial activity seems destined to peter out in one dead end after another. On one occasion, a dream within a dream leads to yet another dream. As the film proceeds, it becomes increasingly clear to the audience that they can rely on nothing they are shown. Reality

"The title's complacent *grandezza* not only characterizes the bourgeoisie itself,
but the visual style of the film, and Buñuel's analytical approach. No other director treats
his characters with such distance and apparent passivity (or indifference);
and none grants them such unconditional freedom to act according to the milieu or
the atmosphere they happen to inhabit – to be new and different in each scene." *Die Zeit*

FERNANDO REY

He turned up in so many films that almost everyone must have seen him sometime – possibly without even noticing it, for his appearances were sometimes fleeting (though always worthwhile). In the 80s, he appeared in so many movies that one critic dared call him "a prop." His filmography comprises around 200 films.

Yet for all that, the Spaniard Fernando Rey (1917–1994) is best known and best loved for his performances in a handful of films by his friend Luis Buñuel, as well as for his major roles in *The French Connection I* and *II* (1971/1975). In the latter movies, he played a sophisticated French drugs czar who's pursued obsessively by a tough, streetwise New York detective (Gene Hackman). The chase scene in the subway is unforgettable: when Rey, the man with the elegant walking-stick and the perfectly-manicured beard, waves nonchalantly as his train draws away from his frustrated nemesis on the platform, it's surely one of the great moments in movie history. Only Rey could have embodied this figure in all its rich ambiguity: gallant and decadent, cultivated and greedy – a memorably nuanced characterization.

His great career with the exiled Spaniard Buñuel began in Mexico with *Viridiana* (1961). There followed *Tristana* (1969/70), *The Discreet Charm of the Bourgeoisie* (*Le Charme discret de la bourgeoisie*, 1972) and *That Obscure Object of Desire* (*Cet obscur objet du désir*, 1977), Buñuel's last film. Though it may be hard to believe, Buñuel discovered Rey when he was playing the part of a corpse; the director was simply blown away by the actor's "expressive power." An encounter of crucial – indeed vital – importance to both…

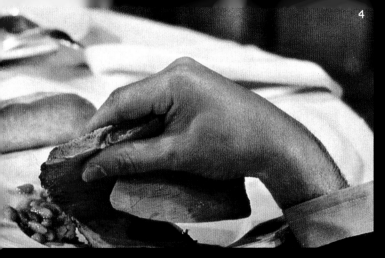

and illusion dissolve and merge into a new actuality, a surreal cinematic universe. Yet however bizarre the events that invade their lives, these six ladies and gentlemen never lose their cool, persevering heroically with their cultivated poses and their gestures of hypocritical friendliness. Quite literally, they never lose face; for when all they have is a succession of masks for every social eventuality, there's no face left to lose.

However elegantly the table is set, it's a uniquely hot, dry and spicy meal that Buñuel serves up to his audience, and it's not for tender palates (though he does include an excellent recipe for an extra dry Martini). In fact the guests at this dinner table are so wonderfully adroit in their blasé bitchiness that it's hard not to end up liking them a little. The subtle pleasure of *schadenfreude* is something one could quite easily acquire a taste for.   SF

"You may note that I haven't really tried to say what the film is about, what it means. And the reason for that is that I don't know. But, I don't really care, either. A poem should not mean, but be, said someone, and if there was a film poem, this is it." *Guardian Weekly*

4   Opportunity grabs: While the party is hiding from terrorists, the ambassador gets what he can.

5   Topsy-turvy: The dead hold a wake while the living sleep. Buñuel adopted and adapted the principles of Carnival.

6   Absolution: A bishop with a shotgun (Julien Bertheau) executes his father's murderer during Confession.

A WOMAN UNDER THE INFLUENCE

1974 - USA - 155 MIN. - DRAMA

DIRECTOR JOHN CASSAVETES (1929–1989) SCREENPLAY JOHN CASSAVETES
DIRECTOR OF PHOTOGRAPHY MITCH BREIT, CALEB DESCHANEL EDITING DAVID ARMSTRONG, TOM CORNWELL,
ROBERT HEFFERNAN MUSIC BO HARWOOD PRODUCTION SAM SHAW for FACES.

STARRING PETER FALK (Nick Longhetti), GENA ROWLANDS (Mabel Longhetti), FRED DRAPER
(George Mortensen), LADY ROWLANDS (Martha Mortensen), KATHERINE CASSAVETES
(Mama Longhetti), MATTHEW LABORTEAUX (Angelo Longhetti), MATTHEW CASSEL
(Tony Longhetti), CHRISTINA GRISANTI (Maria Longhetti), O. G. DUNN (Garson Cross),
MARIO GALLO (Harold Jensen), EDDIE SHAW (Doctor Zepp).

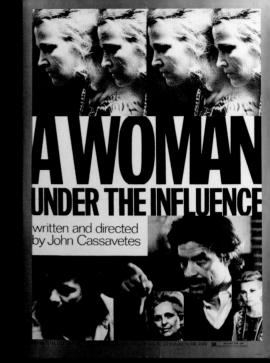

*"Tell me what you want me to be. How you want me to be.
I can be that. I can be anything. Just tell me, Nicky!"*

Two adults try to play house and fail miserably. Two actors infuse their roles with every imaginable contour of human dignity and disgrace, taking their audience hostage for two-and-a-half hours as they unleash the demons of Pandora's box on their rocky marriage.

This was formula that led to one of the greatest cinematic triumphs for independent film-making icon John Cassavetes. In a riveting, powerhouse performance, Gena Rowlands plays a woman on the verge of a mental breakdown. For a long time now, there haven't been words to express what Mabel Longhetti has been feeling, and so she has substituted them with an arsenal of gesticulations and nervous ticks, mimicry and pantomime. She combats the stress of her daily life, which confines her like an iron chastity belt, with deflective hand movements, eye rolls and jerking jaws. These are the mouthed screams of a desperate woman; they pound the audience with an utter devastation that is at times hysterically funny. Peter Falk plays Mabel's husband Nick, a simple blue-collar worker, who has as little control over his words as he does over his own body. He is someone who hollers. His gestures die before completion, often ending in an admonishing pointer finger, or, as on one occasion in the film, in physical abuse. Three children stand in the crossfire as man and wife frantically grasp at straws in the hopes of

pinpointing what originally made them fall in love. The couple are certain of their love for one another, yet they have no idea how to go about loving each other.

A Woman Under the Influence was originally conceived for the stage. The idea was scrapped because seasoned theater veteran Gena Rowlands didn't think she was capable of exerting such an extreme amount of emotional force night after night in front of a live audience. And so, with just a dialog script and no true screenplay, an intimate film was shot almost exclusively within the four walls of a small family residence. No shots were predetermined. The camera was free to roam at will, thus partially accounting for the piece's almost documentary feel. Of course, this atmospheric touch is more the result of Cassavetes' unique directing style, chiseled in diehard method acted techniques. This is illuminated in the film by an act of associative thought processes reflected in Mabel's behavior such as when she improvises the "dying swan" from *Swan Lake*. Here, she not only takes on Cassavetes' dual role of actor-director, but also that of prima ballerina and choreographer. In another scene, the oblivious Nick surprises her at the door with ten work buddies and she instantly transforms herself into a June Cleaver on amphetamines, whipping up a mess hall portion of spaghetti and

1   How much longer will Mabel Longhetti (Gena Rowlands) be able to ward off her nervous breakdown?

2   Loving you is easy 'cos you're beautiful… Mabel's children are her only sanctuary.

3   Was that lonely woman really me? Mabel drinks away her sorrows at a local bar...and falls into the arms of a total stranger.

4   Life of the party: Construction worker, Nick (Peter Falk) loves his wife, but is oblivious to her needs.

5   Big boys don't cry: But they have been known to beat their wives…

"Mabel's not crazy. She's unusual. She's not crazy, so don't say she's crazy!"

Film quote: Nick

doing her best "hostess with the mostest" imitation. Mabel is emotionally electrified when one of the guys breaks into an aria and she implores yet another of the work crew to dance with her. She refuses to take no for an answer, prompting Nick to abruptly silence her. Her spirit and charm have, nonetheless, a miraculous impact on children. Yet upon seeing how the free-spirited Mabel allows the children to run naked through the house, one neighborhood father is convinced that she's off her rocker. Mabel, on the other hand, simply can't understand why he too doesn't just let loose and dance.

Observation of the pictures taken of Cassavetes on the set reveals the actor-director manifesting the same gestures as Mabel, from the ticking Cheshire Cat grin, to the chummy yet invasive hooking an arm around some-

one's shoulder while giving direction. The filmmaker readily encouraged his cast to search for authentic feelings and means of expression that often broke with Hollywood conventions. The product is a family drama and love story, whose tale itself also provides a map of the film's actual genesis.

Be that as it may, the real world is not run according to these rules; it adheres rather to the masculine leadership archetypes seen in Nick. Mabel, as well as all she represents, is too prone to the type of nervous breakdowns that Cassevetes often almost drove his team to. At one point, Nick just stands by and watches as his wife is institutionalized. Completely at a loss as a parent without her, he lets his children sip his beer on one of their family outings. When Mabel is released from the psychiatric hospital six months later, we see how all of his attempts to force his family into neat little roles have failed

JOHN CASSAVETES With his directorial debut, *Shadows* (1959), John Cassavetes (1929–1989) established himself as a permanent fixture in the world of indy-film-making. Today's independent director has him to thank for making it possible to shoot a movie without stepping into financial quicksand. Cassavetes was born in New York in 1929 to Greek immigrant parents. He used his acting to raise funds for his directing projects, appearing in front of the camera in such films as *The Killers* (1964), *The Dirty Dozen* (1967) and *Rosemary's Baby* (1968). Friends and family often played a dual role in Cassavetes' works. Despite the little he could pay them, the actor-director received a high degree of commitment and dedication. Thespians like Seymour Cassel, Peter Falk, Ben Gazzara as well as producer Al Ruban were on board for some of his most ambitious undertakings like *Husbands*, (1970), *Minnie and Moskowitz* (1971), *A Woman Under the Influence* (1974) and *The Killing of a Chinese Bookie* (1976). Gena Rowlands married Cassavetes in 1954 and portrayed the leading roles in many of his pictures such as in *Gloria* (1980). Although Cassavetes' pictures cover a wide range of genres, his constant themes remained individuality conveyed through unforgettable characters prone to double standards, the suffocating mechanisms of conventionality and the full expression of a given personality. Cassavetes is the idol of a long list of cutting-edge filmmakers like Larry Clark of *Kids* fame (1995), and *Happiness* director Todd Solondz (1998).

Nick packs the house full of family and friends to welcome home his "healthy wife" in a gung ho effort to "have a party!" Not to be overlooked in this film is that Nick is not one ounce less out of his mind than Mabel. His relentless need to prove his masculinity leads to disaster time after time, and he appears incapable of recognizing this.

Nonetheless, Cassavetes has no intention of pinning the blame on either of them. The film's leitmotif is much more wrapped up in Nick's schizophrenic and seemingly impossible plea to "just be yourself!" – a philosophy that is possibly to blame for the break-up of his marriage. Cassavetes' own take on the matter shed a bit more light on the subject: "I don't believe that Mabel's collapse is a social problem. It is rooted in personal relationships. Someone can love you and still drive you insane." PB

CHINATOWN ¡

1974 - USA - 131 MIN. - DETECTIVE FILM, DRAMA

DIRECTOR ROMAN POLANSKI (*1933) SCREENPLAY ROBERT TOWNE
DIRECTOR OF PHOTOGRAPHY JOHN A. ALONZO EDITING SAM O'STEEN
MUSIC JERRY GOLDSMITH PRODUCTION ROBERT EVANS for LONG ROAD,
PENTHOUSE, PARAMOUNT PICTURES.

STARRING JACK NICHOLSON (J. J. "Jake" Gittes), FAYE DUNAWAY
(Evelyn Cross Mulwray), JOHN HUSTON (Noah Cross), PERRY LOPEZ
(LAPD Lieutenant Lou Escobar), JOHN HILLERMAN (Russ Yelburton),
DARRELL ZWERLING (Hollis I. Mulwray), DIANE LADD (Ida Sessions),
ROY JENSON (Claude Mulvihill), ROMAN POLANSKI (Man with the knife),
RICHARD BAKALYAN (LAPD Detective Loach).

ACADEMY AWARDS 1974 OSCAR for BEST ORIGINAL SCREENPLAY (Robert Towne).

"I'm just a snoop."

Los Angeles, 1937. When private detective J. J. Gittes (Jack Nicholson) is hired to keep tabs on an unfaithful husband, he assumes it's going to be just another routine job But the investigation takes an unexpected turn. The guy he's been keeping an eye on. a high-ranking official for the city's water and power department is bumped off. His attractive widow Evelyn (Faye Dunaway) retains Gittes' services to find out whodunit. Before he knows it, Gittes stumbles unexpectedly onto a foul smelling real estate scheme, and soon finds himself entangled in one sordid affair after another. Gittes has several bloody run-ins with thugs determined to put an end to his work on the case, and uncovers clues pointing to the involvement of influential power-players in the sinister dealings Even Gittes' alluring employer Evelyn seems to know more about the matter than she's letting on …

Chinatown is considered by many film critics to be not only one of the greatest films of the 70s but of all time. How the movie came to be illustrates like so many other similar moments in Hollywood history, that masterpieces can still be born within the framework of the imperious big studios. Chinatown was simply one of those rare instances when the perfect combination of people came together at just the right time. Jack Nicholson who, at the time was not a solid "A list" star, brought prominent "script doctor" Robert Towne on board the project to write the screenplay. When he got wind of the project, Robert Evans, who was head of production at Paramount, wanted to try his hand at producing a film himself. He finalized an agreement with the writer and actor and secured Roman Polanski, with whom he had collaborated previously on Rosemary's Baby (1968), as the picture's director. (Understandably, Polanski had been working in his native Europe following the brutal death of his wife Sharon Tate [1943–1969] in their Los Angeles home.) When Faye Dunaway was cast as the female lead, yet another not quite famous personality was added to the mix. As one might expect, the shoot was not exactly plain sailing. Evans dubbed the verbal fireworks between Towne and Polanski, "World War III." The problem probably had something to do with the fact that this was first project Polanski directed without writing himself. The product was, nonetheless, an inter-

Chinatown was seen as a Neo-Noir when it was released —
an update on an old genre. Now years have passed and film history
blurs a little, and it seems to settle easily beside the original noirs.
That is a compliment." *Chicago Sun-Times*

1 Portrait of a lady: Femme fatale Evelyn (Faye Dunaway) awakens men's dreams and inspires them to action.

2 In her clutches: The private eye (Jack Nicholson) has lost all professional distance from his seductive client.

3 Masterful execution: Veteran director John Huston plays a brutal patriarch who holds all the cards.

4 Mack the knife: Polanski in a striking cameo as the "nose-slitter."

national smash. *Chinatown* reeled in a total of eleven Oscar nominations, although Robert Towne was the sole person who ended up taking a statuette home.

Yet what makes *Chinatown* truly fascinating, and the reason it attained its instant status as an uncontested masterpiece, is by and large the film's grace in evoking the Golden Age of 1930s–1940s Hollywood, without losing itself in the nostalgia of the era or turning the production into just another stiffly stylized homage. Naturally, Polanski's film draws heavily on classic Bogart characters like detective Philip Marlowe from Howard Hawks' *The Big Sleep* (1946) or his more cynical counterpart Sam Spade from *The Maltese Falcon* (1941), directed by Hollywood legend John Huston. Huston himself plays a pivotal role in *Chinatown* as a ruthless and sickeningly senti-

mental patriarch, who seems to be the key to the entire mystery. Unlike Bogart, Nicholson's character is only capable of being a limited hero. Although J. J. "Jake" Gittes is a likeable, small-time snoop, with a weakness for smutty jokes, the charming sheister fails miserably as a moralist and suffers terribly as a result. The scene featuring Polanski as a gangster who slits open Nicholson's nose is absolutely priceless. The Gittes character also lacks the romantic potential of a Bogart hero. Gittes doesn't embody desires, instead he falters on them. Yet his greatest weakness is Chinatown, the place where his career as a cop came to an end and a synonym for all the irresistible, exotic dangers of the urban jungle. This same sweet taboo seems to echo in Faye Dunaway's character. In the end, Chinatown presents Gittes with a double-edged defeat. Although Towne had originally written a happy

5　Just the facts Ma'am: *Chinatown* evokes classic
　　Hollywood cinema without ever romanticizing it.

6　Still nosing around: J. J. Gittes (Jack Nicholson),
　　bloody but unbowed.

ending, the film's final sequence, which just screams Polanski, sees Gittes inadvertently aiding the forces of evil and losing the love of his life at the same time.

Another great accomplishment of the piece is Polanski and cinematographer John A. Alonzo's triumph in achieving the impact of a black and white Film Noir piece with brilliant color photography. It is uncanny how little the city feels like a movie lot and how convincing the topography looks. Unlike in so many other so-called revisionist noir films, in *Chinatown,* L. A. is not a black, smoldering hell's kitchen but rather a vast, often sunny countryside metropolis still in the early stages of development. The imagery lets the viewer sense that the city and its surrounding valleys exist in spite of the imposing desert. We are also made aware of the colossal pipeline, supplying the city with water, its artificial lifeblood. Water is, in fact, the major resource being manipulated in the story's diabolical real estate venture, a scandal with genuine historical roots in the region. Robert Towne based his screenplay on non-fictional accounts dating back to early 20th century Southern California. It was a time when the foundations for the future riches of the world's movie capital were in construction. The location was chosen primarily on account of the area's year-round sun, ideal for filming, and its affordable purchase price. The boom ushered in a wave of land speculators, corruption and violence. It is a grim bit of Earth that the City of Angels and Hollywood rests upon. A tale that unfolds in *Chinatown*. JH

ROBERT EVANS

Robert Evans (born 1930 in New York), is one of New Hollywood's most illustrious personalities and got his start performing in film at the age of 14. His big break into the business came when actress Norma Shearer, widow of legendary Hollywood tycoon, Irving Thalberg, insisted that Evans play her husband in the *Man of a Thousand Faces* (1957). Dissatisfied with the state of his acting career, he began to work as a freelance producer, without ever producing a single picture, and eventually signed a contract with Paramount in 1965. In the blink of an eye, Evans climbed the rungs of the corporate ladder and emerged as the studio's head of production. He was able to bring the old "mountain" back to its state of former glory as a major studio by taking on a number of blockbuster projects such as *Rosemary's Baby* (1968), *Love Story* (1970), *The Godfather* (1972), *The Godfather – Part II* (1974) and *Chinatown* (1974).

Chinatown marked the first time Evans was able to realize his long harbored ambition of producing a film himself, which garnered him an Academy Award nomination for Best Picture. He left Paramount shortly thereafter to produce film independently, working on films like *Marathon Man* (1976) and *Black Sunday* (1977). These productions were, however, less popular at the box office. In 1984, Evans made headlines for his involvement in the *The Cotton Club* (1984), which not only bombed, but also entangled him in disastrous private scandals. As a result, Evans disappeared from the scene completely for several years. He returned to the business in 1990 with *The Two Jakes*, a further instalment of *Chinatown*, also starring Jack Nicholson. Evans published a book entitled *The Kid Stays in the Picture* (1994) about his personal life story, a constant target of media attention since his start in Hollywood. This gripping autobiography was made into a documentary film in 2002 under the same title.

JAWS ♟♟♟

1975 - USA - 124 MIN. - THRILLER, HORROR FILM

DIRECTOR STEVEN SPIELBERG (*1947) **SCREENPLAY** CARL GOTTLIEB, PETER BENCHLEY, based on his novel of the same name **DIRECTOR OF PHOTOGRAPHY** BILL BUTLER **EDITING** VERNA FIELDS **MUSIC** JOHN WILLIAMS **PRODUCTION** RICHARD D. ZANUCK, DAVID BROWN for ZANUCK/BROWN PRODUCTIONS, UNIVERSAL PICTURES.

STARRING ROY SCHEIDER (Police Chief Martin Brody), ROBERT SHAW (Quint), RICHARD DREYFUSS (Matt Hooper), MURRAY HAMILTON (Mayor Larry Vaughn), LORRAINE GARY (Ellen Brody), CARL GOTTLIEB (Ben Meadows), JEFFREY KRAMER (Lenny Hendricks), SUSAN BACKLINIE (Chrissie), CHRIS REBELLO (Mike Brody), JAY MELLO (Sean Brody).

ACADEMY AWARDS 1975 OSCARS for BEST FILM EDITING (Verna Fields), BEST MUSIC (John Williams), and BEST SOUND (Robert L. Hoyt, Roger Herman Jr., Earl Mabery, John R. Carter).

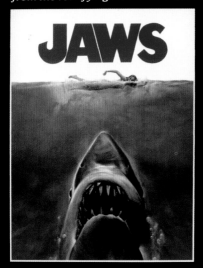

"You're gonna need a bigger boat."

A hot summer night, a beach party, a little too much red wine, and some teenage sex is just the stuff Hollywood horror films are made of. While her drunken companion sleeps off his hangover on the beach, young Chrissie (Susan Backlinie) takes a midnight dip in the water and is torn to pieces by a shark. The fact that the monster with the dead eyes cynically emerges in innocent white from the depths of the water makes it all the more threatening. The shark – the fear and guilt in all of us – awakens our prehistoric terror of the incomprehensible, the truly wild. It is evil incarnate.

But in the small American beach town ironically named Amity, nobody wants to hear about the threat to a safe world and free market economy, least of all from the mouth of visiting New York cop Martin Brody (Roy Scheider) who, to cap it all, is afraid of the water.

Accordingly, the authorities, in the form of the mayor Larry Vaughn (Murray Hamilton), and the profit and pleasure-seeking public win out over Brody, who wants to close the beaches in light of the menacing danger. It comes as no surprise that the town has a new victim the very next day.

A reward of $3,000 for the capture of the shark incites hunting fever in Amity, and the gawking mob on the pier is duly presented with a dead shark. But it is quickly determined that the captured shark can't possibly be the feared killer: upon cutting open its stomach they find a few small fish, a tin can, and a license plate from Louisiana.

It is a motley trio that sets out to capture the beast – a water-shy policeman, a "rich college boy" named Matt Hooper (Richard Dreyfuss), and

2

8

"If *Jaws* was a kind of skeleton key to the angst of the 70s, from the puritanical fear of sex to the war in Vietnam, then its heroes were models of America's wounded masculinity, who meet and join to face a test of character."
Georg Seeßlen

1   Baywatch: Police Chief Martin Brody (Roy Scheider) is fighting nature, the ignorance of those he's trying to protect and his own fears.

2   Beach, blanket, bloodbath: Beautiful Chrissie (Susan Backlinie) is the shark's first victim.

3   Smile for the camera: Three separate models, each seven yards long and weighing over a ton, brought the monster to life. The film crew dubbed the shark "Bruce" – after Steven Spielberg's lawyer.

shark hunting Vietnam veteran Quint (Robert Shaw), a modern Captain Ahab who unsuccessfully attempts to disguise a wounded psyche with a façade of disgust for everything around him. For each of the three men, the shark hunt also turns into a search for their true selves.

The unmistakably sexual aspect of the story of the unnamed monster – a terrifying mixture of phallus and vagina – which afflicts the home and the family has often been pointed out. But *Jaws* is also a film about human fears and character flaws, the overcoming of which gives birth to heroes. That

the story also tells of the capitalistic, self-endangering society, of patriotic America, of mass hysteria, guilt, atonement, and the sacrifice of the individual for the good of the whole is proof of Spielberg's ability to give a simple story plausible readings on multiple levels.

But let's not forget that *Jaws* is one of the most nerve-wracking thrillers of all time. When Spielberg explains that during the filming he felt as if he could direct the audience with an electric cattle prod, it speaks volumes about the cold precision with which, supported by an exceptionally sugges-

THE END OF ARTIFICIAL "Compressors, tanks, winches, pneumatic hoses, welding torches, blow lamps, rigging, generators, copper, iron, and steel wire, plastic material,

"If Spielberg's favorite location is the suburbs, *Jaws* shows suburbanites on vacation."

Chicago Sun-Times

tive soundtrack, he was able to raise the tension and lower it again, all in preparation for the next dramatic highlight.

Just one example of Spielberg's virtuoso story-telling technique is the scene in which the men show one another their scars under deck. In the middle of the scene, the audience is told the story of the *ISS Indianapolis*, the boat with which the Hiroshima bomb was transported to the Pacific. Under fire from Japanese submarines, the crew threw themselves into the ocean and the majority of them were eaten by sharks.

During this sequence, which is actually quite humorous, Spielberg and his authors succeed in setting a counterpoint even before the appearance of the shark illustrates the terror of the story. Quint's tale contains a political dimension. Ultimately, this scene also reveals something about story-telling itself – reality catches you up in a flash. Right when Quint and Hooper attempt to stem their apprehension with loud song, Mr. Spielberg is right there with his electric shocker.

SH

4   Brody's scared of water, but he's about to undergo some shock therapy…

5   Rub a dub dub, three men in a tub: *Jaws* is also a parable about social conflicts in the USA.

6   Shark fin soup: Evil feeds on ignorance and Americans.

ONE FLEW OVER THE CUCKOO'S NEST ♟♟♟♟♟

1975 - USA - 134 MIN. - DRAMA, LITERARY ADAPTATION

DIRECTOR MILOŠ FORMAN (*1932) SCREENPLAY LAWRENCE HAUBEN, BO GOLDMAN, based on the novel of the same name by KEN KESEY and a play by DALE WASSERMAN
DIRECTOR OF PHOTOGRAPHY HASKELL WEXLER, WILLIAM A. FRAKER, BILL BUTLER EDITING LYNZEE KLINGMAN, SHELDON KAHN, RICHARD CHEW (Supervising editor) MUSIC JACK NITZSCHE
PRODUCTION SAUL ZAENTZ, MICHAEL DOUGLAS for FANTASY FILMS, N. V. ZVALUW.

STARRING JACK NICHOLSON (Randle Patrick McMurphy), LOUISE FLETCHER (Nurse Mildred Ratched), WILLIAM REDFIELD (Harding), BRAD DOURIF (Billy Bibbit), WILL SAMPSON (Chief Bromden), DANNY DEVITO (Martini), MICHAEL BERRYMAN (Ellis), PETER BROCCO (Colonel Matterson), DEAN R. BROOKS (Doctor John Spivey), ALONZO BROWN (Miller).

ACADEMY AWARDS 1975 OSCARS for BEST PICTURE (Saul Zaentz, Michael Douglas), BEST DIRECTOR (Miloš Forman), BEST ACTOR (Jack Nicholson), BEST ACTRESS (Louise Fletcher), and BEST ADAPTED SCREENPLAY (Lawrence Hauben, Bo Goldman).

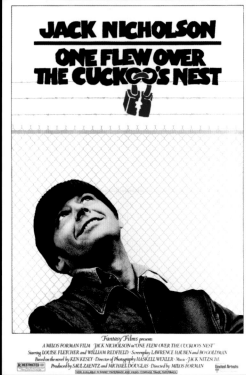

"But I tried didn't I? Goddammit, at least I did that!"

The movie's opening shot evokes an image of paradise lost. Rolling hills are reflected in the glistening water by the rising sun, as a peaceful melody drifts through the air. The last shot is equally utopian. Chief Bromden (Will Sampson), a mountain of a man resident at the psychiatric rehabilitation facility tucked away in this picturesque countryside, wrenches a colossal marble bathroom fixture from its anchored position, hurls it through a window and embarks on the road to freedom. What director Miloš Forman manages to pack into the action that takes place between these two points is a mesmerizing parable about both the urge to capitulate and an ideological system that seeks to crush the individual at any cost. The tale is ingeniously coated in a tragicomic drama about life, death and the state of vegetative indifference exhibited by the residents of an insane asylum.

But all that is about the last thing assault and statutory rape convict, Randle P. McMurphy (Jack Nicholson) has on his mind when he first arrives at the sterile building with barred windows for clinical observation. To McMurphy, the facility serves as a promising alternative to the hard labor he'd be subjected to at the state penitentiary. This is, of course, precisely why higher authorities suspect him of faking his mental ailments. It soon becomes evident that McMurphy is the sole person at the institution still possessing enough fantasy and initiative to combat the current reign of deadening boredom. His opposition comes in the form of the austere head nurse, Mildred Ratched (Louise Fletcher), who has made it her life mission to suck the marrow out of any bit of excitement within the ward in order to assure her patients' eternal sedation. McMurphy, however, slowly undermines her authority. He begins to question trivialities as well as the inalterable daily schedule by instigating "harmless" acts of defiance, even managing to get the patients to sneak out of the clinic and treat them to a fishing trip. Although McMurphy's actions infuse the sequestered men with newfound self-esteem, Nurse Ratched's festering anger reveals her personal disdain for anything other than the prescribed routine. She, of course, defends the

1   It's your move: Randle P. Murphy (Jack Nicholson) thinks he's in a game – and he thinks he can win.

2   Leading by example: Randle is the hero of the other patients in the psychiatric ward.

3   Shake, rattle and roll: Randle encourages his fellow patients to take control of their lives.

"*One flew over the Cuckoo's Nest* is a powerful, smashingly effective movie – not a great movie but one that will probably stir audiences' emotions and join the ranks of such pop-mythology films as *The Wild One*, *Rebel Without a Cause* and *Easy Rider*." *The New Yorker*

prevailing order by enforcing a strict, borderline totalitarian regime rooted in pseudo-democratic doctrines.

To take the film as a critique of modern psychiatric medicine is to misinterpret it. Director Forman has clearly made an attempt at a more monumental allegory about the power structures at play in modern society. Among the poignant final scenes in *One Flew Over the Cuckoo's Nest* is the moment when we discover that the majority of patients at the clinic are there of their own volition. In other words, they have all willingly acquiesced to the tyranny and perpetual humiliation. The counterpoint to this mentality manifests itself in McMurphy's reticence to resign himself to such blind compliance. One of the few actually incarcerated hospital inhabitants, the unforgettable words he utters, following his failed attempt at dislodging a marble bathroom fixture, sum up the plea of Forman's picture: "But I tried didn't I? Goddammit, at least I did that!" Tragically, McMurphy never internalizes the extreme gravity of

JACK NICHOLSON Wily, devious and even lecherous at times, Jack Nicholson still possesses all the qualities required to portray characters driven by animal instincts rather than intellect. His caustic mimicry, gestures and trademark sneer vitalize rebels (*One Flew Over the Cuckoo's Nest*, 1975), psychopaths (*The Shining*, 1980), career killers (*Prizzi's Honor*, 1985) and hardboiled P.I.s alike (*Chinatown*, 1974; *The Two Jakes*, 1990). Some might even regard the sinister, eternally grinning "Joker" in Tim Burton's *Batman* (1988) as the culminating fusion of his classic roles. Hard to believe that for many years it seemed that the movie star born in Neptune, New Jersey in 1937 was not destined to make it big as an actor. In the late 1950s, he joined the team of legendary exploitation film director/producer Roger Corman, performing bit roles in his horror flicks and wannabe rockumentaries, as well as writing screenplays. His screenwriting credits include Monte Hellman's Western *Ride in the Whirlwind* (1965) and Corman's exploration in LSD entitled *The Trip* (1967). The turning point in his career came with his role as a perpetually inebriated lawyer in *Easy Rider* (1969). Dennis Hopper's drama about the disappearance of the American Dream quickly attained cult status and earned Nicholson his first of many Oscar nods. His rise to superstardom reached its inevitable height in the 1970s. Among his many credits and honors, Nicholson has been awarded three Oscars, not to mention the projects he has directed himself. Still very much alive in the business, his more recent movies often feature him as stubborn, eccentric types. These parts attest to Nicholson's immense popularity and continuing role as one of Hollywood's all-time favorite actors.

3

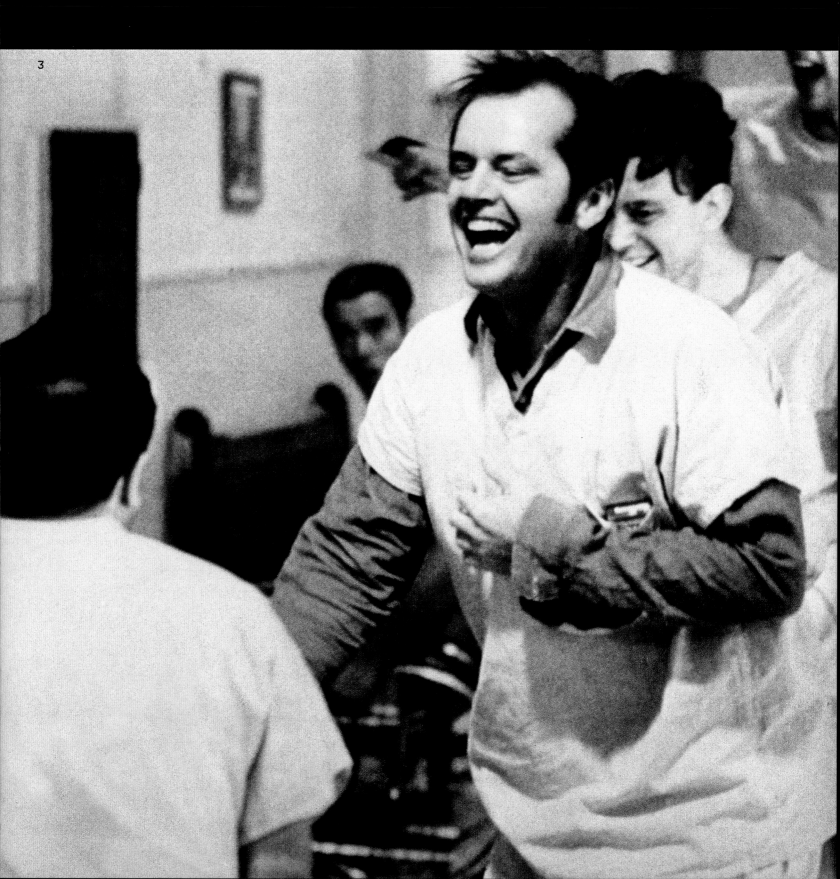

his own predicament and continues to gamble in a poker game where no one can afford to bluff. At one point he is presented with a *deus ex machina* in the form of an open window offering escape. The camera holds its focus on McMurphy's face for some time before a cunning grin finally unfolds across his lips. He will stay and continue on with the "game."

Be that as it may, his tournament is over before he even realizes it. The burgeoning self-confidence and associated mental resilience demonstrated in the wisecracks of the patients cause the hospital staff to implement more drastic physical and psychological measures. The film concludes with a "pacified" McMurphy, who was subjected to a lobotomy, being put out of his misery by his friend, the chief. It is this character who continues what Mc-Murphy has set into motion.

"The 'cuckoo's nest' described by Forman is our very own nest. It's the world we poor lunatics live in, subjected to the bureaucratic rule of one set of oppressors and the economic pressure of another; forever chasing the promise of happiness, which here appears in the guise of liberty – but always obliged to swallow Miss Ratched's bitter little pills." *Le Monde*

TAXI DRIVER

1975 - USA - 113 MIN. - DRAMA

DIRECTOR MARTIN SCORSESE (*1942) SCREENPLAY PAUL SCHRADER
DIRECTOR OF PHOTOGRAPHY MICHAEL CHAPMAN EDITING TOM ROLF, MELVIN SHAPIRO, MARCIA LUCAS
(Editing Supervisor) MUSIC BERNARD HERRMANN PRODUCTION JULIA PHILLIPS, MICHAEL PHILLIPS
for BILL/PHILLIPS, COLUMBIA PICTURES CORPORATION.

STARRING ROBERT DE NIRO (Travis Bickle), CYBILL SHEPHERD (Betsy), JODIE FOSTER (Iris),
HARVEY KEITEL (Sport), ALBERT BROOKS (Tom), PETER BOYLE (Wizard), MARTIN SCORSESE
(Passenger), STEVEN PRINCE (Andy the Gun Dealer), DIAHNNE ABBOTT (Candy Saleswoman),
VICTOR ARGO (Melio).

IFF CANNES 1976 GOLDEN PALM for BEST FILM (Martin Scorsese).

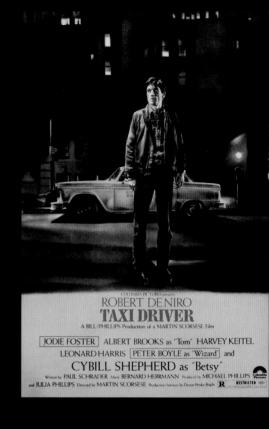

"You talkin' to me?"

The restless, metallic strokes of the musical theme in the opening sequence say it all: this film is a threat. A rising steam cloud hangs over the street and covers the screen in white. As if out of nowhere, a yellow cab penetrates the eerie wall of steam and smoke, gliding through in slow motion. The background music abruptly ends atonally; the ethereal taxi disappears, the cloud closing up behind it. Two dark eyes appear in close up, accompanied by a gentle jazz theme. In the flickering light of the colorful street lamps they wander from side to side, as if observing the surroundings. They are the eyes of Travis Bickle (Robert De Niro), a New York taxi driver who will become an avenging angel.

Even at the premiere in 1976, *Taxi Driver* split the critics. Some saw the main character as a disturbed soul who revels in his role as savior of a young prostitute, for whom he kills three shady characters in an excessively bloody rampage, an act for which the press fetes him as a hero. Others looked more closely and detected a skillfully stylized film language in the melancholy images and a common urban sociopath behind the figure of the madman Travis Bickle: "On every street, in every city, there's a nobody who dreams of being somebody," reads one of the film posters.

Travis can't sleep at night. To earn a few cents he becomes a taxi driver. He'll drive anytime and anywhere, he says in his interview. He will even enter the neighborhoods his colleagues avoid at all costs – the districts with either too little or too much light, in which street gangs loiter around and teenage prostitutes wait for punters under bright neon lights. Travis is given the job. He and his taxi become one and the catastrophe takes its course.

Like Travis, the audience gazes out of the driving taxi into the night. Rarely was New York depicted as impressively. The camera style switches between half-documentary and subjective takes. Bernard Herrmann's sug-

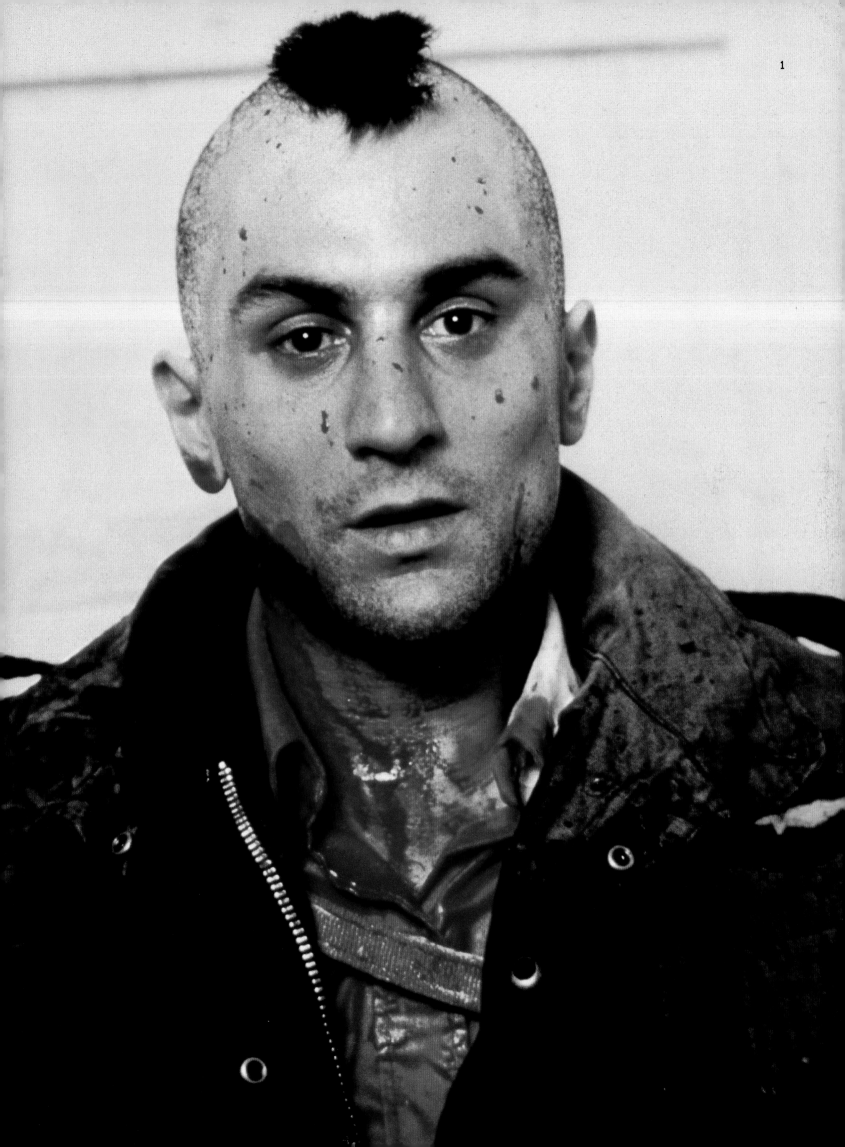

gestive music, which accompanies the film, lends it an acoustic structure, creating a unique combination of image and sound. The taxi driving becomes nothing less than a metaphor of film.

Travis' attempt to build a romantic relationship with campaign assistant Betsy (Cybill Shepherd) fails. He can neither express himself, nor his feelings, which is why in the end he turns to the gun. Isolated and aimless, he wanders through the city. Travis' story resembles the yellow taxi cab that sliced through the cloud of smoke in the opening sequence. He too emerges out of nowhere, briefly appears in the night light of the city, and vanishes again into nothingness.

Travis is no hero, even if many applauded the brutal rampage at the premiere. Violence is naturally an important theme of the film, but the violence is

1   Robert De Niro in *The Last of the Mohicans?*
    Call central casting, quick!

2   Soldier of fortune at a buck a mile: Ex-Marine
    Travis Bickle, at war with New York.

3   Talk to the hand: Travis helps stamp out violent
    crime.

4   This screen ain't big enough for the two of us:
    Both pimp (Harvey Keitel) and taxi driver are used
    to getting their own way.

"Martin Scorsese's *Taxi Driver* is a homage to home from a homeless man; a New York Western, with a midnight cowboy cruising the canyons in a shabby yellow cab." *Der Spiegel*

5

"An utterly strange, disturbing, alarming and fascinating film. Syncretic and glamorous, it is a lurking reptile that changes color like a chameleon; a synthetic amalgam of conflicting influences, tendencies and metaphysical ambitions, raised to the power of a myth: comical, edgy, hysterical."

Frankfurter Rundschau

5   Jodie Foster as the child prostitute, Iris. Nonetheless, it was Foster's older sister who stood in as her body double for the more mature shots.

6   The facts of life: On tonight's episode, Mrs. Garrett tells Tootie what men really want.

7   Remember the Alamo: Election campaigner Betsy (Cybill Shepherd) is the object of Travis's desire.

BERNARD HERRMANN   He made a guest appearance in Hitchcock's *The Man Who Knew Too Much* (1956) as the conductor on the podium of the London Symphony, practically playing himself. He also wrote the music for the film. Born in New York on June 29, 1911, it was Bernard Herrmann who gave a number of film classics the final push towards immortality. He began working for radio, and then moved on to film, collaborating with Alfred Hitchcock, Orson Welles, François Truffaut, Brian De Palma, and Martin Scorsese to name but a few. He gave films like *Vertigo* (1958), *Psycho* (1960), *North by Northwest* (1959), *Citizen Kane* (1941), *The Magnificent Ambersons* (1942), *Fahrenheit 451* (1966), and *Taxi Driver* (1975) an unmistakable musical face, an aura of tonality. No one used the orchestra as eclectically Herrmann. He could make it sound conservative and classical, or send it into strange tonal regions in which the strings, accompanied by sonorous, dark horns, imitated the sounds of swinging metal wires.

Herrmann was fascinated by the sinister romantic literature of the Brontë sisters and by Melville's *Moby Dick*. The sea with its elemental force was an inspiration for the scores of his compositions. He could hear and compose the rising and falling of deep waters. Herrmann was not an affable man, perhaps because he was too much of an artist. He was known for his irascible and perverse behavior. He fell out of favor with Hitchcock during work on *Torn Curtain* (1966). He remained an artist through and through while working on his last soundtrack. He finished it on the day before his death on December 24, 1975. It was the music to *Taxi Driver*.

---

not merely physical, but social. Travis embodies a person who has lost himself in the big city. Robert De Niro gave this type a face and an unmistakable body.

Scorsese is known for creating his films on paper. He draws them like sketches in a storyboard, and time and again he shows that images are his true language. The screenplay was the work of Paul Schrader, and marked the first close collaboration between two film-obsessed men. The scene in which Travis stands before the mirror shirtless, clutching his revolver and picks a fight with himself is unforgettable: "You talkin' to me? Well I'm the only one here. Who do you think you're talking to?" The scene has been cited over and over, but the original remains unattainable. It is a modern classic.

SR

6

STAR WARS ♕♕♕♕♕♕♕

1977 - USA - 121 MIN. - SCIENCE FICTION

DIRECTOR GEORGE LUCAS (*1944) SCREENPLAY GEORGE LUCAS
DIRECTOR OF PHOTOGRAPHY GILBERT TAYLOR EDITING PAUL HIRSCH, MARCIA LUCAS,
RICHARD CHEW MUSIC JOHN WILLIAMS PRODUCTION GARY KURTZ for
LUCASFILM LTD.

STARRING MARK HAMILL (Luke Skywalker), HARRISON FORD (Han Solo),
CARRIE FISHER (Princess Leia Organa), ALEC GUINNESS (Ben "Obi-Wan"
Kenobi), PETER CUSHING (Tarkin), DAVID PROWSE (Darth Vader),
JAMES EARL JONES (Darth Vader's voice), KENNY BAKER (R2-D2),
ANTHONY DANIELS (C-3PO), PETER MAYHEW (Chewbacca), PHIL BROWN
(Owen Lars), SHELAGH FRASER (Beru Lars).

ACADEMY AWARDS 1977 OSCARS for BEST MUSIC (John Williams), BEST FILM EDITING
(Paul Hirsch, Marcia Lucas, Richard Chew), BEST SET DESIGN
(John Barry, Norman Reynolds, Leslie Dilley, Roger Christian), BEST
COSTUMES (John Mollo), BEST SOUND (Don MacDougall, Ray West,
Bob Minkler, Derek Ball), BEST SPECIAL EFFECTS (John Stears, John Dykstra,
Richard Edlund, Grant McCune, Robert Blalack), and SPECIAL PRIZE FOR
SOUND EFFECTS (voices of the aliens and robots, Ben Burtt).

"May the Force be with you!"

There's something rotten in the state of the galaxy. With the blessings of the Emperor, Grand Moff Tarkin (Peter Cushing) and the sinister Lord Vader (David Prowse/James Earl Jones) have been conquering and subjugating one planet system after the other in the old Republic. Tarkin commands a massive spaceship, whose firepower has the ability to annihilate entire planets. This "Deathstar" is the most dangerous weapon in the universe – perhaps with the exception of "The Force," a mysterious, all-pervading energy. Anyone who learns to master this force through years of ascetic training is possessed with superhuman powers. In the past, the Jedi Knights secured justice and kept the peace with the help of "The Force." But now Darth Vader, a renegade Jedi, is one of the last people with control of its powers, forming with Tarkin an almost invincible alliance of evil in the once peaceful expanses of the universe.

Only a small group of rebels resist the might of the Empire and fight to restore the old order. To achieve their aspirations, the construction plans of the "Deathstar", which the rebels have acquired, could be of great assistance. But the spaceship of Princess Leia (Carrie Fisher) is captured just as she is returning to her home planet with the plans in hand. At the last moment she is able to save the blueprint of the "Death Star" inside the droid R2-D2 (Kenny Baker). If this tiny robot can get the plans to the old Jedi Knight Obi-Wan Kenobi (Alec Guinness) in time, there could still be a remote hope for the rebels' cause.

1   May the Force be with you: With a monk's habit and light sabre, Ben "Obi-Wan" Kenobi (Alec Guinness) links medieval mythology to a hi-tech future.

2   Iron lung of evil: Darth Vader (David Prowse) will stop at nothing to conquer the galaxy.

3   Man's best friend according to Lucas: Princess Leia (Carrie Fisher) confides in R2-D2 (Kenny Baker).

The journey of R2-D2 and his companion, the dithering and etiquette-conscious communication robot C-3PO (Anthony Daniels), takes them to the planet Tatooine, where they are purchased by farmer Owen Lars (Phil Brown). His nephew, Luke Skywalker (Mark Hamill) longs for a life more exciting than that of an agricultural worker. He would much rather fight with the rebels against the Empire – just as his father, a legendary Jedi whom he has never met, once did…

Skywalker's dreams of adventure begin to become reality when the two droids meet Obi-Wan. Soon the imperial Storm Troopers are at their heels, and the old Jedi Knight is left with no other alternative but to travel with Luke and the droids to Alderaan, Leia's home planet, bringing the plans of the "Death Star" to help plan a counterattack.

They receive assistance from Han Solo (Harrison Ford), and old pro who, with his ship, the Millennium Falcon, manages to speed away from the fast-approaching imperial cruisers in the nick of time. Even so, they do not reach their destination: Tarkin and Darth Vader have already destroyed the planet Alderaan.

After our heroes free Princess Leia from the "Death Star," nothing stands in the way of the final battle between the Empire and the rebels in the Javin System. The Achilles heel of the gigantic space station is a small ven-

tilation shaft, and in the end, after several intense battles, it is Luke who is able to hit the weak spot and destroy the "Death Star" in a powerful explosion. Only Darth Vader escapes the blazing inferno. And while one battle may have been won in this war in the stars, it won't be long before the Empire strikes back…

George Lucas began working on his star-saga just as his teenage drama, *American Graffiti*, was poised to become the surprise hit of 1973 – a success from which the director profited much less than the studios that produced the film. For Lucas, this experience was the driving motivation never to give control of one of his projects to anyone else again. *Star Wars* was produced entirely by his own company and the special effects were created by Industrial Light & Magic, also a Lucas company. Rounding out the deal was a clause giving rights to merchandising (toys, clothing, etc.) and the use of film music to Lucas, initiating a new period in cinema in which the biggest proceeds of a film were no longer made at the box office. The blockbuster movie was born.

Real success always did depend on reaching the largest possible audience. Lucas stressed over and over that he wrote the screenplay with 8 and 9-year-olds in mind. But in the end, the film was able to connect with virtually every age group, primarily because with his "space opera," Lucas

"I wanted to make a film for kids, something that would present them with a kind of elementary morality. Because nowadays nobody bothers to tell those kids, 'Hey, this is right and this is wrong.'"

George Lucas, interview with David Sheff

"A combination of past and future, Western and space odyssey,
myth and dream world, Star Wars may be the most enduring piece
of escapism ever put on film." *Sacramento Bee*

as neither attempting to depart from old genres, nor to enthusiastically deconstruct them. In fact, his goal was just the opposite. Like his colleague Steven Spielberg, Lucas pursued a higher path, which led him back to the classical narrative form, meeting the expectations of the public and employing the highest levels of technical mastery.

The subject matter of *Star Wars* is akin to a trip through the annals of cultural and film history. Lucas fused elements from the tales of knights and the myths of heroes with the high-tech world of spaceships, was inspired by German and Soviet military uniforms, based the Jedi religion on the Shaman cults of Central America, and created the Empire in the image of an Orwellian dictatorship. The android C-3PO is unmistakably based on the machine woman from Fritz Lang's *Metropolis* (1926), and the concluding hero-honoring ceremony is an obvious reference to Leni Riefenstahl's Nazi party film *The Triumph of the Will* (*Triumph des Willens*, 1935). In short, with *Star Wars* an inter-cultural super-cosmos was created, containing something for every audience member to recognize.

4   Rebels without a shave: Individualists Chewbacca (Peter Mayhew) and Han Solo (Harrison Ford) battle against the evil empire.

5   About face: The imperial storm troopers are trained and ruthless killers.

An overture. In the beginning of *Star Wars* (1977), a long block of text rolls up the screen, setting the stage and recounting the background story. What follows is no singular adventure; it is an entire universe. From the very beginning *Star Wars* was created as a multi-episode project. After the first episode came *Star Wars: Episode V – The Empire Strikes Back* (1980) and then *Star Wars: Episode VI – The Return of the Jedi* (1983). The pre-history of the saga was also conceptualized as a trilogy. Even during the first screenplay drafts, Lucas' Star-world was getting bigger and bigger. This is no exception in the fantasy and science fiction genre. Where new, exotic worlds are created, there will always be questions about how it all began. With the interest in both past and future, the plot possibilities are endless.

Serial science fiction stories were already prevalent and popular in the 1930s. Space heroes like *Flash Gordon* (1936) and *Buck Rogers* (1939) helped their comic forefathers to big screen success. Each 13-part series told of despotic rulers, beautiful women, and heroic men saving the universe; after 20 minutes the plot stopped at the most exciting moment – to be continued next week in this theater!

The *Star-Trek* Universe has been massively popular and has experienced considerable expansion. Since the first episode of the television series about the Starship Enterprise was broadcast in 1966, five spin-off series and ten films have been created, each piece of this long chain of individual stories adding to the colossal inventory of characters, events, time periods, and places that make up this fantastic world.

6 Budget getaway: Protocol droid C-3PO (Anthony Daniels) speaks millions of languages; but unlike brave little R2-D2, he's an exasperating penny-pincher.

7 Putting their lives on the line for a pleasant tomorrow: Princess Leia and Luke Skywalker (Mark Hamill).

8 Everyday life in the not-too-distant future: The furniture of the *Star Wars* universe is sometimes credibly and recognizably shabby.

"It's a terrifically entertaining war story, it has memorable characters and it is visually compelling. What more do we want in movies?" *San Francisco Chronicle*

The real highlight, however, was that Lucas' film, despite its complex plot, tells a story easily reduced to the battle of good versus evil. *Star Wars* is not a story of broken heroes. Lucas sends clearly defined characters into battle, and the audience are never left in doubt as to who will triumph in the end. The result is that the science fiction opus became an effortlessly digestible mixture of vignettes, whose charm lay not in complicated conceptual worlds, but rather in its fantastic moments and visual spectacles. It was these moments that made the film an ideal springboard for the budding entertainment industry of video and computer games. The space battles were replicated and prolonged on consoles and monitors all over the world, helping to reduce the time between episodes...

8

EP

ANNIE HALL 🏆🏆🏆🏆

1977 - USA - 93 MIN. - COMEDY

DIRECTOR WOODY ALLEN (*1935) SCREENPLAY WOODY ALLEN, MARSHALL BRICKMAN
DIRECTOR OF PHOTOGRAPHY GORDON WILLIS EDITING RALPH ROSENBLUM, WENDY GREENE BRICMONT
MUSIC CARMEN LOMBARDO, ISHAM JONES PRODUCTION CHARLES H. JOFFE, JACK ROLLINS
for UNITED ARTISTS.

STARRING WOODY ALLEN (Alvy Singer), DIANE KEATON (Annie Hall), TONY ROBERTS (Rob),
CAROL KANE (Allison), PAUL SIMON (Tony Lacey), COLLEEN DEWHURST (Mother Hall),
JANET MARGOLIN (Robin), SHELLEY DUVALL (Pam), CHRISTOPHER WALKEN (Duane Hall),
SIGOURNEY WEAVER (Alvy's Date), BEVERLY D'ANGELO (TV Actress).

ACADEMY AWARDS 1977 OSCARS for BEST PICTURE (Charles H. Joffe), BEST DIRECTOR (Woody Allen),
BEST ACTRESS (Diane Keaton), and BEST ORIGINAL SCREENPLAY (Woody Allen, Marshall
Brickman).

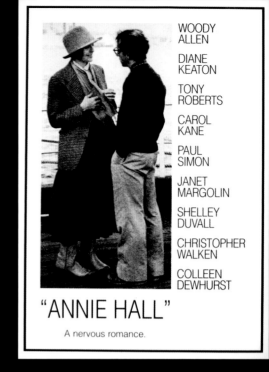

WOODY ALLEN
DIANE KEATON
TONY ROBERTS
CAROL KANE
PAUL SIMON
JANET MARGOLIN
SHELLEY DUVALL
CHRISTOPHER WALKEN
COLLEEN DEWHURST

"ANNIE HALL"

A nervous romance.

"You know, it's one thing about intellectuals, they prove that you can be absolutely brilliant and have no idea what's going on."

"There's an old joke. Two elderly women are at a Catskills mountain resort, and one of them says: 'Boy, the food at this place is really terrible.' The other one says, 'Yeah, I know, and such… small portions.' Well, that's essentially how I feel about life," says *Annie Hall's* actual protagonist, Alvy Singer (Woody Allen) at the top of the film. "(It's) full of loneliness and misery and suffering and unhappiness, and it's all over much too quickly."

Singer is a stand-up comedian, professional cynic and full-time misanthrope. When a big tall blond crew-cutted guy in a record store tells him that Wagner is on sale this week, Jewish Alvy knows exactly how to take it. He also despises Los Angeles for being a city whose only cultural advantage is that you can make a right turn on a red light. What ties this seemingly unrelated hodge-podge of scenes and sketches pieced together by editor Ralph Rosenblum from a heap of over 50,000 feet of film is Alvy's relationship to the movie's title character, Annie Hall.

We meet the couple after the two of them have called it quits for the very last time, and then take an endearing yet heart-breaking trip with them down memory lane to discover what led to the demise of their year-long romance. Annie (Diane Keaton) is the quintessential pseudo-intellectual, a caricature of the urban woman. Alvy brands her as eternally flawed for being born with original sin – she grew up in rural America. On the other hand Alvy's condemning remarks about everyone and everything (including himself) are just his way of concealing his own unique, neurotic blend of self-loathing, self-pity and self-worship, which not even 15 years of therapy could cure him of. As he explains in a TV interview he was deemed "four-P" by a personality assessment test: a hostage in the event of war.

Allen biographer Marion Meade rightly stated that *Annie Hall* could have just as easily been entitled *Alvy Singer* or even better, *Allan Konigsberg*, Woody Allen's given name. The Alvy character is an unmistakable self-portrait of the director, who himself started out as a gag writer for stand-up comics. Up until three weeks before the premiere, Allen insisted that the film be called *Anhedonia* (the debilitating absence of pleasure or the ability to experience it). Arthur Krim, head of United Artists and Allen's paternal role model, allegedly threatened to throw himself out the window if he went through with it.

The almost non-existent cinematic structure of the piece allowed Allen to pack the movie full of amusing quips and snide remarks, more concisely

it supplied him with a vehicle for unabated hilarity. Nonetheless, *Annie Hall* remains a particularly significant work for two main reasons. The first being that the director makes a point of tweaking classic modes of cinematic depictions of reality and storytelling. Whereas he filmed his 1969 piece *Take the Money and Run* (1969) in the style of a news exposé, *Annie Hall* is a veritable cornucopia of narrative conventions and even manages to weave in an animated sequence. Time and again, Alvy directly addresses his audience sitting in the theater. Such is the case in a movie ticket line, when he wishes to one-up and embarrass the wannabe film buff who loudly pontificates, claims to teach a course on TV, Media and Culture at Columbia University and quotes extensively from influential Canadian media theorist Marshall McLuhan. Alvy quickly wins their debate by surreally calling upon McLuhan to

"Personal as the story he is telling may be, what separates this film from Allen's own past work and most other recent comedy is its general believability. His central figures and all who cross their paths are recognizable contemporary types. Most of us have even shared a lot of their fantasies."

Time Magazine

1   He'd never join a club that would have him as a member: Alvy Singer is Woody Allen's filmic alter ego.

2   A walk on the mild side: Neurotic New Yorkers Annie (Diane Keaton), Alvy and Dick (Dick Cavett) analyze life, art, and above all themselves.

3   New York is full of interesting, undiscovered places to hang out...

4   Uppers and downers: Alvy reveres European cinema – and especially Ingmar Bergman.

personally step in and set matters straight. In another memorable sequence, Allen uses a split-screen to illustrate two incompatible worlds, as Alvy's New York Jewish family is compared in similar, juxtaposed dinner scenes to Annie's family. On the left third of the screen is the brightly lit, affluent, politely gracious, aloof and sober Hall family discussing subjects such as the Christmas play and the 4-H Club. On the right two-thirds of the screen is a darkly lit, sloppy and informal, noisily argumentative, competitively babbling Singer family talking about illness (diabetes, heart disease) and unemployment (illustrating that Alvy's argumentative nature and fear of marriage were inherited from his family). The genius of the episode is born out of the actual conversation of the two families that takes place *across* this divided split-screen. This brand of narrative anarchy was both a liberating artistic breakthrough and a triumph for Allen.

The second significant achievement for Allen that came out of *Annie Hall* was the creation of his alter ego, which finally succeeded in distancing him from his purely comic self. Since this picture, Allen's cosmopolitan neurotic has been a free-floating entity who can be readily integrated into the context of more serious pieces like *Hannah and Her Sisters* (1985) and *Husbands and Wives* (1992), or just observe the action from the sidelines as in his 1978 drama, *Interiors* (1978).   SH

DIANE KEATON

In a quirkily perfect performance that won her the Best Actress Oscar, Woody Allen's then flame Diane Keaton reveals Annie Hall's and her own zany yet huggable nature through the character's stumbling, flailing gestures. These are reinforced by self-conscious, shyly banal statements, particularly her self-effacing "La-dee-dah." The similarities between these two women include their over the top and "not quite with it" manner as well as their taste in clothing, which according to Allen, includes an affinity for football jerseys matched to skirts, combat boots and mittens. Given all this, it should come as no surprise that Keaton's original last name supplied the character with hers.

The actress born on January 5, 1946 in Los Angeles, met Allen in 1969 while acting with him in his Broadway play "Play it Again, Sam." A few years later, she appeared for the first time in an often-overlooked performance at the side of Al Pacino in the role of Michael Corleone's wife in Francis Ford Coppola's *Godfather* trilogy (1972, 1974, 1990).

She worked on numerous Woody Allen films, both before and after their relationship came to an end. In 1981, she collaborated with Warren Beatty, with whom she was also romantically involved for some time, on the film *Reds*. Before long, Keaton proved she had what it took to join the male-dominated world of directing and has been making pictures and TV shows, including an episode of the legendary TV show *Twin Peaks*, since the 1980s. Her 1995 work *Unstrung Heroes* is a little-known masterpiece in filmmaking. Her 1996 acting and comedic bravado in *The First Wives Club* (1996) and dramatic eloquence in *Marvin's Room* (1996) reconfirmed her star appeal. Today, it is hard to imagine that this star in her own right was once inextricably tied up with Allen.

THE DEER HUNTER ♟♟♟♟♟

1978 - USA - 183 MIN. - VIETNAM FILM

DIRECTOR MICHAEL CIMINO (*1943) SCREENPLAY DERIC WASHBURN, MICHAEL CIMINO, LOUIS GARFINKLE, QUINN K. REDEKER DIRECTOR OF PHOTOGRAPHY VILMOS ZSIGMOND EDITING PETER ZINNER MUSIC STANLEY MYERS PRODUCTION BARRY SPIKINGS, MICHAEL DEELEY, MICHAEL CIMINO, JOHN PEVERALL for EMI FILMS LTD., UNIVERSAL PICTURES.

STARRING ROBERT DE NIRO (Michael), JOHN CAZALE (Stan), JOHN SAVAGE (Steven), CHRISTOPHER WALKEN (Nick), MERYL STREEP (Linda), GEORGE DZUNDZA (John), CHUCK ASPEGREN (Axel), SHIRLEY STOLER (Steven's Mother), RUTANYA ALDA (Angela), PIERRE SEGUI (Julien).

ACADEMY AWARDS 1978 OSCARS for BEST FILM (Barry Spikings, Michael Deeley, Michael Cimino, John Peverall), BEST DIRECTOR (Michael Cimino), BEST SUPPORTING ACTOR (Christopher Walken), BEST FILM EDITING (Peter Zinner), and BEST SOUND (C. Darin Knight, Richard Portman, Aaron Rochin, William L. McCaughey).

"One shot is what it's all about. A deer has to be taken with one shot."

There are films that lose all their magic as soon as you know how they end; and there are others that keep their thrill even after several viewings. One of the cinema's undying magic moments is the scene at the end of *The Deer Hunter,* in which Nick (Christopher Walken) walks out of the back room of a Saigon gambling den with a red scarf round his head. His old friend Michael (Robert De Niro) steps towards him – he wants him to come home. But Nick can no longer recognize him; he's spent too long with his temple pressed to the barrel of a revolver with just one bullet in the chamber. He's gambled with his life so often, he can't believe it's still his. He moves towards the crowded gaming table with a bunch of banknotes in his hand. Michael tries in vain to persuade him to leave. And suddenly there's a flicker of recognition in Nick's eyes. He laughs, takes the gun, holds it to his head and pulls the trigger.

It's the end of the 60s. Michael, Nick and Steven (John Savage), three friends from a steel town in Pennsylvania, are sent to Vietnam. By coincidence, they meet again in the midst of war. And by misfortune, they end up in the hands of the Vietcong. The prisoners are forced to play Russian Roulette while their captors lay bets on the outcome. Finally, only Michael and Nick are left, face-to-face across the table. Michael demands three bullets instead of one, in order to raise the stakes. His ruse is successful: the two friends overcome the Vietcong guerillas, free Steven from the "tiger cage" (a half-submerged bamboo basket) and flee for their lives. But Michael is the only one who makes it home intact. Steven loses his legs, and Nick gets stuck in Saigon, making money with the game of death.

Only around one-third of this great epic takes place in Vietnam – the middle part. These are among the most impressive images of war ever filmed. The contempt for human life so typical of any war, the hatred, the powerlessness, the fear, and the pride: Michael Cimino brings all these together in a single symbolic action – Russian Roulette. Yet Cimino shows the Americans purely as victims of the Vietnam War, and this provoked a lot of protest, especially in Europe. The Americans, it was claimed, were much more guilty than their opponents of torturing POWs. The film was accused of being racist, and the controversy came to a head at the Berlin Film Festival in

1   War on the home front: Linda (Meryl Streep) and Michael (Robert DeNiro) tackle daily life and its many ghosts.

2   Birds of prey: Michael and Nick (Christopher Walken) on a hunting trip in the mountains.

3   Fun and games in Clairton, Pennsylvania. Cimino shot the Clairton scenes in eight separate locations to breathe life into the fictitious town.

4   Camerawork that is right on target. Cinematographer Vilmos Zsigmond went on to film *Heaven's Gate* (1980) for Cimino.

> "There can be no quarrel about the acting. De Niro, Walken, John Savage, as another Clairton pal who goes to war, and Meryl Streep, as a woman left behind, are all top actors in extraordinary form."
>
> *Time Magazine*

1979, as the Soviet Union, followed by the rest of the Eastern Bloc, withdrew all its films in protest.

But Cimino is not even attempting to provide a political commentary to the Vietnam War. Instead, his film tells the story of people uprooted from everything they used to call home, and it shows the destruction of everything that once made friendship possible. The first hour of the film is devoted to the rituals of the two friends, Michael and Nick. We see their last day in the steelmill; we see them drinking with their buddies from the little community of White Russian immigrants; we see their wild celebrations at Steven's wedding reception, after the Russian Orthodox ceremony. One last time before Vietnam, the friends go hunting in the mountains of Pennsylvania, a pristine contrast to the dirty steel town. Michael's hunting ambition, to kill a deer with

5 Caught in the crossfire: Robert de Niro called this role "his toughest yet" after shooting was completed.

6 "One of the most frightening, unbearably tense sequences ever filmed – and the most violent excoriation of violence in screen history," wrote *Newsweek*.

7 Secret admirer: Back from the war, decorated soldier Michael visits the true love of his life – Nick's girl, Linda (Meryl Streep).

a single shot, will not survive his experiences in Vietnam. Indeed, when he returns in the third part of the film, he'll have difficulties even finding his home – because someone's missing, and he's made a promise. That's why he leaves once more, to search for Nick in Saigon.

At the end, the little group of mourners in the bar will strike up "God Bless America," but their rendition of the hymn is anything but triumphant.

These people are the walking wounded, and each of them has lost something: a friend, physical wholeness, trust in life, or hope for the future. The fault lies with America; and yet America is their home, a part of their very selves. In *The Deer Hunter,* Cimino shows us this painful contradiction, and gives us a subtle, exact and outstandingly photographed portrait of American society after Vietnam.   NM

6

"Equally at ease in the lyrical and the realistic modes, a virtuoso of the shocking image who never loses sight of the whole, a consummate master of his technique, Michael Cimino is a supremely accomplished filmmaker." *Le Monde*

MICHAEL CIMINO   His films are always controversial: *The Deer Hunter* (1978) was showered with Oscars in Hollywood and condemned as a falsification of the Vietnam War in Europe. The epic Late Western *Heaven's Gate* (1980) was hailed as a masterpiece in Europe, and decried as a "catastrophe" in the USA. *Year of the Dragon* (1985), in which a sole cop takes on the Chinese mafia in New York, brought accusations of racism. *The Sicilian* (1987), an opulent biography of the Sicilian popular hero Salvatore Giuliano, was dismissed as historical kitsch.

Michael Cimino (*16.11.1943) came to filmmaking after studying architecture and painting. By the end of the 60s, he was making commercials. In 1973, he joined with John Milius to write the screenplay to *Magnum Force*, starring Clint Eastwood. Cimino's first feature film was *Thunderbolt and Lightfoot* (1974), a tragicomic thriller about a gangster in search of his money, with Eastwood and Jeff Bridges in the leading roles. The debut signaled some of the motifs that would be found throughout Cimino's work: male friendship, detailed milieu studies, and gorgeous landscape panoramas. His expensive obsession with authenticity drove United Artists to bankruptcy, and to this day, *Heaven's Gate* is a synonym for megaflops. Although his last film *The Sunchaser* (1996) was a fairly conventional effort, Michael Cimino is still regarded as one of the most visually brilliant directors in America.

THE TIN DRUM
Die Blechtrommel / Le Tambour

979 - FRG / FRANCE / POLAND / YUGOSLAVIA - 145 MIN. - LITERARY ADAPTATION, DRAMA

DIRECTOR VOLKER SCHLÖNDORFF (*1939) SCREENPLAY JEAN-CLAUDE CARRIÈRE, VOLKER SCHLÖNDORFF, FRANZ SEITZ, based on the novel of the same name by GÜNTER GRASS DIRECTOR OF PHOTOGRAPHY IGOR LUTHER EDITING SUZANNE BARON MUSIC MAURICE JARRE, FRIEDRICH MEYER PRODUCTION FRANZ SEITZ, ANATOLE DAUMAN for BIOSKOP FILM, ARTÉMIS PRODUCTIONS, ARGOS FILMS, HALLELUJAH FILMS.

STARRING DAVID BENNENT (Oskar Matzerath), ANGELA WINKLER (Agnes Matzerath), MARIO ADORF (Alfred Matzerath), DANIEL OLBRYCHSKI (Jan Bronski), KATHARINA THALBACH (Maria), HEINZ BENNENT (Greff), ANDRÉA FERRÉOL (Lina Greff), CHARLES AZNAVOUR (Sigismund Markus), MARIELLA OLIVERI (Roswitha), ILSE PAGÉ (Gretchen Scheffler), OTTO SANDER (The Musician Meyn).

ACADEMY AWARDS 1979 OSCAR for BEST FOREIGN FILM.

IFF CANNES 1979 GOLDEN PALM (Volker Schlöndorff).

"I first saw the light of the world in the form of a 60-watt bulb."

The film starts and ends in a field of potatoes. "I begin long before me," says the narrator, and describes the events that led to the conception of his mother. We see policemen pursuing a man, before a country girl grants him refuge under her voluminous skirts, where matters take their course. The begetting of Oskar, our narrator, is no less strange: his kindly mother Agnes (Angela Winkler) is married to the loudmouthed grocer Alfred Matzerath (Mario Adorf) and in love with the sensitive Pole, Jan Bronski (Daniel

Olbrychski). Oskar is conceived "within this trinity." When he's born, his mother promises him a tin drum; on his third birthday he gets it. And on the same day, already disgusted by the drunken, gluttonous, cacophonous world of the adults around him, he makes an important decision: he's going to stay small. He throws himself down the cellar stairs and immediately stops growing. For the next 18 years, he'll go through life in the body of a three-year-old with a tin drum hanging round his neck. And anyone who tries to take this

"Schlöndorff deliberately looked for a simpler narrative style. Whole fragments of the book were simply left out. Yet I still feel that he's succeeded in casting a new light on the whole story."

Günter Grass, in: Sequenz

1 Toy soldier: On his third birthday, Oskar Matzerath (David Bennent) is given a tin drum...

2 ... and, disgusted at the adult world, he resolves to stop growing immediately.

3 Sins of the fatherland: Oscar's father, grocer Matzerath (Mario Adorf), is a fervent fan of Adolf Hitler.

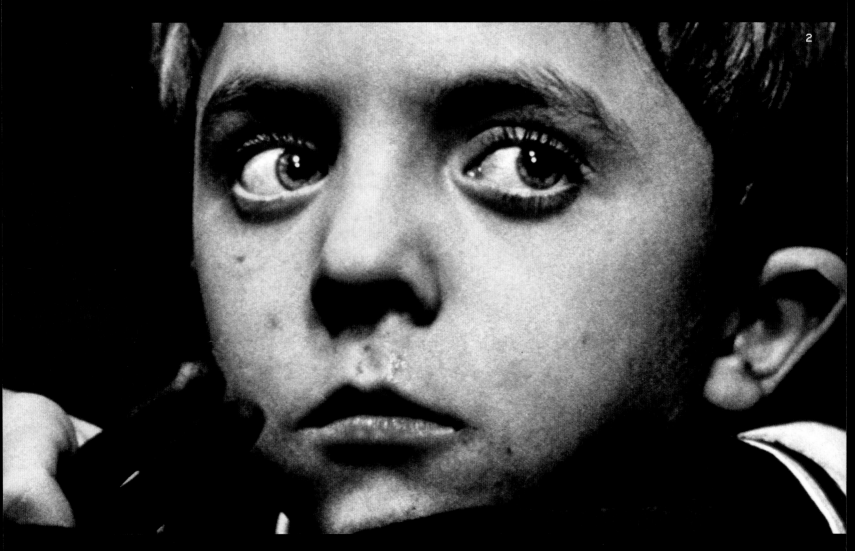

drum away from him will be subjected to little Oskar's unearthly, glass-shattering scream.

Oskar is no normal child. From the day he's born, he can think and make decisions for himself; and his strangeness sets him apart. *The Tin Drum* is an opulent panorama of German-Polish history, seen through the eyes of an outsider. We are witness to the years between 1899 and 1945, from the peaceful co-existence of Germans and Poles in Danzig, to the German attack on the city, to Oskar's flight westwards as the war draws to a close. In the film's final image, the camera watches from the potato field as he fades into the distance. Tectonic shifts in politics are made visible in tiny details, as when Beethoven's portrait makes way for Hitler's. Oskar takes

no sides in all this; he remains an outsider. Once, however, his drumming causes chaos at a Nazi meeting. Oskar carries on drumming till everyone present is swaying happily to the strains of "The Blue Danube." It's reminiscent of the scene in *Casablanca* (1942), where the "Marseillaise" does battle with "Die Wacht am Rhein." On another occasion, Oskar lets the Nazis draw him in: he meets some kindred spirits at a circus, dwarves employed as clowns and later as "a tonic for the troops." Oskar joins them, and soon he too is wearing a Nazi uniform.

If the story is episodic and discontinuous, the cinematic style is a riot. Adapted from the novel by Nobel Prizewinner Günter Grass, the film is a kind of comical yarn, a burlesque bubbling over with ideas, by turns naturalistic

3

VOLKER SCHLÖNDORFF The German weekly *Die Zeit* once had the following to say about Völker Schlöndorff: "Together with Fassbinder, he's undoubtedly the most skilled craftsman in German cinema; but he's not a director whose films can be said to add up to an inimitable style." Yet most of his films can be brought under a single heading: literary adaptations. So Volker Schlöndorff was perhaps an ideal director for *The Tin Drum* (*Die Blechtrommel / Le Tambour*, 1979).

He learned his trade in the Paris of the Existentialists and the *Nouvelle Vague*. He assisted Jean-Pierre Melville and Louis Malle before making *Young Toerless* (*Der junge Törless / Les Désarrois de l'élève Törless*) in 1966 – based on a story by Robert Musil. The works of other great writers would follow: Heinrich von Kleist (*Michael Kohlhaas – der Rebell*, 1969), Marcel Proust (*Swann in Love / Eine Liebe von Swann / Un amour de Swann*, 1983), and Arthur Miller (*Death of a Salesman*, 1985). In the 70s, he turned his attention to the contemporary political scene. Together with his then-wife Margarethe von Trotta, he made *The Lost Honor of Katharina Blum* (*Die verlorene Ehre der Katharina Blum*, 1975), based on a short novel by Heinrich Böll. He then took part in a collective project involving directors such as Alexander Kluge, Rainer Werner Fassbinder and others: *Germany in Autumn* (*Deutschland im Herbst*, 1977/78) described the atmosphere in the country after the abduction of Hanns Martin Schleyer by the Red Army Faction, otherwise known as the Baader-Meinhof Group. In 1999, Schlöndorff returned to this theme, in the drama *Legends of Rita* (*Die Stille nach dem Schuss*), which tells the story of former terrorists gone to ground in East Germany.

"A very German fresco: world history seen and experienced from below. Huge, spectacular images, held together by tiny Oskar." *Volker Schlöndorff*

4   Maid to order: A bellybutton full of sherbet marks Oskar's first sexual experience with servant Maria (Katharina Thalbach).

5   Marching band: Oskar's musical interludes disrupt his mother's regular Thursday rendezvous with Jan.

6   An officer and a gentleman: Oskar falls in love with the midget Roswitha (Mariella Oliveri).

7   The joker's wild: Gambler and ladies' man, Jan Bronski (Daniel Olbrychski), is also an anti-fascist.

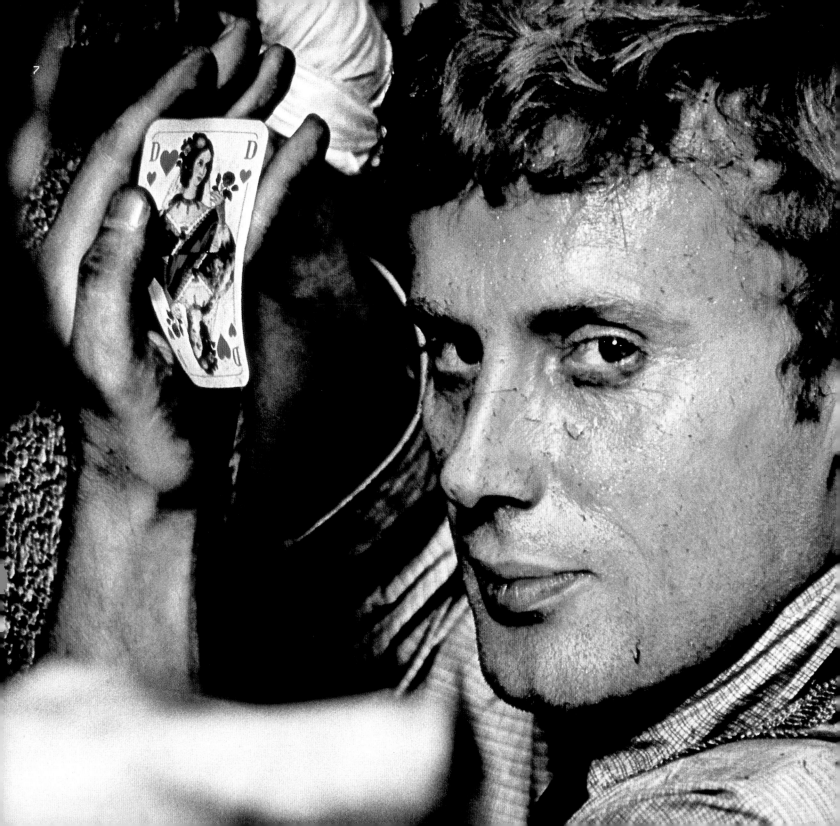

MAD MAX

1979 - AUSTRALIA - 93 MIN. - ACTION FILM, SCIENCE FICTION

DIRECTOR GEORGE MILLER (*1945) SCREENPLAY JAMES MCCAUSLAND, GEORGE MILLER
DIRECTOR OF PHOTOGRAPHY DAVID EGGBY EDITING TONY PATERSON, CLIFF HAYES MUSIC BRIAN MAY
PRODUCTION BYRON KENNEDY for MAD MAX FILMS, KENNEDY MILLER PRODUCTIONS,
CROSSROADS.

STARRING MEL GIBSON (Max Rockatansky), JOANNE SAMUEL (Jessie Rockatansky),
HUGH KEAYS-BYRNE (Toecutter), STEVE BISLEY (Jim Goose), ROGER WARD (Fifi Macaffee),
TIM BURNS (Johnny), VINCENT GIL (Nightrider), GEOFF PARRY (Bubba Zanetti), DAVID BRACKS
(Mudguts), PAUL JOHNSTONE (Cundalini).

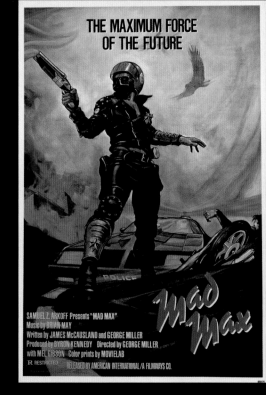

"You've seen it! ...
You've heard it! ...
and you're still asking questions?"

He's simply trying to make sense of it all, policeman Max Rockatansky (Mel Gibson) explains to his wife Jessie (Joanne Samuel), after one of his colleagues is burned alive by a marauding gang of rockers. But he is unable to unearth any explanation.

Max is not alone in his helplessness. Indeed, Australian director George Miller's low-budget production also gives the audience no explanation for the openly waged "war" between cops and rockers. A blend-in at the beginning of the film succinctly identifies the time and location of the plot: "Somewhere in the near future." A street sign on a dusty highway specifies that "Anarchy Road" stretches from this point on, and another sign displays the number of

spectacular car chase between the Nightrider (Vincent Gil), who has declared himself a gas-propelled suicide machine, and the custodians of the law, for whom the murderous race on the desolate country highways is apparently just as much fun as it is for the psychopathic rocker. After several spectacular stunts and half dozen crashes, he stalls — ultimately there is one obstacle too many on the highway.

Logic plays virtually no role in the story of the worn-down "Interceptor," Max, who turns into a merciless avenger after a band of bikers under the leadership of Toecutter (Hugh Keays-Byrne) murders his wife and child: although the adversaries never seek each other out, they continually

1 Officer down: When the highway's a battlefield, there are bound to be some casualties.

2 A light breather: Max (Mel Gibson) will stop at nothing to avenge his murdered family.

3 Remodeling: A rocker practices for the demolition derby.

"*Mad Max* is a Western. It has the same story, but instead of riding horses they are riding motorcycles and cars. People say the Western's dead, but it's not; it's become the car-action film." *Cinema Papers*

Though the plot of *Mad Max* could have sprung directly from a vengeance Western of the 1950s, the scenery and the characters have a comic-like stylization; the protagonists speak in memorable bubbles, and they are motivated by the basic joy of movement.

In a way, *Mad Max* seems like the final stopover in a string of films like Dennis Hopper's *Easy Rider* (1969) and Richard C. Safarian's *Vanishing Point* (1970), which at the beginning of the decade raised the car and/or motorcycle into the consummate expression of individual freedom. But in *Two-Lane Blacktop* (1971) director Monte Hellman had already signified the motormadness of his heroes as an element of their communication disorders. In *Mad Max*, all that is left for the protagonists is pointless violence.

But we should not label this as social criticism – the film is based on the commercial appeal of action and violence, and accentuates them as cleverly constructed highlights within the plot. Ultimately, it is an exploitative product.

Nonetheless, George Miller only seldom dramatizes the violence against people as the focal point of the images, with plot-related aspects remaining in the foreground (at one point a biker's arm is ripped off). Often the enormously violent and powerful impression of the film is a result of the dynamic montage. The most horrifying details are thus left to the viewer's imagination. In the scene in which the bikers kill Max's family, Jessie and the child run into the middle of the street while the rockers steadily approach on their bikes from the distance. After the edit, the bikers have already sped past the cam-

4

4 Car on the barbie: *Mad Max* has some grilling
   action scenes.

5 The bad boys of Melbourne: The future's tax col-
   lectors.

STUNTS A film like *Mad Max* (1979) certainly doesn't belong to those cinematic masterpieces noted for their sleek character portraits or philosophical depths. But even virulent opponents of the film are forced to recognize director George Miller's sovereign command of cinematic forms of expression and the technical brilliance of the stunts coordinated by Grant Page. Presented as a visual attraction, the circus-like perfection of the stunts points to the inception of the cinema – the markets and vaudeville shows where nickelodeons and cinematographs served as entertainment for a wide public. In the early days of the industry (in American films at least), stuntmen were simply extras who realized their chances of employment would increase if they mastered skills not everyone could master. In the labor-divided world of film, a profession quickly developed out of this realization that soon included not only the implementation of actor doubles in dangerous situations, but also the coordination (and dramatization) of action sequences. A special sort of daring was not required, but the opposite: technical perfection and risk minimization are paramount for the stunt coordinator – ultimately a botched take can cost the production not only money, but more importantly, the lives of the stuntmen.

era and Jessie's fate is simply suggested by a stray shoe that tumbles to the side of the road. And when Max belatedly arrives on the scene, the camera retains a wide shot – one can see him sinking over the corpses on the highway in the distance.

Mel Gibson was a completely unknown actor when he made his debut in the role of Max, as a star could not and would not have taken the risk of participating in the production. But the film offers its hero an exceptionally interesting entrance: Miller combines takes of Max's boots, gloves, leather gear, and sunglasses to create the mythical image of the cool policeman. And when we finally get to see the cop's face, we're almost surprised to look into

5

APOCALYPSE NOW ♟♟

1979 - USA - 153 MIN. - WAR FILM

DIRECTOR FRANCIS FORD COPPOLA (*1939) **SCREENPLAY** JOHN MILIUS, FRANCIS FORD COPPOLA, MICHAEL HERR (off-screen commentary), based on motifs from the novella *HEART OF DARKNESS* by JOSEPH CONRAD **DIRECTOR OF PHOTOGRAPHY** VITTORIO STORARO **EDITING** LISA FRUCHTMAN, GERALD B. GREENBERG, RICHARD MARKS, WALTER MURCH **MUSIC** CARMINE COPPOLA, FRANCIS FORD COPPOLA, THE DOORS (Song: "The End") **PRODUCTION** FRANCIS FORD COPPOLA for ZOETROPE CORPORATION, OMNI ZOETROPE.

STARRING MARLON BRANDO (Colonel Walter E. Kurtz), ROBERT DUVALL (Lieutenant Colonel William Kilgore), MARTIN SHEEN (Captain Benjamin L. Willard), FREDERIC FORREST "Chef" Jay Hicks), ALBERT HALL (Chief Quartermaster Phillips), SAM BOTTOMS Lance B. Johnson), LAURENCE FISHBURNE (Tyrone "Clean" Miller), DENNIS HOPPER Photo-journalist), G. D. SPRADLIN (General R. Corman), HARRISON FORD (Colonel G. Lucas).

ACADEMY AWARDS 1979 OSCARS for BEST CINEMATOGRAPHY (Vittorio Storaro), and BEST SOUND Walter Murch, Mark Berger, Richard Beggs, Nathan Boxer).

FF CANNES 1979 GOLDEN PALM (Francis Ford Coppola).

"I love the smell of napalm in the morning."

Vietnam, 1969. Captain Willard (Martin Sheen) is on a top-secret mission to find Colonel Kurtz (Marlon Brando), a highly decorated U.S. Army officer. And when he's located the man, his next task will be to kill him; for Kurtz has clearly gone mad, is defying the control of his superior officers, and now commands a private army in the jungle beyond the Cambodian border. His soldiers are a mixed bag of indigenous people, South Vietnamese, and rogue G.Is, who he uses to his own unauthorized and murderous ends. Willard boards a patrol boat and heads upriver through the rainforest in search of Kurtz; and the further he penetrates into the jungle, the more intensely he and his four comrades experience the horror of war.

No other movie of the 70s received so much attention before it was even released. Francis Ford Coppola was the first director to risk making a big-budget film about the Vietnam War, and he did so with almost demonstrative independence. As his own production company American Zoetrope financed the film, *Apocalypse Now* could be made without the usual assistance – and interference – from the Pentagon. (Even today, such help is practically obligatory when a war film is made in the United States.) Coppola said later that he had originally aimed to make a lucrative action movie. Instead,

the film became an unparalleled nightmare for the celebrated director of *The Godfather* (1972) – and not just in financial terms.

Coppola was looking for a country with a climate similar to Vietnam's so he chose to film in the Philippines. As the necessary infrastructure was lacking, conditions were quite hair-raising from the word go. The military equipment, for instance, was the result of a deal with the dictatorial President Marcos, who was fighting a civil war against communist rebels while the film was being made. As a consequence, helicopters were sometimes requisitioned from the set at short notice and sent off by the military to take part in real battles. Conditions as tough as these made it hard to find stars willing to take part. Initially, the role of Willard was taken by Harvey Keitel, but he was replaced by the little-known Martin Sheen after only three weeks' filming, as his expressive acting was not to Coppola's taste, and he wanted a more passive protagonist. This was an expensive mistake, but harmless in comparison to the problems the director would later face. There was the deadly typhoon that destroyed the expensive sets; the almost fatal heart attack suffered by Martin Sheen; the difficulty of working with the grossly overweight Brando and above all, the trouble caused by the director's own constant departures

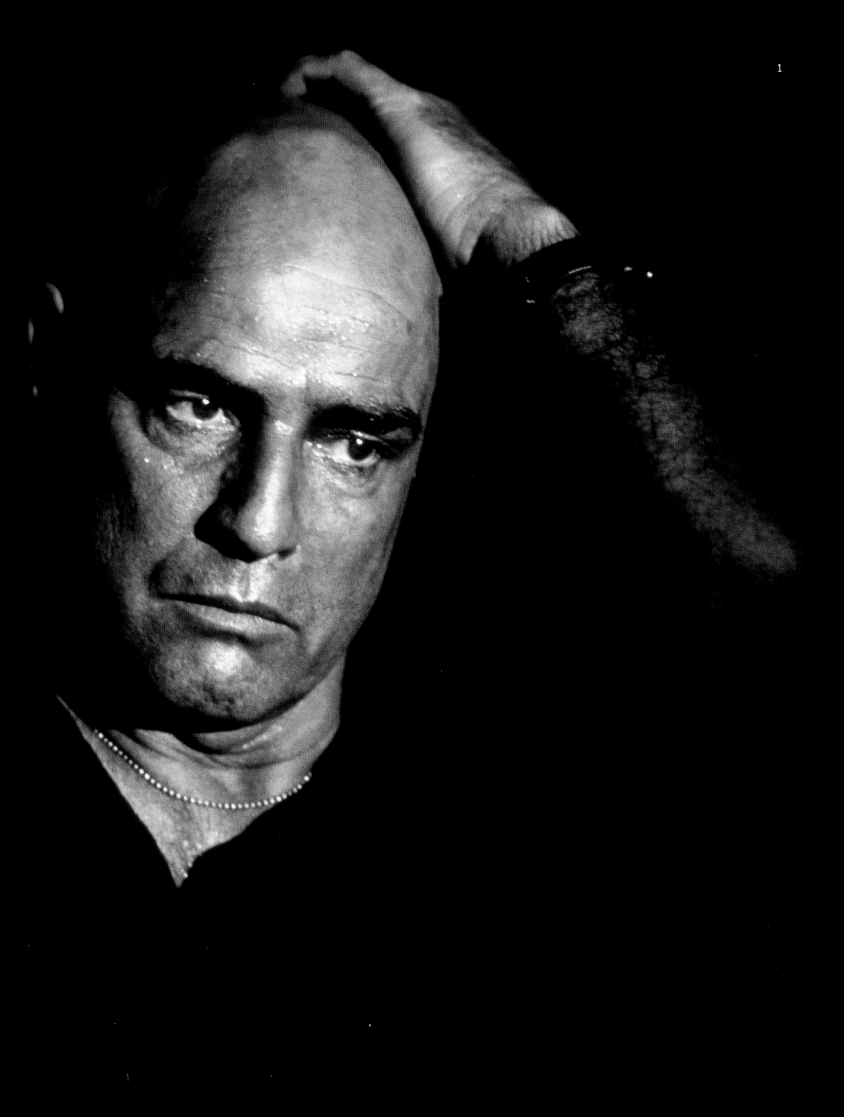

2

1   Tribal titan: Marlon Brando rocked the screen in his role as Colonel Kurtz although he only appeared at the end of the movie.

2   Battle of the Bulge: Captain Willard (Martin Sheen) and the photographer (Dennis Hopper) flesh out the fate of Colonel Kurtz.

3   Duty calls: Filmed on location in the Philippines, *Apocalypse Now's* helicopter was taken off the set and flown into the front lines of battle.

"My film is not a movie. My film is not about Vietnam. It is Vietnam. That's what it was really like. It was crazy."

Francis Ford Coppola, IFF Cannes

from the script. As a result, work had to stop on several occasions, and the filming period expanded from four to 15 months. Soon, the 16 million dollar budget was exhausted, and Coppola – close to physical and mental collapse – was forced to mortgage his own property in order to raise the same sum all over again. The press could smell a disaster of previously unheard of proportions. But though two more years were taken up by post-production, the film ultimately became a box-office hit – despite mixed reviews, and the fact that other "Vietnam movies" had by then already reached the screen.

The legendary status of *Apocalypse Now* is inseparable from the spectacular circumstances of its making. Many people, including Coppola himself, have drawn an analogy between the Vietnam conflict itself and the agonized struggle to complete the film. It's all the more remarkable, then

that Coppola succeeded in freeing himself, gradually but radically, from the superficial realism that tends to typify the war-film genre. The Vietnam War has often been described as a psychedelic experience, but Coppola and his cameraman Vittorio Storaro created images that actually do justice to the description. Willard's trip upriver, inspired by Joseph Conrad's novella *Heart of Darkness*, is a journey into the darkness of his own heart, and so the various stages on his journey acquire an increasingly fantastic, dreamlike quality. At the beginning of his odyssey, Willard encounters the surfing fanatic Lieutenant Colonel Kilgore (Robert Duvall), who sends his squad of choppers in to obliterate a peasant village so that he can enjoy the perfect waves on the neighboring beach. Kilgore's insane euphoria is heightened by the musical accompaniment: Wagner's "Ride of the Valkyrie." At this point, Willard is

4

no more than a passive observer of a monstrous spectacle, which is ironically depicted by Coppola as a kind of hi-tech U.S. Cavalry. It's a grimly satirical scene, in which the director makes masterly use of aesthetic conventions
for his own purposes.

Willard's journey terminates in a realm of the dead: Kurtz's bizarre and
bloody jungle kingdom, a garishly exotic and obscenely theatrical hell-on-
earth. As embodied by Marlon Brando, Kurtz has the quality of a perverted
Buddha. When he first receives Willard in his murky temple residence, both
men are sunk in the surrounding shadows. At the end of the line, in the heart
of darkness, good and evil have grown indistinguishable, and Willard has lost
what distance he ever had; Kurtz has become part of his very self. When

Willard finally kills him, the act – like an archaic ritual – is at once an exor-
cism and a manifestation of the darkness at the heart of mankind, a black
stain no civilization will ever erase. Ultimately, it's the cause and the irre-
ducible essence of war – whatever the epoch, and whatever the weapons
deployed.

In 2001, Coppola brought out *Apocalypse Now Redux*, a director's cut
that was 49 minutes longer. It contains some sequences that had fallen
victim to the cutter's shears, and the director says it's the closest possible
approximation to his original intentions. Yet although the *Redux* version is
undoubtedly somewhat more complex than the original, it constitutes neither
a radical alteration to, nor a significant improvement on the original.   JH

5

4   The river wild: Civilization on a voyage down-
    stream.

5   The buck stops here: Having made it to the end of
    his journey, Willard is prepared to kill Colonel Kurtz.

"It is not so much an epic account of a grueling war as an incongruous, extravagant monument to artistic self-defeat." *Time Magazine*

FRANCIS FORD COPPOLA   Francis Ford Coppola (*7.4.1939 in Detroit) enjoyed a sheltered middle-class childhood in a suburb of New York. His father Carmine was a composer and musician who would later write the music to some of his son's films. Coppola at first studied theatre at the Hofstra University, then film
at UCLA. While still a student, he worked as an assistant director to Roger Corman, who also produced his first feature film, *Dementia 13* (1963).
Coppola made his breakthrough at the early age of 31, when his screenplay to *Patton* (1969) was awarded the Oscar.
A short time later, he was also world-famous as a director – and as the Boy Wonder of the New Hollywood: the Mafia saga *The Godfather* (1972)
became one of the biggest hits in movie history and won three Oscars, including Best Film. Two years later, he topped even this: *The Godfather –
Part II* (1974) scooped six Academy Awards – including Best Director. In the meantime, Coppola had also made an outstanding movie about an alien-
ated surveillance expert: *The Conversation* (1974), which carried off the Golden Palm at the Cannes Festival.
In 1976, Coppola began work on the Vietnam film *Apocalypse Now* (1979), which he produced himself, and which came very close to ruining him.
But after four years in production, that film also won the Golden Palm and two Oscars, and even recouped the huge sum that had been spent making it. Only two years later, however, the failure of the love story *One from the Heart* (1981) drove him into such horrendous debt that he was forced
to sell his production company, American Zoetrope. Though he has since directed other films, such as *The Cotton Club* (1984) and *The Godfather –
Part III* (1990), none have been as successful as his huge hits of the 70s.

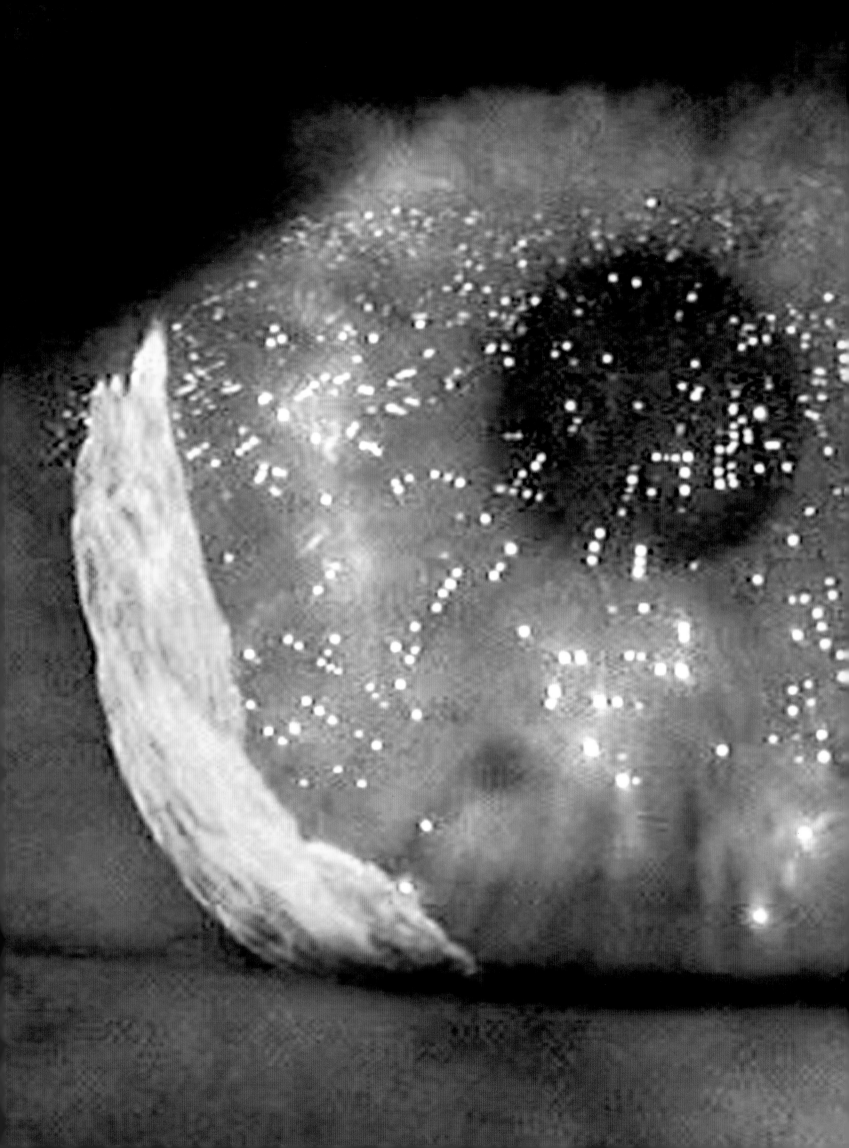

THE 80s
THE CINEMA OF SURFACES

THE CINEMA OF SURFACES
Notes on the Movies of the 80s

.

A city spews fire. The black sky above Los Angeles is rocked by countless explosions. Fireballs erupt from factory smokestacks, the air itself seems to shudder and groan; futuristic flying machines swoop through the city, and a bolt of lightning slashes the horizon. So much light… and yet the darkness seems immune, unscathed, impenetrable. Very close up, the next explosion; and then, as if to counterbalance this vast urban panorama, we see a single human eye, the city lights glittering on its shiny surface. A watchful eye – perhaps the eye of the beholder as such – filling the entire screen; and this eye itself is in turn a kind of screen, or mirror, impassively reflecting the fireballs that loom above the city.

The next shot shows a colossal building complex: two pyramids, symbols of knowledge, power and death. The eye appears again, now recalling an Egyptian hieroglyph. In fact, it is everything at once: a sensory organ, a projection screen and a symbol. The iris lies at its center like an ebony sun, surrounded by starbursts of reflected light. The eye is itself a universe, whole and entire. Even at the start of *Blade Runner* (1982, p. 680), microcosm and macrocosm are mixed, mutually dependent, indivisible.

Gradually, the camera edges in on the pyramids. We peer through a narrow window; inside, a ventilator, a strangely antiquated device in this futuris-tic megalopolis, sluggishly churns the smoky air. The smoker (Morgan Paull) is almost concealed by the smoke; these dense cigarette fumes are his territorial markings and his hiding place. "Next test," announces the loudspeaker. We see that this room is just one among many identical cell-like compartments. The test subject (Brion James), "Leon Kowalski, Waste Management Technician," steps out of the shadows and into the shot, most likely a new employee undergoing a routine initial personal evaluation.

"Come in. Sit down." We are in the personnel department of the Tyrell Corporation – and are immediately confronted with another ominous eye. This time, however, it is the artificial eye of a camera that locks focus on Leon's pupil. This more familiar eye, in turn, shows up on an observation monitor. Following his line of questioning, the sadistic Tyrell Corporation tester deduces that Kowalski is a replicant, a masterpiece of genetic engineering virtually indistinguishable from a human being. The unfortunate tester pays for this discovery with his life.

In this interrogation sequence, Ridley Scott draws a parallel between the human eye and the camera – nature's original and technology's copy. Eye and camera blend and overlap in the course of the scene, as if to demonstrate the origin of one in the other. And each does more than generate mere

images of reality: in both the camera and the eye, where the inner and the outer worlds meet and mingle, perception and identity are organized.

In the 80s, as in no other decade before, filmmakers tackled the very foundation of film aesthetics: the physical and psychic constraints of *seeing*. They set themselves the task of making sight itself visible. Ridley Scott's opening sequence in *Blade Runner* articulates – indeed, realizes – one of the central aspirations of 80s cinema: that a film be more than a mere image; that it create its own aesthetic reality and follow its own laws.

If *Blade Runner* now seems the most significant cult film of the 80s, there are two main reasons for this. First and foremost, the film is filled with breathtaking images of a not-so-distant and not too implausible future. Secondly, it deals with the fundamental question of what it means to be human. It does so in an entirely novel and unexpected manner, without a trace of pretension or false profundity, and the story it tells is gripping. Against his will, the former blade runner Deckard (Harrison Ford) is compelled to hunt down a small group of renegade replicants who have illegally infiltrated the Earth in the hope of extending their genetically preprogrammed, four year lease on life. A "blade runner" is nothing more than a headhunter, something that the sleazy cop Bryant (M. Emmet Walsh) insinuates at the top of the film when he mentions the "skin job" he has lined up for Deckard. The search for the replicants begins, and the director shows us Los Angeles as we've never seen it before.

Critics have often emphasized *Blade Runner*'s sheer visual brilliance, while noting the extent to which the film was influenced by a variety of predecessors. Fritz Lang's *Metropolis* (p. 64), dating back to 1925–26, usually heads the list. This was one of the first films to raise the issue of "artificial humans," and to question the hubris of attempting to create a perfect example of the human species.

The world we are shown in *Blade Runner* knows no difference between day and night. Darkness is constant. With the disappearance of daylight, every last trace of naturalness has become a thing of the past. In this cinematic dystopia, the only sources of light are synthetic. Even the city's immense buildings provide little help in orientation, for the searchlight rays that cross the sky reveal no more than fragments of skyscrapers in the ambient gloom. Here, light and form are inseparable. Giant illuminated billboards are the only visible signs, and the nearest thing to landmarks in this city.

Like light and form, cultures are merging, mixing and congealing; the world's languages have evolved into a bizarre *lingua franca*, a linguistic hodgepodge. Motion itself has changed: in this clogged, overpopulated Babylon, "normal" traffic has become a thing of the past; vehicles have to take off vertically to get anywhere at all. Most of us would be lost in this urban jungle, where inner and outer space, ethnicity and national identity have all been lost in the shuffle.

Man and Superman

Despite the film's tangible desire to overwhelm the audience with images, this imaginary journey to the city of tomorrow also has its philosophical ambitions. Critics did not fail to notice that the protagonist's name – Deckard – evokes that of the French philosopher René Descartes, who claimed to have proved with certainty that human beings can know they exist. The allusion becomes explicit when the replicant Pris (Daryl Hannah) casually pronounces Descartes' signature dictum: "I think, therefore I am." Later, the leader of the replicants, Roy (Rutger Hauer), is granted a closing monolog in which he quotes a poem by Nietzsche that invokes the grandeur and beauty of an infinite universe. Roy's very appearance – blond, athletic, larger-than-life – is reminiscent of the *Übermensch* imagined by Nietzsche.

These philosophical allusions have a common point of departure. Behind the ideas of self-knowledge and the superman, there is an implicit understanding that humanity's ultimate goal and true destiny is to achieve perfection. In the final moments of his life, Roy rejects all this, voicing his willingness to eschew immortality and embrace death. Though all the wonders he has witnessed will disappear with him "like tears in the rain," he can still justify his existence in aesthetic terms. As in Nietzsche's poem, the replicant's ability to perceive the overwhelming splendor of the universe bears

witness to his inalienable dignity. Indeed, in the final showdown between Deckard and Roy that precedes this monolog, it becomes clear that the replicants are in fact the better humans. They can do without the class distinctions that separate "natural" from "artificial" beings – and in the end Roy goes so far as to save his enemy's life.

Scott's film appeared in two different versions. The first accompanied the picture's theatrical release in the 1980s, followed by a director's cut that came out in the 90s. The second version lends even more weight to the supposition that Deckard is himself a replicant. This thesis finds its clearest proof halfway through the film, when Deckard dreams of a unicorn, symbol of freedom and innocence. But the dream is in fact no more than a "memory implant." The truth dawns on the viewer in the film's closing sequence, when Deckard discovers a shiny silver origami unicorn on the floor in front of his apartment. It is immediately clear that the policeman Gaff (Edward James Olmos) must have searched Deckard's rooms, but left the blade runner's sleeping replicant girlfriend Rachael (Sean Young) unscathed – in order to give the couple a chance.

Gaff, a character who is initially depicted in a negative light, embodies a wide range of identities; he is a melange of various races, languages and cultures. By finally putting a positive slant on Gaff, the film comes down in favor of a multi-cultural society that unites and integrates the peoples and languages of the earth.

In its underlying fatalism, *Blade Runner* is clearly inspired by film noir. The mood of the "dark films" which characterized the 40s is an ideal vehicle for the film's epistemological skepticism, the notion that the future will hold no natural or verifiable truths. In the year 2019, Los Angeles is either too bright or too dark. Instead of illuminating, the light blinds. There is nothing but darkness and back-light. This stylistic technique, so typical of Ridley Scott, creates some tremendously potent images, whose very effectiveness supports the film's fundamental skepticism regarding any kind of knowledge or self-knowledge, for we can never know that the self that remembers is really remembering the same self (quite apart from the fact that it's always possible to manipulate people).

Blade Runner might well be subtitled: "An Apology (in the old sense) for Superficies (in the literal sense)." This also goes some way towards explaining why it became such a cult icon in the 80s, a decade in which many directors were obsessed with the surfaces of things. These surfaces, however, are not always recognizable as such. They conceal themselves – like mirrors in the act of reflection, or like the moving images on a TV screen; as long as we are not reminded of the screen's edges we can maintain the illusion that we are genuinely experiencing reality. An interest in surfaces is anything but superficial – although many a critic would have us believe otherwise – for we can only begin to develop an aesthetics of surfaces if we approach the topic with a measure of humility. And in this context, humility means admitting and embracing the relativity and subjectivity of perception.

The replicants' physical appearance allows us no certainty as to whether they are artifacts or "natural" living creatures. And this has a broader significance; for a clear unprejudiced view of *any* aspect of reality is almost as difficult to achieve. What we know depends on what we see; and whether we like it or not, we look at the world through tinted glasses. In this respect, it makes little difference whether our view is colored by our ethnic origin, gender, ideology or most personal desires.

The Dream Machine

Blade Runner is an excellent example of the rapidly growing interest, throughout the 80s, in cinema's peerless capacity to create illusions. While some expressed unease at the knowledge that film and television narratives are merely second-hand realities, others delighted in the power of cinematic spectacles to erase the real world – if only temporarily – from our consciousness. In any case, the decade was marked by an increased questioning of the cinema's means, methods and conventions, and by a close examination of the defining characteristics of cinematic fiction. The renaissance of science fiction movies, for example, was largely due to new developments in technology that made it possible to create ever more perfect illusions. However, this industrialized magic is something that film critics have had more than a little trouble coming to terms with.

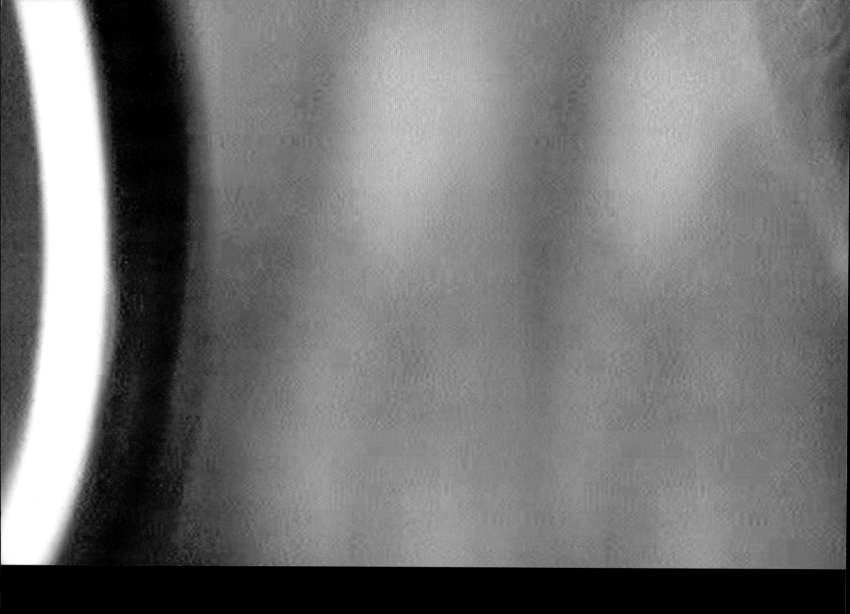

The flawless production design exhibited in movies like *Aliens* (1986), *Total Recall* (1990), *Dune* (1984), *Star Wars: Episode VI – The Return of the Jedi* (1983), *E. T. the Extra-Terrestrial* (1982), *Outland* (1981) and *Back to the Future* (1985) still exhilarates audiences to this very day. All of these films went to extraordinary lengths to create impeccable and unprecedented parallel universes.

Action extravaganzas such as *Lethal Weapon 2* (1989) and *Die Hard* (1987, p. 584) also exploded with miraculous special effects. *F/X* (1985) went so far as to turn the artistry behind visual effects into the subject matter of a blood-curdling thriller. Film publications of the time increasingly focused on the mysterious world of special effects. Yet audiences were not simply succumbing helplessly to the seductive power of the cinematic fantasy. They were discovering and understanding this very potential as a thrilling *subject* for the movies themselves. In short, the decade reinstated high-caliber visual standards and showed a staunch refusal to shy away from spectacle. For the 80s, the cinema was a time machine and a factory of perfect illusions.

The two directors mainly responsible for this shift had established themselves in Hollywood in the 70s. While Steven Spielberg and George Lucas exploited the medium's newfound technical capabilities, they were also willing to resort to crowd-pleasing stock content. If it helped to lure the audience away from the television and back into the theater – so be it. These two filmmakers could evoke a character's fear of heights so effectively that the spectators felt dizzy in their seats. Movies were designed to mesmerize, indeed to overwhelm their audiences; when the house lights were switched on, the spectators should stumble out of the theater, weak at the knees.

When *Star Wars* (1977, p. 606) was released in the late 70s, it was the first in a long line of films to be accompanied by a massive merchandising campaign – the movie as a commercial for itself, so to speak. But only in the 80s did the "blockbuster" become the rule rather the exception. If a film drew the crowds, a sequel was inevitable. The cinema's lost audience was wooed away from television by fast and noisy films that took conscious advantage of the medium's expanding technical possibilities and the unique pleasures of the big-screen experience.

The popularity of the *Indiana Jones* trilogy (1981, 1984, 1988) had little to do with an original storyline. Even before the curtains opened, audiences knew everything would turn out all right in the end. But the plot's predictability detracts nothing from the viewing experience. The audience still has disgusting spiders, unnerving mummies, sadistic villains and countless chase sequences to look forward to. According to Spielberg's stylistic canon, a fast basic tempo with a consistently accelerating momentum is second only to a spectacular opening.

Spielberg's editing technique is superb: just when it seems the tension has to break, he turns the screw a notch further. In Spielberg's adventure films, exaggeration is a matter of principle. It's not enough for Indiana Jones to slip under the descending stone door and barely escape with his life; no,

the director insists on making him reach back under the door to rescue his hat! Film historian Tom Gunning once referred to the industry's early years as the "cinema of attractions" – and the 80s made no attempt to conceal film's lowly origin as a sideshow sensation.

Spielberg's movies of the 80s demonstrate that the cinema is more than just another way of telling a story. The power of the image is of the very

progressively ascending camera as well as the aforementioned editing tech niques revisited in *Raiders of the Lost Ark*. We are intrigued by the tycoon' labyrinth of accumulated treasure – an image of his baffling life – but ar equally aware of what an arduous, nearly impossible task it would be to fin anything tucked away in these walls. Spielberg's intelligent and unpreten tious tribute to Welles is really no more than a sly wink to the audience, reg

ing his greatest triumph with the widely acclaimed *The Last Emperor* (1987). Britain's film business enjoyed a vibrant renaissance, with a generation of directors fired by a passionate opposition to Thatcherism. This interest in politics was something of an anomaly in the European cinema of the time. The "New British Cinema" declared open war on the culture of greed, and directors such as Stephen Frears and Ken Loach produced some politically provocative pieces of film. But the most radical innovations in "ways of seeing" were achieved in the work of Peter Greenaway and Pedro Almodóvar.

In the United States, Jim Jarmusch became the dominant figure in independent cinema, and his influence on European filmmakers is undeniable. The work of the Finnish director Aki Kaurismäki is a case in point: much like Jarmusch's, his films can be seen as a challenge to Hollywood's aesthetic canon. Kaurismäki's laconic heroes are travelers without a destination, people who put attitude before action. Both these directors have a notable liking for long shots and a stationary camera.

In Germany, too, it is hard to identify a common trend. *Fitzcarraldo* (1981, p. 662) was one of Werner Herzog's finest films, while Wim Wenders' *Paris, Texas* (1984) marked a highpoint in the director's mastery of form. The producer Bernd Eichinger became a major player in German cinema, and many of his films have proven their international appeal. As the decade drew to a close, Doris Dörrie's *Men* (*Männer*, 1985) marked the beginning of a

comedy boom that would continue to dominate the German market right into the 90s.

France witnessed a kind of *rapprochement* between Hollywood and the European tradition. The *cinéma du look* pioneered by Jean-Jacques Beineix and Luc Besson marked the arrival of design as an autonomous mode of cinematic expression. This artificial "neon cinema" was an attempt by the younger generation to create original myths and to make a clean break with the intellectual tradition of French film. It was this aesthetic stance that made Beineix and Besson perhaps the most representative figures of their time. All of which goes to show that we can neither speak of a "European cinema" *per se* – nor of any specifically identifiable, monolithic "European audience."

As ever, film criticism in the 80s continued to pit art against commerce. Directors were accused of preferring empty form to substantial content and flashy effects to serious art. These accusations were also targeted at ambitious large-scale productions whose artistic value is now doubted by few people seriously interested in film. One American critic wrote that the exorbitant sum of money Terry Gilliam spent on *Brazil* (1984) had hurt the project more than it helped it, adducing an alleged excess of whimsical ideas as evidence of a "general lack of discipline." *Blade Runner*, too, was sharply criticized for its extreme stylization. The grand illusionists, however, were quite unfazed. Ridley Scott made a robust defense of his film's mannerist style and

the unabashed artificiality of the world he had created: "Sometimes the design is the statement."

It was impossible for the cinema of the 80s to be a medium of enlightenment, for it was less interested in ideas and convictions than in its own seductive power. So it's no accident that directors from the world of advertising, such as Adrian Lyne and Alan Parker, made their mark in the movies by using an extremely stylized cinematic vocabulary with great suggestive force. The brazen artificiality of the Hong Kong cinema also began to attract American and European audiences. Some suggested these films were no more than the slick products of admen and aesthetes addicted to flashy effects. Whether these accusations were justified remains an open question.

In the case of Adrian Lyne's *Jacob's Ladder* (1990), the complaints won't stick. Here, the film's artificiality is a means of rendering the world as seen through the eyes of the Vietnam veteran played by Tim Robbins. His vision is sometimes painfully clear, sometimes fogged and feverish. The audience is intentionally left in the dark as to whether the character is suffering a mental illness or the after-effects of some laboratory-developed drug. Suffice it to say that what's really behind his visions turns out to be a great deal more shocking than either of these possibilities.

In Alan Parker's *Birdy* (1984), certain scenes are saturated with an unreal blue light. These sequences have no intention of providing a naturalistic or realistic view of the world. Instead, they lead the audience into the protagonist's mind. In the end, it's hardly possible to say where his imagination ends and the "real" world begins. Parker's film is an ambitious attempt to depict reality as a subjective state, for his protagonist's world is slippery, not solid, and entirely dependent on mood or situation.

Michael Mann's *Thief / Violent Streets* (1981) demonstrates how a character's entire inner life can be conveyed by means of lighting effects. The overhead lamps at a car dealership become a star-filled sky, and the sparks from a welding torch are a sudden manifestation of joy. Practically the entire film takes place on wet streets in darkness. Many scenes play against a background of display window glass, where reflections of the interiors merge with the light from the street. The hero, a safecracker played by James Caan, has spent most of his life in jail, and now he's on the run again, with both the police and the Mafia hot on his heels. It seems as if his efforts to build up a life of his own are doomed from the very start. Mann drives this home by conjuring up a diffuse limbo, in which the borders between the internal and the external worlds fluctuate and blur. At the film's conclusion, the lights that swish across the hood of a moving car evoke the irrevocable collapse of the safecracker's world. This dissolution of the boundary between the inner and the outer worlds can be observed in many movies of the time, with the camera showing the world through the eyes of the protagonists. In short: the adoption of a subjective point of view is characteristic of 80s cinema.

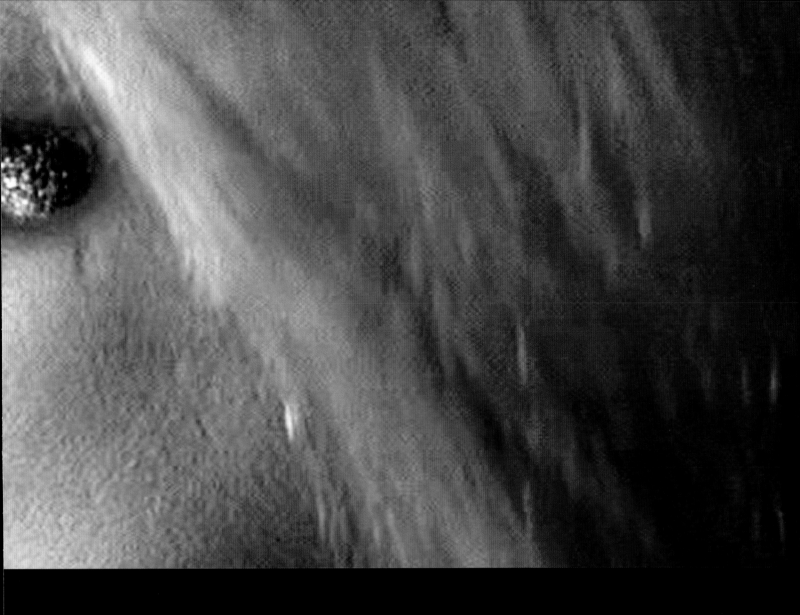

Peckinpah wove a complex cat's cradle out of government red tape, in which it soon becomes impossible to tell who is actually conspiring against whom. Here, even the weather report cannot be taken at face value.

If we grant gadgetry an ever-increasing role in the acquisition of data on our environment, how much will it begin to influence our own perspective on the world? Is the technology nothing more than a means of representing the world? Or have synthetically generated images long since become the blueprint for our own perceptions and memories? In an age in which technology expands the horizons of possibility, film is an art form dedicated to testing the limits of human perception. So it should come as no surprise to us that movies have continued to voice the suspicion that life itself is nothing more than a brilliantly fabricated illusion.

Metamorphosis and Transgression

Besides evincing a fundamental pessimism about the limits of human knowledge and a general fear of deception, this underlying paranoia can also be expressive of a critical attitude towards society. In *Wall Street* (1987, p. 606), Oliver Stone depicts a young stockbroker (Charlie Sheen) learning a few of life's harder lessons. In the process, he comes to see that the world in which he lives and the goals to which he has aspired are nothing more than a sham.

The stylish interiors, the designer desks, the well-groomed surfaces of the people and the objects cannot conceal the nihilism at the heart of it all. This is a world in which everything is sacrificed, irretrievably, to profit. An abstract painting serves as a symbol for this inner and outer void, when Gordon Gekko (Michael Douglas) finds only one thing worthy of mention: the picture's appreciated value. Standing in front of this work of art, he gives his "protégé" a lesson in capitalism. "Illusion has become reality, and the more real it gets, the more strongly it is desired." In the context of the film, these words refer to the absurd, deranged world of the stockmarket traders, but they could equally well apply to the development of the cinema in the 80s. Oliver Stone is entirely capable of playing on both interpretations.

In any case, as always, the audience wants to have its cake and eat it. Movies are expected not only to expose illusions, but first and foremost to create them. The audience wants to see heroes: lone freedom fighters like *Die Hard*'s John McClane, bosom buddies like sergeants Martin Riggs and Roger Murtaugh in *Lethal Weapon* (1987). Yet most of all, moviegoers want to see characters who have been touched by the hand of fate and granted a golden opportunity to shed their petty human limitations and achieve the impossible.

A prime specimen is the frustrated businessman who combats insomnia by combing the city streets. From out of nowhere, a strange woman quite literally "lands" on the hood of his car. Pursued by an armed gang, the man

gallantly helps her escape. Like it or not, the duo must stick together in the hopes of outrunning a mysterious and seemingly all-powerful enemy. Again and again, they succeed in escaping; by the time his odyssey concludes, the hero will see his life through new eyes. We too will see him differently, and perhaps even ourselves as well. This is the very stuff that 80s myths are made of.

John Landis shot *Into the Night* in 1984. The cathartic journey through an unknown world and the encounter with the stranger constituted something close to a shared obsession for the directors of the 80s. In *After Hours* (1985), Martin Scorsese has an IT expert wander the streets of a Kafkaesque New York. In *Something Wild* (1987), Jonathan Demme sends a stodgy businessman the woman of his dreams, who almost drives him insane. In Susan Seidelman's *Desperately Seeking Susan* (1984), a bored housewife loses her memory and finds that there's a whole lot more to life than what home cooking and advice columnists have to offer. The list of films that follow this pattern could easily be extended.

One could interpret this phenomenon as a reaction against the prevailing values of the Reagan era, a rebellion against the dictatorship of normalcy, career and family. And yet the narrative structure of all these films is thoroughly classical. Near the beginning of the film, the main character is confronted with a peculiar situation that threatens to throw his or her life off balance, a crisis which indicates an inner conflict that can only be resolved

by directly addressing the external hazard. Here, we have the fundamental structure of every exciting story in a nutshell.

If this seems to clash with our thesis of a Cinema of Surfaces, the conflict is merely apparent. For when the pressure to conform becomes too great and the outward appearances of things acquire such normative force, the need inevitably arises to pierce through the surface, to take a look behind the foreboding curtain and unmask the powers and mechanisms at work there. The protagonists of the films just listed are paradigmatic heroes, our proxies on the mythical journey to an alien world – a gaudy, threatening and seductive microcosm in which they will finally encounter and face up to themselves.

The alien world can assume a wide variety of forms. It can be a menacing paradise, as in Sydney Pollack's *Out of Africa* (1985) or a hidden yet omnipresent hell on earth, as in David Lynch's *Blue Velvet* (1985). Whatever its precise nature, it is a testing ground for the protagonist, the place where the hero or heroine will be forced to transcend the limitations of the workaday personality. In Alan Parker's music film *The Wall* (1982), these limitations are manifested in the image of the insurmountable wall that had to be destroyed – even at the risk of incurring self-annihilation in the process. The film was based on Pink Floyd's concept-album of the same name, itself a significant creation in its time.

The need for self-transcendence is reflected even more clearly in a number of films that deal with the topic of metamorphosis. In Woody Allen's

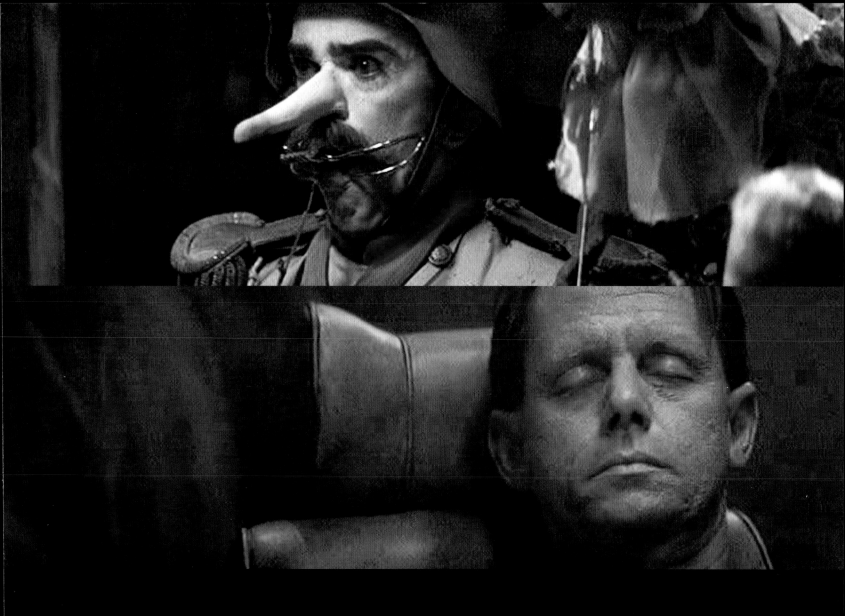

Zelig (1983), a human chameleon develops a desire to identify his true self. In Sydney Pollack's *Tootsie* (1982), the protagonist, played by Dustin Hoffman, can only achieve his full potential by impersonating a woman. Penny Marshall's *Big* (1988) is a fairy-tale take on the transformation theme: a mechanical fortune-teller at a carnival grants a young boy's wish to grow up immediately. He finds it fun, for a while, but his return to harsh reality is as inevitable as it is for the spectator in the cinema.

The examples invoked so far would seem to suggest that the 80s were a decade obsessed with the desire to be something other than what one actually is. Yet it would be easy to compile an equally long list of movies that warn of the dangers of succumbing to such a wish. These films might be said to embody the guilty conscience of escapist fantasy – the voice of morality in 80s cinema, or of reaction, depending on one's point of view. Examples that come to mind include Adrian Lyne's *Fatal Attraction* (1987), in which Dan Gallagher (Michael Douglas) goes through matrimonial hell for his sin of adultery. David Cronenberg's *The Fly* (1985) bears the same kind of message, though here it's voiced in a blatantly sarcastic tone. Anyone who transgresses the boundaries set by nature is found to be guilty of hubris; and in *The Fly*, the proud sinner's punishment is – literally – creeping dissolution.

The unexpected is seen not only as an opportunity but also as a threat. A diffuse feeling of menace haunted the 80s. Domestic politics stagnated while the atomic superpowers held each other at bay, and a dramatic rise in

epidemics culminated in the plague of AIDS. Politicians called for a return to the traditional values of home and family. Yet interestingly – and perhaps strangely in such a climate of social and political tension – the unexpected was increasingly felt to be lurking in the most intimate refuge we possess: in our very selves. Alan Parker's *Angel Heart* (1986) showed a particularly chilling voyage of negative self-discovery, in which the protagonist is forced to realize that his identity is an illusion and that he is nothing more than an instrument of the devil.

In Search of the Lost Secret

It's astonishing how decades so recent can yet seem centuries away. Weren't the 80s thoroughly anti-classical – and less secure than the 70s in matters of taste? And don't the 80s now seem naïve and colorful compared to the cool, elegant decade the 90s tried so hard to be?

We proposed the paradigm of the Surface as the key to understanding the movies of the 80s. The related problems of appearance and reality, true and false identities, aestheticism and the neglect of narrative might of course be pursued further. And it goes without saying that there are other ideas one could explore that might prove equally illuminating. More emphasis might well be placed on just how conservative the decade was, more space might

be devoted to noting how reactionary so many films were, and how indelibly the 80s were marked by the presidency of Ronald Reagan. *First Blood* (1982), *Aliens* (1986), and *Top Gun* (1985) are some of the prime examples that come to mind.

Still, it would be unfair to reduce the 80s to this. Instead of harping on the baleful influence of political stagnation – a perspective on the decade that would force us to see the films as mere compensation mechanisms – we should embrace the escapism, take pleasure in the anarchy and thoroughly enjoy the paranoia. Perhaps the decade's finest achievement was its mistrust of any claim to absolute truth, and its self-liberation from the stranglehold of ideologies.

The 80s were a decade for adventurers, some of them visionaries, and some, perhaps, vainglorious. But what all these films have in common is their desire to restore mystery to the world; and so we will conclude this introduction by recalling the opening scene of Ingmar Bergman's great family chronicle, *Fanny and Alexander* (*Fanny och Alexander*, 1982, p. 668) – a panorama of the turn of the century, and a tale of two childhoods. A frightened boy is running through a house in search of his family. He calls out their names, one by one: "Fanny?! ... Mama?! ... Edith?!," and – finally – "Papa?!" Where are the others? Is he really at home by himself? Has something terrible happened? Have they gone on a trip and forgotten to take him along? Anything is imaginable ... but in reality, Alexander is just playing

make-believe. He's pretending to be alone, abandoned by everyone. And indeed, by the end of the film we will have come to understand that Alexander's imagination more accurately reflects reality than our adult "common sense" would have us believe. In the final scene, his grandmother reads aloud from August Strindberg's *A Dream Play*, summing up the entire plot with its mysterious cast of characters, in words that also encapsulate the cinema of the 1980s: "[in a dream] anything can happen, everything is possible and plausible. Time and space do not exist. Upon an insignificant background of real life events, the imagination spins and weaves new patterns; a blend of memories, experiences, pure inventions, absurdities and improvisations."

Jürgen Müller / Steffen Haubner

RAGING BULL 🏆🏆

1980 - USA - 129 MIN. - BOXING FILM, BIOPIC, DRAMA

DIRECTOR MARTIN SCORSESE (*1942) SCREENPLAY PAUL SCHRADER, MARDIK MARTIN from the autobiography of JAKE LA MOTTA together with JOSEPH CARTER and PETER SAVAGE
DIRECTOR OF PHOTOGRAPHY MICHAEL CHAPMAN EDITING THELMA SCHOONMAKER MUSIC PIETRO MASCAGNI ("Cavalleria Rusticana"), diverse songs arranged by ROBBIE ROBERTSON
PRODUCTION ROBERT CHARTOFF, IRWIN WINKLER for CHARTOFF-WINKLER PRODUCTIONS, UNITED ARTISTS.

STARRING ROBERT DE NIRO (Jake La Motta), CATHY MORIARTY (Vickie La Motta), JOE PESCI (Joey La Motta), FRANK VINCENT (Salvy), NICHOLAS COLASANTO (Tommy Como), THERESA SALDANA (Lenore La Motta), MARIO GALLO (Mario), FRANK ADONIS (Patsy), JOSEPH BONO (Guido), FRANK TOPHAM (Toppy).

ACADEMY AWARDS 1980 OSCARS for BEST ACTOR (Robert De Niro), and BEST EDITING (Thelma Schoonmaker).

"You didn't get me down, Ray!"

It is the beginning of the 1940s and Jake La Motta (Robert De Niro) is one of the top middleweight boxers in the world. He's the "Raging Bull," famous for an almost inhuman ability to take a beating and notorious for his unpredictable attacks. He's not a stylist, he's a brutal puncher whose strength comes from a deep-seated aggression he is unable to control – inside or outside of the ring. The brunt of Jake's aggression is leveled at his wife, but his brother and manager Joey (Joe Pesci) are also forced to weather his temper. Even in his interaction with the Mafiosi from Little Italy, Jake is anything but diplomatic. This erratic behavior contributes to his continually being denied a title fight. He soon meets Vickie (Cathy Moriarty), a blonde beauty who is

already hanging out with the gangsters of Hell's Kitchen, despite being only 15 years old. Jake gets a divorce and marries her. But he is not calmed down. In fact, his jealous outbursts intensify and he terrorizes everyone around him. When he finally gets the chance to fight for the title in 1949, his predictable demise has been years in the making.

Robert De Niro had long dreamed of acting in a cinematic adaptation of Jake La Motta's autobiography. In the midst of shooting of *Alice Doesn't Live Here Anymore* (1974), he tried to convince Martin Scorsese to direct the project. Though initially unsuccessful, De Niro did not relent. He took another shot at it while Scorsese lay in a hospital bed, psychologically and physically

"I put everything I knew and felt into this film, and I thought it would finish my career. I call it 'kamikaze', this way of making films: put all of yourself into it, then forget it and start a new life."

Martin Scorsese, in: Martin Scorsese, David Thompson, Ian Christie (Ed.), Scorsese on Scorsese

1 Blood, sweat and tears: *Raging Bull* captures the sheer physicality of the fights in merciless close-up.

2 Method acting and a few black eyes: In order to give a convincing depiction of "The Bronx Bull," Robert De Niro spent months training as a boxer, and even fought some fights as an amateur. He was rewarded for his efforts with an Oscar.

3 Professional scene-stealer: Joe Pesci (left) worked alongside Robert De Niro in the Scorsese master-pieces *Goodfellas* (1989) and *Casino* (1995).

lacerated by the disaster of *New York, New York* (1977). This time around the director was fascinated by the subject matter, seizing on La Motta's self-destructive life story as a chance to exorcise his own demons. The film therefore focuses less on the boxer's career – the fight scenes are relatively brief – than the story of a man tortured by his own existence, a man who has only himself to blame for his downfall. The fact that La Motta grew up in the same milieu of Italian immigrants that Scorsese knew well from his own childhood intensified his identification with the subject matter.

Raging Bull was the challenge of a lifetime for De Niro. In the role of Jake La Motta, he radically explored the limits of his craft. The convincing

physical presence De Niro lends to the violence La Motta turned on himself and others is as fascinating as it is terrifying. In order to make the fight scenes as believable as possible, he trained – partially under the guidance of La Motta – for months and on several occasions even fought a real bout. Legend has it that De Niro gained over fifty pounds to personify the aging La Motta, who traveled from night club to night club as a fat has-been enter-tainer.

The film's technical quality – its skilful sound design and editing – is just as extraordinary as De Niro's Oscar-winning performance, and the rest of the acting. Michael Chapman deserves a special mention for his excellent

MICHAEL CHAPMAN   Michael Chapman (*21.11.1935 in New York) became one of the most sought-after American cameramen toward the middle of the 70s. He began by working as a camera operator for Gordon Willis, whose "classicism" became a major influence. The films he worked on during this period include Alan J. Pakula's thriller, *Klute* (1971) and Coppola's *The Godfather* (1972). In 1973, Chapman became director of photography for the first time in Hal Ashby's tragicomedy, *The Last Detail*, followed by the Arctic film *The White Dawn* (1974), the first of four collaborations with Philip Kaufman. Chapman worked as operator once again for Spielberg's *Jaws* (1975) before experiencing his real breakthrough with the legendary Scorsese film, *Taxi Driver* (1975), in which he beautifully transmitted the threatening atmosphere of a Film Noir into color images. Chapman proved his mastery of black-and-white photography with another Scorsese film, *Raging Bull* (1980), for which he received his first Oscar nomination, and later with Carl Reiner's lovely Film Noir homage, *Dead Men Don't Wear Plaid* (1981). Chapman built on his reputation in the years that followed, but only real-ly hit the limelight again in 1993 when he received his second Oscar nomination for *The Fugitive*. Chapman repeatedly appears in small roles as an actor, and has been directing films himself since 1983, though without the impact he has had as a cameraman.

4 Sick with jealousy: Mindless violence soon characterizes Jake's relationship with wife Vicky (Cathy Moriarty).

5 & 6 A beached whale: De Niro put on fifty pounds to depict Jake La Motta in his decline.

7 That's *amore*: Martin Scorsese, the son of Sicilian immigrants, depicts the Italian milieu in 40s and 50s New York with a documentary filmmaker's attention to detail.

black-and-white photography, which captures the private life of the boxer with a merciless sobriety that recalls Italian neorealism and the "semi-documentaries" of the 40s. The camera often stands still and focuses on La Motta's violent outbursts. Squeezed into the frame, he resembles an animal caught in a cage, unable to come to terms with the lack of space and powerless to free himself from its constraints. Jake's torturous frustrations are so painfully depicted in these images that the boxing matches begin to seem like a necessary consequence of his life. The extent of his spiritual barrenness becomes clear during the fights. The camera zooms in on the action in the ring, approaching La Motta's subjective perception. Fists pummel body and face from close range, spraying blood and sweat, the images acoustically underscored by dull blows that sound as if they come from the inside out. The violence exploding in these rapidly edited images have an edge of soothing intimacy. It appears that La Motta is only able to truly express himself within the confines of the ring. He is a lonely man for whom punches are not only a reward, but a means of communication. JH

5

"An American masterwork, a fusion of Hollywood genre
with personal vision couched in images and sounds
that are kinetic and visceral, and closer to poetry than pulp."

The Village Voice

FITZCARRALDO
Fitzcarraldo

981 - FRG - 158 MIN. - DRAMA

DIRECTOR WERNER HERZOG (*1942) SCREENPLAY WERNER HERZOG DIRECTOR OF PHOTOGRAPHY THOMAS MAUCH
EDITING BEATE MAINKA-JELLINGHAUS MUSIC POPOL VUH PRODUCTION WERNER HERZOG,
LUCKI STIPETIC for WERNER HERZOG FILMPRODUKTION, PRO-JECT FILMPRODUKTION,
FILMVERLAG DER AUTOREN, ZDF.

STARRING KLAUS KINSKI (Brian Sweeney Fitzgerald, aka "Fitzcarraldo"), CLAUDIA CARDINALE
(Molly), JOSÉ LEWGOY (Don Aquilino), MIGUEL ÁNGEL FUENTES (Cholo), PAUL HITTSCHER
(Orinoco-Paul), HUEREQUEQUE ENRIQUE BOHORQUEZ (Cook), GRANDE OTHELO (Stationmaster),
PETER BERLING (Opera Director).

FF CANNES 1982 SILVER PALM for BEST DIRECTOR (Werner Herzog).

"I will move a mountain!"

It's the beginning of the 20th century, and it feels like there's a Gold Rush on the banks of the Amazon. Actually it's a Rubber Rush, for the market in rubber is booming. And while the businessmen of Iquito rake in the money, Fitzcarraldo (Klaus Kinski) dreams of building an opera house in the middle of the jungle. For the city's rich entrepreneurs, this is no more than another of the eccentric Irishman's mad plans; but after consulting an old map, Fitzcarraldo has a brilliant idea how to finance his dream. On an Amazon tributary, here are countless rubber trees that cannot be exploited because the way is blocked by impassable rapids. Fitzcarraldo's plan is to bypass the rapids by cruising down a neighbouring river until he reaches a point where the two watercourses almost meet; there, he will transport his steamship over land. The adventure begins – but seems doomed to end very quickly

when almost the entire crew abandons ship for fear of the warlike natives. Fitzcarraldo, however, succeeds in winning the Indios over to his side with the help of Enrico Caruso, by winding up the gramophone and broadcasting the tenor's voice into the rainforest. Even when the anticipated narrow strip of land turns out to be a steep hill in the jungle, Fitzcarraldo is undeterred. With the help of the natives, he simply attempts the impossible: dragging the heavy steamship over the mountain.

Fitzcarraldo tells the story of an obsession, and it also seems to be the film of an obsessed man. Werner Herzog had already made a movie with Klaus Kinski in the Peruvian jungle: *Aguirre, Wrath of God* (*Aguirre, der Zorn Gottes*, 1972). But the hair-raising conditions under which this second jungle project took place have been matched, if at all, only by those prevailing when

> "The whole project was total lunacy – the same stark staring madness the film itself is about. It is the sweat-drenched story of a man besotted with the idea of building an opera in the rotting city of Iquitos, for the sole reason that his heart belongs to Caruso." *Die Zeit*

Francis Ford Coppola made *Apocalypse Now* (1979). A documentary by Les Blank, *Burden of Dreams* (1982), provides a gripping account of the making of *Fitzcarraldo*. Shooting was dogged by a series of catastrophes: the loss of the original leading actors, Jason Robards and Mick Jagger; involvement in a border war between Peru and Ecuador; droughts, floods, snakebites and severe accidents. A further shadow was cast by Kinski's notorious outbursts of rage, which (as Herzog reported) were so extreme that an Indio chief even offered to kill him for the director. Herzog, who knew only too well how unpredictable his star could be, had anticipated such problems, and had not

originally planned to cast Kinski; only when Mick Jagger dropped out of the project did Herzog bring Kinski on board as a replacement. But Kinski was without question, ideal for the role; no-one else had his particular charisma, the aura of a lonely and quite possibly insane visionary. It made him the perfect embodiment of a hero who, in the depths of the primeval rainforest, declares the supremacy of art. The leading character is thus a mirror image of the director, to an extent unparalleled in any other Herzog film. In the end *Fitzcarraldo* is a further fruit of the collaboration between Herzog and his "favourite enemy."

4

1 No actor embodies geniality and madness as convincingly as Klaus Kinski.

2 The star and the extras: The Brazilian Indians often felt that Kinski was an intruding presence.

3 No trick photography: The ship was really towed by hand across the mountain of the virgin forest.

4 A most difficult star. On account of his unpredictability, Kinski was not originally considered for the part. But when Mick Jagger and Jason Robards jumped ship, Werner Herzog brought the notorious eccentric on board.

"'I'm a dream-weaver,' says Herzog. Though it's questionable whether we can dream about Fitzcarraldo, we can see enough of Herzog's own vision to let him do the dreaming for us." *Jeune Cinéma*

Alongside Rainer Werner Fassbinder, Wim Wenders and Volker Schlöndorff, Werner Herzog is one of the best-known directors of the "New German Cinema." He was born in Munich on September 5th, 1942, and grew up in a remote rural area. An autodidact, he formed his own film production company in 1963. Since then, he has written, directed and produced more than forty documentaries and feature films; they focus mainly on social outsiders, with whom Herzog clearly sympathises. He attracted great attention with five films starring Klaus Kinski in the leading role: *Aguirre, Wrath of God* (*Aguirre, der Zorn Gottes*, 1972), *Nosferatu* (*Nosferatu – Phantom der Nacht*, 1978), *Woyzeck* (1979), *Fitzcarraldo* (1978–1981) and *Cobra Verde* (1987). In 1999, Herzog looked back on his unusual relationship with the eccentric Kinski in the documentary film *My Favourite Enemy* (*Mein liebster Feind*).

5   *Fitzcarraldo* was the fourth of five Werner Herzog films in which Kinski played the leading role. Their legendary partnership dates back to 1972 when the two teamed up for *Aguirre, Wrath of God* (*Aguirre, der Zorn Gottes*). This project, also shot in a virgin forest, starred Kinski as a power-hungry conquistador.

6   Molly is the only one who believes in Fitzcarraldo's visionary ideas: Claudia Cardinale endows the country madam with an unbridled temper and an equally kind heart characteristic of the lovely Italian actress.

5

6

"… The lensing is top-flight, and Kinski is delightfully mad from start to finish. In fact, Herzog's handling of the thesps, non-professionals in particular, is unique. All said and done, this is a fun film. 'Fitzcarraldo' is an adult daydream. A magnificent one at that." *Variety*

It's possible to argue whether Herzog was justified in his savage determination to see the project through at all costs – a ruthlessness that bears obvious comparisons to Fitzcarraldo himself. What's undeniable is that *Fitzcarraldo*, as a special-effects film, would have been unthinkable without the film team's remarkable readiness to get involved in such a risky, unpredictable project. The film's visionary power is rooted in the fact that one cannot doubt the genuineness of the images it presents; these are pictures we can trust. That ship was really pulled over that mountain by those Indians:

we know it for sure, even though we've never seen anything like it in our lives. Herzog's declared intention as a filmmaker is to show things that may have been dreamt but have never yet been seen; in *Fitzcarraldo*, he succeeds in doing so. These are utterly original images, filled with the pathos of veracity. Today, in the age of digital technology and an ironic self-referential cinema of quotations, the effect of these images on the audience may well be even more overwhelming than it was when the film first came out. *Fitzcarraldo* is first-hand film.

FANNY AND ALEXANDER ♟♟♟♟

Fanny och Alexander

Fanny och Alexander
En film av Ingmar Bergman

982 - SWEDEN / FRANCE / FRG - 187 MIN. - DRAMA, FAMILY FILM

DIRECTOR INGMAR BERGMAN (*1918) **SCREENPLAY** INGMAR BERGMAN **DIRECTOR OF PHOTOGRAPHY** SVEN NYKVIST **EDITING** SYLVIA INGEMARSSON **MUSIC** DANIEL BELL **PRODUCTION** JÖRN DONNER for SWEDISH FILMINSTITUTE, SVT DRAMA, GAUMONT, PERSONAFILM, TOBIS.

STARRING BÖRJE AHLSTEDT (Carl Ekdahl), PERNILLA ALLWIN (Fanny), BERTIL GUVE (Alexander), ALLAN EDWALL (Oscar), EWA FRÖLING (Emilie), JARL KULLE (Gustav Adolf Ekdahl), GUNN WÅLLGREN (Helena Ekdahl), JAN MALMSJÖ (Bishop Edvard Vergerus), HARRIET ANDERSSON (Justina), ANNA BERGMAN (Hanna Schwartz), LENA OLIN (Rosa).

ACADEMY AWARDS 1983 OSCARS for BEST FOREIGN LANGUAGE FILM (Jörn Donner), BEST CINEMATOGRAPHY (Sven Nykvist), BEST ART DIRECTION (Anna Asp, Susanne Linghelm) and BEST COSTUMES (Marik Vos-Lundh).

*"Anything can happen, anything is possible and likely.
Time and space do not exist.
Against a faint background of reality,
imagination spins out and weaves new patterns."*

In the very first scenes of *Fanny and Alexander*, Ingmar Bergman defines his position and signals his intentions. We see a boy looking at a puppet theater. Layer by layer, he lifts up the painted elements of the decoration. In a similar fashion, he will penetrate and see through the fronts and façades of the adult world. The film's perspective is primarily that of a child, and the drama unfolds before the eyes of Bergman's ten-year-old alter ego.

Alexander (Bertil Guve) and his eight-year-old sister Fanny (Pernilla Allwin) are the youngest members of the Ekdahl clan, which runs the theater in a sleepy Swedish town at the beginning of the twentieth century. The grandmother rules the roost with wisdom and forbearance. The Ekdahls' family life is turbulent and colorful, constantly inspiring Alexander to invent new and imaginative games. His ambition is to have a brilliant career on the stage, just like his mother and grandmother, but the death of his father

changes everything. At the end of the year of mourning, Emilie (Ewa Fröling) the young widow, marries the bishop, Edvard Vergerus (Jan Malmsjö). For the sake of love and respectability, she abandons acting and moves into the bishop's residence together with her children. In the strict (and hypocritical atmosphere of their new home, the children are bullied and harassed. But Alexander is a rebel. Instead of saying grace before meals, he mutters unchristian indecencies, and infuriates his stepfather with childish slyness and cruelty. The bishop retaliates mercilessly, and instead of the love of God, the boy makes the acquaintance of the cane and the humiliating methods of the Inquisition. Home is a puritanical hell and it seems like a miracle when Emilie Alexander and Fanny finally manage to escape.

Fanny and Alexander is a baroque and highly dramatic tissue of image in which Ingmar Bergman re-works the raw material of his own childhood

2

3

"*Fanny and Alexander* emerges as a sumptuously produced period piece that is also a rich tapestry of childhood memoirs and moods, fear and fancy, employing all the manners and means of the best of cinematic theatrical from high and low comedy to darkest tragedy with detours into the gothic, the ghostly and the gruesome."

Variety

It is no coincidence that the name Ekdahl reminds us of the photographer's family in Ibsen's play *The Wild Duck*, for this is a story about the need for theater – for imagination – in human life. Ingmar Bergman was the son of a pastor, and the film leaves us in no doubt about his attitude towards sanctimonious clergymen for whom love and the fear of God are no more than instruments of power over their fellow human beings.

Oscar Ekdahl, the father of Alexander and Fanny, dies of a heart attack during a rehearsal of *Hamlet*. His role was the Ghost. Later, he will indeed appear to his son from beyond the grave, offering help and support. In this way, Bergman unhesitatingly extends his naturalist novel of family life to include the supernatural. He goes beyond contrasting the Ekdahl house-

hold's Dionysian love of life with the oppressive discipline of the Episcopal residence, and explores the fundamental conflict between imagination and reason.

The version made for cinema is far from short, with a running time of three-and-a-half hours. However, the four-part TV version, 312 minutes long, is regarded as the Director's Cut. For Bergman, *Fanny and Alexander* was a resume of his entire life and work. Although he has not been idle since, directing a large number of works for the theater and television, he has made no further films for the cinema. *Fanny and Alexander* was, incidentally, the first foreign-language film in history to receive four Oscars.

RF

4

MAGIC LANTERN Alexander possesses not only a puppet theater but a Magic Lantern – Bergman's homage to the medium of moving pictures. This first step towards contemporary cinema was made in the 17th century by Athanasius Kircher, an Austrian Jesuit. The device used a candle and a lens to project an image onto the wall. Inside a casing resembling the normal lanterns of the day, it had a turntable holding little pictures painted on glass. Lens covers were also sometimes used. This entirely mechanical construction made it possible to produce visible movement – sled-rides or windmills with turning blades, for example. Around 1820, the invention of limelight introduced a new phase in cinema history. This novel method of lighting did a lot to further the dissemination of the Magic Lantern and the "Phantasmagorias" that followed. Dissolves and surprising effects with movement now became possible. For the first time, rain, snowfall, fire and the waves of the sea could all be imitated with deceptive accuracy.

1 Peeking into the grown-up world: Alexander (Bertil Guve) and his sister Fanny (Pernilla Allwin).

2 All smiles: A picture perfect Ekdahl family poses with friends and servants for the annual Christmas photo. Fanny and Alexander are seated in the first row.

3 Nothing but the truth: Much like appearing before a court tribunal, Fanny and Alexander often have to account for their actions at Bishop Vergerus' (Jan Malmsjö, right) "humble abode."

4 Bacchanal at the Ekdahl manor: The boisterous Christmas celebration that opens the film instantly puts the audience in festive spirits.

5 Saying their goodnight prayers under the bishop's watchful eye was always a trial for Fanny and Alexander.

6 A visit from the great beyond: Oscar (Allan Edwall), Fanny and Alexander's dearly departed father, appears to his son in the form of a ghost and shares some words of comfort.

5

6

SCARFACE

1982/83 - USA - 170 MIN. - GANGSTER FILM

DIRECTOR BRIAN DE PALMA (*1940) SCREENPLAY OLIVER STONE DIRECTOR OF PHOTOGRAPHY JOHN A. ALONZO
EDITING JERRY GREENBERG, DAVID RAY MUSIC GIORGIO MORODER PRODUCTION PETER SAPHIER,
MARTIN BREGMAN for UNIVERSAL PICTURES.

STARRING AL PACINO (Tony Montana), STEVEN BAUER (Manny Ray), MICHELLE PFEIFFER (Elvira),
MARY ELIZABETH MASTRANTONIO (Gina), ROBERT LOGGIA (Frank Lopez), MIRIAM COLON
(Mama Montana), F. MURRAY ABRAHAM (Omar Swarez), PAUL SHENAR (Alejandro Sosa),
HARRIS YULIN (Bernstein), ÁNGEL SALAZAR (Chi Chi).

"You know what capitalism is? Getting fucked!"

The final scene of this film is the one everybody remembers: Cuban refugee drug lord Tony Montana (Al Pacino) is caught in the gigantic stairwell of his villa, his body riddled with bullets, but he keeps on firing his machinegun unremittingly at his enemies, who stream in through the doorway. Ultimately his body slumps forward, arms spread out in a crucified pose, and he falls headfirst into the fountain in the cavernous foyer. It is a death as violent and merciless as his own life. Perhaps it is a bit too heroic, considering the atrocious trail of murder and mayhem that he left in his wake on the way to the top.

This unsettling epic has often been misunderstood as a brutal action film, but it's a film with many sides. Montana's inability to assert himself without using brute force and his tendency to express affection by humiliating the people he loves lend the film a powerful dramatic effect. Brian De Palma's remake of Howard Hawks' 1932 classic, *Scarface: Shame of a Nation*, was greeted with harsh reviews, mainly on account of its occasional-

ly graphic depictions of violence. In Germany today, *Scarface* on video is still only available in an edited version, 22 minutes shorter than the original. Hawks' *Scarface*, based upon the life of Al Capone, also faced biting criticism because its "negative version of an American entrepreneurial career" (*Film dienst*), went against etiquette.

De Palma's remake shifts the plot to 1980s Miami, when Fidel Castro briefly opened the Cuban border to allow emigrants out, and used the opportunity to rid Cuba of many of its criminals. Tony Montana and his friend Manny Ray (Steven Bauer) belong to this group and quickly rise from dishwashers to drug millionaires in the greed-driven America of the Reagan Era.

Before long, the dark side of this uncompromising and unscrupulous craving for wealth and power comes to the fore. Along with excess comes the beginning of the end. "We're getting sloppy," says Montana to his friend and accomplice, now head of his bodyguards, and drifts further and

"In this country, you gotta make the money first. Then when you get the money, you get the power. Then when you get the power, then you get the women." *Quotation from film: Tony Montana*

1   The slaphappy couple: Tony (Al Pacino) and Elvira's (Michelle Pfeiffer) marriage is soon knocked out by drugs, alcohol and egomania.

2   A great white among sharks: Tony Montana knows no mercy – not even for those who used to watch his back.

3   Lead poisoning: The closing sequence is among the most controversial in film history.

4   Tony sweeps Elvira off her feet with intoxicating glitz.

5   Knowing how the caged bird sings: Elvira wards off boredom with cocaine and cynicism.

6   Paranoia rides wealth's coattails: Montana senses enemies in every corner.

AL PACINO AND ROBERT DE NIRO	Born in 1940 in New York, Alfredo Jacob Pacino was the son of Italian immigrants, just like Robert De Niro. But the similarities between Pacino and De Niro, who is three years younger, do not end there. Both Method actors are best known for specializing in roles as criminals or policemen. After Pacino appeared as Michael Corleone in the first segment of Francis Ford Coppola's *The Godfather* (1972), their paths crossed again in 1974 in the film's sequel, when De Niro played the role of young Vito Corleone. That the two can shine in the romantic genre was proven first by De Niro in *Stanley & Iris* (1989), and two years later by Pacino in *Frankie and Johnny* (1991). The pair was brought together again in Michael Mann's *Heat* in 1995. Both actors also have an equal number of awards to their credit. Though De Niro has been presented with two Oscars, and Pacino just one for his portrayal of a blind ex-general in *Scent of a Woman*, 1992, Pacino, who also acts and directs theatre productions, was honored in Venice in 1994 with a Golden Lion for his lifetime achievements.

further into a drug-induced stupor and paranoia. Suspicion and hate increasingly exert their influence in Montana's stronghold, where he has secluded himself with his drug-addicted wife, Elvira (Michelle Pfeiffer), and his entourage.

Similar to the Tony "Scarface" Camonte (Paul Muni) character in Hawks' version, Tony Montana is also a lost soul, who as his mother (Miriam Colon) predicts, ultimately destroys everyone he loves. And like its predecessor and model, De Palma's film possesses both a psychological and a political dimension. This is hardly surprising considering that the screenplay was written by Oliver Stone.

At one point, Montana explains that society needs men like him, so that people can point a finger at him and still feel righteously innocent. Politicians would rather fight the legalization of drugs than take on organized crime, for black sheep like Montana justify election campaign promises, excuse police brutality and help cover up their own machinations. The powerful don't even need to be corrupt to profit from organized crime. At the end Montana is not gunned down by the police, but by the Mafia. This divergence from Howard Hawks' original could scarcely make its point more effectively – in a decade of Reaganite neo-liberal economic practices, it's a statement as meaningful as it is provocative.   SH

BLADE RUNNER

1982 - USA - 117 MIN. - SCIENCE FICTION, NEO FILM NOIR

DIRECTOR RIDLEY SCOTT (*1937) SCREENPLAY HAMPTON FANCHER, DAVID PEPLOES, based on the novel *DO ANDROIDS DREAM OF ELECTRIC SHEEP?* by PHILIP K. DICK
DIRECTOR OF PHOTOGRAPHY JORDAN CRONENWETH EDITING MARSHA NAKASHIMA, TERRY RAWLINGS
MUSIC VANGELIS PRODUCTION MICHAEL DEELEY for THE LADD COMPANY, BLADE RUNNER PARTNERSHIP.

STARRING HARRISON FORD (Rick Deckard), RUTGER HAUER (Roy Batty), SEAN YOUNG (Rachael), EDWARD JAMES OLMOS (Gaff), M. EMMET WALSH (Bryant), DARYL HANNAH (Pris), WILLIAM SANDERSON (Sebastian), BRION JAMES (Leon), JOE TURKEL (Eldon Tyrell), JOANNA CASSIDY (Zhora), MORGAN PAULL (Holden).

"You're so different. You're so perfect."

Los Angeles, 2019. Earth-toned high-rise temples soar up into smog-covered skies. Factory towers spit fire, and acid rain collects between the neon-illuminated fissures that separate the mammoth buildings. The city has become a mutant hybrid, a futuristic yet archaic urban leviathan. The L. A. streets are home to an exotic blend of races, while whites are housed in forbidding, monolithic skyscrapers. Everyone who can afford it has relocated to one of the "off world colonies." To make this prospect even more enticing, the Tyrell Corporation has designed humanoids called replicants to be used as slave labor on the foreign planets. These synthetic beings are virtually indistinguishable from real humans, but the law forbids them from setting foot on Earth. Yet some of these androids manage to slip through the net, and it is the job of the "blade runners" to hunt them down and "decommission" them. Is this an allusion to the Day of Judgment, where only the innocent can escape the confines of hell? Perhaps. Nothing in this film rich with

philosophical and theological admonishments would seem to indicate the contrary.

Rick Deckard (Harrison Ford) used to work as a blade runner. Now a disillusioned ex-cop, he roams the damp streets with a chip on his shoulder like a film noir crusader. He was the best in the business, which is why the bureau want to reactivate him when a band of four rogue androids, two men and two women, makes their way into L. A. Their "life expectancy" has been programmed to four years. Now, they want to know how much time they have left to live, and they'll do anything to prolong it.

Roy Batty (Rutger Hauer), the leader of these humanoid bandits, is blond, buff and demonic. Meeting his maker Eldon Tyrell (Joe Turkel), a futuristic Dr. Frankenstein, proves an existential disappointment for Roy. Tyrell lives in a pyramid-shaped structure reminiscent of that of the ancient Mayans and sleeps in a bed like the Pope's. Unfortunately, the great creator

is in no position to grant the android a new lease of life, and the fallen angel kills his maker in a dual father-God assassination.

Blade Runner is based on the novel *Do Androids Dream of Electric Sheep?* (1968) by Philip K. Dick, who also wrote the story that inspired *Total Recall* (1990). The film bombed at the box-office, but is nonetheless seen as a milestone in sci-fi. It is a dismal, philosophical fairy tale with mind-boggling sets, sophisticated lighting design and a grandiose score by Vangelis. Alongside *Liquid Sky* (1982) and *The Hunger* (1983), *Blade Runner* is among the most significant 80s New Wave films. One could label it "post-modern" or attribute its power to the director's eclecticism. Scott's mesmerizing *layering* technique showcases his knack for integrating architectural elements, the intricacies of clothing articles, and symbols originating from a wide array of cultures and eras.

The film makes productive use of astoundingly diverse codes, synthesizing their Babylonian confusion into a compact means of communication on the L. A. city streets. In a mélange of Fritz Lang's *Metropolis* (1926), film noir, the imagery of Edward Hopper and the comic book sketches of Moebius, Ridley Scott creates a wildly driven piece that demands its audience to consider the essence of human identity. The film's subtext gradually unfolds throughout its story, raising issues of the conscious and subconscious. The homonymic link between protagonist Deckard and mathematician Descartes is only part of the rich body of motifs that hint at the film's underlying philosophy. Also not to be overlooked are the variations on the "eye" motif throughout the picture. Here, too, the film synthesizes a word's homonymic potential, alluding to the "I" inherent in the word "eye." The eye is a universal symbol

3

1   The other, that's who I am: Rachael (Sean Young), attractive and unapproachable like a film noir vamp. She doesn't know that she's a replicant. Even her memories are just implants.

2   More human than human: Roy Batty (Rutger Hauer) is the *Übermensch* in the Nietzschean sense of the word. The blond beast and yet a slave who suffers and shows compassion.

3   Harrison Ford plays *Blade Runner* Deckard. In hot pursuit of renegade replicants, although perhaps he's one himself.

"*Blade Runner* was *the* science fiction of the 80s. The gritty gray counterpart to Kubrick's *2001*."

epd Film

of recognition and a sense of self-awareness "unique" to humans. Yet in *Blade Runner*, the androids are also equipped with this level of consciousness. "We're not computers, Sebastian, we're physical," Batty declares at one point, laying claim to his humanity as well as his body and physicality, one of the most important topics of the 80s.

For their bodies are precisely what make the androids indistinguishable from their human counterparts. Upon first meeting, Rachael (Sean Young), Eldon Tyrell's secretary, reminds Deckard of the dangers of his occupation when she asks him whether he has ever killed a human by mistake. Her question sensitizes the viewer to the predicament at hand; sometimes the fine line between humans and their replicas is intangible. Rachael herself has sat on both sides of the fence. Although she has always believed herself to be

human, at one point in the film she is forced to confront the reality that she too is an android. There is, however, something "unique" about her. Rachael is the product of an experiment and has been programmed with the memories of Tyrell's niece, which she latches on to as her own. Her memories are rooted in photos. Likewise, it is photos that help Deckard zero in on the whereabouts of the renegade androids. He uses a picture of an empty hotel room as only a 21st century detective would, or at least, as we might have imagined him to from an 80s perspective. Aided by a contraption known as an Esper machine, he enlarges segments of the photo onto a monitor. This provides him with a sort of X-ray vision that allows him to travel into the depths of the image's two-dimensional space. He soon discovers a woman's reflection from within a mirror. The detective embarks on an investigation

4

4 What does it mean to be human? A question the film puts forth in an aesthetically brilliant framework. The film set the standard for 1980s style.

5 Artificial humans are a recurrent phenomenon in both literature and film – from the Greek myth of Pygmalion, E. T. A. Hoffmann's doll Olympia in *The Sandman,* to Fritz Lang's *Metropolis* and Spielberg's *A. I.*, to name but a few. Here, the mannerisms of replicant Pris (Daryl Hannah) almost make her seem like a china doll.

"At first the villain of the piece, he suddenly becomes its mythic, emphatic center. Batty turns Frankenstein's monster to Biblical Adam; Deckard veers from hunter to homomorph." *Film Comment*

RIDLEY SCOTT

Alan Parker dubbed him "the greatest visual stylist working today." With a deep-rooted love for Hollywood, the films of English director Ridley Scott have played an enormous role in determining Tinseltown's film aesthetics for more than twenty years. Whether he is working in sci-fi thrillers like *Alien* (1979) and *Blade Runner* (1982) (a film which would enjoy cult status ten years later with the release of its director's cut), or a feminist road movie like *Thelma & Louise* (1991), Scott's films are a triumph with critics and audiences alike. A graduate of the London Royal College of Art, the *auteur* got his start working for the BBC and then went on to shoot advertising spots with his own production company.

Born in 1937, his first feature film, *The Duellists* (1977) won the prize for best directorial debut at Cannes. Ridley Scott has also enjoyed tremendous success as a producer. Together with his brother Tony Scott (*Top Gun*, 1985), he purchased the Shepperton Studios in 1995. Neither genre nor quality links the resulting films. Fantasy flick *Legend* (1985), featuring a young Tom Cruise, met with a more modest reception, thriller *Someone to Watch Over Me* (1987) was a veritable grand slam, and *Black Rain* (1989) with Michael Douglas, a film on the Japanese Yakuza, is certainly worth seeing. Clearly, in addition to the numerous hits, Scott has also had his share of misses. Columbus glorification *1492: Conquest of Paradise* (1992) as well as *G. I. Jane* (1997) starring Demi Moore bombed at the box-office and were panned by critics. In 2000, Ridley Scott landed himself another smash hit with *Gladiator*, the first big budget Hollywood production about Ancient Rome in more than 30 years. The film reeled in five Oscars at the 73rd Annual Academy Awards.

"We used a lot of real punks for the street scenes in *Blade Runner*. Because I had so much 'crowd', it was better to save time and money by recruiting a huge number of extras: 200 punks, 100 Chinese, another 100 Mexicans."

Ridley Scott in: Film Comment

6 The sun doesn't rise here anymore: Bathed in neon light, the streets of L.A. are ruled by a gangland mix of Chinese, Mexicans and punks.

7 Harrison Ford's laconic and somewhat cynical portrayal of Deckard brings many a film noir protagonist to mind. Not only the visual aesthetics and

characters evoke elements of film noir, but also the voice – over narrative technique, later eliminated in the director's cut, is typical of the genre.

THE FOURTH MAN
De vierde man

1983 - THE NETHERLANDS - 105 MIN. - EROTIC THRILLER

DIRECTOR PAUL VERHOEVEN (*1938) SCREENPLAY GERARD SOETEMAN, based on the novel of the same name by GERARD REVE DIRECTOR OF PHOTOGRAPHY JAN DE BONT EDITING INE SCHENKKAN MUSIC LOEK DIKKER PRODUCTION ROB HOUWER for DE VERENIGDE NEDERLANDSCHE FILMCOMPAGNIE.

STARRING JEROEN KRABBÉ (Gerard Reve), RENÉE SOUTENDIJK (Christine Halsslag), THOM HOFFMAN (Herman), DOLF DE VRIES (Dr. de Vries), GEERT DE JONG (Ria), PAMELA TEVES (Nurse), HANS VEERMAN (Undertaker), HERO MULLER (Josefs), CAROLINE DE BEUS (Adrienne), PAUL NYGAARD (Violinist).

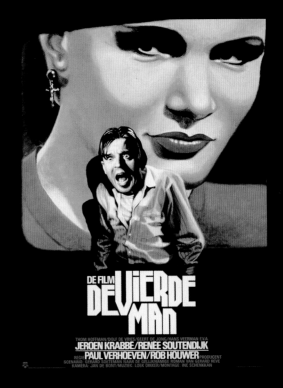

"I lie the truth, until I no longer know whether something really happened or not."

Amsterdam. Writer Gerard Reve (Jeroen Krabbé) no longer knows what to believe: is he hallucinating, or is he the witness to a deadly conspiracy? His lively imagination, fed by the twin sources of strict Catholicism and homo-eroticism, supplies him with plenty of welcome inspiration for his novels, but it begins to take on a deeply disturbing quality when he meets a seductive

pathetic, and invites him back to her place, where they spend the night in a close embrace; but Christine's warm attentions can't save Gerard from his nightmares. In his dream, he sees himself enter a tomb in which three bloody corpses are hanging, and it's clear that a fourth victim is about to be slaugh-tered: Gerard himself. Christine castrates him with a pair of scissors – then

"I don't consider sex the main thing in life, of course, but it's a real possibility for expressing yourself. And I'm always amazed that people fucking each other in films is so completely boring."

Paul Verhoeven, in: Cinema Papers

JAN DE BONT

Paul Verhoeven, born in Amsterdam in 1938, gained international recognition with a series of provocative and visually outstanding films, before making it in Hollywood. His career is closely bound up with that of the cameraman Jan de Bont, responsible for the cinematography on Verhoeven's first major success. *Turkish Delight* (*Turks fruit*, 1973). Even prior to Verhoeven, de Bont had also worked in Hollywood, but *Private Lessons* (1981) was his first film as Director of Photography. He photographed several photographically impressive films, including *Die Hard* (1987), *Black Rain* (1989) and, with Verhoeven as director again, *Basic Instinct* (1992). In 1994, de Bont made his debut as a director with the visceral action thriller *Speed*, a film that set new standards for the genre and became a global box-office hit.

1   Reve (Jeroen Krabbé) wakes up from a ghastly vision: His inner goblins will soon follow him into the outside world.

2   Tactile literature lover or deadly siren: Christine Halsslag (Renée Soutendijk).

3   Homoerotic imagery and Christine Halsslag's mysterious aura pervade Gerard Reve's feverish, waking dreams.

4   If Reve's grueling premonitions are correct, Christine's interlocking embrace will be accompanied by death.

4

Herman dies and Gerard is taken to hospital, suffering from extreme shock. Meanwhile, Christine is outside, flirting with a hunky surfer, before climbing into his car. Is this her fifth victim?

"Every film I've made forms a contrast to the previous one", said Paul Verhoeven, when *The Fourth Man* reached cinemas. "I have a preference for things that are visually spectacular, and feel more drawn to images than sound, although sound, of course, also has an important function." The most spectacular element in this film was Verhoeven's provocative treatment of religious symbols, which many critics regarded as a breaking of taboos. The avowed Catholic Gerard sees Herman, the object of his intense desire, as a crucified Christ – and he approaches him with sexual intentions. Seen in the context of the film's carefully developed supernatural atmosphere, these scenes are thoroughly fitting. Just like Gerard, the viewer is unnerved by a maelstrom of disturbing images and tableaux, whereby it never quite becomes clear whether the notorious drinker, Gerard, is in a delirium or actually living through a series of dreadful events.

This film is a bold and sardonic mixture of Christian motifs, open homosexual eroticism and pure "scary movie." It caused a worldwide furore, and brought Verhoeven a series of awards, including 1984 the International Critics' Award at the Toronto International Film Festival, and the prize for Best Foreign Film from the Los Angeles Film Critics Association.

HK

BLUE VELVET

1985 - USA - 120 MIN. - THRILLER, NEO FILM NOIR

DIRECTOR DAVID LYNCH (*1946) SCREENPLAY DAVID LYNCH
DIRECTOR OF PHOTOGRAPHY FREDERICK ELMES EDITING DUWAYNE DUNHAM
MUSIC ANGELO BADALAMENTI PRODUCTION FRED CARUSO for DE LAURENTIIS
ENTERTAINMENT.

STARRING KYLE MACLACHLAN (Jeffrey Beaumont), ISABELLA ROSSELLINI
(Dorothy Vallens), DENNIS HOPPER (Frank Booth), LAURA DERN
(Sandy Williams), HOPE LANGE (Mrs. Williams), DEAN STOCKWELL (Ben),
GEORGE DICKERSON (Detective Williams), BRAD DOURIF (Raymond),
FRANCES BAY (Aunt Barbara), JACK HARVEY (Mr. Beaumont).

"I'll bet a person could learn a lot by getting into that woman's apartment. You know, sneak in and hide and observe."

The camera sweeps over Lumberton, USA, a charming American small-town, with white picket fences, tulip-filled gardens, and amiable people. Jeffrey Beaumont (Kyle MacLachlan) is on the way to hospital to visit his father, who suffered a heart attack while watering his lawn. While walking home across a field, he pauses to throw rocks at some bottles. He is soon stopped in his tracks – partially hidden by the grass at his feet lies a milky-looking, rotting human ear, covered with crawling ants. The ear is a completely foreign object in this American small-town idyll, and becomes a mesmerically compelling object. Little does he realize that it is to become his entry-ticket into another world. For the moment, he brings the ear to the police.

In Sandy (Laura Dern), the blonde daughter of the investigating detective, Jeffrey finds a hesitant, but eventually more and more curious accomplice and partner. She informs him of a clue in the case that leads to the nightclub singer Dorothy Vallens (Isabella Rossellini). He decides to sneak into her apartment. The thought of forcing his way into this woman's private sphere arouses him more than he will admit to himself, let alone to Sandy.

Blue Velvet is a film about seeing and about the camera as an eye. Jeffrey observes more than he would like to in Dorothy Vallens' apartment. When Dorothy unexpectedly returns, rips the closet door open and orders him out, the boundless terror in his eyes exposes him as a peeping-tom caught

2

red-handed. When Dorothy threatens him and even calls him by name, the object has suddenly become the subject, the subject the object.

The voyeur experiences arousal, pleasure, and power. Director David Lynch plays with these phenomena and makes the viewer an accomplice, but then turns the tables. In Lynch's film, the voyeur is degraded and ultimately becomes the helpless witness of a brutal act. The scene in which Dorothy is brutally raped by the perverted Frank Booth (Dennis Hopper) is just as shocking and disturbing as the shower murder scene in Hitchcock's *Psycho* (1960). And *Blue Velvet* is as important for 1980s cinema as *Psycho* was for film of the early 60s.

The following day, his experience in Dorothy's apartment truly seems like a bad dream to Jeffrey. For just as it would be in a dream, he was alter-

nately observer and participant, and Frank was the representation of the dark side of his soul.

Towards the end of *Blue Velvet*, when the worst is over, the camera shows a close-up of an ear, but this time, it is Jeffrey's own ear. The fissures in the perfect world are apparently sealed, and Jeffrey's journey into the dark depths of the soul is over. But is it entirely over for good, or is this just a temporary respite...

While *Blue Velvet* was initially met with much controversy at the time of its release, its status as one of the best American films of the 80s is indisputable. The film established David Lynch as a visionary of modern cinema, marked the well-deserved comeback of the incomparable Dennis Hopper, and shattered the constricting perception of Isabella Rossellini as merely the flawless daughter of the great Ingrid Bergman.   RF

3

1 Mysterious nightclub singer Dorothy Vallens (Isabella Rossellini) is suspicious of an unannounced visitor.

2 Jeffrey Beaumont (Kyle MacLachlan) is about to drive into the unknown depths of his soul.

3 Under duress: Dorothy forces Jeffrey to take his clothes off and make love to her. Suddenly, there is a knock at the door.

ANGELO BADALAMENTI   Since *Blue Velvet* (1985), Angelo Badalamenti has played a decisive role in each David Lynch project, and it is hard to imagine the Lynch universe

"*Blue Velvet* is a big film about the innocence and perversion that characterises childhood."

David Lynch

4   Shutter speed: Jeffrey bears witness to a bizarre scene from inside Dorothy's closet.

5   Dorothy sings "Blue Velvet" at the Slow Club: Lynch composer Angelo Badalamenti at the piano.

6   Sandy (Laura Dern) is appalled by Dorothy Vallens' morbid power over Jeffrey. Yet Sandy's romantic feelings compel her to help him.

7   "Mommy… Baby wants to fuck!" With her family in his clutches, Frank Booth (Dennis Hopper) strokes Dorothy Vallens with blue velvet.

DEAD RINGERS

1988 - USA / CANADA - 115 MIN. - DRAMA, THRILLER

DIRECTOR DAVID CRONENBERG (*1943) SCREENPLAY BARI WOOD, JACK GEASLAND
DIRECTOR OF PHOTOGRAPHY PETER SUSCHITZKY EDITING RONALD SANDERS MUSIC HOWARD SHORE
PRODUCTION MARC BOYMAN, DAVID CRONENBERG for MANTLE CLINIC II, MORGAN CREEK
PRODUCTIONS, TÉLÉFILM CANADA.

STARRING JEREMY IRONS (Beverly Mantle / Elliot Mantle), GENEVIÈVE BUJOLD (Claire Niveau),
HEIDI VON PALLESKE (Cary), BARBARA GORDON (Danuta), SHIRLEY DOUGLAS (Laura),
STEPHEN LACK (Anders Wolleck), NICK NICHOLS (Leo), LYNNE CORMACK (Arlene),
DAMIR ANDREI (Birchall), MIRIAM NEWHOUSE (Mrs. Bookman).

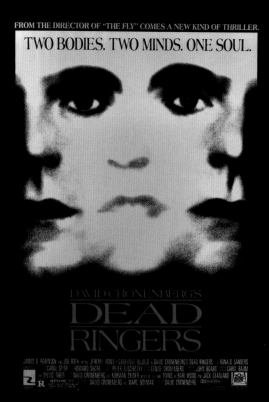

"Pain creates character distortion, it's simply not necessary."

Identical twins Elliot and Beverly Mantle (Jeremy Irons in a dual role) are both renowned physicians. After completing their studies at Cambridge, Mass., the brothers moved out to Toronto where they open up a clinic for gynecology. Aided by state of the art technology, the Mantles specialize in fertilizing the eggs of seemingly barren women. However, there are naturally some patients whom even they cannot help. Such is the case when they discover a physical abnormality in actress Claire Niveau (Geneviève Bujold) that prevents her from ever getting pregnant. Following the diagnosis, Elliot and Claire enter into an affair and it soon becomes clear that the actress has a taste for exotic pleasures. Fascinated by her masochistic tendencies, Elliot decides to contribute to them. Unbeknownst to Claire, Elliot lets brother Beverly slip into his intimate role, once he has had his fill of her. After all, sharing is what these twins do best. But when Beverly falls in love with the fragile actress, the siblings' equilibrium begins to falter.

Until now, the lives of the two brothers have thrived on the perfect balance between their personal and private lives. Elliot's charismatic per-sonality allowed him to play the part of the go-getting daredevil. The rather shy and reserved Beverly, on the other hand, was the brilliant researching strength. Elliot, in turn, would then deftly package his brother's results for the open market. Now and again, they take advantage of their uncanny physical resemblance and trade places. This goes undetected by those around them, as the two are "perceived as a single person," as Elliot puts it. Their complementary Yin and Yang even succeeds in pulling the wool over Claire's eyes. Much time passes before she starts to distinguish the ambivalent behavior of her two lovers, and she is livid upon discovering that her monogamous relationship has grown new feet.

Guilt drives Beverly to drink and drugs. He is torn between wanting to start a new life with Claire independently of his brother, and fearing the prospect of life without him. In a narcotic state, his sleep is tormented by mad visions of Claire vainly trying to sever the twins' shared umbilical cord with her teeth. Elliot, meanwhile, makes a concerted effort to rehabilitate his drug-addicted brother, but is sucked into the same quagmire. He too has started to

3

"*Dead Ringers* is Narcissus' worst nightmare. He wakes up one morning and finds his reflection lying beside him." *epd Film*

...ake "medication" to be "in sync" with Beverly, as he refers to it. This downward spiral soon takes a deadly turn for the two doctors who can live neither with nor without each other.

David Cronenberg's exploration of the phenomenon of twins in *Dead Ringers* (a term from dog racing meaning an identical substitute used to defraud bookmakers) has its roots in biological studies. Himself a former medical student, the director was fascinated by the findings of twin research. Some published reports indicate that identical twins raised apart from each another often develop remarkably similar predispositions, affinities and characteristics. It is Cronenberg's assertion that "the behavior demonstrated by twins turns our entire concept of individuality on its head. We understand that we are dealing with two distinct individuals but are simultaneously thrown for

a loop by their homogeneity. We want to 'see' them as individuals, despite the apparent physical replication we are presented with. It is therefore clear tha we can no longer legitimately view the body as the source of individuality." Cronenberg believes body and soul, as manifested by Elliot and Beverly, to be inseparable. If we limit ourselves to valuing only one of these aspects, as is often the case in the medical field, the other will directly suffer as a result. Fittingly, *Dead Ringers* treats self-renunciation and loss of identity as two slow-moving, malignant processes that accompany physical decay. In late films like *eXistenZ* (1998), Cronenberg takes this reasoning to new heights The human body becomes virtually disbanded in the simulative realms o video games and no longer constitutes a hold on reality.

HM

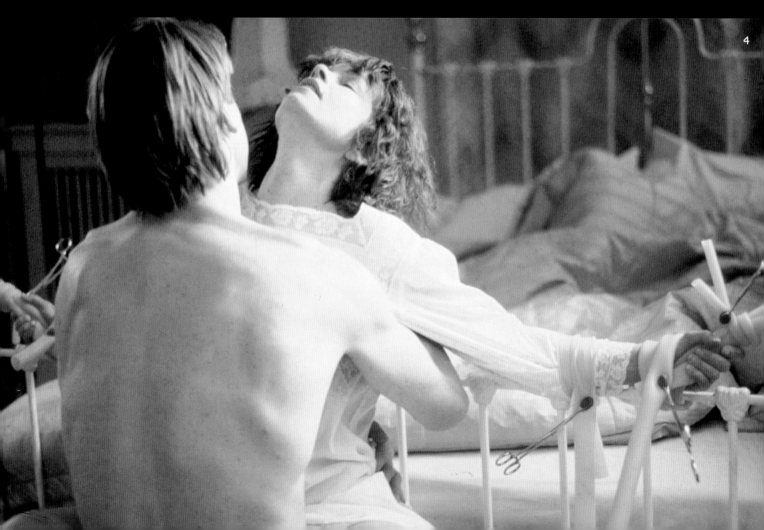

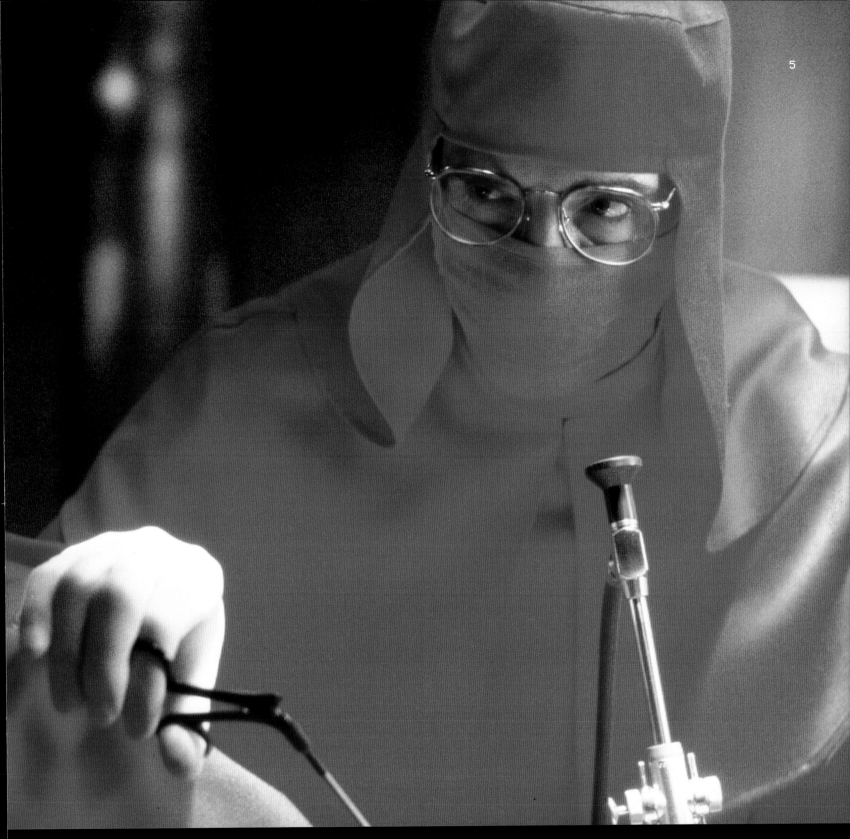

1 Just can't be himself: Beverly Mantle (Jeremy Irons) mourns the loss of his twin brother.

2 One last reunion: Mantle twins Elliot and Beverly.

3 Female intuition: Actress Claire Niveau (Geneviève Bujold) knows she's been had in the worst of ways.

4 Claire falls victim to a little death in Elliot's arms.

5 Quarantine: Good doctor Elliot dissects the ailments of childless mothers at his fertility clinic.

DAVID CRONENBERG Few directors have polarized the masses like David Cronenberg, revered among horror film fans and highbrows alike. Many people first became aware of the Toronto-born Canadian through his first Hollywood film *Videodrome* (1982). Prior to that, the 1943 baby-boomer made a slew of pictures that won him acclaim in sci-fi and horror film circles, including *Fast Company* (1979), *The Brood* (1979) and *Scanners* (1980). Cronenberg's thematic cornerstone is the human body and physical anomalies. He has dazzled audiences time and again with a seemingly limitless arsenal of masterfully executed special effects. As a director he is less interested in the shock value of gore than in the potential of science and technology to alter our relationship to our bodies. *Naked Lunch* (1991), *Crash* (1996) and *eXistenZ* (1998) plunge into the dark side of the engulfing worlds of drugs, cars and video games. He argues that depletion of identity is a typical symptom of addiction whose negative effects are on par with those of physical atrophy.

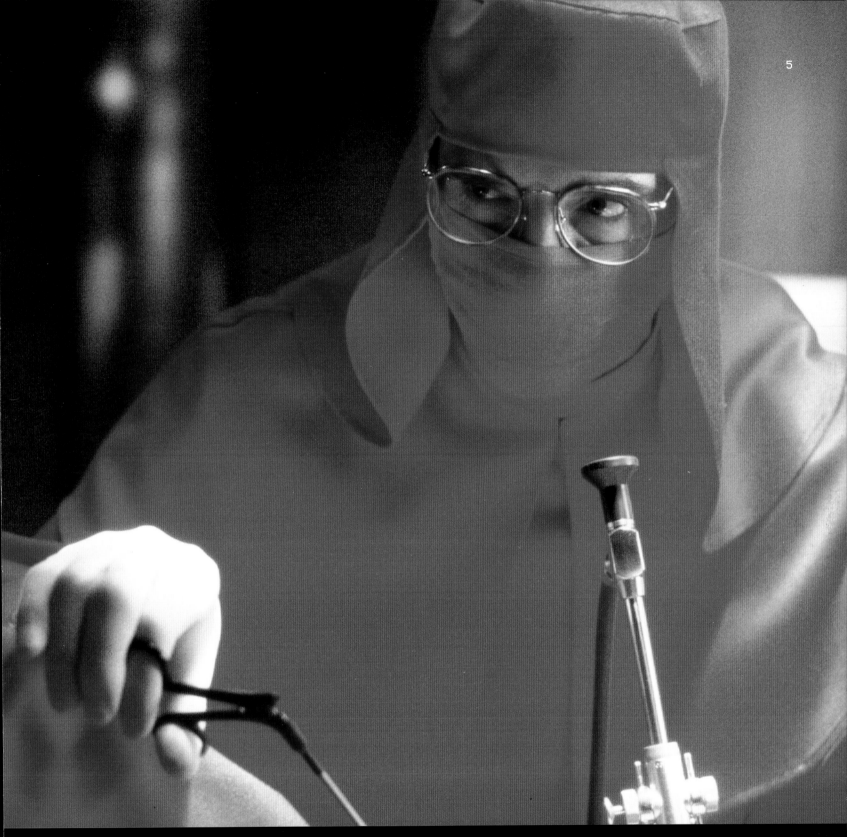

1 Just can't be himself: Beverly Mantle (Jeremy Irons) mourns the loss of his twin brother.

2 One last reunion: Mantle twins Elliot and Beverly.

3 Female intuition: Actress Claire Niveau (Geneviève Bujold) knows she's been had in the worst of ways.

4 Claire falls victim to a little death in Elliot's arms.

5 Quarantine: Good doctor Elliot dissects the ailments of childless mothers at his fertility clinic.

DAVID CRONENBERG Few directors have polarized the masses like David Cronenberg, revered among horror film fans and highbrows alike. Many people first became aware of the Toronto-born Canadian through his first Hollywood film *Videodrome* (1982). Prior to that, the 1943 baby-boomer made a slew of pictures that won him acclaim in sci-fi and horror film circles, including *Fast Company* (1979), *The Brood* (1979) and *Scanners* (1980). Cronenberg's thematic cornerstone is the human body and physical anomalies. He has dazzled audiences time and again with a seemingly limitless arsenal of masterfully executed special effects. As a director he is less interested in the shock value of gore than in the potential of science and technology to alter our relationship to our bodies. *Naked Lunch* (1991), *Crash* (1996) and *eXistenZ* (1998) plunge into the dark side of the engulfing worlds of drugs, cars and video games. He argues that depletion of identity is a typical symptom of addiction whose negative effects are on par with those of physical atrophy.

THE 90ˢ

20 CAMERA SHOTS
FOR 6 SECONDS OF FILM

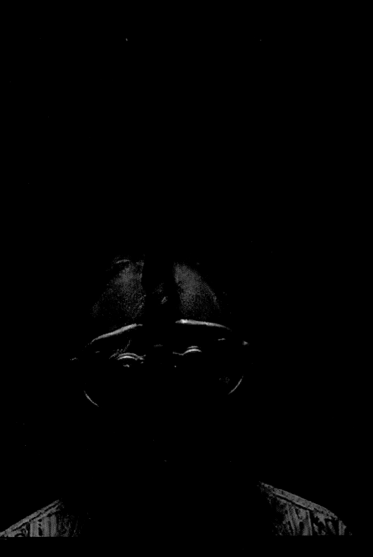

20 CAMERA SHOTS FOR 6 SECONDS OF FILM
Notes on the Movies of the 90s

Movies of the 90s contain imperceptible images. Shots can be accelerated so that they lie below the perception threshold. An example of such acceleration occurs at the end of Jonathan Demme's *The Silence of the Lambs* (1991, p. 716), in what is perhaps the shortest showdown in cinematic history. The exchange of fire between the FBI agent Clarice Starling and the mass-murderer Buffalo Bill takes no more than six seconds, even though it comprises twenty camera shots. It seems odd to devote only six seconds to the most exciting part of a two-hour film, but Demme allows the climax to implode in the true sense of the word and uses extremely powerful visual images.

The director skilfully and expertly creates the build-up to the showdown: after a tense parallel montage, at the end of which we expect the murderer to be caught, it is not the FBI task force that is standing at his door but Clarice on her own. She doesn't know it, but she has found Buffalo Bill. Before she realises who it is standing in front of her, he is able to take refuge in his cellar, where he is holding his latest victim captive. The murderer switches off the light when the FBI agent follows him into the cellar. While her adversary watches, Clarice gropes uncertainly in the dark. Throughout this scene, the audience sees through Buffalo Bill's eyes, his night-vision

device turning everything a ghostly green. During the chase, Clarice's irregular, panic-stricken breathing is all that can be heard. Only when the young agent hears the pistol being cocked behind her is she able to guess the murderer's position. At the speed of light, she spins round and the gunfight begins. In the silence, the cocking of the gun sounds like a thunderclap, as though we are hearing it through Clarice's ears, for in the darkness she has become acutely sensitive to even the tiniest of sounds. When we in turn find ourselves in absolute darkness, we not only hear through the ears of the FBI agent, but also see through her eyes.

The next shot shows the flash from Bill's revolver, which is reflected in the lenses of his night-vision device. The explosion from the gun looks like an abstract painting, and the fight does in fact develop into a symbolic duel. Whereas at first the murderer had the advantage in the darkness, the situation changes when the shooting match begins, as the adversaries dazzle each other when shots are exchanged. The flash from the gunshot allows the camera to show the murderer, who has been hit. This is then followed by a black screen, which lasts longer than the view of the people. Again we see a shot being fired, then another black screen. Now the audience can make out Clarice taking aim, but she is blinded by the shot fired from Bill's pistol.

A black screen and renewed gunfire. The FBI agent shoots with her eyes shut. Another gunshot. Again the audience sees Clarice shooting. A black screen. Bill has been hit a second time. A black screen. The murderer is hit again, and we see the look of agony on his face. A black screen. One shot has hit a window blind, loosening it. The daylight penetrating the cellar reveals a steel helmet and an American flag. The camera then cuts back to the cellar and there, lying on the floor, we see the fatally wounded murderer. With his night-vision device covering his eyes, he looks like a dead insect.

Cinema, television and video

In the cinema, our perception of this sequence is reduced to the knowledge that, after the FBI agent has fired her shots, the murderer lies dead on the floor. It is only in the last few images of this sequence that we return to daylight and viewing at normal speed, whereas what we have just witnessed is for the most part below the perception threshold. It is not until Clarice loads her weapon that it becomes clear what we must have seen. She has actually used up all her ammunition of six cartridges. Although we haven't been able to perceive these six shots consciously, the final images make it possible to come to this conclusion. While the shots are being exchanged, the camera angle changes constantly; we see things alternately through the eyes of the murderer and of the FBI agent. The sequence described here is

barely noticeable in the cinema. To see it at all, you really need to be able to break the picture sequence down into stills using a video recorder.

Clearly, as a means of reproducing scenes, the video recorder has an aesthetic potential comparable to that of a record player or CD player. It allows you to gain expert knowledge, whether you collect the films of a particular director or actor, or are interested in a particular genre.

With regard to video, Martin Scorsese is thoroughly optimistic, seeing in this technology the opportunity for engendering a new enthusiasm for the cinema. In a short article called "The Second Screen", he writes of the new opportunities that the video recorder has opened up. There is now no problem showing films that are hardly known anymore but deserve to be studied, and it is finally possible to compare film scenes directly. He also welcomes the wider distribution it has brought for some of his own films, which now reach a larger audience through video.

The video recorder also enables formal and aesthetic analysis by creating stills. You can study the content and composition of a shot or look at a film sequence in the same way as you can listen again and again to a virtuoso performance of a passage of music, just for the sheer pleasure of it. The growth in the numbers of Hong Kong movie fans is in no small part due to the fact that video makes it possible to appreciate their technical brilliance. Of course, we have never been able to see many of these films in the cinema, viewing them only on video right from the start.

When a director like David Fincher now asks that his films be watched not once but four or five times, this need present no problem for the viewer.

Video can never replace the cinema, of course, but it does enable different forms of perception. Lavish Hollywood productions are created with the aim of making them suitable not only for the one-off cinema experience, but also for repeated viewing on video. The more details intentionally concealed in a film, the more fun you will have in repeated viewings.

In that respect, most films nowadays have three premieres. First they appear in the cinema, then they are brought out on video, and finally they are shown on one of the many television channels. It is doubtful that any development of the last few decades has had a greater influence on filmmaking than videotape. As its use has become more widespread, film and television have come closer together. The video recorder has become the mediating element between the two – and television is certainly no longer second best. With *Star Trek* (from 1979), *The X-Files* (1998), *Mission: Impossible* (1996) and *The Fugitive* (1993), films for the cinema were modelled on famous television series. The same was true of David Lynch's cult series *Twin Peaks* (1989–91), which the director subsequently used as the basis for a film (1992). The barriers between the two media have become permeable. Helen Hunt and George Clooney were popular TV actors long before they became celebrated Hollywood stars, and several of today's prominent directors made music videos or worked for television before they were able to make a full-length feature film.

Seeing and hearing

Technical developments also demonstrate how natural the connection between television and film is today. Televisions are now made with a screen format (16:9) that corresponds to the wide-screen format of the cinema. Larger and larger televisions are being produced and it is now a long time since the cinema screen was the only way of presenting a film. Dolby surround sound systems mean that even at home, the sound and music of a film can be perceived spatially. It is remarkable how far the TV experience has been transformed through developments in technology. Video represents a kind of home movie, not to mention the further development in the form of DVD technology.

It must be acknowledged that such technical progress had its beginnings in cinemas. There too it was digital sound quality, particularly in the multiplex cinemas, that opened up a new cinematic age. You need think only of Steven Spielberg's war film *Saving Private Ryan* (1998), winner of so many Oscars, which in the first 15 minutes gave us a sort of phenomenology of the sounds of war. We can hear how the bullets ricochet off metal, how they hiss into the water or whistle past the soldiers' ears. Whereas the film material at the beginning of *Saving Private Ryan* looks grainy and is reminiscent of the newsreels of the 1940s, the sound is extremely varied. It is as though the images portraying historical events gain authenticity through the soundtrack. We even experience Captain Miller's deafness, when, beside himself in horror at the many dead, for a moment he no longer hears any external noises.

It has long been natural for the audience to see through the eyes of one of the characters in a film and to interpret a panning shot as the subjective view of a person. But in the 90s, we can even hear through the ears of a character in a film. The great success Spielberg enjoyed with *Jurassic Park* (1993) was also due to the convincing use of sound, as we stand in the middle of a stampeding herd of small dinosaurs, or in the unforgettable scene in which a Jeep is pursued by a Tyrannosaurus Rex, whose powerful steps seem to make the whole cinema shake.

In the movies of the 90s, it is impossible to overestimate the importance of sound in making the images so convincing. David Fincher produced a winner in this regard with *Alien³* (1992). In the most gruesome scene of the film, a post-mortem has to be carried out on a young girl, as no one knows whether there is an alien in her body. We see the instruments that are needed to carry out the procedure. We don't see the actual post-mortem itself, but we do hear the child's ribcage being opened up. The scene is almost unbearable and is one of the coldest "images" that modern cinema has produced. Film scenes of this sort illustrate the power sound can exert and that it can be just as effective in its own right as the actual images of a film.

All the examples mentioned concern the reproduction technique of cinema and television as creators of illusion. But has the video also changed the aesthetics of film in the 90s? The example cited above from *The Silence of the Lambs* shows the extreme extent to which images can be accelerated. This becomes clearer when we think, for example, of the influence of music videos, which are largely characterised by brief shots and frequent cuts.

Pictures are shown for only fractions of seconds, so that they are barely perceptible. In the battle scene at the beginning of Ridley Scott's *Gladiator* (2000), the cuts come so quickly that we get no intimation of the significance of a fragment of a second that decides between life and death. At the same time, we are aware of the sudden burst of speed in the sequence. First the legionaries are making meticulous preparations for the battle. Then on the command to attack, the film speeds up and takes us to the heart of the battle, where nothing is thought out in advance, and everything happens intuitively. Such scenes are an assault and a strain on the senses in equal measure. The viewer is all eyes, his intellect suspended.

Remake?

The video recorder has long been viewed as the enemy of the cinema, as though it would corrupt the pure science of film. In an ironic twist, there is an echo of this criticism even in a successful 1990s film. Nora Ephron's *You've Got Mail* (1998) contains the caricature of an art critic who claims in a TV interview that, from a technological point of view, our world is out of kilter. Just think of the video recorder, he says: the idea of a video recorder is that you can record a TV programme if you're going out, but to his mind, the fact that you're going out shows that you don't want to watch the TV programme. As far as he is concerned, the only medium that can be justified is the radio. With his self-absorbed monologue, the critic tries to convince us

that television and video are equally absurd. He maintains that both should be abolished. It becomes clear how serious his assessment is, however, when he casually asks his girlfriend whether she is actually recording the interview. Ephron's film may be dismissed as a romantic comedy, but even so the film poses the important question of the authenticity of the media. Can a love letter be taken seriously when it is sent as an e-mail? Do new technological means of communication make us lose our true personality? Are the contents only credible when they are written on paper? In a crucial scene, the heroine of the film clutches her copy of Jane Austen's *Pride and Prejudice*, as though her identity might be concealed in this book. Thus the film not only tells a love story, but also constantly questions our relationship with the media. These are not just electronic devices that transmit or record specific information, and they are not neutral records of a technical nature. They are rather part of our identity, because we are not just what we stand for, but also what we like, read, listen to and watch.

Ephron's film bears a faint resemblance to Ernst Lubitsch's classic *The Shop Around the Corner* from 1940. Both films tell a love story where the couple get together only by a convoluted route. But fundamentally *You've Got Mail* does not have much in common with the classic film. In only one scene does the director clearly borrow from the original classic: when Meg Ryan and Tom Hanks meet for a blind date with disastrous consequences, you expect the original to outshine the modern version. Meg Ryan is disappointed because, instead of the e-mail friend she had hoped for, she meets only her professional adversary, who, moreover, conceals his e-mail identity. A

heated argument ensues, at the end of which Tom Hanks leaves the bar. This scene makes it clear how mistaken ideals stop people from realising what they really are. In some respects, the film really ends here, and not with its happy ending. However, whereas Lubitsch leaves it up to the audience to judge, Ephron brings an added dimension to the touching closing scene of the film with the use of the song "Somewhere Over the Rainbow" on the soundtrack, thereby deliberately overdoing it and allowing for the possibility of an ironic reading.

Quotation and Hollywood films

It's often said that the cinema of the 1990s is allusive. Video is clearly important here too, as it supports this trend. But others feel that the idea of allusive cinema is a figment of some critics' imagination. These critics are selective when choosing films to prove their hypothesis. People who claim that the cinema of the 1990s is postmodern and allusive cite Francis Ford Coppola's *Dracula* (1992), but not Steven Spielberg's *Schindler's List* (1993). Whereas the first film can be related to many precursors and does actually represent a museum of film history, the second has to be seen in relation to real events of the past. We can also argue against the hypothesis of allusive cinema by saying that there have always been directors who have frequently displayed their knowledge of cinematic history. It was not only in the 1990s that Brian de Palma's works made reference to earlier films; they had been doing so for

years. We need think only of the end of *The Untouchables* (1987), when the American director alludes to the famous scene from Eisenstein's *Battleship Potemkin* (1925, p. 52), in which a pram clatters down a steep flight of steps. He quotes again but less obviously in *Mission: Impossible* (1995), a film which refers to *The Lady From Shanghai* (1948) and represents a homage to its creator, Orson Welles. Thus in de Palma's work, the desire to quote is in no way the exclusive preserve of the 1990s.

Whatever the objections to this idea of the cinema of quotation, it is true that the audience changed in the 1990s. The constant mass-media distribution of films means that there are more viewers who can recognise quotes and therefore know how to appreciate films. It is now much more a matter of course for films to be part of the cultural common knowledge. Without any jury having to rule on it, everybody knows today that *Psycho* (1960, p. 436), *Ben Hur* (1959, p. 390) and *Casablanca* (1942, p. 204) belong to the canon of classic films on which film history is based and from which it continues to develop. In other words, for particular genres, these films set standards that demand quality and originality. Anyone who emphasises the desire to quote in present-day cinema is really only saying that the history of film is not over, but has always represented a starting point and point of reference for filmmakers.

Film and personal reflection

Allusive cinema is a rather vague, general term for a highly creative association with originals, because quotes come in various forms: as remakes, as parodies or as homage. Usually they are allusions used by a director to express his admiration for a particular earlier film or film sequence. Such allusions can be clear, or less obvious. A master of the subtle allusion is the American director, Tim Burton. His film *Edward Scissorhands* (1990) begins with a young girl asking her grandmother where snow comes from. This paves the way for an allegorical trip through the history of film. When the camera leaves the room, we are led over the snow-covered houses of a suburb, until the view rises to a dark castle, in which a light burns. This is an allusion to Orson Welles' *Citizen Kane* (1941, p. 110): the castle with the lit window recalls Charles Foster Kane's huge mansion, Xanadu, and the snow that falls over the artificial-looking suburb harks back to the glass snow-scene that falls from the hand of the dying tycoon. Burton's film quotations attest to his admiration for Welles, who even appears as a character in his film *Ed Wood* (1994). With his reference to the snow-scene, he is also using one of the best cinematic metaphors: expressing in equal measure both childlike innocence and astonishment at the magic of the miniature world. Beyond the glass globe, you look towards a world of your own, dappled with dancing snowflakes, which comes to life in your imagination.

Burton's allusions underline the quality of Orson Welles' classics and make it possible to experience film history visually. The quotes in *Edward*

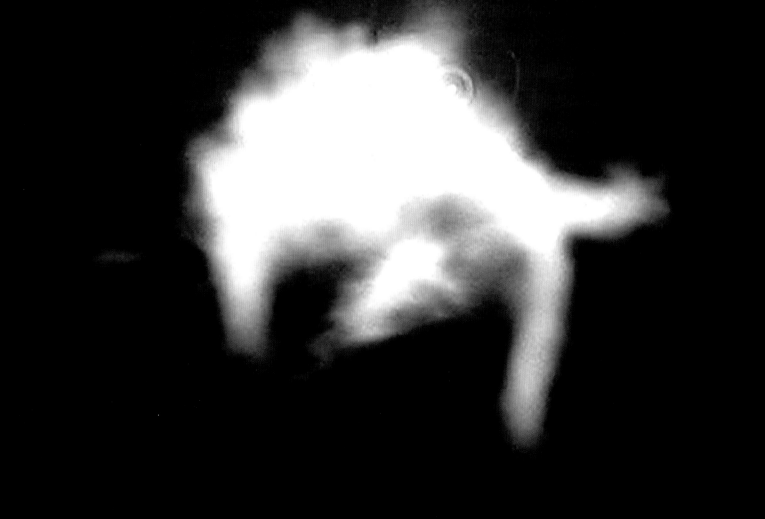

Scissorhands are difficult to recognise precisely because they fit the new context so well. The better a quote is adapted to the new context, the more likely that it will be recognised only by a devotee of the original film.

Danny Boyle is much more direct with his quotes in his film *Trainspotting* (1996). At an important point in the action, he refers to a famous earlier film. At a weekend disco, two boys are talking about their girl-friends. The music is so loud that we cannot hear what they are saying, but have to read subtitles, as in a silent film. The camera approaches the two in a single movement and, in the style of Pop Art, we recognise words such as "Vellozet" or "Synthomon" written on the walls, words which refer back to drinks from the Korova milk bar in Stanley Kubrick's *A Clockwork Orange* (1971, p. 544). Whereas in his film Kubrick lets his camera focus on the face of the principal actor and then pans out, in Doyle's *Trainspotting* the camera gradually zooms in on the two people – an almost direct quote, in which only one element is reversed. This English director's film continues to allude to famous earlier films. The following sequence shows the principal actor of *Trainspotting*, arms folded, standing in front of a poster portraying Robert De Niro as Travis Bickle in the film *Taxi Driver* (1976, p. 600), shooting with two pistols at once. It is not only the poster, but also even the defiant pose with the folded arms that recall Robert De Niro's interpretation of the role. A great many more allusions could be mentioned. In retrospect, the off-screen monologue at the start of the film seems to be a clear parallel with the open-ing monologue from *A Clockwork Orange*. The film also alludes to the record cover of the Beatles' "Abbey Road" LP, and there are shots that bring to mind

Richard Lester's Beatles films. This is not merely an expression of Doyle's admiration for the films in question, for these references to "Swinging London" give added meaning to the film. They tell of the end of a particular form of pop culture that is being replaced by techno. What has changed is a youth culture that is defined by saying no. Unlike Tim Burton, the English director produces his allusions so that they are clearly recognisable, almost to the point of being literal re-enactments.

Quotations do not, however, necessarily have to refer to what are regarded as great film classics: we need think only of the *Scream* trilogy (1996, 1997, 1999), which contains constant allusions to successful horror films such as *Nightmare on Elm Street* (from 1984) or *Halloween* (from 1978). What links the audience and the film characters in this way is detailed knowledge of these horror thrillers. The attraction of the sequel lies precise-ly in the fact that games are constantly being played with the audience's sense of anticipation. We think we know how the plot will develop, and, as a result, we are fooled time and again, because nothing turns out quite as expected. In the 1990s, cinematic self-reflection is no longer the exclusive prerogative of the *auteur* film, but a component part of mainstream cinema.

Non-linear narration

Along with speeding up pictures and the desire to quote, the third formal fea-ture of the movies of the 90s was the exploration of non-linear narration. The

(1978, p. 618); and Bruce Willis, familiar to many as the amoral hero of numerous action films, plays a boxer with character who ultimately remains incorruptible. Such allusions and identification of the actors with their roles make any reality outside of the film disappear.

In the labyrinth of images

The time structure of the film is even more radical. After Vincent Vega has been shot dead, he reappears in a subsequent scene. Of course, this is only possible because Tarantino muddies the chronology of his story. The film does not begin with the earliest scene chronologically, but jumps ahead, without the viewer being aware. This move is a stroke of genius, because it can highlight something that is a matter of principle: films take place not as a sequence starting from the present, but in a time called Future II. They run in the "past future". With *Pulp Fiction*, we find ourselves in a time warp that we can no longer leave. The killer, Vincent Vega, is shot dead when he is guarding the apartment of the boxer, Butch, who has betrayed their joint boss, Marsellus. When Vega reappears in the next but one scene, it can only be a flashback. The story has gone back to the beginning and we find out the macabre events that happened at the end of Jules' and Vincent's first job. Even if the audience can make out a logical connection between the individual episodes, it becomes clear during the film that even more things could have happened in the course of events that are initially assumed to repre-

sent the time line. Time seems infinitely divisible and another incident can always be revealed as having taken place between the episodes that are already known to the audience. It is like a person who rambles on in conversation, and always finds new pegs for more stories. In this anecdotal narrative device, the chronology of the episodes, which can be reconstructed only in retrospect, occurs in the background. Instead, events both comical and macabre keep the viewer in suspense and make any questions about a narrative logic subordinate. The attraction of such a narrative device lies in solving the riddle that sends the viewer into a pictorial labyrinth. We have the impression of being led through different genres, almost like an ironic allusion to channel hopping on evening television.

Dangerous fictions

There are many more buzz words that we could have chosen apart from those discussed, and the idea of genre is a case in point. Whereas at the beginning of the decade you might have had the impression that more and more films were mixing the genres in a new and interesting way, at the end of the decade, with *Titanic* (1997) and *Saving Private Ryan*, single-varietal genre films of apparently long-outmoded types came back into being.

Another important trend, which has become increasingly apparent over the decade, is the growth in the use of digital images. *Toy Story* (1995) was the first totally computer-generated full-length feature film. Whole lavish his-

toric sets are now simulated using computers, like the Coliseum in Ridley Scott's *Gladiator* or the luxury liner surging through the sea in James Cameron's *Titanic*. The first example of this was George Lucas' *Star Wars: Episode 1 – The Phantom Menace* (1999), with its sensational stunts. It is hard to predict further developments in this field, but they seem likely to affect the action film most.

The buzz words of acceleration, allusive cinema and non linear narration represent three paradigms that characterise, not cinema as a whole admittedly, but the important films of the 1990s. These are linked with the assertion that video is a prerequisite for all three phenomena. Acceleration throws up the question of the relationship between time and perception; allusions link the past with the present; and finally, non linear narration is a sort of mind-game, which makes it clear that television and cinema do not portray an image of reality, but have been re-creating it for years. Thus some films have explained this epistemological question at the end of the 1990s with a pessimistic perspective. Think of Peter Weir's media satire *The Truman Show* (1998), or Terry Gilliam's *Twelve Monkeys* (1995), David Cronenberg's *eXistenZ* (1999) and Larry and Andy Wachowski's *The Matrix* (1999) – all these films unsettle the viewer and ask whether people are not in fact deceived about the real character of the world. The relativity of perception, the reporting of events through the media and the displacement of the reality of this world combine to become the theme. It may be that the media give us the illusion of reality, that we only ever encounter it vicariously through duplicates, or a gigantic conspiracy is in progress. Such films bear

witness to the uneasiness with which we have left the first millennium and entered the second. The extent to which such a feeling of unease and the concomitant apocalyptic ideas are due to the pessimism typical of the end of an era, remains to be seen.

Film, television and video are everywhere in the modern world. The more time we spend in front of cinema and television screens, the more critically we must examine the possibilities and limits of these media. In so doing, we will be forced to the conclusion that there will probably never be a natural or appropriate use of media, even if we knew what such a thing was. Voluntarily limiting oneself, say to only one film a week? One film a day might be more realistic. Everyone knows that good films are addictive. In this respect, the situation is no better for cinema than it is for the older media like the radio or the book. Criticism of the media has been around since before the advent of television. Centuries ago, reading too many novels led a Spaniard by the name of Don Quixote to do battle with windmills and think that he was a knight. A classic case of losing your grip on reality because of media consumption. In spite of any illusions, we can certainly neither dispute the good intentions of this sad-faced knight nor fail to admit that he experienced a thing or two.

Jürgen Müller

THE SILENCE OF THE LAMBS ♟♟♟♟♟

1991 - USA - 118 MIN. - THRILLER

DIRECTOR JONATHAN DEMME (*1944) SCREENPLAY TED TALLY, based on the novel of the same name by THOMAS HARRIS DIRECTOR OF PHOTOGRAPHY TAK FUJIMOTO MUSIC HOWARD SHORE PRODUCTION GARY GOETZMAN, EDWARD SAXON, KENNETH UTT, RON BOZMAN for STRONG HEART PRODUCTIONS (for ORION).

STARRING JODIE FOSTER (Clarice Starling), ANTHONY HOPKINS (Dr Hannibal Lecter), SCOTT GLENN (Jack Crawford), TED LEVINE (Jame Gumb), ANTHONY HEALD (Dr Frederick Chilton), BROOKE SMITH (Catherine Martin), DIANE BAKER (Senator Ruth Martin), KASI LEMMONS (Ardelia Mapp), ROGER CORMAN (FBI Director Hayden Burke), GEORGE A. ROMERO (FBI Agent in Memphis).

ACADEMY AWARDS 1992 OSCARS for BEST PICTURE, BEST SCREENPLAY based on material previously produced or published (Ted Tally), BEST DIRECTOR (Jonathan Demme), BEST ACTOR (Anthony Hopkins) and BEST ACTRESS (Jodie Foster).

"I'm having a friend for dinner."

Clarice Starling (Jodie Foster), daughter of a policeman shot in the line of duty, wants to join the FBI. At the FBI Academy in Woods, Virginia, she races over training courses, pushing herself to the limit. Wooden signs bear the legend "HURT-AGONY-PAIN: LOVE IT" – they're not just there to exhort the rookies to excel, they also reveal the masochism involved. The movie goes through the whole range of this theme, from heroic selflessness to destructive self-hate. Jack Crawford (Scott Glenn), who is Starling's boss and the head of the FBI's psychiatric department, sends her to Baltimore to carry out a routine interview with an imprisoned murderer who is resisting questioning. As well as being a psychiatrist, the prisoner is also an extreme pathological case who attacked people and ate their organs. For eight years

Dr Hannibal "The Cannibal" Lecter (Anthony Hopkins) has lived in the window-less cellar of a high security mental hospital. Crawford hopes the interview will provide clues to the behaviour of a second monster, a killer known as "Buffalo Bill" who skins his female victims and has so far skilfully evaded the FBI. Crawford's plan works, and the professorial cannibal agrees to discuss the pathology of mass murderers with his visitor Clarice – on one condition. Lecter will give her expert advice on Buffalo Bill in exchange for the tale of her childhood trauma. "Quid pro quo" – she lays bare her psyche, he gives her a psychological profile of her suspect. The gripping dialogue that develops between the ill-matched couple can be understood on many levels. On one hand, we see a psychoanalyst talking to his patient, on the

2

3

1 The naked man and the dead: "Buffalo Bill" (Ted Levine) uses a sewing machine to make himself a new identity from the skin of his victims; above him are butterflies, a symbol of that metamorphosis.

2 The staring matches between Starling (Jodie Foster) and Lecter (Anthony Hopkins) are a battle for knowledge: Lecter is to help the FBI build a profile of the killer; Starling is to surrender the secret of her childhood.

3 The pair meet in the lowest part of the prison system, a basement dungeon from the underworld.

4 The eyes have it: in the serial killer genre, eyes become a tool for appropriation, destruction and penetration.

other, a young detective interrogating an unpredictable serial killer, and that ambiguity is the determining quality in Lecter and Starling's relationship. Both follow their own aims unerringly, refusing to give way, and the struggle that results is one of the most brilliant and sophisticated duels in cinema history. The daughter of a US senator falls into the hands of Buffalo Bill, and suddenly the FBI is under increasing pressure to find the murderer. Lecter's chance has come. In return for his help in capturing Jame Gumb alias Buffalo Bill (Ted Levine), he asks for better conditions and is transferred to a temporary prison in Memphis. He kills the warders and escapes in the uniform of a policeman, whose face he has also removed and placed over his own. His last exchange with Starling takes place over the telephone, when he rings from a Caribbean island to congratulate her on her promotion to FBI agent and bids her farewell with the words: "I'm having a friend for dinner". After hanging up, Lecter follows a group of tourists in which the audience recognise the hated Dr Chilton (Anthony Heald), director of the secure mental hospital in Baltimore, who clearly will be Lecter's unsuspecting dinner "guest".

The Silence of the Lambs marked a cinematic high point at the beginning of the 90s. It is impossible to categorise in any one genre as it combines

several. There are elements from police movies (where crime does not pay), but it's also a thriller that borrows much from real historical figures: the model for both Gumb and Lecter is Edward Gein (1906–1984), who was wearing braces made from his victims' skin when arrested in 1957.

But *The Silence of the Lambs* is also a movie about psychiatry. Both murderers are presented as psychopaths whose "relation" to one another forms the basis for criminological research, even though their cases are not strictly comparable. The movie was so successful that it became one of the most influential models for the decade that followed, enriching cinema history to the point of plot plagiarism and quotation.

Suspense and Deception

Hannibal Lecter had already appeared on the silver screen before *The Silence of the Lambs*. In 1986, Michael Mann filmed Thomas Harris' 1981 novel *Red Dragon* under the title *Manhunter*. Five years later, Jonathan Demme refined the material, and the changing perspectives of his camera work give what is fundamentally a cinematic re-telling of *Beauty and the*

4

The Silence of the Lambs is just plain scary – from its doomed and woozy camera angles to its creepy Freudian context." *The Wahington Post*

Beast a new twist. Demme films his characters from both within and without.

The director plays with the fluid border between external and internal reality, between memory and the present, as when we see Clarice's childhood in two flashbacks for which we are completely unprepared. Jodie Foster's eyes remain fixed on the here and now while the camera zooms beyond her into the past, probing her psychological wounds. During the final confrontation between Clarice and Jame Gumb, the perspective changes repeatedly. We see the murderer through Clarice's eyes but we also see the young FBI agent through the eyes of Jame, who seeks out his victims in the dark using infrared glasses.

This changing perspective in the movie's final scenes emphasises the extreme danger that Clarice is in. Other sequences are straightforward trickery, like the changing perspectives in the sequence which builds up to the finale. A police contingent has surrounded the house where they expect to find Jame Gumb, and black police officer disguised as a deliveryman rings the bell. On the other side of the door, we hear the bell ring. Jame dresses and answers the door. The police break into the house, whilst we see the murderer open the door to find Clarice standing before him – alone. In the next take, the police storm an empty house. This parallel montage combines two places that are far apart, two actions with the same aim, two houses, of which one is only seen from outside, the other from inside. We are made to

5   6

5   The cannibal clasps his hands. Cage and pose are reminiscent of Francis Bacon's portraits of the pope.

6   Lecter overpowers the guards with their own weapons: one policeman is given a taste of his own pepper spray.

7   The monster is restrained with straitjacket and muzzle; the powers of the state have the monopoly on violence for the time being.

8   A policeman is disembowelled and crucified on the cage. With his outstretched arms, he looks like a butterfly.

7

think that both actions are happening in the same place. The parallel montage is revealed as a trick and increases the tension: we suddenly realise that Clarice must face the murderer alone.

More than one film critic assumed that this ploy meant that even Hollywood films had moved into an era of self-reflexivity. Instead of consciously revealing a cinematic device, however, the parallel montage serves primarily to heighten the movie's atmosphere of danger and uncertainty. Nevertheless, *The Silence of the Lambs* works on both levels, both as exciting entertainment and as a virtuoso game with key cultural figures and situations. Some critics went so far as to interpret the perverted killer Buffalo Bill as Hades, god of the underworld, and although analyses like that may be interesting, they are not essential to an understanding of the film or its success.

At the 1992 Oscar awards, *The Silence of the Lambs* carried off the so-called Big Five in the five main categories, something which only two films (*It Happened One Night* (1934) and *One Flew Over the Cuckoo's Nest* (1975) had managed previously. Ten years after his escape, Hannibal Lecter appeared again on the silver screen (*Hannibal*, 2001). Jodie Foster refused to play the role of Clarice for a second time and was replaced by Julianne Moore (*Magnolia*) and Ridley Scott took over from Jonathan Demme as director.   RV

8

"I go to the cinema because I feel like being shocked." *Jonathan Demme*

10

9 In "Buffalo Bill's" basement lair, Starling is just about to be plunged into total darkness …

10 … where she has to feel her way blindly, straining to hear, while "Buffalo Bill" watches her through infra-red goggles.

PARALLEL MONTAGE A process developed early in the history of cinema. Editing enables two or more events happening in different places to be told and experienced at the same time. The best-known kind of parallel montage in movies is the "last-minute rescue", where images of an endangered or besieged character are juxtaposed in rapid succession with those of the rescuers who are on their way. Action movies use such sequences over and over as a means of increasing the tension, and the device has remained basically the same from David Griffith's 1916 film *Intolerance* to today's thrillers. Parallel montage allows us to be a step ahead of the figures in a film. We are allowed to know things that the characters do not themselves realise, and we are also in several places at the same time, an experience which is only possible in fiction.

FORREST GUMP ♟♟♟♟♟♟

1994 - USA - 142 MIN. - COMEDY

DIRECTOR ROBERT ZEMECKIS (*1952) **SCREENPLAY** ERIC ROTH, based on the novel of the same name by WINSTON GROOM **DIRECTOR OF PHOTOGRAPHY** DON BURGESS **MUSIC** ALAN SILVESTRI **PRODUCTION** WENDY FINERMAN, STEVE TISCH, STEVE STARKEY, CHARLES NEWIRTH for PARAMOUNT.

STARRING TOM HANKS (Forrest Gump), ROBIN WRIGHT (Jenny Curran), GARY SINISE (Lt. Dan Taylor), SALLY FIELD (Mrs Gump), MYKELTI WILLIAMSON (Benjamin Buford "Bubba" Blue), MICHAEL CONNER HUMPHREYS (Forrest as a boy), HANNA HALL (Jenny as a girl), TIFFANY SALERNO (Carla), MARLA SUCHARETZA (Lenore), HALEY JOEL OSMENT (Forrest Junior).

ACADEMY AWARDS 1995 OSCARS for BEST PICTURE, BEST ACTOR (Tom Hanks), BEST DIRECTOR (Robert Zemeckis), BEST VISUAL EFFECTS (Allen Hall, George Murphy, Ken Ralston, Stephen Rosenbaum), BEST FILM EDITING (Arthur Schmidt), and BEST ADAPTED SCREENPLAY (Eric Roth).

"Shit happens!"

A bus stop in Savannah, Georgia. A man with the facial expression of a child sits on the bench, a small suitcase next to him and a box of chocolates in his hand. While he is waiting for the bus, he tells the story of his life to the others sitting around him.

The story begins sometime in the 1950s in a place called Greenbow in Alabama. Here Forrest Gump (Michael Conner Humphreys), a young boy named after a hero from the Civil War, is growing up without a father. He is different from the other children: his IQ of 75 is way below average, and as his mother (Sally Field) says, his spine is as bent as a politician's morals. But his mother is a strong-willed woman, and she manages to balance out these defects. She makes her boy wear leg braces and although she's prepared to

use her body to convince the headmaster that Forrest doesn't need to go to a special school, she teaches her son morals: "Dumb folks are folks who act dumb", being one of the many pearls of wisdom from her rich repertoire.

Forrest, who is friendly and unsuspecting, doesn't have an easy life. No one wants to sit next to him on the school bus, apart from Jenny (Hanna Hall), who soon becomes his only friend. When Forrest is being teased by his school mates for the thousandth time, she tells him to run away. Forrest always does what people tell him, and suddenly he discovers hidden gifts like speed and endurance. The leg braces shatter, and with them the limitations of his simple mind fall away. Swifter than the wind, Forrest runs and runs and runs through his youth.

Years later, when he's almost an adult, Forrest is running away from his schoolmates again and by mistake ends up on a football field. Simple-minded Forrest is offered a college scholarship and a place on an All-American football team.

"Life is like a box of chocolates. You never know what you're gonna get" – another gem from Mrs Gump's treasury. There's a lot in this for Forrest. Thanks to his knack for being in the right place at the right time, his football career is followed by military service and the Vietnam War, where he becomes not only a war hero but also a first-class table tennis player. After the war he fulfils a promise he made to Bubba (Mykelti Williamson), his friend and comrade in arms, and he makes his fortune as the captain of a shrimp-

ing boat. He becomes even richer when he invests his millions in what he believes to be a fruit firm by the name of "Apple".

Forrest Gump's life is a 40-year, long-distance run through American post-war history. He shakes hands with Presidents Kennedy and Nixon, shows Elvis Presley the hip thrust and inspires John Lennon's song "Imagine". He invents the Smiley as well as the "Shit happens" sticker. By pure chance his finger is always on the pulse of the times. He gets mixed up in a protest action for racial integration, in a demonstration against the Vietnam War and accidentally witnesses the Watergate Affair.

Just as Forrest's career and his experiences of American history are unintentional, his meetings with the love of his life, Jenny (Robin Wright), are

"Hanks is a kid again in director Robert Zemeckis' *Forrest Gump*. Slow-witted and likeable, Forrest races through the rubble of the 50s, 60s and 70s." *Time Magazine*

1   As simple as they come: Forrest Gump (Tom Hanks) fulfils the American dream in his own way.

2   A safe seat: one of his mother's sayings was "Dumb folks are folks who act dumb" and this stays with him all his life.

3   Jenny (Hanna Hall) is Forrest's (Michael Conner Humphreys) only friend. She sticks by him, even though everybody teases him because he is so slow physically and mentally.

4   A woman's wiles: Forrest's single mother (Sally Field) uses everything in her power, even her own body, to ensure that her son leads a normal life.

3

4

also unplanned. Instead of fulfilling her dream and becoming a folksinger she has ended up a junkie hanging round the hippie scene, singing in a third-rate night club. When his mother dies, Forrest moves back to Greenbow, where he has a short but unsuccessful affair with Jenny. Once more, Forrest tries to run away from his destiny and he runs through America for three years without a concrete destination, accompanied by a growing band of followers.

Director Robert Zemeckis is known for being a specialist in technically demanding entertainment movies. He literally turned Meryl Streep's head in *Death Becomes Her* (1992) and his *Back to the Future* trilogy suggests that he has a weakness for time travel (*Back to the Future I-III*, 1985, 1989, 1990).

Forrest Gump, adapted by Eric Roth from the novel of the same name by Winston Groom, is also a strange journey into the past.

With the help of George Lucas' special effects firm Industrial Light & Magic (ILM), Zemeckis uses sophisticated visual tricks and original film footage to create the illusion that Forrest was actually present at various historical occasions. For the scene where Forrest shakes hands with President Kennedy in the Oval Office, the digital technicians of ILM used archive material with the real people cut out and a superimposed image of Forrest Gump. Tom Hanks was filmed in front of a blue screen and this was combined with the archive film by computer. Computer technology is present throughout *Forrest Gump*, though audiences are unlikely to notice it. With its help

"Throughout, Forrest carries a flame for Jenny, a childhood sweetheart who was raised by a sexually abusive father and is doomed to a troubled life. The character's a bit obvious: Jenny is clearly Forrest's shadow – darkness and self destruction played against his lightness and simplicity." *San Francisco Chronicle*

thousand real extras were transformed into a hundred thousand simulated demonstrators.

The naive boy-next-door image which Tom Hanks had developed elsewhere made him the ideal actor for this part, which one critic described as "Charlie Chaplin meets Lawrence of Arabia". His Forrest Gump is the counterpart of Josh Baskin, the twelve-year-old who grows into the body of a man overnight in Penny Marshall's comedy *Big* (1988).

Forrest Gump is not a direct reflection of contemporary history, but it does reflect a distinctly American mentality. History is personalised and shown as a series of coincidences. The moral of the movie is as simple as

CHUNGKING EXPRESS
Chongqing Senlin

1994 - HONG KONG - 97 MIN. - DRAMA

DIRECTOR WONG KAR-WAI [WANG JIAWEI] (*1958) **SCREENPLAY** WONG KAR-WAI
MUSIC ROEL A. GARCIA, FRANKIE CHAN [CHEN SHUNQI]
DIRECTOR OF PHOTOGRAPHY CHRISTOPHER DOYLE, ANDREW LAU [LIU WEIQIANG]
PRODUCTION CHAN YI-KAN [CHEN YIJIN] for JET TONE PRODUCTIONS.

STARRING BRIGITTE LIN [Lin Qingxia] (woman with the blond wig),
KANESHIRO TAKESHI [He Qiwu] (# 223), TONY LEUNG [Liang Chaowei]
(# 663), FAYE WONG [Wang Jinwen] (Faye), VALERIE CHOW [Shou Jialing]
(Stewardess), "PIGGY" CHAN [Chen Jinquan], GUAN LINA, HUANG ZHIMING,
LIANG ZHEN, ZUO SONGSHEN.

"California Dreamin'"

To begin with, *Chungking Express* was just occupational therapy for Wong Kar-Wai: he had a couple of months' break in the middle of a big production called *Ashes of Time* (*Dung che sai duk*, 1992–94) and he wanted to fill it in by knocking out a short movie. He started out with little more than a couple of clearly defined characters and locations to go with them. The internal links and the plot, were all to be found in the process of filming.

April 30, 1994. A woman (Brigitte Lin) in a garish blond wig and enormous sunglasses has to pass on a packet of drugs, but she loses it and has to go and look for it. At the same time policeman He Qiwu – officer no. 223 – sits in a snack bar drowning his sorrows, as his girl friend left him exactly a month ago. Since then he has survived on cans of pineapple whose sell-by date is today, symbolising the end of his love. Gloomily he gets more and more drunk and empties his last can of pineapple. To cap it all, today is his 25th birthday. He decides to fall in love with the first woman who comes into the snack bar. Enter the blonde with the sunglasses, worn out from a chaotic day and looking for comfort.

Another policeman – officer no. 663 – has also split up with his girl friend, an air hostess. She has left her key to his apartment in his regular bar with Faye the waitress, who constantly listens to the promises of "California Dreamin'". Faye has secretly been in love with the policeman for a long time and has absolutely no intention of passing on the keys. She starts creeping into his apartment everyday. Sometimes she simply cleans up, often she plays some kind of trick, swaps labels on tin cans, dissolves sleeping pills in drinks or puts new fish in his aquarium. One day she finds a message from the policeman: he wants to meet her and arranges a date in the Restaurant California.

The particular conditions of the movie's production, meant that Wong had to fight not only with his inspiration but also with the plans of his film team, who were booked up for months ahead. Apparently the set was the scene of the most extraordinary comings and goings as both the actors and the technicians were constantly disappearing off to other film sets. Wong improvised a lot and filmed lots of individual scenes that had to be self-con-

tained, as it was unclear how the scenes would fit together at the end. Despite the movie's transitory character, this gives every moment a high degree of concentration. Wong withdrew to the editing room with the piece-meal material and two months later, *Chungking Express* was finished.

The movie became Wong Kar-Wai's greatest international success, the blonde with the sunglasses the icon of a whole generation and Chris Doyle one of the most important cameramen of the 90s. Wong Kar-Wai became a style. Wong Kar-Wai came to mean loose plots structured like poems, eccentric voice-overs, bright colours, spectacular hand-held camera work and outlandish picture composition: an urbane cinema of memories, where romance is only possible in retrospect, set in a city which is constantly changing, which denies its past and which will soon cease to exist. OM

"It's beautiful, simple, funny and smart. I wish more films were like it." *Le Monde*

CHRISTOPHER DOYLE   Christopher Doyle was born in Sydney in 1952. His work together with director Wong Kar-Wai, whose movies he filmed from *Days of Being Wild* (*A Fei zhengzhuan*, 1990) onwards, made him into one of the most-imitated cameramen of the 90s. His sensitive approach to colour combined with precise hand-held camera work came to express the melancholy of the period's *fin-de-siècle* school of international art films. As Doyle now lives in Hong Kong, he has taken a Cantonese name: Duk Ke-feng (= lord, master, like the wind). As well as his work as a cameraman, he also directs music videos and commercials – for the fashion designer Yoji Yamamoto, for example. After several years of somewhat chaotic work, Doyle presented his first feature-length movie *Away with Words* in 1999.

1   "[I'm the] DJ of my own films." *Wong Kar-Wai*

2   Self-reflection, Hong Kong style: Cantonese pop superstar Faye Wong [Wang Jinwen] as Faye in a typical Wong game with the identities of his actors.

3   Another icon of 1990s cinema: Oriental hit-woman Brigitte Lin [Lin Qingxia] in a blonde wig.

4   "There is so little space in Hong Kong that you would have no chance with a fixed camera. You have to work with a hand-held camera." *Cameraman Christopher Doyle*

5   "The scenes in *Chungking Express* […] are set in places that he [Wong Kar-Wai] himself frequents, such as the 'Midnight-Express' Fast-Food Stand in the Lan Kwai Fong district." *Production Manager & Chief Editor William Chang*

PULP FICTION 🏆

1994 - USA - 154 MIN. - GANGSTER FILM

DIRECTOR QUENTIN TARANTINO (*1963) **SCREENPLAY** QUENTIN TARANTINO, ROGER ROBERTS AVARY
DIRECTOR OF PHOTOGRAPHY ANDRZEJ SEKULA **MUSIC** VARIOUS SONGS **PRODUCTION** LAWRENCE BENDER for
JERSEY FILMS, A BAND APART (for MIRAMAX).

STARRING JOHN TRAVOLTA (Vincent Vega), SAMUEL L. JACKSON (Jules Winnfield), UMA THURMAN
(Mia Wallace), HARVEY KEITEL (Winston Wolf), VING RHAMES (Marsellus Wallace),
ROSANNA ARQUETTE (Jody), ERIC STOLTZ (Lance), QUENTIN TARANTINO (Jimmie),
BRUCE WILLIS (Butch Coolidge), MARIA DE MEDEIROS (Fabienne), CHRISTOPHER WALKEN
(Koons), TIM ROTH (Ringo/Pumpkin), AMANDA PLUMMER (Yolanda/Honeybunny).

IFF CANNES 1994 GOLDEN PALM.

ACADEMY AWARDS 1995 OSCAR for BEST ORIGINAL SCREENPLAY (Quentin Tarantino, Roger Roberts
Avary).

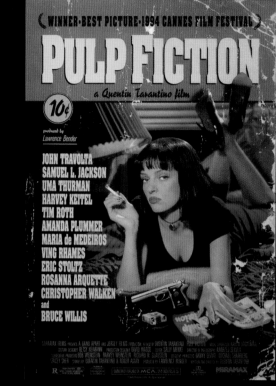

"Zed's dead, baby. Zed's dead."

After his amazing directorial debut *Reservoir Dogs* (1991), Quentin Tarantino had a lot to live up to. The bloody studio piece was essentially a purely cinematic challenge, and such an unusual movie seemed difficult to beat. But Tarantino surpassed himself with *Pulp Fiction*, a deeply black gangster comedy. Tarantino had previously written the screenplay for Tony Scott's uninspired gangster movie *True Romance* (1993) and the original script to Oliver Stone's *Natural Born Killers* (1994). At the beginning of his own movie, he presents us with another potential killer couple. Ringo and Yolanda (Tim Roth and Amanda Plummer), who lovingly call each other Pumpkin and Honeybunny, are sitting having breakfast in a diner and making plans for their future together. They are fed up of robbing whisky stores whose multi-cultural owners don't even understand simple orders like "Hand over the cash!" The next step in their career plan is to expand into diners – why not start straight away with this one? This sequence, which opens and concludes *Pulp Fiction* serves a framework for the movie's other three inter-woven stories, which overlap and move in and out of chronological sequence. One of the protagonists is killed in the middle of the movie, only to appear alive and well in the final scene, and we only understand how the stories hang together at the very end.

The first story is "Vincent Vega and Marsellus Wallace's Wife". Vincent and Jules (John Travolta and Samuel L. Jackson), are professional assassins on their way to carry out an order. Their boss Marsellus Wallace (Ving Rhames) wants them to bring him back a mysterious briefcase. A routine job, as we can tell from their nonchalant chit-chat. Their black suits make them look as if they have stepped out of a 40s *film noir*. Vince is not entirely happy, as he has been given the job of looking after Marsellus' wife Mia (Uma Thurman) when the boss is away. In gangster circles, rumour has it that Vincent's predecessor was thrown out of a window on the fourth floor – apparently for doing nothing more than massaging Mia's feet.

"The Golden Watch", the second story in the film, is the story of has-been boxer Butch Coolidge (Bruce Willis). He too is one of Marsellus' "niggers" as the gangster boss calls all those who depend on him. Butch has accepted a bribe and agreed to take a dive in after the fifth round in his next fight. At the last minute, he decides to win instead and to run away with the money and his French girlfriend Fabienne (Maria de Medeiros).

In the third story, "The Bonnie Situation", a couple of loose narrative strands are tied together. Jules and Vincent have done their job. However, on the way back, Vincent accidentally shoots his informer who is sitting in the

"Hoodlums Travolta and Jackson — like modern-day Beckett characters — discuss foot massages, cunnilingus and cheeseburgers on their way to a routine killing job. The recently traveled Travolta informs Jackson that at the McDonald's in Paris, the Quarter Pounder is known as 'Le Royal'. However a Big Mac's a Big Mac, but they call it 'Le Big Mac'." *The Washington Post*

begins like a kitsch scene from any Vietnam movie, but quickly deteriorates into the scatological and absurd when Walken tells the boy in great detail about the dark place where his father hid the watch in the prison camp for so many years.

Tarantino has an excellent feel for dialogue. His protagonists' conversations are as banal as in real life, they talk about everything and nothing, about potbellies, embarrassing silences or piercings. He also lays great value on those little details which really make the stories, for example the toaster, which together with Vincent's habit of long sessions in the bathroom will cost him his life – as he prefers to take a detective story rather than a pistol into the lavatory.

Tarantino's treatment of violence is a theme unto itself. It is constantly present in the movie, but is seldomly explicitly shown. The weapon is more important than the victim. In a conventional action movie, the scene where Jules and Vincent go down a long corridor to the apartment where they will kill several people would have been used to build up the suspense, but in Tarantino's film Vincent and Jules talk about trivial things instead, like two office colleagues on the way to the canteen.

One of the movie's most brutal scenes comes after Vincent and Mia's restaurant visit. The pair of them are in Mia's apartment, Vincent as ever in the bathroom, where he is meditating on loyalty and his desire to massage Mia's feet. In the meantime Mia discovers his supply of heroin, thinks it is cocaine and snorts an overdose. Vincent is then forced to get physical with her, but not in the way he imagined. To bring her back to life, he has to plant an enormous adrenaline jab in her heart.

Pulp Fiction also shows Tarantino to be a master of casting. All the roles are carried by their actors' larger-than-life presence. They are all "cool": Samuel L. Jackson as an Old-Testament-quoting killer, and Uma Thurman in a black wig as an enchanting, dippy gangster's moll. Bruce Willis drops his habitual grin and is totally convincing as an ageing boxer who refuses to give up. Craggy, jowly John Travolta plays the most harmless and good-natured assassin imaginable. If *Pulp Fiction* has a central theme running through it, then it's the "moral" which is present in each of the three stories. Butch doesn't run away when he has the opportunity but stays and saves his boss's life. Vincent and Jules live according to strict rules and principles and are very moral in their immoral actions. Vincent is so loyal that it finally costs him his life. Jule's moment of revelation comes when the bullets aimed at him miraculously miss. Coincidence or fate? Jules, who misquotes a Bible passage from Ezekiel before each of the murders he commits, decides that henceforth he will walk the path of righteousness. In the last scene when Ringo and Honeybunny rob the diner, Ringo tries to take the mysterious shiny briefcase. He fails to spot Jules draw his gun and under normal circumstances he would be a dead man. But Jules, who has decided to turn over a new leaf, has mercy on both of them –and that's not normal circumstances.　　　APO

4

5

"Tarantino's guilty secret is that his films are cultural hybrids. The blood and gore, the cheeky patter, the taunting mise-en-scène are all very American — the old studios at their snazziest."

Time Magazine

1 Do Mia's (Uma Thurman) foot massages turn into an erotic experience?

2 The Lord moves in mysterious ways: Jules (Samuel L. Jackson) is a killer who knows his Bible by heart.

3 Completely covered in blood: Vincent (John Travolta) after his little accident.

4 Everything's under control: as the "Cleaner" Mister Wolf (Harvey Keitel) takes care of any dirty work that comes up.

5 Echoes of *Saturday Night Fever*: Mia and Vincent risk a little dance.

6 In his role as Major Koons Christopher Walken plays an ex-Vietnam prisoner-of-war as he did in *The Deer Hunter*.

7

"Split into three distinct sections, the tale zips back and forth in time and space, meaning that the final shot is of a character we've seen being killed 50 minutes ago." *Empire*

PULP — Cheap novels in magazine format, especially popular in the 30s and 40s, owing their name to the cheap, soft paper they were printed on. The themes and genres of these mostly illustrated serial novels and short stories ranged from comics to science fiction to detective stories. The first pulp stories appeared in the 1880s in the magazine *The Argosy*. In the 1930s there were several hundred pulp titles available, but by 1954 they had all disappeared – pulp was replaced by the cinema, the radio and above all, the new paperback book.

7 Will his pride desert him? Boxer Butch (Bruce Willis) gets paid every time he loses in the ring.

8 You gotta change your life! Jules and Vincent talk about chance and predestiny.

9 Hand over the cash! Yolanda (Amanda Plummer) carries out …

10 … the plan that she and Ringo (Tim Roth) hatched a few moments before.

8

L. A. CONFIDENTIAL 🏆🏆

1997 - USA - 138 MIN. - POLICE FILM, DRAMA, NEO FILM NOIR

DIRECTOR CURTIS HANSON (*1945) SCREENPLAY CURTIS HANSON, BRIAN HELGELAND based on the novel *L. A. CONFIDENTIAL* by JAMES ELLROY DIRECTOR OF PHOTOGRAPHY DANTE SPINOTTI
MUSIC JERRY GOLDSMITH PRODUCTION CURTIS HANSON, ARNON MILCHAN, MICHAEL G. NATHANSON for REGENCY ENTERPRISES.

STARRING RUSSELL CROWE (Bud White), KEVIN SPACEY (Jack Vincennes), GUY PEARCE (Ed Exley), KIM BASINGER (Lynn Bracken), DANNY DEVITO (Sid Hudgeons), JAMES CROMWELL (Dudley Smith), DAVID STRATHAIRN (Pierce Patchett), RON RIFKIN (D. A. Ellis Loew), MATT MCCOY (Brett Chase), PAUL GUILFOYLE (Mickey Cohen).

ACADEMY AWARDS 1998 OSCARS for BEST SUPPORTING ACTRESS (Kim Basinger), and BEST ADAPTED SCREENPLAY (Curtis Hanson, Brian Helgeland).

"Why did you become a cop? – I don't remember."

Sun, swimming pools, beautiful people: "Life is good in L.A., it's a paradise …" That Los Angeles only exists in commercials. In *L. A. Confidential* – set in the early 50s – the city looks quite different, and is a morass of crime and corruption. Three policemen try to combat this with varying dedication and varying motives. Ambitious young police academy graduate Ed Exley (Guy Pearce) is a champion of law and order, and his testimony against his colleagues in an internal police trial catapults him straight to the top of the station house hierarchy. Bud White (Russell Crowe) is a hardened cynic who is prepared to extract confessions with force, but cannot stand violence against women and Jack Vincennes (Kevin Spacey) is nothing more than a corrupt phoney who uses his police job to get in with the entertainment

industry. He is advisor to the television series "Badge Of Honor" and sets up stories for Sid Hudgeons (Danny DeVito), slimy reporter on the gossip magazine "Hush-Hush".

Exley's first case is a spectacular bloodbath in the Nite Owl bar. Five lie dead in the bathroom, killed with a shotgun. Three back youths seen near the scene of the crime are swiftly arrested, and with his brilliant interrogation technique, Exley gets them to admit to having kidnapped and raped a Mexican girl. While White frees the victim and shoots her captor, the three blacks escape from police custody. Exley hunts them down and shoots them dead. He is hailed as a hero and awarded a medal, and it would seem that that is the end of the case. But it doesn't seem to quite add up, and Exley

"It's striking to see how the elegance and lightness of touch in the atmosphere of *L. A. Confidential* seem both to derive from and influence the actors." *Cahiers du cinéma*

3

4

1   He may have deserved it much more for this film, but Russell Crowe didn't win an Oscar until 2001 for *Gladiator*.

2   Bud White (Russell Crowe) doesn't waste any time with the kidnapper of the Mexican girl.

3   Kim Basinger's Oscar for the part of Lynn Bracken brought her long-overdue universal acclaim.

4   A Christmas angel: Lynn out on business until late in the evening with her employer.

5   A few moments of melancholy apart, Bud White doesn't let the corruptness of the world get to him.

6   Brief moments of happiness: is there a future for Bud and Lynn's love?

7   Lynn the prostitute's little trick: she does herself up to look like 1940s glamour star Veronica Lake.

White and Vincennes continue their investigations until they discover a conspiracy which reaches up into the highest echelons of police and city administration, involving drugs, blackmail, and a ring of porn traders.

L. A. Confidential is a reference to the first and perhaps most brazen American gossip magazine "Confidential" (1952–1957), and Hudgeons, the reporter played by Danny DeVito (who is also the off-screen narrator) is an alter ego of Robert Harrison, its infamous editor. Hudgeons gets his kicks from filth and sensationalism, and typifies the moral decadence that seems to have infected the entire city. The police make deals with criminals, the cops who uncover the conspiracy are far from blameless and even the naive greenhorn Exley looses his innocence in the course of the film.

Director Curtis Hanson conjures up the brooding atmosphere of the film noir crime movies of the 40s and 50s, but *L. A. Confidential* is far more than a throwback of a simple nostalgia trip. Cameraman Dante Spinotti shoots clear images free from any patina of age and avoids typical genre references like long shadows. The crime and the corruption seem even more devastating when told in pictures of a sunny, crisp Los Angeles winter. The plot is complex and difficult to follow on first viewing, but Hanson does not emphasise this so much as individual scenes which condense the city's amorality into striking images, like Vincennes saying he can no longer remember why he became a cop. Above all, the director focuses on his brilliant ensemble. Australians Russell Crowe and Guy Pearce, who were virtually unknown before the movie was made, make a great team with the amazing Kevin Spacey. Kim Basinger is a worthy Oscar winner as prostitute and Veronica Lake look-alike Lynn.

HJK

5

6

"When I gave Kevin Spacey the script, I said I think of two words: Dean Martin."

Curtis Hanson in: Sight and Sound

8

JAMES ELLROY: L. A.'S INDEFATIGABLE CHRONICLER

His own life sounds like a crime story. James Ellroy was born in Los Angeles in 1948. When he was ten, his mother fell victim to a sex killer, a crime he works through in his 1996 novel *My Dark Places*. The shock threw Ellroy completely off the rails: drugs, petty crime and 50 arrests followed, and he came to writing relatively late. His first novel *Brown's Requiem* was published in 1981 and made into a movie with the same name in 1998. He then wrote a novel trilogy on the figure of the policeman Lloyd Hopkins. The first of this series *Blood on the Moon* (1984) was filmed in 1988 as *Cop* starring James Woods in the title role. Ellroy's masterpiece is the L. A. tetralogy, novels on historical crimes from the period 1947 to 1960. *L. A. Confidential* is the extensive third volume of the series; it took Hanson and co-author Brian Helgeland a whole year and seven different versions to adapt it as a screenplay.

8 Tabloid reporter Sid Hudgeons (Danny DeVito) loves digging up other people's dirt.

9 Officer Vincennes (right) likes to take Hudgeons and a photographer along to his arrests.

10 Vincennes (Kevin Spacey) makes sure that first and foremost he's looking after number one.

11 Officer Ed Exley (Guy Pearce) earns praise from the press and from his boss Dudley Smith (James Cromwell, right).

9

FACE/OFF

1997 - USA - 138 MIN. - ACTION FILM

DIRECTOR JOHN WOO (*1946) SCREENPLAY MIKE WERB, MICHAEL COLLEARY
DIRECTOR OF PHOTOGRAPHY OLIVER WOOD MUSIC JOHN POWELL PRODUCTION DAVID PERMUT, BARRIE M. OSBORNE, TERENCE CHANG, CHRISTOPHER GODSICK for DOUGLAS-REUTHER PRODUCTION, WCG ENTERTAINMENT.

STARRING JOHN TRAVOLTA (Sean Archer), NICOLAS CAGE (Castor Troy), JOAN ALLEN (Eve Archer), ALESSANDRO NIVOLA (Pollux Troy), GINA GERSHON (Sasha Hassler), DOMINIQUE SWAIN (Jamie Archer), NICK CASSAVETES (Dietrich Hassler), HARVE PRESNELL (Victor Lazarro), COLM FEORE (Dr Malcolm Walsh), CCH POUNDER (Dr Hollis Miller).

"In order to catch him, he must become him."

Sepia pictures, images in someone's memory. A father rides with his son on a carousel horse. A shot rings out. The father is wounded and the son is killed. Six years later L. A. cop Sean Archer (John Travolta) still hasn't caught up with Castor Troy (Nicolas Cage), the psychopathic sharp shooter who killed his son. He gets another chance at a private airfield. Castor and his brother Pollux (Alessandro Nivolla) are about to take off, and Archer tries to stop them.

A shoot-out ensues where Pollux is arrested and Castor is injured and falls into a coma. But Archer still hasn't shaken off Castor Troy's evil legacy. His brother is carrying a disc that contains information on a gigantic bomb attack in Los Angeles, but the whereabouts of the bomb is a mystery. Pollux insists that he will only speak to his brother. To find out the truth about the bomb, a team of scientists from a secret project make Archer an unbelievable offer.

The parallel between hunter and hunted is a well-worn theme: the cop has to empathise with the criminal in order to predict his next move. Many movies have used this device, perhaps none so systematically as *Heat* (1995), where cop Al Pacino and gangster Robert De Niro meet for a tête-à-tête. *Face/Off*'s director John Woo takes the motif to new heights when he turns the cop into the gangster. With the help of the latest medical technology, Archer is given the face, stature and voice of the gangster Troy. He already knows more than enough about Troy's story, deeds and accomplices as he has been chasing him for years. To get the information out of him, Archer is admitted to the high security prison where Pollux is being kept. The mission remains a secret, and not even Archer's boss or his wife know anything about it. At any time, with the help of the same techniques, he can be given back his own body. But suddenly that escape route is suddenly blocked. Troy wakes out of his coma and appears in the prison – as Archer.

4

1   A shock: police officer Archer (John Travolta)
    wearing the face of the villain he has been pursu-
    ing like a man possessed for the last six years.

2   "Ridiculous chin", says Castor (Nicolas Cage)
    when Archer's face is fixed onto his.

3   The parallel between the hunter and the hunted is
    a well-known film motif, but nobody has ever
    taken it as far as John Woo.

4   It's not easy for Archer: locked up in the body of
    Castor in a high-tech jail.

5   The momen
    arch-enemy

6   Sean and E
    son. Their g
    film.

JOHN TRAVOLTA   John Travolta's career began in 1975 with the role of Vinnie Barbarino in the popular television series *Welco*
in the dance movies *Saturday Night Fever* (1977) and *Grease* (1978) was based on his clichéd roles as attrac
practically disappeared from the screen in the 1980s. He wasn't able to return to Hollywood's premiere lea
the off-beat killer Vincent Vega in *Pulp Fiction* (1994). Since then, Travolta has established himself as a ver
home in comedy roles as in action films (for example, *Operation: Broken Arrow*, 1995) or in existential dra
has become one of Hollywood's biggest earners in the 1990s: following *Pulp Fiction*, which made him 140,0
to 20,000,000 dollars.

He has had the cop's face put on and shot the scientists and the people who
witnessed the "swap". Archer manages to escape from the prison and has
to make his way as an outlaw while Troy lives in his comfortable home with
his wife and daughter.

Two movies gave new life to the Hollywood Action Film genre in the
90s: *Speed* (1994) and *Face/Off*. *Speed* is a fast-paced, light-footed celebration of pure movement, whereas *Face/Off* – despite its virtuoso action
scenes – has dark, elegiac undertones and a much more complex plot.
Archer is a tragic figure from the outset, first losing his son and then his life.
The idea of changing bodies might seem far-fetched, but it offers the director plenty of opportunities to play with the hunter/hunted motif. John Woo

goes through all of them one by one. Tro
subtle kind of gangster: he defuses hi
decides he wants to run the whole polic
holds Troy's son in his arms as he usec
Eve is delighted with the reawakened p
like a new man.

The doppelgänger motif reaches a
Archer and Troy stand on two sides of a
own reflections, each of them wearing th
al stylisation typical of Woo is everywher
in a church, or the slow motion billowin

5

"Woo is such an action wizard that he can make planes or speed boats kick box, but his surprising strength this time is more on a human level."

New York Times

6

THE CELEBRATION
Festen (Dogme 1)

998 - DENMARK - 106 MIN. - DRAMA

DIRECTOR THOMAS VINTERBERG (*1969) SCREENPLAY THOMAS VINTERBERG, MOGENS RUKOV DIRECTOR OF PHOTOGRAPHY ANTHONY DOD MANTLE MUSIC MORTEN HOLM PRODUCTION BRIGITTE HALD, MORTEN KAUFMANN for NIMBUS FILM.

STARRING ULRICH THOMSEN (Christian), THOMAS BO LARSEN (Michael), PAPRIKA STEEN (Helene), HENNING MORITZEN (Helge), BIRTHE NEUMANN (the mother), TRINE DYRHOLM (Pia), HELLE DOLLERIS (Mette), BJARNE HENRIKSEN (Chef), GBATOKAI DAKINAH (Gbatokai), KLAUS BONDAM (Master of Ceremonies), THOMAS VINTERBERG (Taxi Driver), JOHN BOAS (Grandfather).

FF CANNES 1998 SPECIAL JURY PRIZE.

"Here's to the man who killed my sister, a toast to a murderer."

A dogma is a religious teaching or a doctrine of belief. When four Danes got together to draw up ten commandments in 1995, baptised them "Dogme 95" and described them as a cinematic vow of chastity, it seemed a bizarre act of self-chastisement in a post-ideological age. Perhaps, critics suggested, the whole thing was a bid for freedom at a time of computer animation and post-modern indifference. They wanted to do away with all the trappings of technology and to get back to the basics: strict classical form following crazy, ornate Baroque. Perhaps, the sceptics replied, it was nothing more than a publicity stunt: Tarantino meets *It's A Wonderful Life*.

Nobody could have guessed at that point that the same four Danes would go on to open an agency that watches over the keeping of the commandments and distributes certificates. By the beginning of 2001 a dozen films had been adjudged worthy to promote themselves as "produced in accordance with the rules of the Dogme Manifesto". Both the manifesto and the certification process are inspired by deadly seriousness tempered with a certain dose of ironic humour, and certificates can cost anything from nothing at all to 2000 dollars, according to the budget of the film in question. One of the signatories, Thomas Vinterberg, director of the first brilliant Dogme film *The Celebration*, admitted in an interview that the whole thing oscillates between being "a game and in deadly earnest".

That is also a good description of *The Celebration*'s relationship to its subject matter: whenever viewers attempt to look at it purely as a comedy or solely as drama, it is guaranteed to topple over into the opposite. Drama and comedy are most likely to meet at their extremes. *The Celebration* is not exactly a black comedy, more a bitter reckoning with the deceptive façade of the institution of family life. The best ideas often come from a new look at traditional models and the movie's departure point is very simple: patriarch Helge (Henning Moritzen) is celebrating his 60th birthday with his family at a country mansion. The party turns into a night of grim revelations and innumerable skeletons are dragged out of the family closet.

Basically, the film is about the accusations of the oldest son Christian (Ulrich Thomsen). He claims that he and his twin sister were abused by their father, and that this was the reason for his sister's recent suicide. After a shocked pause, the guests return to the festivities as if nothing had happened. At first, Christian's repeated accusations are received with the same equanimity as the table speeches of Grandfather (John Boas) who always tells the same anecdote. Later his mother (Birthe Neumann) attempts to smooth over the situation and finally his hot-tempered youngest brother Michael (Thomas Bo Larsen) explodes. It takes a message from the next world to convince those present of Christian's story.

The Discreet Charm
of the Dogme Commandments

Some critics consider the Dogme commandments to be a self-important waste of time, but the rules for the use of natural sound and hand-held cameras result in films that look like home movies, giving a picture and sound quality which contributes greatly to the believability of their story lines. At first sight, high-resolution video shot without artificial light and transferred onto 35mm looks like an amateur recording of a private birthday party. The unusual, often underexposed or unfocused pictures force the audience to concentrate. Like a source of purity and liberation, they contrast with the family's repression of the party's shocking revelations. The Dogme films'

rejection of skilfully produced, artificial images gives them a feeling of undiluted directness and a whole new pallet of expressive means. This is the attack of the documentary hand-held camera on the bastion of the feature film – direct cinema as a presentation of the truth in fiction.

Once spectators get used to the grainy, wobbly pictures, which have quite a different beauty from polished Hollywood pictures, the movie itself is highly coherent both visually and dramatically. The camera angles have been chosen with extreme care: there is a bird's eye view from the corner of the room, a jump shot over a fence and a camera hidden behind the banisters. Furniture or objects often obstruct the camera's viewfinder. There are two possible interpretations of this: firstly, a blocked viewpoint implies that the place of filming is treated spontaneously and that potential obstacles are dealt with as they arise. Secondly, obscured viewpoints give the movie a documentary feel, as if the camera were a hidden witness or a passer-by.

1   The patriarch Helge shortly before his fall from power: Henning Moritzen, Birthe Neumann.

2   Michael (Thomas Bo Larsen) lets himself be waited on by his ex-lover (Birgitte Simonsen).

3   "When my sister died a couple of months ago, it became clear to me that with all the baths he took, Helge was a very clean man." Christian (Ulrich Thomsen) accuses his father.

4   Chopped-off heads, blurred images and natural lighting – camera technique applying the Dogme 95 resolutions.

5   Two brothers still fighting for their father's favour: Christian is thrown out of the house at the instigation of his younger brother Michael.

The plot follows the classic division in three acts with Christian as the hero and focal point overcoming opposition and obstacles. At the beginning he only has the support of the hotel staff who have known him since he was little, like the chef Kim, who spirits away the guests' keys so that they are isolated in the country house like the guests in Buñuel's *The Exterminating Angel* (*El ángel exterminador*, 1962). But Mexico or Denmark, 1962 or 1998, bourgeois charm is revealed to be nothing but a veneer of civilisation that peels away all too easily.

With great intensity and directness, Vinterberg and his actors show how the respectable bourgeois atmosphere is rapidly transformed into hate-filled racism, how finally the aggressive brother Michael changes sides and erupts against his father instead of shouting at his wife and children, his sister's black boyfriend and his brother. The abyss in *The Celebration* lurks just below the surface: the official face of the family only just manages to con-

cear the grimace behind it. Vinterberg is so committed and uncompromising he almost seems like a descendent of the iconoclasts of the '68 generation

Vinterberg grew up in a hippy commune. In interviews, he often points out that the Catholic terminology of the Dogme Manifesto came from co-signatory Lars von Trier and has nothing to do with him. He prefers the communist component implicit in the word "Manifesto". To him, this artistic manifesto is also a compelling call to revolt, a return to the basics of collective filmmaking and an appeal for the rejection of production hierarchies, so as a protest against the cult of the auteur, the director's name is not allowed to appear on the film. The aim above all is to reclaim film from the spirit of post-modernism. Dogma means nothing less than forgetting everything you've already seen and done, beginning again from the beginning, and reinventing cinema. Vinterberg is still filled with awe and wonder in the face of "living pictures" and he shares this with his audience.   MH

DOGME 95   **1.** Shooting must be done on location. Props and sets must not be brought in. **2.** The sound must never be produced apart from the images or vice versa. **3.** The camera must be hand-held. **4.** The film must be in colour. Special lighting is not acceptable. (If there is too little light for exposure the scene must be cut or a single lamp be attached to the camera) **5.** Optical work and filters are forbidden. **6.** The film must not contain superficial action. (Murders, weapons, etc. must not occur.) **7.** Temporal and geographical alienation are forbidden. (That is to say that the film takes place here and now.) **8.** Genre movies are not acceptable. **9.** The film format must be Academy 35mm. **10.** The director must not be credited.

"Something terrible happens and everyone says, 'Let's have another cup of coffee, let's sing a song and have a dance'. That is typical of the Danes."

Thomas Vinterberg in: Zoom

ALL ABOUT MY MOTHER

Todo sobre mi madre

1999 - SPAIN / FRANCE - 101 MIN. - MELODRAMA

DIRECTOR PEDRO ALMODÓVAR (*1951) **SCREENPLAY** PEDRO ALMODÓVAR
DIRECTOR OF PHOTOGRAPHY AFFONSO BEATO **MUSIC** ALBERTO IGLESIAS **PRODUCTION** AGUSTIN ALMODÓVAR,
CLAUDE BERRI for EL DESEO, RENN PRODUCTIONS, FRANCE 2 CINÉMA.

STARRING CECILIA ROTH (Manuela), ELOY AZORÍN (Estéban), MARISA PAREDES (Huma Rojo),
PENÉLOPE CRUZ (Sister Rosa), ANTONIA SAN JUAN (Agrado), CANDELA PEÑA (Nina),
ROSA MARÍA SARDÀ (Rosa's mother), FERNANDO FERNÁN GÓMEZ (Rosa's father),
TONI CANTÓ (Lola), CARLOS LOZANO (Mario).

IFF CANNES 1999 SILVER PALM for BEST DIRECTOR (Pedro Almodóvar).

ACADEMY AWARDS 2000 OSCAR for BEST FOREIGN LANGUAGE FILM.

"The only genuine thing about me is my feelings."

The loss of a child is the worst thing that can happen to a mother. Manuela (Cecilia Roth) never mentioned the child's father, even when asked, but now that she is completely on her own she continues her son's search for his other parent. Bowed by suffering and yet filled with strength she is driven back deep into her own past, and she travels from Madrid to Barcelona, from her present existence back to an earlier one. The people she meets on this journey to the end of the night generally only appear on our screens as the bad crowd in television crime series, as pathetic informers or more likely as corpses. Here, transsexuals and junkie prostitutes, pregnant nuns and touchy divas are not only the main characters, but with all their failings and weaknesses, they also win our sympathy.

In her search for comfort, Manuela eventually finds the father of her dead son Estéban (Eloy Azorín), and he has now become a dark angel of death, a terminally ill transsexual who earns his living as a prostitute. Eighteen years ago when they were a couple he was also called Estéban, but now (s)he calls herself Lola (Toni Cantó). Although (s)he was once attractive, those days are long gone: Estéban the First no longer exists and Lola is not long for this world either. Nevertheless, at the end of the movie a third Estéban is born, giving us a utopian hope against all the odds.

The audience shares Manuela's perspective and the Spanish director guides us skilfully through the glittering microcosm of Barcelona's transsex-

ual scene. Almodóvar however has no intention of giving us a documentary he does not claim to portray objective reality in an authentic manner, and neither is it his intention to teach us a lesson in pity. Instead he takes all the expressive means at the disposal of a melodrama to their extreme: tears blood, blows, violence, fucking, birth, love, hate, life and death. The plot may sound unlikely, but nothing seems artificial or false and that is the true miracle of this movie, an effect due in no small part to its fantastic actresses.

They all play actresses in the movie as well: Manuela does role plays with hospital employees to teach them how to deal with the families of deceased patients, and when Nina (Candela Peña), partner of the theatre diva Huma (Marisa Paredes) can't go on stage because she's too doped up Manuela takes her place. The faithful companion Agrado (Antonia San Juan) is perhaps the greatest actress in the true sense of the word; her body has been operated on innumerable times until it is nothing but artificial illusion One of the best scenes is where she has to announce the cancellation of a play but manages to whip up the disappointed audience into storms of enthusiasm with an autobiographic monologue. This movie about mothers is also dedicated to all actresses who have ever played actresses.

At their best Almodóvar's men are senile like the father (Fernando Fernán Gómez) of AIDS sufferer Rosa (Penélope Cruz), but for the most part men are conspicuous by their absence. However, even in his short appear

3

1 Women in the mirror: Marisa Paredes (with lip-pencil) and Cecilia Roth.

2 Three women, three different stories: Manuela (Cecilia Roth, left), whose son died, and Rosa (Penélope Cruz, right), whose son provides a glim-

mer of hope at the end of the film, on either side of Rosa's mother (Rosa María Sardà).

3 The actress Huma Rojo (Marisa Paredes), larger than life, looks through the railings at her fan Estéban (Eloy Azorín), who is soon to die.

4 Penélope Cruz, *shooting star* of Spanish cinema, finds herself on the road to Hollywood.

5 It's the "End of the line for desire" not only for the dreams of Almodóvar's heroines, but also as a play in the film.

ances the double father Estéban/Lola – who is in theory the villain of the piece – is given a dignity which no other character acquires in the course of the whole movie. Almodóvar respects every single human emotion, however bizarre his characters might appear. "The only genuine thing about me is my feelings," says Agrado, the faithful transsexual girlfriend in *All About My Mother*. This also applies to Almodóvar's movie, where feelings always remain genuine despite the visual artistry. And that's more than can be said of most films. MH

"*All About My Mother* is all about art, women, people, life, and death, and must be one of the most intense films I've ever made."

Pedro Almodóvar in: Cahiers du cinéma

PEDRO ALMODÓVAR   In the 1980s Almodóvar was hailed as an icon of Spain's gay subculture and was a welcome guest at international festivals. His biting satire ensured that midnight showings of his films were invariably sold out and eventually he became a great figure of European art cinema. In the 90s he was awarded all of cinema's most important prizes and came to be considered one of the most important contemporary filmmakers. He started off being provocative for the sake of it, but gradually he has given his figures depth and complexity whilst still taking a critical look at conventional bourgeois family life and sexual morals. Nowadays Almodóvar is seen as part of the great tragicomic tradition alongside directors such as Fassbinder or Buñuel.

AMERICAN BEAUTY ♟♟♟♟♟

999 - USA - 121 MIN. - DRAMA

DIRECTOR SAM MENDES (*1965) SCREENPLAY ALAN BALL DIRECTOR OF PHOTOGRAPHY CONRAD L. HALL
MUSIC THOMAS NEWMAN PRODUCTION BRUCE COHEN, DAN JINKS for DREAMWORKS SKG, JINKS/
COHEN COMPANY.

STARRING KEVIN SPACEY (Lester Burnham), ANNETTE BENING (Carolyn Burnham), THORA BIRCH
(Jane Burnham), WES BENTLEY (Ricky Fitts), MENA SUVARI (Angela Hayes), PETER GALLAGHER
(Buddy Kane), CHRIS COOPER (Colonel Frank Fitts), ALLISON JANNEY (Barbara Fitts), SCOTT
BAKULA (Jim Olmeyer), SAM ROBARDS (Jim "JB" Berkley).

ACADEMY AWARDS 2000 OSCARS for BEST PICTURE, BEST ACTOR (Kevin Spacey), BEST
CINEMATOGRAPHY (Conrad L. Hall), BEST DIRECTOR (Sam Mendes), and BEST ORIGINAL
SCREENPLAY (Alan Ball).

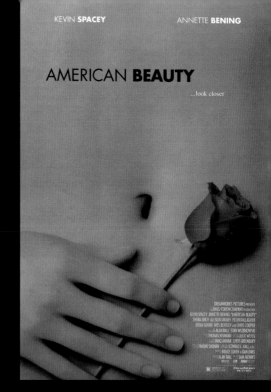

"You have no idea what I'm talking about, I'm sure. But don't worry, you will someday."

In one year's time Lester Burnham (Kevin Spacey) will be dead: that much we learn right at the beginning of the movie. And he already knows this himself, for he's the one who tells his own story. A dead man speaks to us from off screen, and the strangest thing about it is his amused detachment. With a sweeping movement making the off-screen narration seem like a message of salvation, the camera moves down on the world from above and closes in on the dismal suburban street where Lester lives. We are introduced to the situation in which he finds himself: his marriage to Carolyn (Annette Bening) is over, and she considers him a failure, while his daughter Jane (Thora Birch) hates him for not being a role model. The only highpoint of Lester's sad daily routine is masturbating under the shower in the morning while his wife gathers roses in the garden to decorate the dinner table where they conduct their daily fights.

Family happiness, or whatever passed for it, only ever existed in the photos that Lester often looks at to remind himself of his past, and of the interest in life which he once had but which is now buried under the pressure of conformity. It is only when he falls in love with Angela (Mena Suvari), his daughter's Lolita-like friend, that he rediscovers his zest for life. This second spring changes Lester, but his wife Carolyn meanwhile is doing worse and worse as a property dealer. He reassesses his position and discovers old and forgotten strengths. She by contrast becomes inextricably entwined in the fatal cycle of routine and self-sacrifice. As Lester puts it, trying to live as though their life were a commercial nearly destroys them both. Outward

conformity and prosperity results in inner impoverishment. The business mantras that Carolyn repeats over and over to herself to bolster her self-confidence sound increasingly ridiculous under the circumstances.

At this point, it becomes abundantly clear what we are intended to understand by "American Beauty". The title is not a reference to the seductive child-woman who helps Lester break out of the family prison – that would be too superficial. The subject of *American Beauty* is the question of the beauty of life itself. Mendes' movie is about whether or not it is possible to live a fulfilling life in a society where superficiality has become the norm. To put it in more philosophical terms, *American Beauty* uses the expressive means of drama and satire to go through all the possibilities for leading an honest life in a dishonest environment. Sadly this turns out to be impossible or at least Lester's attempt ends in death.

It's a gem of a movie, thanks to Sam Mendes' careful use of film techniques. He never exposes his characters to ridicule and he protects them from cheap laughs by giving them time to develop. He also gives depth to their relationships and arranges them in dramatic constellations. Mendes' experience as a theatre director shows in a number of carefully staged scenes whose strict form is well suited to the Burnham's oppressive and limited family life. Many scenes put us in mind of plays by Samuel Beckett, like the backyard sequence where Rick teaches Lester not to give in to circumstance. The symmetrical arrangements of characters around the table or the television are further reminders of family dramas on the stage.

2

3

4

1 A seductively beautiful image.

2 Hollywood's new bright young things: saucy Angela (Mena Suvari) …

3 … and sensitive Jane (Thora Birch).

4 Carolyn Burnham (Annette Bening) on the brink of madness.

5 Liberation from the familial cage brings happiness to Lester Burnham (Kevin Spacey).

"At first the film judges its characters harshly; then it goes to every effort to make them win back their rights." *Frankfurter Allgemeine Zeitung*

In an important subplot, Lester's daughter Jane falls in love with Rick, the boy next door, who is never seen without his video camera and films constantly, to "remind himself", as he says. He documents the world and discovers its beauty in grainy video pictures of dead animals and people. It is his father, the fascist ex-marine Colonel Frank Fitts – brilliantly acted by Chris Cooper – who in a moment of emotional turmoil shoots Lester Burnham and thereby fulfils the prophecy made at the beginning of the film. The hopeless struggle between internal and external beauty comes to a bloody end, but the issue remains open. The movie points to a vague possibility for reconciling these two opposites, but at the end this seems to have been an illusion. Despite our right to the "pursuit of happiness", material and spiritual wealth seem to be mutually exclusive, and the good life remains a promise of happiness which is yet to be fulfilled. With irony and humour *American Beauty* shows that modern American society's mental state is by no means as rosy as the initiators of the Declaration of Independence would have hoped.

BF

KEVIN SPACEY What would the cinema of the 90s have been without Kevin Spacey? Born in 1959, this friendly looking actor with his ordinary face portrayed some of the most complex and disturbing characters of the decade with impressive depth. Nobody demonstrated so clearly the difference between being and appearance, between a deceptive façade and the brutal reality behind it as drastically as Kevin Spacey playing John Doe, "The Man Without Qualities" in *Se7en* (1995), or the sinister Keyser Soze who pulls the strings in *The Usual Suspects* (1995). Spacey is an enigmatic minimalist who needs only a few striking gestures, and with cool irony can play great emotional cinema as he shows in the role of Lester Burnham in *American Beauty*. When he dies at the turning point of a story – as he does in *L.A. Confidential* – it's a great loss, both for us and for the movie.

"When I made *American Beauty*, I wanted the film's vision to offer every spectator a very intimate experience. I hope it's a universal work, which helps one understand life that little bit better."

Sam Mendes in: Le Figaro

6   Grotesque victim of his own ideology: sinister neighbour Colonel Fitts (Chris Cooper) shortly before his surprise coming out.

7   Scenes from a marriage in ruins.

8   Wes Bentley is very convincing as Ricky Fitts, the introverted young man from next door.

9   Jane is fascinated by Ricky's puzzling hobby.

10   Life's true beauty can only be appreciated in a video image.

MAGNOLIA

1999 - USA - 188 MIN. - DRAMA, EPISODIC FILM

DIRECTOR PAUL THOMAS ANDERSON (*1970) SCREENPLAY PAUL THOMAS ANDERSON
DIRECTOR OF PHOTOGRAPHY ROBERT ELSWIT MUSIC JON BRION, AIMEE MANN PRODUCTION PAUL THOMAS
ANDERSON, JOANNE SELLAR for GHOULARDI FILM COMPANY, NEW LINE CINEMA,
THE MAGNOLIA PROJECT.

STARRING JOHN C. REILLY (Jim Kurring), TOM CRUISE (Frank T. J. Mackey), JULIANNE MOORE
(Linda Partridge), PHILIP BAKER HALL (Jimmy Gator), JEREMY BLACKMAN (Stanley Spector),
PHILIP SEYMOUR HOFFMAN (Phil Parma), WILLIAM H. MACY (Quiz Kid Donnie Smith),
MELORA WALTERS (Claudia Wilson Gator), JASON ROBARDS (Earl Partridge).

IFF BERLIN 2000 GOLDEN BEAR.

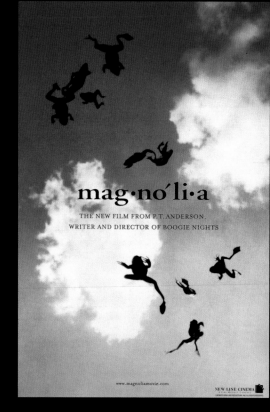

"It would seem that we're through with the past, but it's not through with us."

According to Quentin Tarantino, the plot of *Pulp Fiction* (1994) is three stories about a story. Shortly before that, the film virtuoso Robert Altman gave the episodic movie new elegance with *Shorts Cuts* (1993), where many short stories revolve around a centre, overlap, move away from each other again and form new combinations. Although director Paul Thomas Anderson originally tried to play down the link, *Magnolia* can definitely be seen in relation to these earlier movies. The denial was probably just the reaction of a promising young filmmaker who wanted audiences to take a second look at his *Boogie Nights* (1997).

At the centre of the tragicomedy *Magnolia* is Big Earl Partridge (Jason Robards), a TV tycoon of the worst kind. He lies dying, a wilting magnolia. Earl is the key figure, the man behind the scenes and the origin of all evils. His name alone is a programme for the movie … Earl is the only figure who always stays in the same place, unable to move from his deathbed. When the camera looks down on him from above and the mighty fanfare from Richard Strauss's *Also sprach Zarathustra* sounds, it's not just an ironic reference to

his once all-powerful influence, but also to the end of Stanley Kubrick's *2001 – A Space Odyssey* (1968). There we see the astronaut David Bowman as an old man alone on a big bed, shortly before the next evolutionary leap transforms him into the famous foetus from the final shot of 2001 and the cycle of human development moves onto a higher plane. Earl's end also signifies new beginnings, but before that can come about all the suffering that he has brought into the world must be dealt with. And that is no easy task.

With great humour and sympathy, *Magnolia* tells the stories of all the people on whose lives he has had such a lasting influence. First of all comes Earl's son Frank (Tom Cruise) who trains frustrated men to become super-macho in his "Seduce and Destroy" seminars. He got this motto from his father, who destroyed his wife with his complete lack of consideration. Now, shortly before his death, the shallow patriarch searches for his lost son, who he had abandoned as a teenager when his mother fell ill with cancer. When the two come together at the end, their broken relationship is shown in all its misery. Earl's young wife Linda (Julianne Moore) only married him for his

1

2

"Almost exactly in the middle is *Magnolia* – which lasts for three hours and isn't a second too long – so close to its characters that we can almost feel their breath."

Frankfurter Allgemeine Zeitung

1 Prodigal son (Tom Cruise) and hated father (Jason Robards).

2 Relationship at an end: scenes from a marriage on its deathbed. Julianne Moore in the role of Linda Partridge.

3 The incarnation of law and order: good-natured police officer Jim Kurring (John C. Reilly).

4 Claudia (Melora Walters), abused by her own father and addicted to drugs, provides an optimistic ending to the film.

5 Phil (Philip Seymour Hoffman), the carer of ailing patriarch Earl, demonstrates patience and sensitivity.

6 Confessions under duress: homosexual Donnie (William H. Macy) becomes the victim of his inferiority complex.

money. She realises the shallowness of her own character and starts to go through a crisis of identity. Quiz master Jimmy Gator (Philip Baker Hall) presents the bizarre show "What Do Kids Know?" for Big Earl Partridge TV Productions, where three children compete against three adults answering general knowledge questions. Jimmy has absorbed his boss's way of thinking to such a degree that his extramarital affairs even include his daughter Claudia, who is now a cocaine addict and funds her habit with occasional prostitution. When the neighbours complain about her loud music, she gets a visit from a policeman who promptly falls in love with her, and even greater confusion ensues. Finally, there are the two child prodigies who have become famous through the quiz show. Former child star Donny now tries vainly to chat up a good looking barman and Stanley wets his pants at the show's decisive moment, as the production team's strict rules don't allow him to go to the lavatory before the broadcast.

The movie's interpersonal conflicts run along the fault lines between parents and children and men and women. All these relationships have been ruined by an inability to build up and maintain friendships, and by the impossibility of any real communication. *Magnolia* is an affectionate but cynical critique of the medium of television, and all the people in the movie seem to be trying to emulate its clichés. Behind everything is the television magnate Earl. The characters' lives are nothing more than television made flesh, absurd TV drama on the wrong side of the screen.

The movie begins with a macabre, satirical undertone and it becomes increasingly sarcastic and even cynical. An amused, concise voice-over at the beginning talks about the absurdity of life and denies the existence of coincidence, and the film goes on to prove that thesis. Although at first the episodes appear to be a transitory collection of unconnected events, a dense network of links gradually appears. The movie draws the audience into a

PAUL THOMAS ANDERSON Paul Thomas Anderson first worked as a production assistant on television films, video productions and game shows in Los Angeles and New York, before leaving the New York University Film School after only two days to get back to the practical side of things again. He developed his short film *Cigarettes and Coffee* (1993) into his first feature film *Hard Eight*, which was presented at the 1996 Cannes Film Festival. *Boogie Nights* (1997) was nominated for three Oscars. His innovative directing style doesn't balk at confusing plots or complex characters, and he is not afraid to break taboos. Paul Thomas Anderson is considered one of the most promising young directors around today.

7   The strain of the TV quiz is written all over the   8   Donnie runs into more and more trouble.   9   Learning from children: a hard task even for
    face of young genius Stanley (Jeremy Blackman).   compère Jimmy Gator (Philip Baker Hall)

whirl of failed relationships and unfulfilled yearnings for freedom, love and mutual respect. This descent influences the movie's images, and their rhythm becomes slower and their colours darker, and spectators start to feel that the downward spiral could go on forever. But *Magnolia* is anything but a pessimistic movie: shortly before the final catastrophe, all the figures suddenly begin to sing the same song wherever they happen to be. After the initial surprise, this absurd directorial idea turns out to be a wonderful trick, which counteracts the seemingly inevitable end with off-beat humour in a

manner not dissimilar to the song at the end of *Monty Python's Life of Brian* (1979). When it rains frogs at the very end, spectators heave a sigh of relief along with the characters in the movie. This surreal event makes it clear that anything is possible in this movie. We may not be able to believe our eyes, but "it did happen" as the text under the pictures tells us. The event shakes the characters out of their lethargy and reminds them of the incredible opportunities that life can offer. And a small smile into the camera in the final shot holds the key to the way out of this crisis whose name is life.   BR

"*Magnolia* takes a long run-up, then jumps and lands in the middle of our present. It is the first film of the new millennium."

Frankfurter Allgemeine Zeitung

"The film pauses for a moment: suicides forget to press the trigger, addicts forget their fix, and those in pain their pain.
Then the play is over, the world appears fresh once more, the dead are buried and the living are given a second chance." *Süddeutsche Zeitung*

10   Tom Cruise in the unusual role of a repulsive advocate of machismo.

11   Victim of self-delusion: Julianne Moore is a convincing Beauty and the Beast.

CROUCHING TIGER, HIDDEN DRAGON ♟♟♟♟

Wo hu zang long

2000 - CHINA / HONG KONG / TAIWAN / USA - 120 MIN. - MARTIAL ARTS FILM, FANTASY

DIRECTOR ANG LEE (*1954) **SCREENPLAY** JAMES SCHAMUS, WANG HUI LING, TSAI KUO JUNG, based on a novel by WANG DU LU **DIRECTOR OF PHOTOGRAPHY** PETER PAU **MUSIC** TAN DUN **PRODUCTION** BILL KONG, HSU LI KONG, ANG LEE for UNITED CHINA VISION, SONY, COLUMBIA, GOOD MACHINE, EDKO FILMS.

STARRING CHOW YUN-FAT (Li Mu Bai), MICHELLE YEOH (Yu Shu Lien), ZHANG ZIYI (Jiao Long Yu/Jen), CHANG CHEN (Xiao Hu Luo/Lo), LUNG SIHUNG (Sir Te), CHENG PEI-PEI (Jade Fox), LI FAZENG (Yu), GAO XIAN (Bo), HAI YAN (Madam Yu), WANG DEMING (Tsai).

ACADEMY AWARDS 2001 OSCARS for BEST FOREIGN LANGUAGE FILM, BEST CINEMATOGRAPHY (Peter Pau), BEST MUSIC (Tan Dun), BEST ART DIRECTION (Tim Yip).

"Sharpness is a state of mind"

Crouching Tiger, Hidden Dragon is in every sense a fairy tale, while still remaining a classic martial arts film. This is no contradiction, the martial arts film genre is a perfect medium for telling fairy tales and has never been afraid of the extreme exaggeration that is necessary to film the fantastic. In Crouching Tiger, Hidden Dragon, the world of the fairytale is already evoked by the setting: the synthesised studio shots, the fantastic landscapes shot on location in the People's Republic of China, and the original costumes and architecture. The historic reconstruction of an idyllic past goes hand in hand with its stylisation. Into this opulent scenario steps Wu-dan master Li Mu Bai (Chow Yun-Fat). Wu-Dan is a style of swordsmanship that teaches self-negation and internal strength. Sharp wits become the practitioner's greatest weapon. Li Mu Bai wishes to turn his back on his earlier life as a swordsman, in search of greater enlightenment, and therefore entrusts his fabled sword "Green Destiny" to the keeping of the State Administrator in Peking. The sword is delivered by his female colleague Yu Shu Lien (Michelle Yeoh), who is bound to him in a sort of Platonic imprisonment through a secret bond of unspoken love. Jen (Zhang Ziyi), the daughter of an aristocratic family

also lives in the city but is trapped in the gilded cage of her social circumstances. She is being forced into an arranged marriage. Jen has a servant and companion who is interested in far more than her socially appropriate upbringing. She is in fact the witch Jade Fox, wanted by the police for the murder of Li Mu Bai's teacher. Not only does she assist the beautiful Jen in maintaining her flawless looks and behaviour, she also secretly trains her in various martial arts. Jen much prefers adventure to the dreariness of her sheltered life in the city. A lengthy flashback relates how she fell in love with the desert bandit Lo following his assault on her caravan. In spite of his wild appearance, Lo is a warm-hearted person. As a pair, they counterbalance Li Mu Bai and Yu Shu Lien. Although their youth makes it easier for them to ignore social constraints, their love is also destined for an unhappy end.

But before the film leads us into this web of relationships, a crime occurs: the priceless sword is stolen. A furious chase ensues, but the masked thief just manages to escape. The film's repeated chase-scenes where the participants follow each other over rooftops, through alleyways and even over treetops may at first appear absurd, but are in fact an integra

1

part of Chinese folk mythology. By collaborating with the same team that choreographed the fight-scenes in *The Matrix* (1999), Ang Lee reaches new heights of intercultural film style in *Crouching Tiger, Hidden Dragon*. The stolen sword acts as a kind of "McGuffin", carrying the story forward without playing an important role in its outcome. Even before all the relationships in the film are clearly established, transformations begin. During the chase and fight-scenes they are literally set in motion. At times, the camera work reduces the action into dancing graphic patterns. Where the human eye can only discern lines of motion – in the rapid oscillation between long and short-range shots – the fight-scenes nonetheless remain carefully controlled. They are a reflection of the same ethic of discipline and self-control that governs social behaviour in the film. The art of fighting is also a social art.

"A faithful heart makes wishes come true"

Ang Lee's *Crouching Tiger, Hidden Dragon* is a remarkable martial arts film. While respecting the conventions of the genre, it is also a fascinating vehicle for the portrayal of tragic-romantic love stories in a poetic setting. The movie owes its persuasiveness to the manner in which Ang Lee extends the boundaries of the genre without betraying its innate virtues. As in his other films – especially *Eat, Drink, Man, Woman* (1994), *The Wedding Banquet*

1 Fairylike grace and unbridled energy are not mutually exclusive: beautiful and wilful Jen (Zhang Ziyi) casts her spell over the film.

2 The sword of power is reason, and nobody knows this better than the monk Li Mu Bai (Chow Yun-Fat).

3 Love beyond death: earthly barriers are no obstacle. Michelle Yeoh in the role of Hu Shu Lien.

"Sword and sabre shiver and redound like lovers in this portrait of contrasted temperaments locked in battle. This is a whirligig of literal revenges, slings and arrows ... Ang Lee enters the ranks of his past masters." *Libération*

(1993), *Sense and Sensibility* (1995), *The Ice Storm* (1997), and *Ride with the Devil* (1999), the film whose production practically coincided with *Crouching Tiger, Hidden Dragon,* Lee's strength lies in the careful balance between the powerful visual images and the mastery of epic storytelling. This reflects Lee's equal experience of western and eastern culture. *Crouching Tiger, Hidden Dragon* has reflective moments where it devotes itself to its protagonists' personal concerns, but then it erupts into phases of extreme action, before settling effortlessly back into contemplative situations. The film never loses its rhythm, and great attention is paid to every detail.

Crouching Tiger, Hidden Dragon combines images of the director's youth in Taiwan with a story from the fourth book of a pentology by Du Lu Wang. The novel is a product of East Asian popular literature comparable with the penny-romance, featuring stereotyped heroes and predictable love

stories. Ang Lee adapts this cultural tradition with great skill. In his version, virtues like bravery, friendship, and honour turn out to be impossible ideals. He does not reject them, but takes leave of them with melancholy regret and not before he has pointed a way out of the resulting emptiness.

In contrast to the value system of a male-dominated society, the film emphasises womanly virtues. In an irony typical of Ang Lee's films, the fate of the male protagonist lies in the hands of three women who are all struggling for independence from the patriarchal norm. Finally, *Crouching Tiger, Hidden Dragon* is an ideal film realisation of the principle of Yin and Yang: contemplative stillness and furious action, peaceful dialogue and sword battles, the cramped city and the wide-open Chinese landscapes. The balanced harmony of its composition makes *Crouching Tiger, Hidden Dragon* a fairy tale constructed on an epic scale. BR

"The choreography was new to me. It had its roots in the Peking Opera, and they are completely different from the Western method of producing action scenes."

Ang Lee in: epd Film

4 At the moment of maximum concentration, body and soul fuse together.

5 Jen's desire for a life full of adventure and love is being fulfilled, but not quite as she imagines.

5

6   In the fantasy world of *Crouching Tiger, Hidden Dragon* the normal laws of physics don't apply.

7   During the fight, the rival women's bodies hover and fly through space with no apparent efforts.

8   Brigand Lo (Chang Chen) makes a good haul.

MARTIAL ARTS FILMS   Generally, martial arts films are films featuring oriental combat sports and their accompanying philosophical traditions. The plots normally revolve around a hero figure whose sense of loyalty and justice free him from moral scruples in meting out vengeance to evil-doers. The martial arts film developed into a mass product in Hong Kong and gradually shifted its focus away from psychological complexity towards the representation of spiritual states through choreographed motion, and dynamic movement therefore takes on a metaphorical perspective. In the 70s martial arts found their way into American action movies via Hong Kong cinema. Martial arts movies had an increasing influence in the 80s on the related genres of gangster movies, historical epics and even comedy. Alongside Bruce Lee and the no less popular Jackie Chan, directors like John Woo or Tsui Hark have made martial arts acceptable within the action movie genre, giving it a whole new dimension.

1920 OSCARS

1 The first-ever Academy Award for Best Actor went to Germany's Emil Jannings. In *The Last Command* (1928) and *The Way of All Flesh* (1928) he once again turned in a dazzling performance as a humiliated and demoralized old man.

2 In the late 1920s, Janet Gaynor was mainly cast as the wide-eyed innocent. In 1927/1928 she won the Oscar for Best Actress in a Leading Role for two romantic master-pieces: F. W. Murnau's *Sunrise* (1927) and *Seventh Heaven* (1927), in which she co-starred with Charles Farrell, pictured here.

1927/28
BEST PICTURE SUNRISE – A SONG OF TWO HUMANS
(in "Unique and Artistic Picture" category)
BEST PICTURE WINGS (in "Best Production" category)
BEST DIRECTOR LEWIS MILESTONE for *Two Arabian Knights* (Comedy)
BEST DIRECTOR FRANK BORZAGE for *Seventh Heaven* (Drama)
BEST ACTRESS JANET GAYNOR in *Seventh Heaven,
Sunrise – A Song of Two Humans* and *Street Angel*
BEST ACTOR EMIL JANNINGS in *The Last Command* and *The Way of All Flesh*
BEST ORIGINAL SCREENPLAY BEN HECHT for *Underworld*
BEST ADAPTED SCREENPLAY BENJAMIN GLAZER for *Seventh Heaven*
BEST TITLE WRITING JOSEPH FARNHAM, GEORGE MARION JUN.
BEST CINEMATOGRAPHY CHARLES ROSHER, KARL STRUSS for *Sunrise – A Song of Two Humans*
BEST ART DIRECTION WILLIAM CAMERON MENZIES for *The Dove* and *Tempest*
BEST ENGINEERING EFFECTS ROY POMEROY for *Wings*

1928/29
BEST PICTURE THE BROADWAY MELODY
BEST DIRECTOR FRANK LLOYD for *The Divine Lady*
BEST ACTRESS MARY PICKFORD in *Coquette*
BEST ACTOR WARNER BAXTER in *In Old Arizona*
BEST SCREENPLAY HANNS KRÄLY for *The Patriot*
BEST CINEMATOGRAPHY CLYDE DE VINNA for *White Shadows in the South Seas*
BEST ART DIRECTION CEDRIC GIBBONS for *The Bridge of San Luis Rey*

1929/30
BEST PICTURE ALL QUIET ON THE WESTERN FRONT
BEST DIRECTOR LEWIS MILESTONE for *All Quiet on the Western Front*
BEST ACTRESS NORMA SHEARER in *The Divorcee*
BEST ACTOR GEORGE ARLISS in *Disraeli*
BEST SCREENPLAY FRANCES MARION for *The Big House*
BEST CINEMATOGRAPHY JOSEPH T. RUCKER, WILLARD VAN DER VEER for *With Byrd at the South Pole*
BEST ART DIRECTION HERMAN ROSSE for *King of Jazz*
BEST SOUND RECORDING DOUGLAS SHEARER for *The Big House*

3 Where the boys are: Spencer Tracy retains his title as the reigning Best Actor in the business for his work in *Boys Town*. That same year, 1938, co-star Mickey Rooney (right) received an honorary acting Oscar.

4 1939 was a very good year: *Gone With The Wind* is proclaimed Hollywood's Best Picture, making producer David O. Selznick a giant among men in what was arguably the greatest year in American filmmaking.

1930 OSCARS

1931
BEST PICTURE CIMARRON
BEST DIRECTOR NORMAN TAUROG for *Skippy*
BEST LEADING ACTRESS MARIE DRESSLER in *Min and Bill*
BEST LEADING ACTOR LIONEL BARRYMORE in *A Free Soul*
BEST SUPPORTING ACTRESS NOT AWARDED
BEST SUPPORTING ACTOR NOT AWARDED

1932
BEST PICTURE GRAND HOTEL
BEST DIRECTOR FRANK BORZAGE for *Bad Girl*
BEST LEADING ACTRESS HELEN HAYES in *The Sin of Madelon Claudet*
BEST LEADING ACTOR WALLACE BEERY in *The Champ* and FREDRIC MARCH in *Dr. Jekyll and Mr. Hyde*
BEST SUPPORTING ACTRESS NOT AWARDED
BEST SUPPORTING ACTOR NOT AWARDED

1933
BEST PICTURE CAVALCADE
BEST DIRECTOR FRANK LLOYD for *Cavalcade*
BEST LEADING ACTRESS KATHARINE HEPBURN in *Morning Glory*
BEST LEADING ACTOR CHARLES LAUGHTON in *The Private Life of Henry VIII*
BEST SUPPORTING ACTRESS NOT AWARDED
BEST SUPPORTING ACTOR NOT AWARDED

1934
BEST PICTURE IT HAPPENED ONE NIGHT
BEST DIRECTOR FRANK CAPRA for *It Happened One Night*
BEST LEADING ACTRESS CLAUDETTE COLBERT in *It Happened One Night*
BEST LEADING ACTOR CLARK GABLE in *It Happened One Night*
BEST SUPPORTING ACTRESS NOT AWARDED
BEST SUPPORTING ACTOR NOT AWARDED

1935
BEST PICTURE MUTINY ON THE BOUNTY
BEST DIRECTOR JOHN FORD for *The Informer*
BEST LEADING ACTRESS BETTE DAVIS in *Dangerous*
BEST LEADING ACTOR VICTOR MCLAGLEN in *The Informer*
BEST SUPPORTING ACTRESS NOT AWARDED
BEST SUPPORTING ACTOR NOT AWARDED

1936
BEST PICTURE THE GREAT ZIEGFELD
BEST DIRECTOR FRANK CAPRA for *Mr. Deeds Goes to Town*
BEST LEADING ACTRESS LUISE RAINER in *The Great Ziegfeld*
BEST LEADING ACTOR PAUL MUNI in *The Story of Louis Pasteur*
BEST SUPPORTING ACTRESS GALE SONDERGAARD in *Anthony Adverse*
BEST SUPPORTING ACTOR WALTER BRENNAN in *Come and Get It*

1937
BEST PICTURE THE LIFE OF EMILE ZOLA
BEST DIRECTOR LEO MCCAREY for *The Awful Truth*
BEST LEADING ACTRESS LUISE RAINER in *The Good Earth*
BEST LEADING ACTOR SPENCER TRACY in *Captains Courageous*
BEST SUPPORTING ACTRESS ALICE BRADY in *In Old Chicago*
BEST SUPPORTING ACTOR JOSEPH SCHILDKRAUT in *The Life of Emile Zola*

1938
BEST PICTURE YOU CAN'T TAKE IT WITH YOU
BEST DIRECTOR FRANK CAPRA for *You Can't Take It With You*
BEST LEADING ACTRESS BETTE DAVIS in *Jezebel*
BEST LEADING ACTOR SPENCER TRACY in *Boys Town*
BEST SUPPORTING ACTRESS WALTER BRENNAN in *Kentucky*
BEST SUPPORTING ACTOR FAY BAINTER in *Jezebel*

1939
BEST PICTURE GONE WITH THE WIND
BEST DIRECTOR VICTOR FLEMING for *Gone with the Wind*
BEST LEADING ACTRESS VIVIEN LEIGH in *Gone with the Wind*
BEST LEADING ACTOR ROBERT DONAT in *Goodbye, Mr. Chips*
BEST SUPPORTING ACTRESS HATTIE MCDANIEL in *Gone with the Wind*
BEST SUPPORTING ACTOR THOMAS MITCHELL in *Stagecoach*

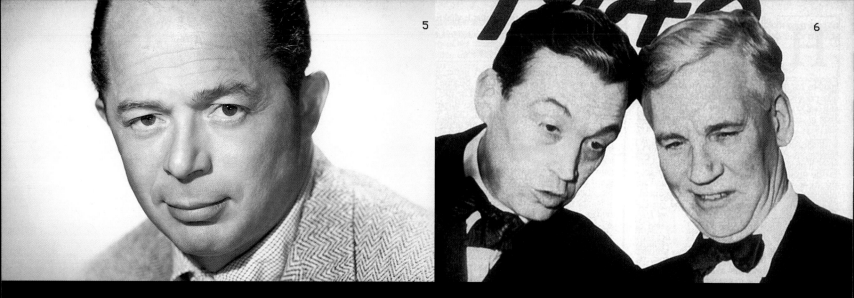

5 Wilder at heart: *The Lost Weekend* is applauded with Oscars for its accomplishments in direction and script adaptation.

6 A regular gem: John Huston helps his father Walter (right) strike it big as a supporting actor in *The Treasure of Sierra Madre*.

1940 OSCARS

1940
BEST PICTURE REBECCA
BEST DIRECTOR JOHN FORD for *The Grapes of Wrath*
BEST LEADING ACTRESS GINGER ROGERS in *Kitty Foyle*
BEST LEADING ACTOR JAMES STEWART in *The Philadelphia Story*
BEST SUPPORTING ACTRESS JANE DARWELL in *The Grapes of Wrath*
BEST SUPPORTING ACTOR WALTER BRENNAN in *The Westerner*

1941
BEST PICTURE HOW GREEN WAS MY VALLEY
BEST DIRECTOR JOHN FORD for *How Green Was My Valley*
BEST LEADING ACTRESS JOAN FONTAINE in *Suspicion*
BEST LEADING ACTOR GARY COOPER in *Sergeant York*
BEST SUPPORTING ACTRESS MARY ASTOR in *The Great Lie*
BEST SUPPORTING ACTOR DONALD CRISP in *How Green Was My Valley*

1942
BEST PICTURE MRS. MINIVER
BEST DIRECTOR WILLIAM WYLER for *Mrs. Miniver*
BEST LEADING ACTRESS GREER GARSON in *Mrs. Miniver*
BEST LEADING ACTOR JAMES CAGNEY in *Yankee Doodle Dandy*
BEST SUPPORTING ACTRESS TERESA WRIGHT in *Mrs. Miniver*
BEST SUPPORTING ACTOR VAN HEFLIN in *Johnny Eager*

1943
BEST PICTURE CASABLANCA
BEST DIRECTOR MICHAEL CURTIZ for *Casablanca*
BEST LEADING ACTRESS JENNIFER JONES in *The Song Of Bernadette*
BEST LEADING ACTOR PAUL LUKAS in *Watch on the Rhine*
BEST SUPPORTING ACTRESS KATINA PAXINOU in *For Whom the Bell Tolls*
BEST SUPPORTING ACTOR CHARLES COBURN in *The More The Merrier*

1944
BEST PICTURE GOING MY WAY
BEST DIRECTOR LEO MCCAREY for *Going My Way*
BEST LEADING ACTRESS INGRID BERGMAN in *Gaslight*
BEST LEADING ACTOR BING CROSBY in *Going My Way*
BEST SUPPORTING ACTRESS ETHEL BARRYMORE in *None But the Lonely Heart*
BEST SUPPORTING ACTOR BARRY FITZGERALD in *Going My Way*

1945
BEST PICTURE THE LOST WEEKEND
BEST DIRECTOR BILLY WILDER for *The Lost Weekend*
BEST LEADING ACTRESS JOAN CRAWFORD in *Mildred Pierce*
BEST LEADING ACTOR RAY MILLAND in *The Lost Weekend*
BEST SUPPORTING ACTRESS ANNE REVERE in *National Velvet*
BEST SUPPORTING ACTOR JAMES DUNN in *A Tree Grows in Brooklyn*

1946
BEST PICTURE THE BEST YEARS OF OUR LIVES
BEST DIRECTOR WILLIAM WYLER for *The Best Years of Our Lives*
BEST LEADING ACTRESS OLIVIA DE HAVILLAND in *To Each His Own*
BEST LEADING ACTOR FREDRIC MARCH in *The Best Years of Our Lives*
BEST SUPPORTING ACTRESS ANNE BAXTER *in The Razor's Edge*
BEST SUPPORTING ACTOR HAROLD RUSSELL in *The Best Years of Our Lives*

1947
BEST PICTURE GENTLEMAN'S AGREEMENT
BEST DIRECTOR ELIA KAZAN for *Gentleman's Agreement*
BEST LEADING ACTRESS LORETTA YOUNG in *The Farmer's Daughter*
BEST LEADING ACTOR RONALD COLMAN in *A Double Life*
BEST SUPPORTING ACTRESS CELESTE HOLM in *Gentleman's Agreement*
BEST SUPPORTING ACTOR EDMUND GWENN in *Miracle on 34th Street*

1948
BEST PICTURE HAMLET
BEST DIRECTOR JOHN HUSTON for *Treasure of Sierra Madre*
BEST LEADING ACTRESS JANE WYMAN in *Johnny Belinda*
BEST LEADING ACTOR LAURENCE OLIVIER in *Hamlet*
BEST SUPPORTING ACTRESS CLAIRE TREVOR in *Key Largo*
BEST SUPPORTING ACTOR WALTER HUSTON in *Treasure of Sierra Madre*

1949
BEST PICTURE ALL THE KING'S MEN
BEST DIRECTOR JOSEPH L. MANKIEWICZ for *A Letter to Three Wives*
BEST LEADING ACTRESS OLIVIA DE HAVILLAND in *The Heiress*
BEST LEADING ACTOR BRODERICK CRAWFORD in *All the King's Men*
BEST SUPPORTING ACTRESS MERCEDES MCCAMBRIDGE in *All the King's Men*
BEST SUPPORTING ACTOR DEAN JAGGER in *Twelve o'Clock High*

8

1950 OSCARS

7 Stage fright: Actress Bette Davis (left) proves she's anything but over the hill when *All About Eve* receives a total of six Academy Awards. If the film's two leading actresses hadn't both been nominated for an Oscar, Davis may have taken one home herself.

8 Rulers of the waves: Humphrey Bogart and Katharine Hepburn brave love's tumultuous waters aboard the *African Queen* – and Bogart's valor is rewarded with an Oscar for Best Actor in a Leading Role.

1950
BEST PICTURE ALL ABOUT EVE
BEST DIRECTOR JOSEPH L. MANKIEWICZ for *All About Eve*
BEST LEADING ACTRESS JUDY HOLLIDAY in *Born Yesterday*
BEST LEADING ACTOR JOSÉ FERRER in *Cyrano de Bergerac*
BEST SUPPORTING ACTRESS JOSEPHINE HULL in *Harvey*
BEST SUPPORTING ACTOR GEORGE SANDERS in *All About Eve*

1951
BEST PICTURE AN AMERICAN IN PARIS
BEST DIRECTOR GEORGE STEVENS for *A Place in the Sun*
BEST LEADING ACTRESS VIVIEN LEIGH in *A Streetcar Named Desire*
BEST LEADING ACTOR HUMPHREY BOGART in *The African Queen*
BEST SUPPORTING ACTRESS KIM HUNTER in *A Streetcar Named Desire*
BEST SUPPORTING ACTOR KARL MALDEN in *A Streetcar Named Desire*

1952
BEST PICTURE THE GREATEST SHOW ON EARTH
BEST DIRECTOR JOHN FORD for *The Quiet Man*
BEST LEADING ACTRESS SHIRLEY BOOTH in *Come back, Little Sheba*
BEST LEADING ACTOR GARY COOPER in *High Noon*
BEST SUPPORTING ACTRESS GLORIA GRAHAME in *The Bad and the Beautiful*
BEST SUPPORTING ACTOR ANTHONY QUINN in *Viva Zapata!*

1953
BEST PICTURE FROM HERE TO ETERNITY
BEST DIRECTOR FRED ZINNEMANN for *From Here to Eternity*
BEST LEADING ACTRESS AUDREY HEPBURN in *Roman Holiday*
BEST LEADING ACTOR WILLIAM HOLDEN in *Stalag 17*
BEST SUPPORTING ACTRESS DONNA REED in *From Here to Eternity*
BEST SUPPORTING ACTOR FRANK SINATRA in *From Here to Eternity*

1954
BEST PICTURE ON THE WATERFRONT
BEST DIRECTOR ELIA KAZAN for *On the Waterfront*
BEST LEADING ACTRESS GRACE KELLY in *The Country Girl*
BEST LEADING ACTOR MARLON BRANDO in *On the Waterfront*
BEST SUPPORTING ACTRESS EVA MARIE SAINT in *On the Waterfront*
BEST SUPPORTING ACTOR EDMOND O'BRIEN in *The Barefoot Contes...*

1955
BEST PICTURE MARTY
BEST DIRECTOR DELBERT MANN for *Marty*
BEST LEADING ACTRESS ANNA MAGNANI in *The Rose Tattoo*
BEST LEADING ACTOR ERNEST BORGNINE in *Marty*
BEST SUPPORTING ACTRESS JO VAN FLEET in *East of Eden*
BEST SUPPORTING ACTOR JACK LEMMON in *Mister Roberts*

1956
BEST PICTURE AROUND THE WORLD IN EIGHTY DAYS
BEST DIRECTOR GEORGE STEVENS for *Giant*
BEST LEADING ACTRESS INGRID BERGMAN in *Anastasia*
BEST LEADING ACTOR YUL BRYNNER in *The King and I*
BEST SUPPORTING ACTRESS DOROTHY MALONE in *Written on the Wind*
BEST SUPPORTING ACTOR ANTHONY QUINN in *Lust for Life*

1957
BEST PICTURE THE BRIDGE ON THE RIVER KWAI
BEST DIRECTOR DAVID LEAN for *The Bridge on the River Kwai*
BEST LEADING ACTRESS JOANNE WOODWARD in *The Three Faces of Eve*
BEST LEADING ACTOR ALEC GUINNESS in *The Bridge on the River Kwai*
BEST SUPPORTING ACTRESS MIYOSHI UMEKI in *Sayonara*
BEST SUPPORTING ACTOR RED BUTTONS in *Sayonara*

1958
BEST PICTURE GIGI
BEST DIRECTOR VINCENTE MINNELLI for *Gigi*
BEST LEADING ACTRESS SUSAN HAYWARD in *I Want to Live!*
BEST LEADING ACTOR DAVID NIVEN in *Separate Tables*
BEST SUPPORTING ACTRESS WENDY HILLER in *Separate Tables*
BEST SUPPORTING ACTOR BURL IVES in *The Big Country*

1959
BEST PICTURE BEN-HUR
BEST DIRECTOR WILLIAM WYLER for *Ben-Hur*
BEST LEADING ACTRESS SIMONE SIGNORET in *Room at the Top*
BEST LEADING ACTOR CHARLTON HESTON in *Ben-Hur*
BEST SUPPORTING ACTRESS SHELLEY WINTERS in *The Diary of Anne Frank*
BEST SUPPORTING ACTOR HUGH GRIFFITH in *Ben-Hur*

1960 OSCARS

9   Epic greatness: David Lean and Sam Spiegel on the set of *Lawrence of Arabia*, winner of seven Oscars.

10   Double Indemnity: Julie Christie enjoys more critical acclaim in 1965 than any other big-name screen star with a Best Actress Oscar for *Darling* and the many wins of *Doctor Zhivago*.

1960
BEST PICTURE   THE APARTMENT
BEST DIRECTOR   BILLY WILDER for *The Apartment*
BEST LEADING ACTRESS   ELIZABETH TAYLOR in *Butterfield 8*
BEST LEADING ACTOR   BURT LANCASTER in *Elmer Gantry*
BEST SUPPORTING ACTRESS   SHIRLEY JONES in *Elmer Gantry*
BEST SUPPORTING ACTOR   PETER USTINOV in *Spartacus*

1961
BEST PICTURE   WEST SIDE STORY
BEST DIRECTOR   ROBERT WISE, JEROME ROBBINS for *West Side Story*
BEST LEADING ACTRESS   SOPHIA LOREN in *Two Women*
BEST LEADING ACTOR   MAXIMILIAN SCHELL in *Judgment at Nuremberg*
BEST SUPPORTING ACTRESS   RITA MORENO in *West Side Story*
BEST SUPPORTING ACTOR   GEORGE CHAKIRIS in *West Side Story*

1962
BEST PICTURE   LAWRENCE OF ARABIA
BEST DIRECTOR   DAVID LEAN for *Lawrence of Arabia*
BEST LEADING ACTRESS   ANNE BANCROFT in *The Miracle Worker*
BEST LEADING ACTOR   GREGORY PECK in *To Kill a Mockingbird*
BEST SUPPORTING ACTRESS   PATTY DUKE in *The Miracle Worker*
BEST SUPPORTING ACTOR   ED BEGLEY in *Sweet Bird of Youth*

1963
BEST PICTURE   TOM JONES
BEST DIRECTOR   TONY RICHARDSON for *Tom Jones*
BEST LEADING ACTRESS   PATRICIA NEAL in *Hud*
BEST LEADING ACTOR   SIDNEY POITIER in *Lilien auf dem Felde*
BEST SUPPORTING ACTRESS   MARGARET RUTHERFORD in *Hotel International*
BEST SUPPORTING ACTOR   MELVYN DOUGLAS in *Hud*

1964
BEST PICTURE   MY FAIR LADY
BEST DIRECTOR   GEORGE CUKOR for *My Fair Lady*
BEST LEADING ACTRESS   JULIE ANDREWS in *Mary Poppins*
BEST LEADING ACTOR   REX HARRISON in *My Fair Lady*
BEST SUPPORTING ACTRESS   LILA KEDROVA in *Zorba the Greek*
BEST SUPPORTING ACTOR   PETER USTINOV in *Topkapi*

1965
BEST PICTURE   THE SOUND OF MUSIC
BEST DIRECTOR   ROBERT WISE for *The Sound of Music*
BEST LEADING ACTRESS   JULIE CHRISTIE in *Darling*
BEST LEADING ACTOR   LEE MARVIN in *Cat Ballou*
BEST SUPPORTING ACTRESS   SHELLEY WINTERS in *A Patch of Blue*
BEST SUPPORTING ACTOR   MARTIN BALSAM in *A Thousand Clowns*

1966
BEST PICTURE   A MAN FOR ALL SEASON
BEST DIRECTOR   FRED ZINNEMANN for *A Man for all Seasons*
BEST LEADING ACTRESS   ELIZABETH TAYLOR in *Who's Afraid of Virginia Woolf?*
BEST LEADING ACTOR   PAUL SCOFIELD in *A Man for all Seasons*
BEST SUPPORTING ACTRESS   SANDY DENNIS in *Who's Afraid of Virginia Woolf?*
BEST SUPPORTING ACTOR   WALTER MATTHAU in *The Fortune Cookie*

1967
BEST PICTURE   IN THE HEAT OF THE NIGHT
BEST DIRECTOR   MIKE NICHOLS for *The Graduate*
BEST LEADING ACTRESS   KATHARINE HEPBURN in *Guess Who's Coming to Dinner*
BEST LEADING ACTOR   ROD STEIGER in *In the Heat of the Night*
BEST SUPPORTING ACTRESS   ESTELLE PARSONS in *Bonnie and Clyde*
BEST SUPPORTING ACTOR   GEORGE KENNEDY in *Cool Hand Luke*

1968
BEST PICTURE   OLIVER!
BEST DIRECTOR   CAROL REED for *Oliver!*
BEST LEADING ACTRESS   BARBRA STREISAND in *Funny Girl* /
KATHARINE HEPBURN in *The Lion In Winter*
BEST LEADING ACTOR   CLIFF ROBERTSON in *Charly*
BEST SUPPORTING ACTRESS   RUTH GORDON in *Rosemary's Baby*
BEST SUPPORTING ACTOR   JACK ALBERTSON in *The Subject Was Roses*

1969
BEST PICTURE   MIDNIGHT COWBOY
BEST DIRECTOR   JOHN SCHLESINGER for *Midnight Cowboy*
BEST LEADING ACTRESS   MAGGIE SMITH in *The Prime of Miss Jean Brodie*
BEST LEADING ACTOR   JOHN WAYNE in *True Grit*
BEST SUPPORTING ACTRESS   GOLDIE HAWN in *Cactus Flower*
BEST SUPPORTING ACTOR   GIG YOUNG in *They Shoot Horses, Don't They?*

11 Showstopper: Liza Minnelli in *Cabaret*.

12 Straight through the heart: According to the *Deer Hunter's* Michael Cimino "One shot is what it's all about."

1970 OSCARS

1970
BEST PICTURE PATTON
BEST DIRECTOR FRANKLIN J. SCHAFFNER for *Patton*
BEST LEADING ACTRESS GLENDA JACKSON in *Women in Love*
BEST LEADING ACTOR GEORGE C. SCOTT in *Patton*
BEST SUPPORTING ACTRESS HELEN HAYES in *Airport*
BEST SUPPORTING ACTOR JOHN MILLS in *Ryan's Daughter*

1971
BEST PICTURE THE FRENCH CONNECTION
BEST DIRECTOR WILLIAM FRIEDKIN for *The French Connection*
BEST LEADING ACTRESS JANE FONDA in *Klute*
BEST LEADING ACTOR GENE HACKMAN in *The French Connection*
BEST SUPPORTING ACTRESS CLORIS LEACHMAN in *The Last Picture Show*
BEST SUPPORTING ACTOR BEN JOHNSON in *The Last Picture Show*

1972
BEST PICTURE THE GODFATHER
BEST DIRECTOR BOB FOSSE for *Cabaret*
BEST LEADING ACTRESS LIZA MINNELLI in *Cabaret*
BEST LEADING ACTOR MARLON BRANDO in *The Godfather (the award was declined)*
BEST SUPPORTING ACTRESS EILEEN HECKART in *Butterflies Are Free*
BEST SUPPORTING ACTOR JOEL GREY in *Cabaret*

1973
BEST PICTURE THE STING
BEST DIRECTOR GEORGE ROY HILL for *The Sting*
BEST LEADING ACTRESS GLENDA JACKSON in *A Touch of Class*
BEST LEADING ACTOR JACK LEMMON in *Save the Tiger*
BEST SUPPORTING ACTRESS TATUM O'NEAL in *Paper Moon*
BEST SUPPORTING ACTOR JOHN HOUSEMAN in *The Paper Chase*

1974
BEST PICTURE THE GODFATHER – PART II II
BEST DIRECTOR FRANCIS FORD COPPOLA for *The Godfather – Part II*
BEST LEADING ACTRESS ELLEN BURSTYN in *Alice Doesn't Live Here Anymore*
BEST LEADING ACTOR ART CARNEY in *Harry and Tonto*
BEST SUPPORTING ACTRESS INGRID BERGMAN in *Murder on the Orient Express*
BEST SUPPORTING ACTOR ROBERT DE NIRO in *The Godfather – Part II*

1975
BEST PICTURE ONE FLEW OVER THE CUCKOO'S NEST
BEST DIRECTOR MILOŠ FORMAN for *One Flew Over the Cuckoo's Nest*
BEST LEADING ACTRESS LOUISE FLETCHER in *One Flew Over the Cuckoo's Nest*
BEST LEADING ACTOR JACK NICHOLSON in *One Flew Over the Cuckoo's Nest*
BEST SUPPORTING ACTRESS LEE GRANT in *Shampoo*
BEST SUPPORTING ACTOR GEORGE BURNS in *The Sunshine Boys*

1976
BEST PICTURE ROCKY
BEST DIRECTOR JOHN G. AVILDSEN for *Rocky*
BEST LEADING ACTRESS FAYE DUNAWAY in *Network*
BEST LEADING ACTOR PETER FINCH in *Network*
BEST SUPPORTING ACTRESS BEATRICE STRAIGHT *in Network*
BEST SUPPORTING ACTOR JASON ROBARDS in *All the President's Men*

1977
BEST PICTURE ANNIE HALL
BEST DIRECTOR WOODY ALLEN for *Annie Hall*
BEST LEADING ACTRESS DIANE KEATON in *Annie Hall*
BEST LEADING ACTOR RICHARD DREYFUSS in *The Goodbye Girl*
BEST SUPPORTING ACTRESS VANESSA REDGRAVE in *Julia*
BEST SUPPORTING ACTOR JASON ROBARDS in *Julia*

1978
BEST PICTURE THE DEER HUNTER
BEST DIRECTOR MICHAEL CIMINO for *The Deer Hunter*
BEST LEADING ACTRESS JANE FONDA in *Coming Home*
BEST LEADING ACTOR JON VOIGHT in *Coming Home*
BEST SUPPORTING ACTRESS MAGGIE SMITH in *California Suite*
BEST SUPPORTING ACTOR CHRISTOPHER WALKEN in *The Deer Hunter*

1979
BEST PICTURE KRAMER VS. KRAMER
BEST DIRECTOR ROBERT BENTON for *Kramer vs. Kramer*
BEST LEADING ACTRESS SALLY FIELD in *Norma Rae*
BEST LEADING ACTOR DUSTIN HOFFMAN in *Kramer vs. Kramer*
BEST SUPPORTING ACTRESS MERYL STREEP in *Kramer vs. Kramer*
BEST SUPPORTING ACTOR MELVYN DOUGLAS in *Being There*

13 Knock out! Robert De Niro sees red in *Raging Bull*.

14 Simply brilliant: Dustin Hoffman lights up the screen as the autistic Raymond Babbitt. His role in *Rain Man* got him an Oscar in 1988.

1980 OSCARS

1980
BEST PICTURE ORDINARY PEOPLE
BEST DIRECTOR ROBERT REDFORD for *Ordinary People*
BEST LEADING ACTRESS SISSY SPACEK in *Coal Miner's Daughter*
BEST LEADING ACTOR ROBERT DE NIRO in *Raging Bull*
BEST SUPPORTING ACTRESS MARY STEENBURGEN in *Melvin and Howard*
BEST SUPPORTING ACTOR TIMOTHY HUTTON in *Ordinary People*

1981
BEST PICTURE CHARIOTS OF FIRE
BEST DIRECTOR WARREN BEATTY for *Reds*
BEST LEADING ACTRESS KATHARINE HEPBURN in *On Golden Pond*
BEST LEADING ACTOR HENRY FONDA in *On Golden Pond*
BEST SUPPORTING ACTRESS MAUREEN STAPLETON in *Reds*
BEST SUPPORTING ACTOR SIR JOHN GIELGUD in *Arthur*

1982
BEST PICTURE GANDHI
BEST DIRECTOR RICHARD ATTENBOROUGH for *Gandhi*
BEST LEADING ACTRESS MERYL STREEP in *Sophie's Choice*
BEST LEADING ACTOR BEN KINGSLEY in *Gandhi*
BEST SUPPORTING ACTRESS JESSICA LANGE in *Tootsie*
BEST SUPPORTING ACTOR LOUIS GOSSET JR. in *An Officer and a Gentleman*

1983
BEST PICTURE TERMS OF ENDEARMENT
BEST DIRECTOR JAMES L. BROOKS for *Terms of Endearment*
BEST LEADING ACTRESS SHIRLEY MACLAINE in *Terms of Endearment*
BEST LEADING ACTOR ROBERT DUVALL in *Tender Mercies*
BEST SUPPORTING ACTRESS LINDA HUNT in *The Year of Living Dangerously*
BEST SUPPORTING ACTOR JACK NICHOLSON in *Terms of Endearment*

1984
BEST PICTURE AMADEUS
BEST DIRECTOR MILOŠ FORMAN for *Amadeus*
BEST LEADING ACTRESS SALLY FIELD in *Places in the Heart*
BEST LEADING ACTOR F. MURRAY ABRAHAM in *Amadeus*
BEST SUPPORTING ACTRESS PEGGY ASHCROFT in *A Passage to India*
BEST SUPPORTING ACTOR HAING S. NGOR in *The Killing Fields*

1985
BEST PICTURE OUT OF AFRICA
BEST DIRECTOR SYDNEY POLLACK for *Out of Africa*
BEST LEADING ACTRESS GERALDINE PAGE in *The Trip to Bountiful*
BEST LEADING ACTOR WILLIAM HURT in *Kiss of the Spider Woman*
BEST SUPPORTING ACTRESS ANJELICA HUSTON in *Prizzi's Honor*
BEST SUPPORTING ACTOR DON AMECHE in *Cocoon*

1986
BEST PICTURE PLATOON
BEST DIRECTOR OLIVER STONE for *Platoon*
BEST LEADING ACTRESS MARLEE MATLIN in *Children of a Lesser God*
BEST LEADING ACTOR PAUL NEWMAN in *The Color of Money*
BEST SUPPORTING ACTRESS DIANNE WIEST in *Hannah and Her Sisters*
BEST SUPPORTING ACTOR MICHAEL CAINE in *Hannah and Her Sisters*

1987
BEST PICTURE THE LAST EMPEROR
BEST DIRECTOR BERNARDO BERTOLUCCI for *The Last Emperor*
BEST LEADING ACTRESS CHER in *Moonstruck*
BEST LEADING ACTOR MICHAEL DOUGLAS in *Wall Street*
BEST SUPPORTING ACTRESS OLYMPIA DUKAKIS in *Moonstruck*
BEST SUPPORTING ACTOR SEAN CONNERY in *The Untouchables*

1988
BEST PICTURE RAIN MAN
BEST DIRECTOR BARRY LEVINSON for *Rain Man*
BEST LEADING ACTRESS JODIE FOSTER in *The Accused*
BEST LEADING ACTOR DUSTIN HOFFMAN in *Rain Man*
BEST SUPPORTING ACTRESS GEENA DAVIS in *The Accidental Tourist*
BEST SUPPORTING ACTOR KEVIN KLINE in *A Fish Called Wanda*

1989
BEST PICTURE DRIVING MISS DAISY
BEST DIRECTOR OLIVER STONE for *Born on the Fourth of July*
BEST LEADING ACTRESS JESSICA TANDY in *Driving Miss Daisy*
BEST LEADING ACTOR DANIEL DAY-LEWIS in *My Left Foot*
BEST SUPPORTING ACTRESS BRENDA FRICKER in *My Left Foot*
BEST SUPPORTING ACTOR DENZEL WASHINGTON in *Glory*

15 Jonathan Demme gave a new countenance to evil, and won 5 Oscars in 1991.

16 A master of the ironic storyline: Quentin Tarantino won an Oscar for *Pulp Fiction* in 1994.

1990 OSCARS

1990
BEST PICTURE DANCES WITH WOLVES
BEST DIRECTOR KEVIN COSTNER for *Dances with Wolves*
BEST LEADING ACTRESS KATHY BATES in *Misery*
BEST LEADING ACTOR JEREMY IRONS in *Reversal of Fortune*
BEST SUPPORTING ACTRESS WHOOPI GOLDBERG in *Ghost*
BEST SUPPORTING ACTOR JOE PESCI in *GoodFellas*

1991
BEST PICTURE THE SILENCE OF THE LAMBS
BEST DIRECTOR JONATHAN DEMME for *The Silence of the Lambs*
BEST LEADING ACTRESS JODIE FOSTER in *The Silence of the Lambs*
BEST LEADING ACTOR ANTHONY HOPKINS in *The Silence of the Lambs*
BEST SUPPORTING ACTRESS MERCEDES RUEHL in *The Fisher King*
BEST SUPPORTING ACTOR JACK PALANCE in *City Slickers*

1992
BEST PICTURE UNFORGIVEN
BEST DIRECTOR CLINT EASTWOOD for *Unforgiven*
BEST LEADING ACTRESS EMMA THOMPSON in *Howards End*
BEST LEADING ACTOR AL PACINO in *Scent of a Woman*
BEST SUPPORTING ACTRESS MARISA TOMEI in *My Cousin Vinny*
BEST SUPPORTING ACTOR GENE HACKMAN in *Unforgiven*

1993
BEST PICTURE SCHINDLER'S LIST
BEST DIRECTOR STEVEN SPIELBERG for *Schindler's List*
BEST LEADING ACTRESS HOLLY HUNTER in *The Piano*
BEST LEADING ACTOR TOM HANKS in *Philadelphia*
BEST SUPPORTING ACTRESS ANNA PAQUIN in *The Piano*
BEST SUPPORTING ACTOR TOMMY LEE JONES in *The Fugitive*

1994
BEST PICTURE FORREST GUMP
BEST DIRECTOR ROBERT ZEMECKIS for *Forrest Gump*
BEST LEADING ACTRESS JESSICA LANGE in *Blue Sky*
BEST LEADING ACTOR TOM HANKS in *Forrest Gump*
BEST SUPPORTING ACTRESS DIANNE WIEST in *Bullets Over Broadway*
BEST SUPPORTING ACTOR MARTIN LANDAU in *Ed Wood*

1995
BEST PICTURE BRAVEHEART
BEST DIRECTOR MEL GIBSON for *Braveheart*
BEST LEADING ACTRESS SUSAN SARANDON in *Dead Man Walking*
BEST LEADING ACTOR NICOLAS CAGE in *Leaving Las Vegas*
BEST SUPPORTING ACTRESS MIRA SORVINO in *Mighty Aphrodite*
BEST SUPPORTING ACTOR KEVIN SPACEY in *The Usual Suspects*

1996
BEST PICTURE THE ENGLISH PATIENT
BEST DIRECTOR ANTHONY MINGHELLA for *The English Patient*
BEST LEADING ACTRESS FRANCES MCDORMAND in *Fargo*
BEST LEADING ACTOR GEOFFREY RUSH in *Shine*
BEST SUPPORTING ACTRESS JULIETTE BINOCHE in *The English Patient*
BEST SUPPORTING ACTOR CUBA GOODING JR. in *Jerry Maguire*

1997
BEST PICTURE TITANIC
BEST DIRECTOR JAMES CAMERON for *Titanic*
BEST LEADING ACTRESS HELEN HUNT in *As Good As It Gets*
BEST LEADING ACTOR JACK NICHOLSON in *As Good As It Gets*
BEST SUPPORTING ACTRESS KIM BASINGER in *L. A. Confidential*
BEST SUPPORTING ACTOR ROBIN WILLIAMS in *Good Will Hunting*

1998
BEST PICTURE SHAKESPEARE IN LOVE
BEST DIRECTOR STEVEN SPIELBERG for *Saving Private Ryan*
BEST LEADING ACTRESS GWYNETH PALTROW in *Shakespeare in Love*
BEST LEADING ACTOR ROBERTO BENIGNI in *Life is Beautiful*
BEST SUPPORTING ACTRESS JUDI DENCH in *Shakespeare in Love*
BEST SUPPORTING ACTOR JAMES COBURN in *Affliction*

1999
BEST PICTURE AMERICAN BEAUTY
BEST DIRECTOR SAM MENDES for *American Beauty*
BEST LEADING ACTRESS HILARY SWANK in *Boys Don't Cry*
BEST LEADING ACTOR KEVIN SPACEY in *American Beauty*
BEST SUPPORTING ACTRESS ANGELINA JOLIE in *Girl Interrupted*
BEST SUPPORTING ACTOR MICHAEL CAINE in *The Cider House Rules*

795

GENERAL INDEX

IMPRINT

CREDITS

The publishers would like to thank the distributors, without whom many of these films would never have reached the big screen.

Columbia Tri Star, Filmverlag der Autoren, MGM, Paramount, RKO, Tobis, 20th Century Fox, United Artists, Universal, Warner Bros.

Academy Award® and Oscar® are the registered trademark and service mark of the Academy of Motion Picture Arts and Sciences.

If, despite our concerted efforts, a distributor has been unintentionally omitted, we apologise and will amend any such errors brought to the attention of the publishers in the next edition.

COPYRIGHT

Pages *2, 6-31, 399*:
Nosferatu – Eine Symphonie des Grauens
Friedrich Wilhelm Murnau/Prana-Film GmbH
Page *402*:
Breakfast at Tiffany's
Blake Edwards/Paramount Pictures
Page *314*:
Marcel Jeanne © VG Bild-Kunst, Bonn 2008
Pages *185-189*:
© Walt Disney Pictures
Pages *477-481*:
© Photos Georges Pierre
Pages *315-317*:
© Photos Leo Mirkine
Pages *329-333, 423-427*:
© Reporters Associati s.r.l.
Page *278*:
© 1950 Kadokawa Pictures, Inc.

PHOTOGRAPHS

defd and CINEMA, Hamburg
Deutsche Kinemathek, Berlin *(pp. 43-45, 117-123, 624)*
Deutsches Filminstitut – DIF e.V./Deutsches
    Filmmuseum, Frankfurt *(p. 662)*
British Film Institute (BFI), London
Bibliothèque du Film (BiFi), Paris
Herbert Klemens Filmbild Fundus
    Robert Fischer, Munich
Ciné-Images, Paris *(p. 110)*
Photofest, New York *(pp. 32, 36, 42, 104, 144)*
The Kobal Collection, London/New York
    (pp. 190, 212, 780)

© 2008 TASCHEN GmbH
Hohenzollernring 53, D-50672 Köln
www.taschen.com

PROJECT MANAGEMENT

Anne Gerlinger, Cologne

TEXTS

Ulrike Bergfeld (UB), Philipp Bühler (PB),
Malte Hagener (MH), Jörn Hetebrügge (JH),
Heinz-Jürgen Köhler (HJK), Petra Lange-Berndt (PLB),
Nils Meyer (NM), Lars Penning (LP),
Stephan Reisner (SR), Burkhard Röwekamp (BR),
David Gaertner (DG), Eckhard Pabst (EP),
Steffen Haubner (SH), Jörg Schweinitz (JS),
Oliver Küch (OK), Eric Stahl (ES), Rainer Vowe (RV),
Katja Kirste (KK), Harald Keller (HK), Anne Pohl (APO),
Robert Fischer (RF), Helmut Merschmann (HM),
Steffen Lückehe (SL), Olaf Möller (OM),
Anka Ziefer (AZ)

EDITING

20S: Gill Paul, Grapevine Publishing
    Services Ltd., London
30s and *40s*: Daniela Klein for English Express, Berlin
50s, 60s, 70s and *80s*: Daniela Klein for English
    Express, Berlin, and Jonathan Murphy, Brussels
90s: Jonathan Murphy, Brussels

TECHNICAL EDITING

David Gaertner, Bertram Kaschek and Malte Hagener, Berlin, and Steffen Haubner, Hamburg

ENGLISH TRANSLATIONS

20s: Isabel Varea, Caroline Durant, Karen Waloschek
    and Monika Bloxam, for Grapevine Publishing
    Services Ltd., London
30s, 40s, 50s and *60s*: Patrick Lanagan,
    Shaun Samson for English Express, Berlin
70s and *80s*: Daniel A. Huyssen, Patrick Lanagan
    and Shaun Samson for English Express, Berlin
90s: Deborah Caroline Holmes, Vienna, Harriet Horsfield
    in association with First Edition Translations Ltd.,
    Cambridge, Katharine Hughues, Oxford

DESIGN

Sense/Net, Andy Disl and Birgit Reber, Cologne

PRODUCTION

Ute Wachendorf, Cologne

To stay informed about upcoming TASCHEN titles, please request our magazine at www.taschen.com/magazine or write to TASCHEN America, 6671 Sunset Boulevard, Suite 1508, USA-Los Angeles, CA 90028, contact-us@taschen.com, Fax: +1-323-463.4442. We will be happy to send you a free copy of our magazine which is filled with information about all of our books.

Printed in China
ISBN 978-3-8365-0860-5